T0305320

Securities Finance

THE FRANK J. FABOZZI SERIES

Securities Finance

Securities Lending and Repurchase Agreements

FRANK J. FABOZZI

STEVEN V. MANN

EDITORS

WILEY

John Wiley & Sons, Inc.

For general information on our other products and services or for technical support, please contact our Customer Care Department within the United States at (800) 762-2974, outside the United States at (317) 572-3993 or fax (317) 572-4002.

Wiley also publishes its books in a variety of electronic formats. Some content that appears in print may not be available in electronic books. For more information about Wiley products, visit our web site at www.wiley.com.

ISBN-13 978-0-471-67891-5
ISBN-10 0-471-67891-0

Printed in the United States of America

10 9 8 7 6 5 4 3 2 1

Contents

Securities finance involves secured borrowing and lending transactions that are motivated for various reasons such as obtaining securities for settlement, financing inventory positions, and generating incremental income by lending securities. At one time, securities finance consisted of securities lending arrangements for equities and bonds and repurchase agreements (repos) for bonds. While these two forms of securities finance still dominate today, other methods commonly used include contracts for differences, equity swaps, and single stock futures as well as equity repos.

The purpose of this book is to provide investors and traders with an enhanced understanding of the various arrangements in the securities finance market. It is our hope that the knowledge gained will enable readers to make a more informed choice about their participation in this expanding market.

The book is divided in three parts. The 12 chapters in Part One cover securities lending, also commonly referred to as *stock lending*. Chapter 1 by Mark Faulkner describes securities lending as well as benefits for lenders and borrowers of securities participating in the market, the different types of securities lending transactions, mechanics of the transaction, the role of intermediaries, and the risks faced by the lenders of securities. The critical role of securities finance in capital markets is discussed by the staff of State Street in Chapter 2. Finding the most suitable route to participate in the securities lending market and the issue of selecting a suitable counterparty are the subjects of Chapter 3 by Mark Faulkner, focusing on the lending of international equities with regard to both lending and nonlending institutions.

The traditional programs available to institutional investors seeking to enter the securities lending market are also reviewed by Anthony Nazzaro in Chapter 4. An innovative program offering an alternative route to the market is the auction process developed by eSecLending. In Chapter 5, Daniel Kiefer of CalPERS and Judith Mabry of eSecLending describe this new option available to principal lenders. At one time, simply computing the revenues produced by a securities lending program was adequate in assessing the potential benefits for market participants and for managing a program. Today, this is not adequate. Rather, market participants evaluate the decision to participate and manage the process based on the risk-adjusted expected return.

To help understand the risks in a securities lending transaction involving bonds, Chapter 6, prepared by one of the editors, provides background information about the characteristics of these securities and their risks. In the United States, programs involving lending against cash collateral are the most common form of collateral management model and recently cash-based lending has become more popular outside the United States. In cash-based lending programs, it is critical that liquidity risks be controlled. In Chapter 7, Ed Blount and Aaron Gerdeman explain how to manage liquidity risks.

An analytical framework for aiding lenders in making decisions on the appropriateness of any type of collateral program (cash or securities) and understanding how they could amend proposed programs to reflect their particular risk/reward tolerance is described in Chapter 8 by Mark Faulkner. In Chapter 9, Peter Economou explains how reporting performance on a risk-adjusted basis can provide lenders with the information for proactively managing the securities lending process.

The participants in a securities lending transaction must consider legal, regulatory, tax, and accounting issues. The last three chapters in Section One deal with these issues. In Chapter 10, Charles Dropkin explains how to develop effective guidelines for managing legal risks for U.S.-based participants. He identifies certain key legal and regulatory issues that market participants must understand and follow in order to have an effective compliance program and describes mechanisms that can be included in programs for reducing insolvency risk. The Federal income tax consequences of securities lending transactions are detailed in Chapter 11 by Richard Shapiro. Statement of Financial Accounting Standard 140 is the primary accounting literature on securities lending transactions. In determining the accounting treatment, the basic concept is control. In Chapter 12, Susan Peters offers guidance regarding the recording and financial treatment of loaned securities.

Part Two covers bond financing by means of repurchase agreements (repos). The first chapter in this section, Chapter 13, prepared by the editors, explains a repo transaction, the types of repo transactions, and the mechanics of the transaction. The focus of the chapter then turns to the analysis of a repo transaction from the investor's perspective and illustrates the calculations with Bloomberg screens. While the focus of Chapter 13 is the U.S. repo market, Richard Comotto covers the European repo market in Chapter 14. Because of the unique characteristics of agency *mortgage-backed securities* (MBS), a special form of repo has developed, dollar rolls. Before the editors describe dollar rolls in Chapter 16, one of the editors provides an overview of agency MBS in Chapter 15. A historical and analytical framework for assessing the effect of dollar rolls on the MBS market and strategies employed by asset managers (including valuation dynamics) is explained in Chapter 17 by Anand Bhattacharya, Paul Jacob, and William Berliner.

Part Three contains only one chapter (Chapter 18) coauthored by the editors and describes alternative vehicles to securities lending for equity financing. These alternatives are equity repo and linear derivative contracts (i.e., nonoptions) which include contracts for differences and single stock futures, and equity swaps.

We would like to extend our profound appreciation to the contributing authors and Jim Daraio Capital Markets Management for permission to use some of the exhibits in Chapter 16.

Frank J. Fabozzi
Steven V. Mann

Frank J. Fabozzi, Ph.D., CFA, CPA is the Frederick Frank Adjunct Professor of Finance in the School of Management at Yale University. Prior to joining the Yale faculty, he was a Visiting Professor of Finance in the Sloan School at MIT. Professor Fabozzi is a Fellow of the International Center for Finance at Yale University and the editor of the *Journal of Portfolio Management*. He earned a doctorate in economics from the City University of New York in 1972. In 1994 he received an honorary doctorate of Humane Letters from Nova Southeastern University and in 2002 was inducted into the Fixed Income Analysts Society's Hall of Fame. He is the honorary advisor to the Chinese Asset Securitization Web site.

Steven V. Mann, Ph.D., is Professor of Finance at the Moore School of Business, University of South Carolina. He has coauthored four previous books and numerous articles in the area of investments, primarily fixed-income securities and derivatives. Professor Mann is an accomplished teacher, winning 20 awards for excellence in teaching and has received two awards for outstanding research. He also works as a consultant to investment/commercial banks and has conducted training programs for financial institutions throughout the United States.

Contributing Authors

William S. Berliner — Countrywide Securities Corporation
Anand K. Bhattacharya — Countrywide Securities Corporation
Ed Blount — The ASTEC Consulting Group
Richard Comotto — University of Reading, England
Charles E. Dropkin — Proskauer Rose LLP
Peter Economou — State Street
Frank J. Fabozzi — Yale University
Mark C. Faulkner — Spitalfields Advisors
Aaron J. Gerdeman — The ASTEC Consulting Group
Paul Jacob — Countrywide Securities Corporation
Daniel E. Kiefer — CalPERS
Judith G. Mabry — eSecLending
Steven V. Mann — University of South Carolina
Anthony A. Nazzaro — A. A. Nazzaro Associates
Susan C. Peters — eSecLending
Richard J. Shapiro — Ernst & Young LLP
State Street

Securities Lending

One

Securities Lending

An Introduction to Securities Lending

Mark C. Faulkner
Managing Director
Spitalfields Advisors

ecurities lending—the temporary transfer of securities on a collateralized basis—is a major and growing activity providing significant
benefits for issuers, investors, and traders alike. These are likely to
include improved market liquidity, more efficient settlement, tighter
dealer prices and, perhaps, a reduction in the cost of capital. This chapter describes securities lending, the motivation for lenders and borrowers to participate, the role of intermediaries, market mechanics, and the
risks faced by the lenders of securities.

WHAT IS SECURITIES LENDING

Securities lending is an important and significant business that describes
the market practice whereby securities are temporarily transferred by
one party (the lender) to another (the borrower). The borrower is
obliged to return the securities to the lender, either on demand, or at the

The author is grateful for the assistance provided by David Rule, Simon Hills, Dag-
mar Banton, John Serocold, Andrew Clayton, Joyce Martindale, Susan Adeane,
Habib Motani, Niki Natarajan, Andrew Barrie, Jackie Davis, and Bill Cuthbert.

end of any agreed term. For the period of the loan the lender is secured by acceptable assets delivered by the borrower to the lender as collateral.

Securities lending today plays a major part in the efficient functioning of the securities markets worldwide. Yet it remains poorly understood by many of those outside the market.

In some ways, the term "securities lending" is misleading and factually incorrect. Under English law and in many other jurisdictions, the transaction commonly referred to as "securities lending" is, in fact ...

> a disposal (or sale) of securities linked to the subsequent reacquisition of equivalent securities by means of an agreement.

Such transactions are collateralized and the "rental fee" charged, along with all other aspects of the transaction, is dealt with under the terms agreed between the parties. It is entirely possible and very commonplace that securities are borrowed and then sold or on-lent.

There are some consequences arising from this clarification:

1. Absolute title over both the securities on loan and the collateral received passes between the parties.
2. The economic benefits associated with ownership—e.g., dividends, coupons, etc.—are "manufactured" back to the lender, meaning that the borrower is entitled to these benefits as owner of the securities but is under a contractual obligation to make equivalent payments to the lender.
3. A lender of equities surrenders its rights of ownership, e.g., voting. Should the lender wish to vote on securities on loan, it has the contractual right to recall equivalent securities from the borrower.

Appropriately documented securities lending transactions avoid taxes associated with the sale of a transaction or transference fees.

Different Types of Securities Loan Transaction

Most securities loans in today's markets are made against collateral in order to protect the lender against the possible default of the borrower. This collateral can be cash or other securities or other assets.

Transactions Collateralized with Other Securities or Assets

Noncash collateral would typically be drawn from the following collateral types:

- Government bonds
  - Issued by G7, G10 or Non-G7 governments
- Corporate bonds
  - Various credit ratings
- Convertible bonds
  - Matched or unmatched to the securities being lent
- Equities
  - Of specified indices
- Letters of credit
  - From banks of a specified credit quality
- Certificates of deposit
  - Drawn on institutions of a specified credit quality
- Delivery by value ("DBVs")[1]
  - Concentrated or unconcentrated
  - Of a certain asset class
- Warrants
  - Matched or unmatched to the securities being lent
- Other money market instruments

The eligible collateral will be agreed upon between the parties, as will other key factors including:

- Notional limits
  - The absolute value of any asset to be accepted as collateral
- Initial margin
  - The margin required at the outset of a transaction
- Maintenance margin
  - The minimum margin level to be maintained throughout the transaction
- Concentration limits
  - The maximum percentage of any issue to be acceptable, e.g., less than 5% of daily traded volume
  - The maximum percentage of collateral pool that can be taken against the same issuer, that is, the cumulative effect where collateral in the

---

[1] *Delivery by Value* is a mechanism in some settlement systems whereby a member may borrow or lend cash overnight against *collateral*. The system automatically selects and delivers collateral securities, meeting pre-determined criteria to the value of the cash (plus a margin) from the account of the cash borrower to the account of the cash lender and reverses the transaction the following morning.

form of letters of credit, CD, equity, bond and convertible may be issued by the same firm

Exhibit 1.1 shows collateral being held by a *tri-party agent*. This specialist agent (typically a large custodian bank or international central securities depository) receives only eligible collateral from the borrower and hold it in a segregated account to the order of the lender. The tri-party agent marks this collateral to market, with information distributed to both lender and borrower (in the diagram, dotted "Reporting" lines). Typically the borrower pays a fee to the tri-party agent.

Exhibit 1.2 provides an illustration of cash flows on a securities against collateral other than cash for a transaction in the United Kingdom.

There is debate within the industry as to whether lenders, which are flexible in the range of noncash collateral that they are willing to receive, are rewarded with correspondingly higher fees. Some argue that they are; others claim that the fees remain largely static, but that borrowers are more prepared to deal with a flexible lender and, therefore, balances and overall revenue rise.

The agreement on a fee is reached between the parties and would typically take into account the following factors:

- Demand and supply
  - The less of a security available, other things being equal, the higher the fee a lender can obtain
- Collateral flexibility
  - The cost to a borrower of giving different types of collateral varies significantly, so that they might be more willing to pay a higher fee if the lender is more flexible

EXHIBIT 1.1   Noncash Collateral Held by a Third-Party Agent

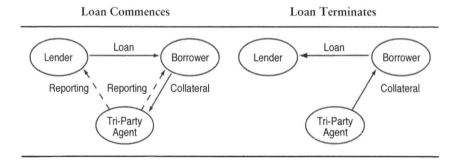

EXHIBIT 1.2   Cash Flows on a Securities Loan Against Collateral Other than Cash
The return to a lender of securities against collateral other than cash derives from the
fee charged to the borrower. A cash flow of this transaction reads as follows:

Transaction date	13 June 2005
Settlement date	16 June 2005
Term	Open
Security	XYZ Limited
Security price	£10.00 per share
Quantity	100,000 shares
Loan value	£1,000,000.00
Lending fee	50 basis points (100ths of 1%)
Collateral	UK FTSE 100 Concentrated DBVs
Margin required	5%
Collateral required	£1,050,000.00 in DBVs
Daily lending income	£1,000,000.00 × 0.005 × (1/365) = £13.70

Should the above transaction remain outstanding for one month and be returned on
16 July 2005 there will be two flows of revenue from the borrower to the lender.

On 30 June fees of £191.80 (£13.70 × 14 days)
On 31 July fees of £219.20 (£13.70 × 16 days)

Thus total revenue is £411.00 against which the cost of settling the transaction (loan
and collateral) must be offset.

Note: For purposes of clarity, the example assumes that the value of the security
on loan has remained constant, when in reality the price would change daily resulting in a mark to market event, different fees chargeable per day and changes
in the value of the collateral required. Open loan transactions can also be re-rated
or have their fee changed if market circumstances alter. It is assumed that this did
not happen either.

- The size of the manufactured dividend required to compensate the
  lender for the posttax dividend payment that it would have received
  had it not lent the security
  - Different lenders have varying tax liabilities on income from securi-
    ties; the lower the manufactured dividend required by the lender, the
    higher the fee it can negotiate.[2]

---

[2] An explanation of how securities lending can be motivated by the different tax status of borrowers and lenders is discussed later in this chapter.

- ▦ The term of a transaction
    - ■ Securities lending transactions can be open to recalls or fixed for a specified term; there is much debate about whether there should be a premium paid or a discount for certainty. If a lender can guarantee a recall-free loan then a premium will be forthcoming. One of the attractions of repo and swaps is the transactional certainty on offer from a counterpart
- ▦ Certainty
    - ■ As explained later in this chapter, there are trading and arbitrage opportunities, the profitability of which revolves around the making of specific decisions. If a lender can guarantee a certain course of action, this may mean it can negotiate a higher fee

Transactions Collateralized with Cash

Cash collateral is, and has been for many years, an integral part of the securities lending business, particularly in the United States. The lines between two distinct activities, securities lending and cash reinvestment, have become blurred and to many U.S. investment institutions securities lending is virtually synonymous with cash reinvestment. This is much less the case outside the United States, but consolidation of the custody business and the important role of U.S. custodian banks in the market means that this practice is becoming more prevalent. The importance of this point lies in the very different risk profiles of these increasingly intertwined activities.

The revenue generated from cash-collateralized securities lending transactions is derived in a different manner from that in a noncash transaction (see Exhibit 1.3). It is made from the difference or "spread" between interest rates that are paid and received by the lender (see Exhibit 1.4).

EXHIBIT 1.3   Cash-Collateral Securities Transaction

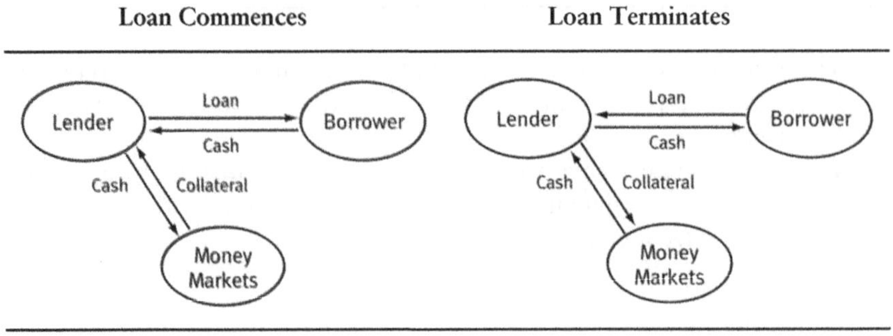

EXHIBIT 1.4 Cash Flows on a Securities Loan Collateralized with Cash

Transaction date	13 June 2005
Settlement date	16 June 2005
Term	Open
Security	XYZ Limited
Security price	£10.00 per share
Quantity	100,000 shares
Loan value	£1,000,000.00
Rebate rate	80 basis points
Collateral	USD cash
Margin required	5%
Collateral required	$1,718,850.00 (£1,050,000.00 × 1.67)
Reinvestment rate	130 basis points
Daily Lending Income	$23.87 or £14.58 ($1,718,850.00 × 0.005 × (1/360))

FX Rate assumed of £1.00 = $1.637

If the above transaction remains outstanding for one month and is returned on 16 July 2005, there will be two flows of cash from the lender to the borrower. These are based upon the cash collateral, and the profitability of the lender comes from the 50 basis points spread between the reinvestment rate and the rebate rate.

$1,718,850 × 0.008 × (1/360)) = $38.20

Payments to the borrower:

On 30 June $534.80 ($38.20 × 14 days)
On 31 July $611.20 ($38.20 × 16 days)

The lender's profit will typically be taken as follows:

On 30 June £204.12 (£14.58 × 14 days)
On 31 July £233.28 (£14.58 × 16 days)

Thus total revenue is £437.40 against which the cost of settling the transactions (loan and collateral) must be offset.

Note: For purposes of clarity, this example assumes that the value of the security on loan has remained constant for the duration of the above transaction. This is most unlikely; typically the price would change daily resulting in a mark to market and changes to the value of the collateral required. Open loan transactions can also be re-rated or have their rebate changed if market circumstances alter. It is assumed that this did not happen either.

The marginal increase in daily profitability associated with the cash transaction at a 50 bps spread compared with the noncash transaction of 50 bps is due to the fact that the cash spread is earned on the collateral which has a 5% margin as well as the fact that the USD interest rate convention is 360 days and not 365 days as in the United Kingdom.

Reinvestment guidelines are typically communicated in words by the beneficial owner to their lending agent, and some typical guidelines might be as follows:

Conservative
- Overnight G7 Government Bond repo fund
- Maximum effective duration of 1 day
- Floating-rate notes and derivatives are not permissible
- Restricted to overnight repo agreements

Quite Conservative
- AAA rated Government Bond repo fund
- Maximum average maturity of 90 days
- Maximum remaining maturity of any instrument is 13 months

Quite Flexible
- Maximum effective duration of 120 days
- Maximum remaining effective maturity of 2 years
- Floating-rate notes and eligible derivatives are permissible
- Credit quality: Short-term ratings: A1/P1, long-term ratings: A-/A3 or better

Flexible
- Maximum effective duration of 120 days
- Maximum remaining effective maturity of 5 years
- Floating-rate notes and eligible derivatives are permissible
- Credit quality: Short-term ratings: A1/P1, long-term ratings: A-/A3 or better

Some securities lending agents offer customized reinvestment guidelines while others offer reinvestment pools.

Other Transaction Types

Securities lending is part of a larger set of interlinked securities financing markets. These transactions are often used as alternative ways of achieving similar economic outcomes, although the legal form and accounting and tax treatments can differ. The other transactions are described in the following subsections.

Sale and Repurchase Agreements

Sale and repurchase agreements or repos involve one party agreeing to sell securities to another against a transfer of cash, with a simultaneous agreement to repurchase the same securities (or equivalent securities) at a specific price on an agreed date in the future. It is common for the terms "seller" and "buyer" to replace the securities lending terms "lender" and "borrower." Most repos are governed by a master agreement called the TBMA/ISMA Global Master Repurchase Agreement (GMRA).[3]

Repos occur for two principal reasons: either to transfer ownership of a particular security between the parties or to facilitate collateralized cash loans or funding transactions.

The bulk of bond lending and bond financing is conducted by repurchase agreements (repos) and there is a growing equity repo market. An annex can be added to the GMRA to facilitate the conduct of equity repo transactions.

Repos are much like securities loans collateralized against cash, in that income is factored into an interest rate that is implicit in the pricing of the two legs of the transaction.

At the beginning of a transaction, securities are valued and sold at the prevailing "dirty" market price (i.e., including any coupon that has accrued). At termination, the securities are resold at a predetermined price equal to the original sale price together with interest at a previously agreed rate known as the repo rate.

In securities-driven transactions (i.e., where the motivation is not simply financing) the repo rate is typically set at a lower rate than prevailing money market rates to reward the "lender" who invests the funds in the money markets and, thereby, seek a return. The "lender" often receives a margin by pricing the securities above their market level.

In cash-driven transactions, the repurchase price typically is agreed at a level close to current money market yields, as this is a financing rather than a security-specific transaction. The right to substitute repoed securities as collateral is agreed by the parties at the outset. A margin is often provided to the cash "lender" by reducing the value of the transferred securities by an agreed "haircut" or discount.

Buy/Sell Backs

Buy/sell backs are similar in economic terms to repos but are structured as a sale and simultaneous purchase of securities, with the purchase agreed for a future settlement date. The price of the forward purchase is typically calculated and agreed by reference to market repo rates.

---

[3] The Public Securities Association ("PSA"), now called the Bond Market Association ("BMA"), is a U.S. trade association. The International Securities Market Association ("ISMA") is the self-regulatory organization and trade association for the international securities market.

The purchaser of the securities receives absolute title to them and retains any accrued interest and coupon payments during the life of the transaction. However, the price of the forward contract takes account of any coupons received by the purchaser.

Buy/sell back transactions are normally conducted for financing purposes and involve fixed income securities. In general a cash borrower does not have the right to substitute collateral. Until 1996, the bulk of buy/sell back transactions took place outside of a formal legal framework with contract notes being the only form of record. In 1995, the GMRA was amended to incorporate an annex that dealt explicitly with buy/sell backs. Most buy/sell backs are now governed by this agreement.

Exhibit 1.5 compares the three main forms of collateralized securities loan transaction.

LENDERS AND INTERMEDIARIES

The securities lending market involves various types of specialist intermediary which take principal and/or agency roles. These intermediaries separate the underlying owners of securities—typically large pension or other funds, and insurance companies—from the eventual borrowers of securities, whose usual motivations are described later in this chapter.

Intermediaries

Agent Intermediaries
Securities lending is increasingly becoming a volume business and the economies of scale offered by agents that pool together the securities of different clients enable smaller owners of assets to participate in the market. The costs associated with running an efficient securities lending operation are beyond many smaller funds for which this is a peripheral activity. Asset managers and custodian banks have added securities lending to the other services they offer to owners of securities portfolios, while third party lenders specialize in providing securities lending services.

Owners and agents "split" revenues from securities lending at commercial rates. The split will be determined by many factors including the service level and provision by the agent of any risk mitigation, such as an indemnity. Securities lending is often part of a much bigger relationship and therefore the split negotiation can become part of a bundled approach to the pricing of a wide range of services.

EXHIBIT 1.5 Summary of Collateralized Loan Transactions

Characteristic	Securities Lending		Repo		Buy/sell Back
	Cash Collateral	Securities/Other Noncash Collateral	Specific Securities (securities driven)	General Collateral (cash driven)	
Formal method of exchange	Sale with agreement to make subsequent reacquisition of equivalent securities	Sale with agreement to make subsequent reacquisition of equivalent securities	Sale and repurchase under terms of master agreement	Sale and repurchase under terms of master agreement	Sale and repurchase
Form of exchange	Securities vs. cash	Securities vs. collateral (Note: Often free of payment but sometimes delivery versus delivery)	Securities vs. cash (Note: Often delivery versus payment)	Cash vs. securities (Note: Often delivery versus payment)	Cash vs. securities (Note: Often delivery versus payment)
Collateral type	Cash	Securities (bonds and equities), letters of Credit, DBVs, CDs	Cash	General collateral (bonds) or acceptable collateral as defined by buyer	Typically bonds
Return is paid to the supplier of	Cash collateral	Loan securities (not collateral securities)	Cash	Cash	Cash
Return payable as	Rebate interest (i.e., return paid on cash lower than comparable cash market interest rates)	Fee, e.g., standard fees for FTSE 100 stocks are about 6–8 basis points (i.e., 0.06–0.08% p.a.)	Quoted as repo rate, paid as interest on the cash collateral (lower than general collateral repo rate)	Quoted as repo rate, paid as interest on the cash	Quoted as repo rate, paid through the price differential between sale price and repurchase price

13

EXHIBIT 1.5 (Continued)

| Characteristic | Securities Lending | | Repo | | Buy/Sell Back |
	Cash Collateral	Securities/Other Noncash Collateral	Specific Securities (securities driven)	General Collateral (cash driven)	
Initial margin	Yes	Yes	Yes	Yes	Possible
Variation margin	Yes	Yes	Yes	Yes	No (only possible through close out and repricing)
Overcollateralization	Yes (in favour of the securities lender)	Yes (in favour of the securities lender)	No	Possible (if any, in favour of the cash provider)	Possible (if any, in favour of the cash provider)
Collateral substitution	Yes (determined by borrower)	Yes (determined by borrower)	No	Yes (determined by the original seller)	No (only possible through close out and repricing)
Dividends and coupons	Manufactured to the lender	Manufactured to the lender	Paid to the original seller	Paid to the original seller	No formal obligation to return income normally factored into the buy-back price
Legal set off in event of default	Yes	Yes	Yes	Yes	No
Maturity	Open or term	Open or term	Open or term	Open or term	Term only
Typical asset type	Bonds and equities	Bonds and equities	Mainly bonds, equities possible	Mainly bonds, equities possible	Almost entirely bonds
Motivation	Security specific dominant	Security specific	Security specific	Financing	Financing dominant
Payment	Monthly in arrears	Monthly in arrears	At maturity	At maturity	At maturity

14

Asset Managers

It can be argued that securities lending is an asset-management activity—a point that is easily understood in considering the reinvestment of cash collateral. Particularly in Europe, where custodian banks were, perhaps, slower to take up the opportunity to lend than in the United States, many asset managers run significant securities lending operations.

What was once a back-office low profile activity is now a front office growth area for many asset managers. The relationship that the asset managers have with their underlying clients puts them in a strong position to participate.

Custodian Banks

The history of securities lending is inextricably linked with the custodian banks. Once they recognized the potential to act as agent intermediaries and began marketing the service to their customers, they were able to mobilize large pools of securities that were available for lending. This in turn spurred the growth of the market.

Most large custodians have added securities lending to their core custody businesses. Their advantages include: the existing banking relationship with their customers; their investment in technology and global coverage of markets, arising from their custody businesses; the ability to pool assets from many smaller underlying funds, insulating borrowers from the administrative inconvenience of dealing with many small funds and providing borrowers with protection from recalls; and experience in developing as well as developed markets.

Being banks, they also have the capability to provide indemnities and manage cash collateral efficiently—two critical factors for many underlying clients.

Custody is so competitive a business that for many providers it is a loss-making activity. However, it enables the custodians to provide a range of additional services to their client base. These may include foreign exchange, trade execution, securities lending, and fund accounting.

Third-Party Agents

Advances in technology and operational efficiency have made it possible to separate the administration of securities lending from the provision of basic custody services, and a number of specialist third-party agency lenders have established themselves as an alternative to the custodian banks. Their market share is currently growing from a relatively small base. Their focus on securities lending and their ability to deploy new technology without reference to legacy systems can give them flexibility.

Principal Intermediaries

There are three broad categories of principal intermediary: broker dealers, specialist intermediaries, and prime brokers. In contrast to the agent intermediaries, principal intermediaries can assume principal risk, offer credit intermediation, and take positions in the securities that they borrow. Distinctions between the three categories are blurred. Many firms would be in all three.

In recent years securities lending markets have been liberalized to a significant extent so that there is little general restriction on who can borrow and who can lend securities. Lending can, in principle, take place directly between beneficial owners and the eventual borrowers. But typically a number of layers of intermediary are involved. What value do the intermediaries add?

A beneficial owner may well be an insurance company or a pension scheme while the ultimate borrower could be a hedge fund. Institutions are often reluctant to take on credit exposures to borrowers that are not well recognized, regulated, or who do not have a good credit rating, which would exclude most hedge funds. In these circumstances, the principal intermediary (often acting as prime broker) performs a credit intermediation service in taking a principal position between the lending institution and the hedge fund.

A further role of the intermediaries is to take on liquidity risk. Typically they will borrow from institutions on an open basis—giving them the option to recall the underlying securities if they want to sell them or for other reasons—while lending to clients on a term basis, giving them certainty that they will be able to cover their short positions.

In many cases, as well as serving the needs of their own propriety traders, principal intermediaries provide a service to the market in matching the supply of beneficial owners that have large stable portfolios with those that have a high borrowing requirement. They also distribute securities to a wider range of borrowers than underlying lenders, which may not have the resources to deal with a large number of counterparts.

These activities leave principal intermediaries exposed to liquidity risk if lenders recall securities that have been on lent to borrowers on a term basis. One way to mitigate this risk is to use in-house inventory where available. For example, proprietary trading positions can be a stable source of lending supply if the long position is associated with a long-term derivatives transaction. Efficient inventory management is seen as critical and many securities lending desks act as central clearers of inventory within their organizations, only borrowing externally when netting of in-house positions is complete. This can require a significant technological investment. Other ways of mitigating "recall risk" include arrangements to borrow securities from affiliated investment management firms, where regulations permit, and bidding for exclusive (and certain) access to securities from other lenders.

On the demand side, intermediaries have historically been dependent upon hedge funds or proprietary traders that make trading decisions. But a growing number of securities lending businesses within investment banks have either developed "trading" capabilities within their lending or financing departments, or entered into joint ventures with other departments or even in some cases their hedge fund customers. The rationale behind this trend is that the financing component of certain trading strategies is so significant that without the loan there is no trade.

Broker Dealers

Broker dealers borrow securities for a wide range of reasons:

■ Market making
■ To support proprietary trading
■ On behalf of clients

Many broker dealers combine their securities lending activities with their prime brokerage operation (the business of servicing the broad requirements of hedge funds and other alternative investment managers). This can bring significant efficiency and cost benefits. Typically within broker dealers the fixed income and equity divisions duplicate their lending and financing activities.

Specialist Intermediaries

Historically, regulatory controls on participation in stock lending markets meant that globally there were many intermediaries. Some specialized in intermediating between stock lenders and market makers in particular, for example, U.K. Stock Exchange Money Brokers ("SEMB"). With the deregulation of stock lending markets, these niches have almost all disappeared.

Some of the specialists are now part of larger financial organizations. Others have moved to parent companies that have allowed them to expand the range of their activities into proprietary trading.

Prime Brokers

Prime brokers serve the needs of hedge funds and other "alternative" investment managers. The business was once viewed, simply, as the provision of six distinct services, although many others such as capital introduction, risk management, fund accounting, and startup assistance have now been added (see Exhibit 1.6).

EXHIBIT 1.6 Services Provided by Prime Brokers

Profitable Activities	Part of the Cost of Being in Business
Securities lending	Clearance
Leverage of financing provision	Custody
Trade execution	Reporting

Securities lending is one of the central components of a successful prime brokerage operation, with its scale depending on the strategies of the hedge funds for which the prime broker acts. Two strategies that are heavily reliant on securities borrowing are long/short equity and convertible bond arbitrage.

The cost associated with the establishment of a full-service prime broker is steep, and recognized providers have a significant advantage. Some of the newer entrants have been using total return swaps, contracts for difference, and other derivative transaction types to offer what has become known as "synthetic prime brokerage." Again securities lending remains a key component of the service as the prime broker will still need to borrow securities in order to hedge the derivatives positions it has entered into with the hedge funds, for example, to cover short positions. But it is internalized within the prime broker and less obvious to the client.

Beneficial Owners

Those beneficial owners with securities portfolios of sufficient size to make securities lending worthwhile include pension funds, insurance and assurance companies, mutual funds/unit trusts, and endowments.

Beneficial Owner Considerations

When considering whether and how to lend securities, beneficial owners first need to consider organization characteristics and portfolio characteristics.

Organization characteristics include management motivation, technology investment, and credit risk appetitive. With regards to management motivation, some owners lend securities solely to offset custody and administrative costs, while others are seeking more significant revenue. Lenders vary in their willingness to invest in technological infrastructure to support securities lending. The securities lending market consists of organizations with a wide range of credit quality and collateral capabilities. A cautious approach to counterpart selection (AAA only) and restrictive collateral guidelines (G7 Bonds) will limit lending volumes.

Portfolio characteristic include size, holdings size, investment strategy, investment strategy, tax jurisdiction and position, and inventory attractiveness. With respect to size, other things being equal, borrowers prefer large portfolios. Loan transactions generally exceed $250,000. Lesser holdings are of limited appeal to direct borrowers. Holdings of under $250,000 are probably best deployed through an agency programme, where they can be pooled with other inventories. Active investment strategies increase the likelihood of recalls, making them less attractive than passive portfolios. Borrowers want portfolios where they need liquidity. A global portfolio offers the greatest chance of generating a fit. That said, there are markets that are particularly in demand from time to time and there are certain borrowers that have a geographic or asset class focus.

With respect to tax jurisdiction and position, borrowers are responsible for "making good" any benefits of share ownership (excluding voting rights) as if the securities had not been lent. They must "manufacture" (i.e., pay) the economic value of dividends to the lender. An institution's tax position compared to that of other possible lenders is therefore an important consideration. If the cost of manufacturing dividends or coupons to a lender is low then its assets will be in greater demand. Finally, regarding inventory attractiveness, "hot" securities are those in high demand while *general* collateral or general collateral securities are those that are commonly available. Needless to say, the "hotter" the portfolio, the higher the returns to lending.

Routes to the Market

Having examined the organization and portfolio characteristics of the beneficial owner, we must now consider the various possible routes to market. The possible routes to the securities lending market are briefly discussed below. A more detailed discussion is provided in Chapter 3.

Using an Asset Manager as Agent   A beneficial owner may find that the asset manager they have chosen, already operates a securities lending programme. This route poses few barriers to getting started quickly.

Using a Custodian as Agent   This is the least demanding option for a beneficial owner, especially a new one. They will already have made a major decision in selecting an appropriate custodian. This route also poses few barriers to getting started quickly.

Appointing a Third-Party Specialist as Agent   A beneficial owner, who has decided to outsource, may decide it does not want to use the supplier's asset manager(s) or custodian(s), and instead appoint a third-party specialist. This route may mean getting to know and understand a new provider prior to getting started. The opportunity cost of any delay needs to be factored into the decision.

Auctioning a Portfolio to Borrowers   Borrowers demand portfolios for which they bid guaranteed returns in exchange for gaining exclusive access to them. There are several different permutations of this auctioning route:

- Do-it-yourself auctions
- Assisted auctions
- Agent assistance
- Consultancy assistance
- Specialist "auctioneer" assistance

This is not a new phenomenon but one that has gained a higher profile in recent years and discussed in more detail in other chapters in this book. A key issue for the beneficial owner considering this option is the level of operational support that the auctioned portfolio will require and who will provide it. The key issue here is finding the best auctioneer.

Selecting One Principal Borrower   Many borrowers effectively act as wholesale intermediaries and have developed global franchises using their expertise and capital to generate spreads between two principals that remain unknown to one another. These principal intermediaries are sometimes separately incorporated organizations, but more frequently, parts of larger banks, broker-dealers or investment banking groups. Acting as principal allows these intermediaries to deal with organizations that the typical beneficial owner may choose to avoid for credit reasons such as, hedge funds.

Lending Directly to Proprietary Principals   Normally, after a period of activity in the lending market using one of the above options, a beneficial owner that is large enough in its own right, may wish to explore the possibility of establishing a business "in house," lending directly to a selection of principal borrowers that are the end-users of their securities. The proprietary borrowers include broker-dealers, market makers and hedge funds. Some have global borrowing needs while others are more regionally focused.

Choosing Some Combination of the Above   Just as there is no single or correct lending method, so the options outlined above are not mutually exclusive. Deciding not to lend one portfolio does not preclude lending to another; similarly, lending in one country does not necessitate lending in all. Choosing a wholesale intermediary that happens to be a custodian in the United States and Canada does not mean that a lender cannot lend Asian assets through a third-party specialist, and European assets directly to a panel of proprietary borrowers.

THE BORROWING MOTIVATION

One of the central questions commonly asked by issuers and investors alike is "Why does the borrower borrow my securities?" Before considering this point, let us examine why issuers might care.

If securities were not issued, they could not be lent. Behind this simple tautology lies an important point. When initial public offerings are frequent and corporate merger and acquisition activity is high, the securities lending business benefits. In the early 2000s, the fall in the level of such activity depressed the demand to borrow securities leading to a depressed equity securities lending market (i.e., fewer trading opportunities, less demand, and fewer "specials") and issuer concern about the role of securities lending, such as whether it is linked in any way to the decline in the value of a company's shares or whether securities lending should be discouraged.

How many times does an issuer discussing a specific corporate event stop to consider the impact that the issuance of a convertible bond, or the adoption of a dividend reinvestment plan might have upon lending of their shares? There is a significant amount of information available on the "long" side of the market and correspondingly little on the short side. Securities lending activity is not synonymous with short selling. But it is often, although not always, used to finance short sales (discussed next) and might be a reasonable and practical proxy for the scale of short-selling activity in the absence of full short sale disclosure. It is, therefore, natural that issuers would want to understand how and why their securities are traded.

Borrowers, when acting as principals, have no obligation to tell lenders or their agents why they are borrowing securities. In fact, they may well not know themselves as they may be on-lending the securities to proprietary traders or hedge funds that do not share their trading strategies openly. Some prime brokers are deliberately vague when borrowing securities as they wish to protect their underlying hedge fund customer's trading strategy and motivation.

This section explains some of the more common reasons behind the borrowing of securities. In general, these can be grouped into: (1) borrowing to cover a short position (settlement coverage, naked shorting, market making, arbitrage trading); (2) borrowing as part of a financing transaction motivated by the desire to lend cash; and (3) borrowing to transfer ownership temporarily to the advantage of both lender and borrower (tax arbitrage, dividend reinvestment plan arbitrage).

Borrowing to Cover Short Positions

Settlement Coverage

Historically, settlement coverage has played a significant part in the development of the securities lending market. Going back a decade or so, most securities lending businesses were located in the back offices of their organizations and were not properly recognized as businesses in their own right. Particularly for less liquid securities—such as corporate bonds and equities with a limit free float—settlement coverage remains a large part of the demand to borrow.

The ability to borrow to avoid settlement failure is vital to ensure efficient settlement and has encouraged many securities depositories into the automated lending business. This means that they remunerate customers for making their securities available to be lent by the depository automatically in order to avert any settlement failures.

Naked Shorting

Naked shorting can be defined as borrowing securities in order to sell them in the expectation that they can be bought back at a lower price in order to return them to the lender. Naked shorting is a directional strategy, speculating that prices will fall, rather than a part of a wider trading strategy, usually involving a corresponding long position in a related security.

Naked shorting is a high-risk strategy. Although some funds specialize in taking short positions in the shares of companies they judge to be overvalued, the number of funds relying on naked shorting is relatively small and probably declining.

Market Making

Market makers play a central role in the provision of two-way price liquidity in many securities markets around the world. They need to be able to borrow securities in order to settle "buy orders" from customers and to make tight, two-way prices.

The ability to make markets in illiquid small capitalization securities is sometimes hampered by a lack of access to borrowing, and some of the specialists in these less liquid securities have put in place special arrangements to enable them to gain access to securities. These include guaranteed exclusive bids with securities lenders.

The character of borrowing is typically short term for an unknown period of time. The need to know that a loan is available tends to mean that the level of communication between market makers and the securities lending business has to be highly automated. A market maker that goes short and then finds that there is no loan available would have to buy that security back to flatten its book.

Arbitrage Trading

Securities are often borrowed to cover a short position in one security that has been taken to hedge a long position in another as part of an "arbitrage" strategy. Some of the more common arbitrage transactions that involve securities lending are described in the following subsections.

Convertible Bond Arbitrage

Convertible bond arbitrage involves buying a convertible bond and simultaneously selling the underlying equity short and borrowing the shares to cover the short position). Leverage can be deployed to increase the return in this type of transaction. Prime brokers are particularly keen on hedge funds that engage in convertible bond arbitrage as they offer scope for several revenue sources:

- Securities lending revenues
- Provision of leverage
- Execution of the convertible bond
- Execution of the equity

Pairs Trading or Relative Value "Arbitrage"   This in an investment strategy that seeks to identify two companies with similar characteristics whose equity securities are currently trading at a price relationship that is out of line with their historical trading range. The strategy entails buying the apparently undervalued security while selling the apparently overvalued security short, borrowing the latter security to cover the short position. Focusing on securities in the same sector or industry should normally reduce the risks in this strategy.

Index Arbitrage   In this context, arbitrage refers to the simultaneous purchase and sale of the same commodity or stock in two different markets in order to profit from price discrepancies between the markets.

In the stock market, an arbitrage opportunity arises when the same security trades at different prices in different markets. In such a situation, investors buy the security in one market at a lower price and sell it in another for more, capitalizing on the difference. However, such an opportunity vanishes quickly as investors rush in to take advantage of the price difference.

The same principle can be applied to index futures. Being a derivative product, index futures derive their value from the securities that constitute the index. At the same time, the value of index futures is linked to the stock index value through the opportunity cost of funds (borrowing/lending cost) required to play the market.

Stock index arbitrage involves buying or selling a basket of stocks and, conversely, selling or buying futures when mispricing appears to be taking place.

Financing

As broker dealers build derivative prime brokerage and customer margin business, they hold an increasing inventory of securities that requires financing.

This type of activity is high volume and takes place between two counterparts that have the following coincidence of wants: One has cash that they would like to invest on a secured basis and pick-up yield. The other has inventory that needs to be financed

In the case of bonds, the typical financing transaction is a repo or buy/sell back. But for equities, securities lending and equity, repo transactions are used.

Tri-party agents are often involved in this type of financing transaction as they can reduce operational costs for the cash lender and they have the settlement capabilities the cash borrower needs to substitute securities collateral as their inventory changes.

Temporary Transfers of Ownership

Temporary transfers of ownership are driven by tax arbitrage and dividend plan reinvestment arbitrage opportunities.

Tax Arbitrage   Tax driven trading is an example of securities lending as a means of exchange. Markets that have historically provided the largest opportunities for tax arbitrage include those with significant tax credits that are not available to all investors—examples include Italy, Germany and France.

The different tax positions of investors around the world have opened up opportunities for borrowers to use securities lending transactions, in effect, to exchange assets temporarily for the mutual benefit of purchaser, borrower and lender. The lender's reward comes in one of two ways: either a higher fee for lending if they require a lower manufactured dividend, or a higher manufactured dividend than the posttax dividend they would normally receive (quoted as an "all-in rate").

For example, an offshore lender that would normally receive 75% of a German dividend and incur 25% withholding tax (with no possibility to reclaim) could lend the security to a borrower that, in turn, could sell it to a German investor who was able to obtain a tax credit rather than incur withholding tax. If the offshore lender claimed the 95% of the dividend that it would otherwise have received, it would be making a significant pick-up (20% of the dividend yield), while the borrower might make a spread of between 95% and whatever the German investor was bidding. The terms of these trades vary widely and rates are calculated accordingly.

Dividend Reinvestment Plan Arbitrage   Many issuers of securities create an arbitrage opportunity when they offer shareholders the choice of taking a dividend or reinvesting in additional securities at a discounted level.

Income or index tracking funds that cannot deviate from recognized securities weightings may have to choose to take the cash option and forgo the opportunity to take the discounted reinvestment opportunity.

One way that they can share in the potential profitability of this opportunity is to lend securities to borrowers that then take the following action:

- Borrow as many guaranteed cash shares as possible, as cheaply as possible
- Tender the borrowed securities to receive the new discounted shares
- Sell the new shares to realize the "profit" between the discounted share price and the market price
- Return the shares and manufacture the cash dividend to the lender

MARKET MECHANICS

This section outlines the processes in the life of a securities. Specifically, the following are discussed:

- Negotiation of loan deals
- Confirmations
- Term of loan
- Term trades
- Putting securities "on hold"
- Settlements, including how loans are settled and settlement concerns
- Termination of loans
- Redelivery, failed trades and legal remedies
- Corporate actions and voting

There are other issues that are unique to specific countries. These include any tax arrangements and reporting of transactions to an exchange or other authority/regulator.

Loan Negotiation

Traditionally securities loans have been negotiated between counterparts (whose credit departments have approved one another) on the phone, and followed up with written or electronic confirmations. Normally the borrower initiates the call to the lender with a borrowing requirement. However, proactive lenders may also offer out in-demand securities to their approved counterparts. This would happen particularly where one borrower returns a security and the lender is still lending it to others in the market, they will contact them to see if they wish to borrow additional securities.

Today, there is an increasing amount of bilateral and multilateral automated lending whereby securities are broadcast as available at particular rates by email or other electronic means. Where lending terms are agreeable, automatic matching can take place.

An example of an electronic platform for negotiating equity securities loan transactions is EquiLend, which began operations in 2002 and is backed by a consortium of financial institutions. EquiLend's stated objective is to:

> Provide the securities lending industry with the technology to streamline and automate transactions between borrowing and lending institutions and ... introduce a set of common protocols. EquiLend will connect borrowers and lenders through a common, standards-based global equity lending platform enabling them to transact with increased efficiency and speed, and reduced cost and risk.

EquiLend is not alone in this market; for example, SecFinex offers similar services in Europe.

Confirmations

Written or electronic confirmations are issued, whenever possible, on the day of the trade so that any queries by the other party can be raised as quickly as possible. Material changes during the life of the transaction are agreed between the parties as they occur and may also be confirmed if either party wishes it. Examples of material changes are collateral adjustments or collateral substitutions. The parties agree who will take responsibility for issuing loan confirmations.

Confirmations would normally include the following information:

- Contract and settlement dates
- Details of loaned securities
- Identities of lender and borrower (and any underlying principal)
- Acceptable collateral and margin percentages
- Term and rates
- Bank and settlement account details of the lender and borrower

Term of Loan, and Selling Securities While on Loan

Loans may either be for a specified term or open. Open loans are trades with no fixed maturity date. It is more usual for securities loans to be open or "at call," especially for equities, because lenders typically wish to preserve the flexibility for fund managers to be able to sell at any time. Lenders are able to sell securities despite their being on open loan because they can usually be recalled from the borrower within the settlement period of the market concerned. Nevertheless open loans can remain on loan for a long period.

Term Trades—Fixed or Indicative?

The general description "term trade" is used to describe differing arrangements in the securities lending market. The parties have to agree whether the term of a loan is "fixed" for a definite period or whether the duration is merely "indicative" and, therefore, the securities are callable. If fixed, the lender is not obliged to accept the earlier return of the securities; nor does the borrower need to return the securities early if the lender requests it. Accordingly, securities subject to a fixed loan should not be sold while on loan.

Where the term discussed is intended to be "indicative," it usually means that the borrower has a long-term need for the securities but the lender is unable to fix for term and retains the right to recall the securities if necessary.

Putting Securities "On Hold"

Putting securities "on hold" (referred to in the market as "icing" securities) is the practice whereby the lender will reserve securities at the request of a borrower on the borrower's expected need to borrow those securities at a future date. This occurs where the borrower must be sure that the securities will be available before committing to a trade that will require them.

While some details can be agreed between the parties, it is normal for any price quoted to be purely indicative, and for securities to be held to the following business day. The borrower can "roll over" the arrangement (i.e., continue to "ice" the securities) by contacting the holder before 9 A.M., otherwise it terminates.

Key aspects of icing are that the lender does not receive a fee for reserving the securities and they are generally open to challenge by another borrower making a firm bid. In this case the first borrower would have 30 minutes to decide whether to take the securities at that time or to release them.

"Pay-to-Hold" Arrangements

A variation of icing is "pay-to-hold," where the lender does receive a fee for putting the securities on hold. As such, they constitute a contractual agreement and are not open to challenge by other borrowers.

Settlements

Securities lenders need to settle transactions on a shorter timeframe than the customary settlement period for that market. Settlement will normally be through the lender's custodian bank and this is likely to apply regardless of whether the lender is conducting the operation or delegating to an agent. The lender will usually have agreed a schedule of guaranteed settlement times for its securities lending activity with its custodians. Prompt settlement information is crucial to the efficient monitoring and control of a lending programme, with reports needed for both loans and collateral.

In most settlement systems securities loans are settled as "free-of-payment" deliveries and the collateral is taken quite separately, possibly in a different payment or settlement system and maybe a different country and time zone. For example, U.K. equities might be lent against collateral provided in a European International Central Securities Depository or U.S. dollar cash collateral paid in New York. This can give rise to what is known in the market as "daylight exposure," a period during which the loan is not covered as the lent securities have been delivered but the collateral securities have not yet been received. To avoid this exposure some lenders insist on precollateralization, so transferring the exposure to the borrower.

The CREST system for settling U.K. and Irish securities is an exception to the normal practice as collateral is available within the system. This enables loans to be settled against cash intraday and for the cash to be exchanged, if desired, at the end of the settlement day for a package of DBV securities overnight. The process can be reversed and repeated the next day.

Termination of the Loan

Open loans may be terminated by the borrower returning securities or by the lender recalling them. The borrower will normally return borrowed securities when it has filled its short position. A borrower will sometimes refinance its loan positions by borrowing more cheaply elsewhere and returning securities to the original lender. The borrower may, however, give the original lender the opportunity to reduce the rate being charged on the loan before borrowing elsewhere.

Redelivery, Failed Trades, and Legal Remedies

When deciding which markets and what size to lend in, securities lenders consider how certain they can be of having their securities returned in a timely manner when called, and what remedies are available under the legal agreement (discussed later) in the event of a failed return.

Procedures to be followed in the event of a failed redelivery are usually covered in legal agreements or otherwise agreed between the parties at the outset of the relationship. Financial redress may be available to the lender if the borrower fails to redeliver loaned securities or collateral on the intended settlement date. Costs that would typically be covered include:

- Direct interest and/or overdraft incurred
- Costs reasonably and properly incurred as a result of the borrower's failure to meet its sale or delivery obligations
- Total costs and expenses reasonably incurred by the lender as a result of a "buy-in" (i.e., where the lender is forced to? purchase securities in the open market following the borrower's failure to return them)

Costs that would usually be excluded are those arising from the transferee's negligence or willful default and any indirect or consequential losses. An example of that would be when the nonreturn of loaned securities causes an onward trade for a larger amount to fail. The norm is for only that proportion of the total costs which relates to the unreturned securities or collateral to be claimed. It is good practice, where possible, to consider "shaping" or "partialling" larger transactions (i.e., breaking them down into a number of smaller amounts for settlement purposes) so as to avoid the possibility of the whole transaction failing if the transferor cannot redeliver the loaned securities or collateral on the intended settlement date.

Corporate Actions and Votes

The basic premise underlying securities lending is to make the lender "whole" for any corporate action event—such as a dividend, rights or bonus issue—by putting the borrower under a contractual obligation to make equivalent payments to the lender, for instance by "manufacturing" dividends. However a shareholder's right to vote as part owner of a company cannot be manufactured. When securities are lent, legal ownership and the right to vote in shareholder meetings passes to the borrower, who will often sell the securities on. Where lenders have the right to recall securities, they can use this option to restore their holdings and voting rights. The onus is on the borrower to find the securities, by borrowing or purchasing them in the market if necessary. This can damage market liquidity, which is a risk that intermediaries manage.

It is important that beneficial owners are aware that when shares are lent the right to vote is also transferred. For example, in the United Kingdom, the Securities Lending and Repo Committee's (SLRC) code of guidance states in Section 2.5.4 that lenders should make it clear to clients that voting rights are transferred. A balance needs to be struck between the importance of voting and the benefits derived from lending the securities. Beneficial owners need to ensure that any agents they have made responsible for their voting and stock lending act in a co-ordinated way.

Borrowing securities in order to build up a holding in a company with the deliberate purpose of influencing a shareholder vote is not necessarily illegal in the United Kingdom. However, institutional lenders have recently become more aware of the possibility, and tend not to see it as a legitimate use of securities borrowing.

A number of market bodies throughout the world have been addressing the relationship between securities lending and voting. For example, a recent report by Paul Myners, to the U.K. Shareholder Voting Working Group made the following recommendation:

> Stocklending is important in maintaining market liquidity but borrowing of shares for the purpose of voting is not appropriate ... it is important that beneficial owners are fully aware of the implications for voting if they agree to their shares being lent. In particular, when a resolution is contentious I start from the position that the lender should automatically recall the related stock, unless there are good economic reasons for not doing so.[4]

Internationally, a working group of the International Corporate Governance Network is currently examining best practices for long-

---

[4] "A Review of the Impediments to Voting UK Shares," available at www.investmentfunds.org.uk.

term investors in relation to securities lending and voting. The SLRC is also considering additions to its code in this area.

FINANCIAL RISKS AND RISK MANAGEMENT

This section reviews the main financial risks in securities lending and how lenders usually manage them. More detailed discussion of these risks is provided in other later chapters.

Financial risks in securities lending are primarily managed through the use of collateral and netting. As described earlier in this chapter, collateral can be in the form of securities or cash. The market value of the collateral is typically greater than that of the lent portfolio. This margin is intended to protect the lender from loss and reflect the practical costs of collateral liquidation and repurchase of the lent portfolio in the event of default. Any profits made in the repurchase of the lent portfolio are normally returned to the borrower's liquidator. Losses incurred are borne by the lender with recourse to the borrower's liquidator along with other creditors.

When Taking Cash as Collateral

Because of its wide acceptability and ease of management, cash can be highly appropriate collateral. However, the lender needs to decide how best to utilize this form of collateral. As described earlier in this chapter, a lender taking cash as collateral pays rebate interest to the securities borrower, so the cash must be reinvested at a higher rate to make any net return on the collateral. This means the lender needs to decide on an appropriate risk-return trade-off. In simple terms, reinvesting in assets that carry one of the following risks can increase expected returns: a higher credit risk: a risk of loss in the event of defaults or a longer maturity in relation to the likely term of the loan. Many of the large securities lending losses over the years have been associated with reinvestment of cash collateral.

Typically, lenders delegate reinvestment to their agents (e.g., custodian banks). They specify reinvestment guidelines, such as those set out earlier in this chapter. There is a move towards more quantitative, risk-based approaches, often specifying the "value-at-risk" in relation to the different expected returns earned from alternative reinvestment profiles. Agents do not usually offer an indemnity against losses on reinvestment activity so that the lender retains all of the risk while their agent is paid part of the return.

When Taking Other Securities as Collateral

Compared with cash collateral, taking other securities as collateral is a way of avoiding reinvestment risk. In addition to the risks of error, systems failure and fraud always present in any market, problems then arise on the default of a borrower. In such cases the lender will seek to sell the collateral securities in order to raise the funds to replace the lent securities. Transactions collateralized with securities are exposed to a number of different risks that are described below.

Reaction and Legal Risk

If a lender experiences delays in either selling the collateral securities or repurchasing the lent securities, it runs a greater risk that the value of the collateral will fall below that of the loan in the interim. Typically, the longer the delay, the larger the risk.

Mispricing Risk

The lender will be exposed if either collateral securities have been overvalued or lent securities undervalued because the prices used to mark-to-market differ from prices that can actually be traded in the secondary market. One example of mispricing is using mid rather than bid prices for collateral. For illiquid securities, obtaining a reliable price source is particularly difficult because of the lack of trading activity.

Liquidity Risk

Illiquid securities are more likely to be released at a lower price than the valuation used. Valuation "haircuts" are used to mitigate this risk (i.e., collateral is valued at, for example, 98% or 95% of the current market value). The haircuts might depend upon:

- The proportion of the total security issue held in the portfolio—the larger the position, the greater the haircut
- The average daily traded volume of the security: the lower the volume, the greater the haircut
- The volatility of the security; the higher the volatility, the greater the haircut

Congruency of Collateral and Lent Portfolios (Mismatch Risk)

If the lent and collateral portfolios were identical, then there would be no market risk. In practice, of course, the lent and collateral portfolios are often very different. The lender's risk is that the market value of the lent securities increases but that of the collateral securities falls before rebalancing can be effected. Provided the counterpart has not defaulted, the lender will be able to call for additional collateral on any adverse collateral/loan price movements. However, following default, it will be exposed until it has been able sell the collateral and replace the lent securities.

The size of mismatch risk depends on the expected covariance of the value of the collateral and lent securities. The risk will be greater if the value of the collateral is more volatile, the value of the lent securities is more volatile, or if their values do not tend to move together, so that the expected correlation between changes in their value is low. For example, in deciding whether to hold U.K. government securities or U.K. equities to collateralize a loan of BP shares, a lender would have to judge whether the greater expected correlation between the value of the U.K. equities and the BP shares reduced mismatch risk by more than the lower expected volatility in the value of the government securities.

Many agent intermediaries will offer beneficial owners protection against these risks by agreeing to return (buy-in) lent securities immediately for their clients following a fail, taking on the risk that the value of the collateral on liquidation is lower.

Securities Lending Using Other Securities as Collateral: A Worked Example

The following illustration described one approach to estimating the risk exposure to a lender taking securities as collateral. Assume that lender ABC has loaned Borrower 1 a range of equities in the U.K., U.S., Japanese, and Malaysian markets. Collateral is mainly in the form of U.K. gilts at various maturities, sterling cash deposits, and U.S. long-dated Treasury bonds. The gross margin is £25 million or 4.5% of loan inventory. Exhibit 1.7 summarizes the situation.

Exhibit 1.8 shows the type of data on which a detailed analysis of mismatch risk might be based: the average daily liquidity in each asset class; the volatility of each asset class; the average residual risk on particular securities within each asset class; and a matrix of correlations between various asset classes.

Realistic Valuations

The first consideration is whether the valuation prices are fair. Assuming the portfolios have been conservatively valued at bid and offer (not mid) prices, then the lender might require some adjustment (haircut) to reflect concentration and price volatility of the different assets. For example, in the case of the sterling cash collateral, the haircut might be negligible. However, for the Malaysian equity portfolio, a high adjustment might

EXHIBIT 1.7   Summary of ABC's Lent and Collateral Position with Borrower 1

Asset Class	Loan Inventory (£m)	Number of Loan Positions	Collateral Inventory (£m)	Number of Collateral Positions	Gross Margin (£m)
Total	55.0	43	575.0	10	25.0
FTSE 100	100.0	5	75.0	2	−25
FTSE 250	200.0	10			−200
U.K. 20-year Bonds			300.0	5	300
U.K. Cash			100.0		100
U.S. Equities	100.0	15			−100
Japanese Equities	50.0	3			−50
Malaysian Equities	100.0	10			−100
U.S. Long Bonds			100.0	3	100

Source: Barrie & Hibbert.

be sought on the assumption that it would probably cost more than £100 million to buy back this part of the lent portfolio. Required haircuts might be based on the average daily liquidity for the asset class, the price volatility of the asset class and the residual risk on individual securities, taken from Exhibit 1.8.

Exhibit 1.9 shows how necessary haircuts could affect the valuation. For example, the lent Malaysian equities have been revised upwards to £101.4 million. This reflects the lower liquidity and higher volatility of the Malaysian equities, which outweigh the risk reduction brought by diversifying the risk on the lent portfolio. The lender's margin has thus effectively been reduced from £25 million to £16.2 million or 2.9%.

Risk Calculation (Postdefault)
Using the adjusted portfolios, the lender can then calculate the risk of a collateral shortfall in the event of the borrower defaulting. Broadly, this will need to assess the volatility of each asset class, the correlation between them and the residual risk of securities within them to derive a range of possible scenarios from which probabilities of loss and the most likely size of losses on default can be estimated. Working on the assumption that the lender can realize its collateral and replace its lent securities in a reaction time of 20 days, Exhibit 1.10 shows the results for the portfolio, together with some sensitivity analysis in case market volatility and liquidity that has been significantly changed. By increasing

EXHIBIT 1.8 Data Used to Drive the Analysis

Asset Class	Average Daily Liquidity (£m)	Asset Risk	Average Stock Residual Risk (% p.a.)	Correlation Assumptions							
				FTSE 100	FTSE 250	U.K. 20-Year Bonds	U.K. Cash	U.S. Equities	Japanese Equities	Malaysian Equities	U.S. Long Bonds
FTSE 100	5.80	18%	20%	1.00	0.93	0.38	-0.01	0.70	0.31	0.64	0.26
FTSE 250	1.00	20%	30%	0.93	1.00	0.30	-0.09	0.65	0.37	0.61	0.23
U.K. 20-year Bonds	20.00	9%	3%	0.38	0.30	1.00	-0.02	0.09	0.12	0.08	0.12
U.K. Cash		1%	3%	-0.01	-0.09	-0.02	1.00	-0.04	-0.09	-0.07	-0.02
U.S. Equities	9.40	20%	24%	0.70	0.65	0.09	-0.04	1.00	0.26	0.64	0.68
Japanese Equities	1.40	25%	22%	0.31	0.37	0.12	-0.09	0.26	1.00	0.30	0.13
Malaysian Equities	0.90	34%	29%	0.64	0.61	0.08	-0.07	0.64	0.30	1.00	0.39
U.S. Long Bonds	20.00	14%	5%	0.26	0.23	0.12	-0.02	0.68	0.13	0.39	1.00

Source: Barrie & Hibbert.

EXHIBIT 1.9   Adjusted Collateral and Lent Portfolio Values

Asset Class	Adjusted Loan Inventory (£m)	Adjusted Collateral Inventory (£m)	Net Margin (£m)
FTSE 100	100.7	73.8	−26.9
FTSE 250	203.8		−203.8
U.K. 20-year Bonds		299.7	299.7
U.K. Cash		100.0	100.0
U.S. Equities	100.2		−100.2
Japanese Equities	51.0		−51.0
Malaysian Equities	101.4		−101.4
U.S. Long Bonds		99.8	99.8

Source: Barrie & Hibbert.

EXHIBIT 1.10   Risk Analysis for Borrower 1 under Different Assumptions

Scenario	Probability of Loss on Default	Expected Loss on Default (£m)
Base Case	26%	4.0
Asset Risk Increased by 50%	33%	8.0
Reduce Liquidity by 50%	31%	5.1

Source: Barrie & Hibbert.

the volatility assumption or reducing the liquidity assumption, the probability and scale of expected losses increase.

The final sensitivity is reaction time and Exhibit 1.11 shows how the probability and expected size of losses decrease if the lender can realize the collateral and replace the lent securities more quickly.

This framework can be used to understand how possible changes in ABC's programme with Borrower 1 might affect the risks. Exhibit 1.11 summarizes some of the possible changes that could be made, in each case leaving the base case portfolio unchanged in other respects.

Netting

Netting is an important element of risk management given that market participants will often have many outstanding trades with a counterpart. If there is a default the various standard industry master agreements for securities lending should provide for the parties' various obligations under different securities lending transactions governed by a master

EXHIBIT 1.11   Risk Analysis for Borrower 1 under Different Lending Policies

Policy	Probability of Loss on Default	Expected Loss on Default (£m)
Base case portfolios	26%	4.0
Reaction time = 10 days	19%	1.8
Reaction time = 3 days	5%	0.2
Halve the concentration (i.e., double the number of securities lent and collateral)	20%	2.7
£10m more in cash collateral	15%	1.9
No Malaysian lending + Reduction in cash collateral	17%	1.7
Matched collateral/Lent exposure & concentration + Residual collateral in cash	14%	0.7

Source: Barrie & Hibbert.

agreement to be accelerated—that is, payments become due at current market values. So instead of requiring the parties to deliver securities or collateral on each of their outstanding transactions gross, their respective obligations are valued (i.e., given a cash value) and the value of the obligations owed by one party are set off against the value of the obligations owed by the other, and it is the net balance that is then due in cash.

This netting mechanism is a crucial part of the agreement. That is why there is so much legal focus on it. For example, participants need to obtain legal opinions about the effectiveness of netting provisions in jurisdictions of overseas counterparts, particularly in the event of a counterpart's insolvency.

That is also why regulators of financial firms typically expect legal opinions on the robustness of netting arrangements before they will recognize the value of collateral in reducing counterpart credit exposures for capital adequacy purposes.

CHAPTER 2

Securities Lending, Liquidity, and Capital Market-Based Finance

State Street

As the advantages that deep, liquid capital markets offer to national economies—most notably, enhanced capacity for economic growth—become more evident, policymakers in nations around the world are seeking ways to foster capital market growth. As capital markets evolve, they divide risk even more finely—by evolving new financial instruments such as options and futures (derivatives) and new investment vehicles and strategies such as mutual funds and hedged investments. The single most important quality that securities markets need to function successfully and to grow is *liquidity*—the ability to buy or sell substantial investment positions quickly, smoothly, and with minimal market impact. One of the most important factors in fostering liquidity is the evolution of a broad array of securities lending functions. The ability to borrow securities is, in fact, a key element in the development of advanced capital markets. Wherever securities lending has not yet become accepted practice, the evolution of national or regional capital markets is stunted—limiting their ability to efficiently allocate capital to economic development.

Today, more and more governments, multinational agencies and scholars recognize that capital markets play an indispensable role in economic development, and that securities lending enables these markets to work much better and to evolve. In recent years, many nations have been moving to remove legal and regulatory obstacles to securities lending and to actively encourage more participation in the practice as a way to spur the growth of their domestic capital markets.

The world's leading central banks themselves engage in the closely-related practice of using repurchase transactions (repos) in government securities markets as an element in managing their monetary policies. These institutions have also been encouraging a wider array of private securities firms to participate in this market alongside them. The growing official consensus in favor of capital markets and the increased recognition by policymakers of securities lending's function as an important market "lubricant" will ensure that securities lending remains a central element in twenty-first-century capital markets.

THE GREAT TRANSITION: THE RISE OF CAPITAL MARKET-BASED FINANCE

The financial history of the world's most developed economies through the twentieth century centers on a single theme—the "securitization of finance"—as capital markets grew to supplement, even to displace, traditional banks as the prime intermediaries between borrowers and lenders of capital.[1] The last decades of the twentieth century saw capital markets in the most developed nations come to eclipse traditional, bank-dominated financial systems. Fueled by a multitrillion dollar wave of pension and retirement savings, capital markets in the United States, the United Kingdom, and other leading economies have grown well past the scale of the total holdings of their national banking systems.

Capital markets in these nations have, in fact, replaced banks as the dominant source of corporate finance. In the United States, for example, this process of "disintermediation" is so far advanced that less than 30% of corporate finance now comes from traditional commercial banks. Some of the most dynamic growth areas in these nations' banking industries now center on the transformation of traditional bank products such as mortgages or credit-card debt into "securitized" products that can be traded on the capital markets.

The forces driving the rise of capital markets remain strong. These range from the aging of the global population, the attendant multitrillion dollar rise in retirement savings, the continuing triumph of capitalism itself, progress in the application of both raw computing power and quantitative strategies to investing, the explosive growth of derivatives and hedge funds, and today, the ubiquitous availability of information to guide and execute investment and trading strategies on a global basis.

---

[1] Ron Chernow, *The Death of the Banker: The Decline and Fall of the Great Financial Dynasties and the Triumph of the Small Investor* (New York: Vintage Books, Random House, 1997).

A growing number of economists and policymakers, backed up by day-to-day experience, now share a consensus view: robust capital markets, which offer a full array of modern financial products and practices, contribute to long-term national economic growth by encouraging entrepreneurship and innovation, even given periodic market corrections.[2]

Capital markets can finance economic growth more efficiently than traditional bank-lending systems that depend on making a "spread" of interest rate revenue over the banks' costs of funds. Capital markets can more easily diversify and distribute risk by dividing shares in the equity ownership or portions of the debt involved in financing enterprises into stocks and bonds, which in turn can be much more widely dispersed among investors than traditional bank loans.

The availability of active markets for shares in new enterprises then enables venture capitalists to make a range of investments in a variety of high-risk ventures—in the hope that one or more spectacularly successful IPOs will more than make up for other ventures' failures and losses. Traditional commercial banks, by contrast, cannot risk lending to an array of unproven startups—however promising—because banks cannot earn enough additional interest on those new firms that succeed to make up for capital they are likely to lose when other, unproved borrowers fail.

In addition, as capital markets evolve further, they can "split the atom" of risk even more finely—by creating new financial instruments such as options and futures and new investment vehicles and strategies such as mutual funds, exchange traded funds and hedged investments. These provide investors new ways to increase returns and manage risks, and to do so more cost effectively.

Given these dynamic, growth-fostering advantages, it is no surprise that both developed and emerging nations are actively seeking to follow the same process of financial evolution so evident in the United States, the United Kingdom, and other capital market leaders. The movement away from communist economic regimes in the 1980s and 1990s has spawned a huge expansion in the number of global stock markets that money managers and institutional investors have to consider—from fewer than 80 in the early 1980s to more than 160 by the turn of the twenty-first century.

Much of that growth has been concentrated among the world's most advanced securities markets—notably New York and London—where market capitalization on the leading exchanges multiplied tenfold in the 1990s. As the strategic growth advantage that developed capital markets offer to national economies becomes more evident, policymakers in

---

[2] Ross Levine and Sara Zervos, "Stock Markets, Banks, and Economic Growth," IFC, World Bank, 1999.

many nations are coming to view capital market development as imperative to their nations' futures, to their ability to finance new high-tech industries and to their competitiveness in a globalizing economy.

Over and above their "growth advantage," the development of deep, liquid capital markets also offers nations the benefit of greater financial system stability. As Federal Reserve Board Chairman Alan Greenspan has noted, the existence of strong capital markets alongside well-regulated banking systems may help insulate a nation's whole financial system from systemic risk by providing alternate sources of liquidity and financing that can be tapped when either banking systems or securities markets are in short-term crisis.[3]

This is not to suggest that capital markets represent some magic elixir for economic growth, or that traditional banks are moribund. Even when accompanied by well-developed rule of law, advanced accounting standards and free flow of information, capital markets can, at times, overinflate or depress underlying economic value, creating "bubbles" and "panics." As the Fed Chairman noted, the central banks' ability to inject liquidity into the financial system through banks was essential in containing the financial "contagion" that had frozen many securities markets in the wake of the 1997–1998 Asian financial crisis.

The key point is that having advanced capital markets and strong banking systems gives nations both greater competition in the provision of capital and the possibility of turning to complementary financing systems, and eliminates the need to simply rely on one or the other. The "securitization" of the U.S.-based mortgage industry, for example, helped keep housing finance flowing, which limited the depth of the 1990–1991 U.S. recession precisely because banks could repackage and sell their mortgage loans into capital markets.

Financial Complexity and "Intensification"

Besides their sheer scale, the world's most developed capital markets have become vastly more complex and transnational in scope. Companies doing business in and serving these capital markets—both buy-side institutional investors and sell-side brokerage firms—have expanded their horizons from national to global markets as they seek to manage the largest pools of long-term investment capital in history.

Investors have also changed their own investment and trading habits in a process that some analysts have dubbed "financial intensification." This refers to both the vast proliferation of new financial instruments—mainly options, futures and other derivatives that inves-

---

[3] Alan Greenspan, "Remarks Before the World Bank Group and the International Monetary Fund, Program of Seminars," Washington, D.C., September 27, 1999.

tors use to manage and mitigate risk—and to the dramatic rises in trading volumes as investors engage these new instruments to conduct trading and investment strategies that often produce vastly higher turnover.

Taken together, the rise of cross-border investing and the proliferation of financial instruments that serve to arbitrage differences between national capital markets, points to the emergence of a single truly global capital market which is subject to the "law of one price" as domestic price and regulatory differences erode.[4] Individual nations' markets, then, become nodes in this emerging global network, and their success depends on the extent that national policymakers make their markets attractive to domestic and foreign investors.

Clearly, what capital markets need above all to grow, to become liquid, and to sustain increasing volumes of transactions is capital—preferably sustainable flows of long-term, "patient" investment. The prime source for funding the rise of late twentieth century capital markets has been domestic pension savings and the evolution of collective investment vehicles. It is no coincidence that the nations with the highest ratios of equity market capitalization to *gross domestic product* (GDP)—the United States, the United Kingdom, the Netherlands, for example—also have the most well-developed systems of pension, collective fund, and personal retirement savings. While domestic pension savings have been a prime fuel for their growth, the most advanced capital markets also benefit from their openness to cross-border investing, which grew explosively in the 1990s.

For nations whose capital markets are less developed, one clear lesson is that the removal of obstacles to foreign investment is itself a prerequisite for the development of effective capital markets.[5] Improving regulatory transparency is also necessary to boost foreign investment. Transparency leads to business predictability for foreign entities that are expanding to new markets and taking the risk of dealing with many uncertainties. In turn, the ability of a given national or regional securities market to attract capital—whether from domestic savings and pension funds or from offshore investors—depends critically on the creation of efficient, well-regulated mechanisms for handling rising transaction flows, settling trades and mitigating risk.

---

[4] Lowell Bryan and Diana Farrell, *Market Unbound: Unleashing Global Capitalism* (New York: John Wiley & Sons, Inc., 1996).
[5] World Trade Organization, "Opening Markets in Financial Services and the Role of the GATS," September 22, 1997.

THE CENTRAL ROLE OF LIQUIDITY

The single most important quality that successful securities markets must foster is liquidity—the ability to buy or sell substantial investment positions quickly, smoothly, and with minimal market impact. As an analysis from the Counterparty Risk Management Policy Group put it: "Market liquidity is a precondition for the smooth pursuit of *all financial activities*, including the pricing of financial products, the risk management of financial institutions, and the conduct of monetary policy."[6]

There is, of course, a notorious circularity in analyzing the root sources of liquidity because it is, to a large degree, a self-fulfilling phenomenon. Investor confidence spurs a general willingness to trade, the participation of many transactors deepens markets and smoothes trading, and these qualities of a market further raise investors' confidence. Liquidity is, or can be, the function of such a "virtuous circle."

Definitions of liquidity range beyond the ability to deploy capital into and out of a market in an "efficient" way—that is, without excessive transaction costs or impacts on securities prices. Micro-analysis of a given market measures its liquidity in at least three dimensions:

- Tightness—how far transaction prices diverge from midmarket prices—a metric generally visible in the size of bid-asked spreads
- Depth—how large a volume of trades can be processed without significantly affecting prevailing market prices or the amount of orders on market-makers' books in a given timeframe
- Resiliency—how quickly price fluctuations resulting from trade are dissipated and/or how quickly imbalances in order flows are adjusted and price recovery occurs[7]

In a somewhat broader sense, liquidity includes the ability of market participants to make money by trading when a market is moving downward as well when that market is trending upwards. Liquidity also relies on efficient price information and settlement systems, low transactions pricing and spreads, and low infrastructure and tax costs.

These overall features of a market's efficiency, all of which contribute liquidity to traders and investors in a market, are continually evolving. National laws and regulations, systems for trade settlements and record-keeping, provisions for the security of investors' own data and for greater

---

[6] Counterparty Risk Management Policy Group, "Improving Counterparty Risk Management Practices," June 1999.

[7] BIS-CGFS, "Market Liquidity: Research Findings and Selected Policy Implications," May 1999.

transparency of financial information provided to the market—these elements can all enhance liquidity if they are well designed and implemented. Alternatively, regulatory restrictions on short-selling or hedge funds and other, even more inhibiting measures—such as capital controls or transaction taxes—can discourage investors and erode liquidity.

Ultimately, liquidity is a function of investors' confidence that they can buy and sell their investments when they want to in markets that may fluctuate but which will not stall or fail. Clearly investor confidence—or its withdrawal—has a self-reinforcing impact on any market's liquidity. Fostering such confidence, then, has to be a central aim for national authorities intent on developing their capital markets. One way that governments and central banks foster liquidity directly is through implicit assurances that they will provide market participants with funds to keep orderly trading underway and mitigate trading freeze-ups or panicky sell-offs if market crises do occur.

Offering a specific asset class—such as long-term government bonds—with specific policy assurances that the government will keep the market liquid, can also be a useful way to ensure that even amid the evaporation of liquidity from some markets, at least some benchmark asset that the rest of the market relies on to price other risks and values will continue trading freely until confidence generally can be restored.[8]

Another way to encourage liquidity is for national regulatory authorities to allow and encourage more market participants to engage in lending and borrowing securities already outstanding in the nations' equity and bond markets. (Such permission, even encouragement, is already common in most markets for government bonds, because most central banks are themselves major "players" in these markets.) Regulators can further assist by understanding and encouraging the use of swaps, options and other derivatives, which encourage liquidity by enabling traders and investors to mitigate their risks.

Evolution of the U.S. Securities Lending Market

The development of a broad array of securities lending activities can provide a very significant source of liquidity to any well-developed capital market. A brief review of how securities lending has evolved in the U.S. market—the world's deepest and most liquid securities investment and trading arena—can help illustrate the critical role that securities lending practices play in providing liquidity to increasingly vast capital markets which are executing increasingly complex trading strategies.

Historically, the earliest evidence of securities lending in the United States can be traced back to the market for U.S. government war debt

---

[8] BIS-CGFS, May 1999.

following the Declaration of Independence in 1776. But a considerably more robust market for private securities lending in both the American and British stock and bond markets developed throughout the 1800s.

From those centuries-old origins well into the mid-twentieth century, the lending and borrowing of securities evolved as a private, ad hoc practice usually done directly between investors or broker/dealers. It was not until the 1960s, in the United States, that securities lending began to develop as a substantial day-to-day market of its own served by specialized institutions and practitioners.

The most important factor driving the emergence of the modern securities lending industry was the revival of interest in stock market investing brought about in the 1960s by the U.S. economy's booming growth. Many of the leading firms on Wall Street not only notched record profits, but also drew a level of individual and institutional investment not seen since before the "Crash" of 1929 and the subsequent Great Depression.

As rapid economic growth fueled a booming equity market on Wall Street, first individuals and increasingly, pension funds, rushed to invest. Many corporations too, took advantage of rising share prices to issue equity-related hybrid securities convertible into common stock. Other companies used their rising stock as "currency" to take part in a wave of corporate takeovers and restructurings.

Both of these developments opened new opportunities for professional traders to "arbitrage" between common stock and hybrids—or between the stocks of acquiring or target firms engaged in takeover battles. The bull market also revived interest in American Depositary Receipts (ADRs), an instrument developed in the late 1920s to represent foreign shares traded in markets in other countries. Not least, as stock prices soared, more bearish speculators sold shares short in hopes that prices would later decline.

By the early 1970s, both stock exchanges and securities firms were struggling to cope with the huge upsurge of trading brought on by these overlapping waves of change. The result was a series of major back office snarls, some severe enough to lead to the collapse of major Wall Street trading firms and an explosion in settlement failures. These symptoms of operational dysfunction—and classic market illiquidity—were eased in the course of the 1970s by two developments. First, the trade settlement process was increasingly automated and the back office paper jams eased. Second, a true securities lending industry began to emerge that was able to reduce trade fails substantially by providing borrowed assets to arbitrageurs, short-sellers and other traders who needed securities that they did not own to conduct their investment strategies.

The growth of institutionalized securities lending was a timely development for U.S. markets because it paralleled a further surge in the demand-side of the securities lending equation. This was brought about by the boom in option trading and other derivatives in the mid-1970s set off by the application to capital markets of the Black-Scholes option-pricing model. This analytical tool provided traders with a more reliable formula for gauging the value of put and call options on stocks. With a reliable metric for measuring values in the options markets, volume exploded. And trading strategies based on options required the borrowing and lending of shares for hedging as well as for arbitrage. As the so-called "derivatives revolution" rolled on, the investment strategies born of the Black-Scholes model laid the groundwork for a fresh wave of financial innovation centered on new derivatives, index arbitrage, and other complex investment and trading strategies throughout the 1980s and 1990s—all of which drove demand from dealers and investors for borrowed securities to execute their trades and hedge their market risks.

On the supply side, U.S. custodian banks moved to meet demand for borrowed securities in the 1970s by devising lending services for such institutional clients as insurance companies, corporate investment portfolios, and, later, college endowment funds. Legislation soon permitted pension funds to join the quest for enhanced returns by engaging in securities lending. By the mid-1980s, the majority of large institutional investors in the United States were using securities lending routinely as a way to earn extra income to offset custodial fees—and securities lending in the United States had itself become a thoroughly institutionalized industry.

The key lesson of this U.S. experience is simple: Securities lending and capital markets evolve in tandem.

Securities Lending: Key to Market Liquidity

In mobilizing the securities already outstanding in a market, securities lending has the effect of increasing the total supply of assets available to support trading and settlement. This enables the outstanding stock of assets, in effect, to do "double duty" in the service of market liquidity by converting otherwise sterile holdings into a dynamic, internally generated source of finance that can support higher trading volumes and more sophisticated trading strategies.

By turning existing stocks and bonds into financing sources for further transactions, a well-developed securities lending business can minimize trading friction, improve efficiency, reduce settlement fails, and lower transaction costs across an entire capital market. The benefits are multiple. Risk mitigation is made easier by the options that securities lending provides to investors wanting to balance "long" positions with off-setting "short" positions. Indeed, *all* market participants benefit— not just those who engage in securities lending or borrowing.

The development of a sophisticated securities lending industry has, in fact, played a central role in enhancing the liquidity of those markets that have managed to successfully "leap" to maturity. Indeed, market "maturity" may best be defined as the level of liquidity that can attract significant investment from large global investors.

In country after country through the 1980s and 1990s, new or revitalized capital markets began their economic "take-offs" by first attracting increased attention from domestic investors and from the most venturesome of foreign investors. Almost by definition, it is this first wave of inward investment that makes an emerging market actually "emerge." To continue growing, a capital market needs to draw investment that is more stable and longer-term—from larger investors who are typically much more risk-averse than the pioneers.

This has required capital marketplaces around the world to improve and automate their settlement processes, to establish central securities depositories (where they did not yet exist) and to "decertify" securities ownership and unclog paper flows.

As these changes take hold and investment in a given market rises, further pressures build—for better data, for greater transparency, and for the creation of derivatives or short-selling practices that increasingly larger investors need to hedge their investment risks. The demand for means to hedge exposures is particularly acute among global pension funds.

Bound by fiduciary standards of prudence, many institutional investors are virtually obliged to use derivatives, repos, and other instruments to manage their investment exposures. The rise of markets in derivatives instruments, in turn, depends on the ability of players in the real or "underlying" securities markets to engage in substantial short-selling and securities lending, and so to sustain liquidity amid rising transaction volumes.

In markets where securities lending is underdeveloped—or explicitly discouraged by regulatory or cultural barriers—evolution to a world-class level is simply stunted, at least until these barriers are removed.

As this market development pattern has replayed time after time, more and more governments, multilateral agencies like the World Bank and economists have come to acknowledge the catalytic role of capital markets in economic development. Institutions like the Bank for International Settlements are also acknowledging the role of securities lending in helping securities markets to function well.

A new consensus is emerging: the ability to borrow securities is an indispensable element in the development of advanced, effective capital markets.[9] Indeed, the greater the turnover in a market, the more important

---

[9] Technical Committee of the International Organization of Securities Commissions (IOSCO), "Securities Lending Transactions: Market Development and Implications," Bank for International Settlements (BIS) Committee on Payment and Settlement Systems (CPSS), July 1999.

securities lending becomes. Securities lending, in short, is no longer an ad hoc, back-office operation that enables borrowers to trade on securities they currently do not own. Nor is securities lending merely a low-risk way for institutional investor lenders to earn a few more basis points or cut custody fees on their holdings. Securities lending as an industry has, in fact, matured to become a major source of internal financing that any capital market needs to achieve world-class, twenty-first century practice.

Little wonder that a report by the Bank for International Settlements and the International Organization of Securities Commissions concluded that

> Securities lending markets are a vital component of domestic and international finance markets, providing liquidity and greater flexibility to securities, cash, and derivatives markets ... Securities lending activity will continue to increase and become an even more integral component of financial markets in the future.[10]

Sophisticated regulators and policymakers in many nations now recognize that securities lending provides the liquidity that lubricates their capital market engines. And, as a 1998 report by the Committee on the Global Financial System notes:

> Investors are more willing to transact and take positions in markets where they expect liquidity to continue at a high level for the foreseeable future ... and market liquidity tends to be enhanced when instruments can be substituted for one another, since the market for each of them will be less fragmented.[11]

This growing recognition by governments and regulators of the value of securities lending should not be surprising. It stems, in large part, from central banks' and monetary authorities' own reliance on the closely-related practice of using *repurchase agreements* (repos) in their government debt markets as a key element in monetary policy—a development we will turn to shortly. However, we will first explain how securities lending finances liquidity.

How Securities Lending Finances Liquidity

To better understand how securities lending concretely contributes to market liquidity, consider the structure of a specific equity lending

---

[10] IOSCO/BIS Report, July 1999.

[11] BIS-CGFS, "A Review of Financial Market Events in Autumn 1998," October 1999.

transaction in its simplest form. In basic equity lending, a counterparty borrows stocks against a collateral obligation. The borrowed shares are cycled back into the trading market and the collateral (if cash) is used to purchase additional instruments, generally short-term money market or other fixed-income instruments. Both components of the transaction— the lent securities and the reinvested collateral—inject additional securities or cash into capital markets, enhancing liquidity both directly and indirectly.

The increased supply of assets that lending makes available to support transactions in a given market facilitates that market's efficiency in the pricing and settlement of transactions, which helps the market's trading flow move more smoothly and with less market impact. This is virtually a dictionary definition of what liquidity means.

However, securities lending also enhances liquidity indirectly. That is because the smoother transaction flows that lending facilitates contribute to investors' confidence that they can trade with less risk of "fails" or market freeze-ups. This holds true not only for the simple example cited above, but for the whole array of complex trading strategies that have evolved over recent decades, all of which depend on a robust securities lending market for their execution.

As a market grows in value and trading volume, market participants create new instruments and trading strategies that increase demand for borrowed securities. Securities lending thus evolves from a settlement and back office function to the supplying of securities to cover short positions to the supplying of lent securities to support global trading strategies.

By reintroducing shares, bonds or other financial instruments back into the market on a cost-efficient and timely basis, securities lending enables market participants to use these assets in ways that rebalance prices, diversify risk, minimize trade and settlement fails and allow positions to be exchanged even when parties to a trade do not own the securities being traded.

Here is a further example from the world of arbitrage, one of the heavy generators of demand for securities lending in today's marketplace. Arbitrage trading, the object of which is to capture price differences for the same security or its equivalent in different markets, generates continual demand for securities borrowing as arbitrageurs seek to exploit often minimal and transitory price differences between securities that they may not own. The arbitrageur's profit is often minuscule. But he repeats this strategy all day long, whenever the price spread gets out of line on either the high or low side. That makes him an omnipresent "rebalancer" of prices— and an incessant contributor to liquidity on both sides of the market. And although arbitrageurs seek profit from inefficient pricing, it is their trading, often supported by borrowed securities, that keeps bringing prices back in line and makes overall markets more efficient.

In ADR arbitrage, for instance, the arbitrageur trades back and forth between a depositary receipt traded in the United States and the actual shares traded in, say, Frankfurt, capturing price discrepancies as they arise. The arbitrageur borrows securities as needed to execute his trade—and in the process deepens trading volume and pushes the prices back in line. Similarly, index arbitrage keeps pricing in line between a basket of shares and an index futures contract.

The more complex strategy of "risk arbitrage" in corporate merger and acquisition deals also rebalances and adds liquidity to securities markets. When one company offers its shares to buy another company, the arbitrage strategy is often to purchase the target company's shares, borrow shares of the acquiring company and sell them short to capture the premium, often 20% or more, that the acquirer is offering as an incentive to the target company's shareholders. When, or if, the deal goes through, the arbitrageur can capture the premium by delivering his (or her) shares in the target company in exchange for the acquiring company's shares, which he then returns to the securities lender.

Target companies sometimes object to risk arbitrage activity on grounds that a large proportion of its shares in arbitrageurs' hands will swing a shareholder vote in favor of the deal. But risk arbitrage—and the securities lending that makes it possible—benefits the market by absorbing a large portion of the acquisition risks, bringing pricing in line with those risks, and adding trading liquidity that permits shareholders in the target company to sell their shares and capture a portion of the premium before the deal goes through.

Recognizing Securities Lending's Key Role

The decade of the 1990s was bracketed by two major policy reports that resoundingly endorsed the role of securities lending in capital market development—and urged nations to do more to encourage it. The first was a 1989 report by the Group of 30 (G-30) on clearing and settlement systems. One of the report's recommendations urged governments and regulators to facilitate securities lending in order to reduce the high rates of trading "fails" that were discouraging cross-border investors and rendering domestic capital markets illiquid and prone to paralysis.[12]

The G-30's call to take down regulatory and taxation barriers that inhibit securities lending received increasingly positive response through the 1990s. Japan, Australia, the United Kingdom, Switzerland, Italy,

---

[12] Group of Thirty, "Clearance and Settlement in the World's Securities Markets," March 1989.

France, and other nations acted to remove legal and regulatory obstacles to securities lending and to actively encourage more participation in lending, swaps and securities "sell-buy-back" agreements by both domestic and foreign entities.[13]

At the same time, in the form of repurchase agreements, securities lending has become a vital tool of modern monetary policy though the activity of central banks themselves in government securities markets. Leading central banks all now use an active repo trading strategy to add liquidity to their sovereign debt markets, to stabilize their currencies, and to attract foreign investment.

Amid the explosive growth of global capital markets—and the increasing use of securities lending and hedging techniques by central banks and governments—the decade of the 1990s closed with this conclusion from a joint study by BIS and IOSCO:

> Securities lending has become a central part of securities market activity in recent years, to the point where the daily volume of securities transactions for financing purposes considerably exceeds that of outright purchase and sale transactions.[14]

Repo and Securities Lending

Securities lending and the market in repos have similar characteristics but with different legal structures. They both follow the same transaction structure whereby a security is transferred vs. a collateral obligation. Repo transactions are outright sales of a security accompanied by an agreement to buy the security back at a specified price on a specified date—sometimes as soon as the next day. Thus they can be used as either a securities borrowing or cash borrowing vehicle. In effect, the repo seller lends the security against cash collateral, while the repo buyer lends cash against the security as collateral.

Like a securities loan, repo may have the effect of bringing divergent prices back into line, of lowering the cost of financing and trading strategies, and of "splitting the atom of risk."

By the 1990s, the repo market was quite sophisticated. As the July 1999 IOSCO/BIS report described it:

> In the U.S. Treasury repo market, brokers began to run matched book portfolios to provide liquidity to their customers and to use the repo market to take positions on the short end of the yield curve. For example, a broker might lend securities on repo for one

---

[13] IOSCO/BIS Report, July 1999.
[14] IOSCO/BIS Report, July 1999.

month and finance them for one week, in the expectation that repo financing rates would fall. Thus repo grew beyond a straightforward financing market to become a money market instrument in its own right, as an alternative to interbank deposit and Treasury bill/certification of deposit markets.[15]

Perhaps most significantly, repo has evolved to be an important tool in managing monetary policy for a number of central banks around the world. As noted by the Committee on the Global Financial System in its report on Implications of the Repo Market for Central Banks,

> For the central banks that use them, repos have often become the most important monetary policy instrument. In a number of G-10 central banks, the proportion of repos used in the refinancing of the domestic financial sector is over 70%.[16]

Repo and securities lending are related transactions with related functions. They are linked by their similarity in providing a supply of securities, increasing trading volumes, diversifying risk, and helping to keep financial markets running smoothly. These very similar practices are, in fact, linked across markets. As the Committee of the Global Financial System notes:

> In some instances, the supply of securities in repo markets can be increased by stock-lending agreements . . . (such agreements) allow institutions that hold securities but do not want to (or are not allowed to) participate in the repo markets to earn a higher return . . . Since repo markets support securities markets, securities issuers sometimes take steps to promote them.[17]

In addition to the increased liquidity that loans of securities inject into a capital market by directly facilitating various trading strategies, the collateral that is posted against borrowed securities also benefits the markets.

When cash is pledged as collateral, the general practice is to reinvest it in short-term, money-market instruments, because securities lenders have to price, purchase, sell and settle on a daily basis and holding any illiquid instrument in a short-term fund would be excessively risky. The need to invest such collateral, in turn, generates substantial, continuing demand from securities lenders for reliable money-market investments—adding breadth and depth to markets for supranational, corporate and

---

[15] IOSCO/BIS Report, July 1999.

[16] BIS-CGFS, "Implications of Repo Markets for Central Banks," March 1999.

[17] BIS-CGFS, March 1999.

securitized short-term debt. Where noncash collateral is accepted, lenders will generally approve only issues that can readily be priced, traded, and liquidated for a cash position in order to protect securities loans.

THE EMERGING OFFICIAL CONSENSUS: FOSTERING CAPITAL MARKETS AND SECURITIES LENDING

As governments, multinational agencies, and scholars recognize both the catalytic role of capital markets in economic development and the ways that securities lending keeps markets liquid, a growing number of nations are removing legal and regulatory obstacles to securities lending. Some are actively encouraging more participation in the practice by both domestic and foreign entities.

Recent developments around the globe indicate that nations are continuing to recognize the merits of securities lending and to encourage the practice through reforms. Official support is particularly notable in the closely-related arena of repo transactions in government securities markets—which have become central to the operations of the largest and most powerful monetary authorities in the world.

CONCLUSION

If the 1990s saw the rise of capital markets as the prime vehicles for financing the most dynamic economies in the world, the first decade of the twenty-first century will see these markets truly come of age. Growing awareness of the powerful competitive advantages that well-developed capital markets bring to national economies will spur their further development worldwide. The continued global movement towards pension and savings reforms will provide trillions of dollars in mass-based investment capital to help world securities markets grow.

Nations that want to harness these vast, stable flows of long-term funds to spur their capital markets will, in turn, need to open themselves to the full array of legal, regulatory and transaction mechanisms that make securities markets work. Derivatives, hedging, and securities lending are among the key elements that any market will need to make available to attract investors and grow.

As the representatives of securities regulators and central banks concluded in the 1999 IOSCO/BIS report:

Today, securities lending markets are a vital component of domestic and international finance markets, providing liquidity and greater flexibility to securities, cash, and derivatives markets . . . Securities lending activity will continue to increase and become an even more integral component of financial markets in the future.[18]

The increased official recognition by policymakers and central banks that they need to stimulate securities lending in general and repo markets in particular promises to make securities lending a central element in the growth of twenty-first century capital markets. This implies that as astonishing as the rise of securities lending has been over the past 20 years, the industry's best days are yet to come.

---

[18] IOSCO/BIS Report, July 1999.

CHAPTER 3

Finding a Route to Market: An Institutional Guide to the Securities Lending Labyrinth

Mark C. Faulkner
Managing Director
Spitalfields Advisors

F inding the most suitable route to market and the issue of selecting a counterpart are at the heart of the securities lending business. In this chapter, we discuss these issues for the benefit of institutions whose core businesses do not include securities lending. We focus on the lending of international equities with regard to both lending and nonlending institutions.

WHICH COMES FIRST—THE DESIRE TO LEND OR THE ROUTE TO MARKET?

How do explorers plan expeditions? Do they first choose a destination, and then plan the route? Or, do they plan a route and thus reach a destination by default? Explorers have doubtless done both.

How do institutions approach lending? Do they first decide to lend, and then find the appropriate route to market? Or, do they become seduced by the proponent of a particular route and slip into the decision to lend?

Historical precedent suggests that it is ultimately possible to reach a satisfactory conclusion in whatever order these decisions are made. Continents are discovered whether people sail off looking for them or not.

Today, when we want to explore a known place, we usually identify the destination and, perhaps, the motivation for embarking on the journey before we select the route. So how should institutions approach the lending market? Before we tackle this question, let us explore whether such a market exists and whether it is accurate to call it a *market*. If it does exist, institutions should understand the kind of market that it is. What are its characteristics? What drives it?

Approaching a peripheral activity, for that is what securities lending is for most institutions, requires caution and patience. Navigating this labyrinth is not easy, nor is it impossible. Despite what any marketer of the business may tell you, it is no more "rocket science" than it is a "free lunch."

MARKET CHARACTERISTICS

Any market can be defined as a meeting place for supply and demand. The securities lending business qualifies as a market in its own right, given that definition. Lending institutions and a wide variety of intermediaries provide the supply to meet demands of other intermediaries or principal borrowers.

When we look at the source of the demand, the status of securities lending as a market in its own right is somewhat less obvious. The core market driver is a demand for securities that comes from proprietary traders selling the cash market short, frequently to hedge long derivative positions. If we accept this fact, we see that the securities lending market is subordinate to, and dependent on, the cash and derivative securities markets.

The securities lending market is also tied closely to other securities financing markets in the form of the repo, swaps, and prime brokerage products. The recent use of repurchase agreements (repo) for equity securities, as well as bonds, in Europe is a case in point.

In the repo market, equity lending desks of brokers, dealers, and banks finance their long equity inventory as if they were bonds. Many of these positions, of course, exist either as a result of financing customer strategies or because securities have been borrowed in anticipation of making onward deliveries. Which comes first, the borrow or the repo?

Securities lending is part of the broader securities financing business. The number of firms renaming departments is clear evidence of this fact.

MARKET SIGNIFICANCE

If the derivatives market is the engine, then securities lending is the oil; it brings much needed liquidity to the marketplace—at a price. This oil is expensive. Some estimates suggest that international securities lending revenues (i.e., excluding those in U.S. domestic market) exceed $1.5 billion per year. It is the search for a share of this revenue that draws institutions from their core activities toward the less familiar world of securities lending.

Securities lending is a specialist activity with its own conventions, practices, and rules. As in any business, it is most rewarding to be an expert. Pension funds hire experienced managers to invest assets to meet the demands of their pensioners. Insurance companies manage assets to meet their liabilities. Securities lending experts focus upon matching supply and demand of lendable securities.

The key factor distinguishing securities lending from many other areas of the financial services sector is its almost complete lack of transparency. This lack of transparency is to the benefit of the experts.

MARKET TRANSPARENCY

The securities lending market is so opaque that it reminds some observers of the bankruptcy business in the United States during the 1980s. Information and experience is highly concentrated in the hands of a relatively small number of firms and people. There are very few screens on which prices are displayed and fewer still where you can get more than an indicative quote.

The market remains this way because it is in the interests of the dominant players to keep it so. More transparency is not in their interest, or so they believe. This lack of transparency does more than restrict the number of institutions bringing supply to the market. It also hampers the speed of any institutional entry.

Most service providers would agree that an informed customer is a better customer. This is not the widely held view in the securities lending business. Such an attitude has not only held the market back, but also led to the development of numerous myths.

MARKET MYTHS

We can dispel some of the more popular market myths.

■ "Everyone should lend." As our examination will show, this business is not for everyone. That said, everyone *should be* an informed observer. Portfolios and trading strategies change. What is once an unattractive portfolio, from a lending perspective, may become attractive in the future.

■ "Lending is risk-free." While it is true that the risks can be identified, managed, and minimized, no one should expect to be rewarded in this business without accepting some risk.

■ "Cash is the only safe form of collateral." Cash has to be managed and invested to produce a yield, and cash reinvestment is not without its risks. In Europe, fiscal regimes have historically encouraged using securities and letters of credit as collateral. Recently, equities, convertible bonds, and even equity warrants have been accepted as part of collateral portfolios along with the more typical government bonds. The significant losses in the securities lending business are associated almost exclusively with the taking of cash as collateral.

■ "Good collateral makes a good counterpart out of a bad one." Collateral should be seen as insurance against counterpart default. An unrated counterpart with little capital should be seen for what it is, not what it gives you as collateral. Good collateral, in terms of the type of assets and haircut taken, can provide merely a degree of increased comfort.

■ "There is one route to market." In fact, there are several different routes to market, each with its own advantages and disadvantages. The different routes are not mutually exclusive, as some may have you believe.

■ "Indemnification eliminates all risk." Indemnities vary considerably in quality. Some will eliminate most of the risks associated with participation in this business; others are not worth the paper they are written upon. Ultimately one has to recognize that this form of insurance and protection is not without cost. Furthermore, no matter what the indemnification says, one is always exposed to the risk that the indemnifier will not perform.

■ "A level playing field exists." Irrespective of an institution's sense of fairness and desire to treat all counterparts equally, one has to recognize that they are not equal in all respects. Triple A-rated banks are different from single B-rated broker/dealers and should be treated accordingly. The fact that they are not treated differently is a testament to good marketing on behalf of the disadvantaged and an unwilling-ness on behalf of many institutions to make difficult decisions. In the money markets, a lender of cash explicitly differentiates between bor-rowers by setting different rates, margins, collateral requirements, and duration limits. Such differentiation is rare in the securities lending business, with the result that an unlevel playing field is artificially lev-eled. This is not in the long-term interest of the lending community.

■ "The market is mature." There remains a significant imbalance between international supply and international demand in certain countries and for particular securities. Why else would any potential new lender be courted by so many borrower suitors? New firms con-tinue to enter the market, and certain intermediaries continue to oper-ate profitably. The rise of third-party agent lenders is just the latest phenomenon in a market that continues to develop and change. Even where the market exhibits signs of maturity, such as in the U.S. equity market, there remains significant room for revenue generation.

■ "Standardized legal contracts fit all scenarios." Standardized contracts bring the benefits of consistency, and can save on legal expenditure, but they should be seen more as a starting point than a solution. The vagar-ies of cross-border securities lending transactions mandate careful con-sideration before choosing to use one of several standard documents without amendment.

■ "Tax arbitrage drives the market." Fiscal authorities around the globe are, quite rightly, fixated upon the collection of taxes due them. When it comes to securities lending, however, their collecting zeal seems to know no bounds. Rather than see the cost of manufacturing a dividend for what it is, namely, a cost associated with borrowing securities (that borrowers seek to minimize), the tax authorities see a dividend arbi-trage behind every trade. This is certainly not the case. While it is true that tax arbitrage does take place, and that the securities lending mar-ket plays a role in facilitating it, it is equally true that the largest non-dollar lending market is the Japanese market. Here the historically low dividend yields play a minimal role in borrower motivation.

ORGANIZATIONAL CHARACTERISTICS

Before expending any energy on securities lending beyond your organi-zation, you need to spend some time considering the characteristics that your organization and portfolios exhibit. Working on the assumption that it is unlikely that an institution will reinvent itself or adopt a new trading strategy just to facilitate the lending of securities, this approach could save significant resources and frustration.

To simplify the approach, we divide institutional characteristics into two groups—organizational and portfolio-specific. We acknowledge that all organizations differ but feel that some general characteristics are comon across geographical and sectoral boundaries. For the purposes of this analysis, we assume that the regulatory situation affecting any lending decision is known and clear, admittedly an extreme simplifying assumption.

Management Motivation

Every lender is in it for the money. Some may view lending as a peripheral activity to help offset custody and administrative cost and, whatever the merits of their portfolio, may never change this view. Others see lending as a valuable contributor to revenues and a potential source of competitive advantage, and act accordingly.

It is important that the activity be sponsored by a wide cross section of the organization and that the fund managers are motivated to provide their support. As any operations manager will tell you, running a program without the understanding and commitment of the fund managers is fraught with peril. Senior managers need to understand the motivation behind their organization's potential involvement, and move forward only when a degree of consensus is reached.

Technology

While a variety of vendor systems can alleviate a significant amount of the technological strain associated with participating in securities lending, successful participants commit significant resources to internal systems. Borrowers will want to receive available inventory as frequently as possible. Lenders will need: (1) to avoid lending the same securities twice; (2) to deal with sales of inventory by their fund managers; (3) to process both recalls and returns; and (4) to effect any "buy-ins" as necessary. These are not particularly difficult tasks, but each needs to be recognized and addressed.

Credit

A lender's collateral flexibility, be it in terms of cash reinvestment parameters or the ability to accept lower-grade securities, will be rewarded. Like any other market, the securities lending market is a meeting place for organizations with a wide range of credit quality and collateral capabilities. A borrower's credit rating may be inversely related to its propensity to borrow. If an institution has a cautious approach to counterpart selection and a low tolerance for risk, this must be recognized by management charged with researching securities lending. This is not to say that securities lending cannot be conducted profitably, but rather that the route to market selected has to be consistent with the institution's general risk profile.

Do-it-Yourself or Outsource

Some organizations have a propensity to outsource services; others do not. Understanding this fundamental organizational trait, prior to talking to potential counterparts, will enable managers to identify routes that are not likely to be suitable, and to focus on those that exhibit more of an organizational "fit."

PORTFOLIO CHARACTERISTICS

Our analysis of the characteristics of the portfolio or portfolios that might be available for lending has the dual benefit of further exploration of the viability of participation and, should one decide to take the next step, a start on evaluating the merits of a portfolio.

Size of the Total Portfolio

Size is not everything, but it helps. Borrowers covet large portfolios more than they do small ones. A concentrated portfolio of even $50 million of the right securities, of course, is worth investigating.

Size of Individual Holdings

Individual holdings of under $250,000 are of limited appeal to direct borrowers as the average loan transaction size is in the order of $500,000. Generally, holdings of less than $750,000 are likely to be best deployed through the lender's participation in an efficient pooled lending program.

Investment Strategy: Active or Passive

Active trading, which increases the likelihood of recalls, reduces the attractiveness of the inventory. It is often better for a borrower not to borrow a security than to borrow it and have it recalled. Recalls tend to come at the most inopportune times, and can cause significant strain in a lender-borrower relationship. Passive portfolios are ideal lending portfolios, although if you have the same inventory as everyone else, lending revenues are going to be low.

Geographic and Sectoral Diversification of the Portfolio

A broad geographic and sectoral distribution within a portfolio is a positive factor from a lending perspective. The securities markets of the world are in a constant state of flux, and at any given moment a particular country or sector may become a focus of demand. Borrowers like lenders who offer a wide geographic range of liquidity. They understand that the profitability of lending in certain markets may be marginal, and they direct compensating business toward lenders who provide service in such markets.

Tax Position or Jurisdiction of the Beneficial Owner

Borrowers are responsible for "making good" any benefits of share ownership that would have accrued to the lender had the securities not been lent—excluding voting rights. Borrowers, in the case of dividends, must "manufacture" (i.e., pay) the economic value of these to the lender.

The manufacturing of dividends is a major cost component of borrowing securities. A borrower with $100 million of German securities outstanding that yield an average of 3%, for example, could save $450,000 if the manufactured dividend obligation could be reduced by 15% ($100,000,000 × 3% × 15%).

An institution's tax position at a particular time is a given, but understanding your standing compared to that of your peers is valuable when one is researching the viability of lending.

By way of an example, U.K. pension funds would usually reserve 85% of the dividend on a Dutch equity. The U.K. Inland Revenue has decided, however, that if that fund were to lend those securities over the dividend date then a borrower must pay 85% to the lender, and 15% to the Inland Revenue. This rule means that U.K. pension funds are less attractive as lenders than, for example, U.S. pension funds.

Attractiveness of the Lendable Inventory

The definition of a security's attractiveness, like so many things in the securities lending business, made rather inaccessible by the adoption of simple code words. "Hot" securities are those in high demand, and general collateral or "GC" securities are those that are commonly available. Needless to say, the "hotter" your portfolio, the more lending merit it has. "Hotness" is difficult to assess without approaching potential counterparts, but as a rough rule of thumb, non-Japanese Asian securities are hot, as are less liquid and tax-advantaged securities worldwide.

In conclusion, if an institution is revenue hungry, with good technology, passively managing a global inventory of large holdings of hot securities, and domiciled in Bermuda, the lending case is particularly strong.

THE SIX ROUTES TO MARKET

Should the organizational and portfolio characteristics exhibited by an institution seem encouraging, the next step is to assess what routes to market are available. The key thing to remember is that there are options, and, despite what anyone may tell you, the choice of route is not a straightforward black or white decision.

Don't Go to the Market

While not going to the market will not endear a potential lender to the proponent of any route to the market, this may indeed be the right decision for a given organization. If, however, the organizational and portfolio characteristics are favorable, there should be a route or routes that offer the required return for a given level of risk and effort.

Use Your Global/Domestic Custodian as Agent

Using your global/domestic custodian is the least demanding route for a lender, especially for one new to the business. Assuming the acceptability of any indemnifications and confidence in the custodian, this route offers few barriers to getting started quickly. Levels of both risk and effort are low, but so too is the cost, in the form of reduced revenues.

The competitive pressures in the custody business are intense and, in securities lending, banks feel they have discovered a money machine—not unlike their old view of the foreign exchange business. If banks succeed at securities lending, they will not only generate significant revenues to support technological investments and cross-subsidize their core business, but they will also retain their customers. No wonder they are keen to lend your assets!

Appoint a Third-Party Specialist as Agent

If a lender decides not to lend itself, but at the same time believes that the custodian cannot offer the service required, the answer may be to appoint a third-party specialist. In the United States, the demand for this option is born out of frustration with custodial performance. Elsewhere it is typically a response to the increasingly competitive nature of the business and the propensity for institutions, which could lend directly, to outsource to specialists.

Agent intermediaries are sometimes separately incorporated organizations, but are more frequently parts of larger bank, broker-dealer, or investment banking groups. The third-party agent lending specialists represent the most fashionable and fastest growing sector of the business. For a firm already in the lending business, the low marginal cost of entry and significant potential rewards are two very good reasons for setting up a specialist agent.

Select Intermediary as Principal

Many wholesale intermediaries have developed global franchises and use their expertise and capital to generate spreads between two princi-pals that remain unknown to one another. These principal intermediar-ies again are sometimes separately incorporated organizations, but more frequently parts of larger bank, broker-dealer, or investment banking groups. Acting as principal gives these intermediaries the freedom to deal with organizations that the typical institution may choose to avoid.

The classic principal intermediary is the prime broker—borrowing from institutions and banks to lend to "hedge funds." The technology required to support such a business is a significant barrier to entry, and without the technology lending would be impossible. Given the opaque nature of these relationships, it is impossible for the lender to determine where the securities are going, in particular if they are being on loan or used by the intermediaries' own traders.

Lend Directly to Proprietary Principal

As institutions understand the market dynamic more, they may wish to consider lending directly to the organizations that are the final end users of the securities they supply. The proprietary borrowers include broker-dealers, market makers, and hedge funds. Some exhibit global demand, while others are more regionally focused.

Choose Some Combination of the Above

Just as there is no one right route to market, neither are the options we have outlined mutually exclusive. Choosing not to lend one portfolio does not preclude the lending of another, just as lending in one country does not mean one has to lend in all of them. Choosing a wholesale intermediary that happens to be your custodian in the United States and Canada does not mean that you cannot lend your Asian assets through a third-party specialist and your European assets directly to a panel of proprietary borrowers.

TYPICAL MARKETING STRATEGIES

The right route to market is a route that is consistent with meeting your realistic objectives. The challenge of finding the right route is not made any easier by the different marketing messages that institutions receive from the securities lending professionals. Besides marketing their own firm's merits, borrowers adopt certain arguments to encourage an institution to take a particular route.

While it is impossible to detail all the potential marketing strategies that a gifted professional might select, we can identify some of the more frequently used ones.

Do Not Go to the Market

It would be most unusual to hear "don't go to the market" unless the portfolio in question were particularly unattractive, but there are times when an attrractive portfolio, with significant revenue-generating potential, draws this response. It really means: "We can't do it, so you shouldn't." Such a reaction is often expressed as the taking of the "moral high ground," and most frequently comes from custodian banks.

This is not to say that there are not genuine instances when the best advice is not to lend, but rather that an institution hearing this line should question whether it is getting good advice or merely an excuse for an inability to perform.

Use Your Global/Domestic Custodian as Agent

The administrative straightforwardness of using a custodian bank makes it the conservative option. Custodians will argue that they are perfectly positioned to clear, report, and process your lending activity in as near a troublefree and seamless manner as is possible. They will give you directed or discretionary options so that you can effectively select your own principals. They will manage collateral in accordance with your investment guidelines and make a great deal of their indemnifications (but only to the extent that they offer them). They will argue about their global reach, commitment, and risk management controls until any thinking person would view any option other than this route to market with extreme caution.

Custodians continue to reap the benefit of planting the seeds of doubt in many an institutional mind. They do so because it sells.

Appoint a Third-Party Specialist as Agent

Fed up with being a small fish in a large pond? A large fish in a large pond? Fed up dealing with Jacks of all trades who are masters of none? Want a partner to help you get fair value from your lending inventory? These are just some of the lines you might expect from a specialist agent.

They would argue that advances in technology have eliminated many of the administrative and communications barriers that once made this route difficult to navigate. They may suggest furthermore that they can achieve a higher utilization rate for securities, and obtain more income per loan. They will attack custodial programs as inefficient and run by nonexperts.

Specialists may also argue that many custody programs are victims of their own success. How they do this is determined largely by the size of your portfolios. If the inventory is small, the argument may be: "The custody lending pool that you are in is so large that you are never going to get the kind of utilization that you might in our smaller pool. You will be relatively more important to us and, while remaining a small fish, will swim in a smaller pond." Should the inventory be large, expect to hear: "Your lending inventory utilization is being undermined by the custody bank's automated allocation algorithms. There are too many lenders in the custody pool who are getting their fair share of loans at your expense, loans you might be able to satisfy on your own. Why not become a big fish in our smaller pond?"

Select Intermediary as Principal

If you are looking for the wholesale distribution of your assets through a securities specialist who can coordinate the demands of many proprietary borrowers and take advantage of them as a principal, then the intermediary route is for you. This is a real departure point for an institution.

Wholesaling requires establishing a desk, incurring fixed costs, and adopting a professional approach to the lending of your securities, although taking this route without such a commitment is avoidable if you sign an exclusive arrangement with one principal and outsource your collateral management function. This might make sense for an entry level institution that wishes to earn while it learns for a specified period of time, but it is less likely to be the optimal approach for a large and attractive portfolio in the longer term.

Intermediaries will make much of their captive demand, be it from prime brokerage customers or affiliated proprietary trading desks. The key trade-off to assess when exploring this route is whether taking it will generate revenue that will justify the commensurate increase in commitment required and concentration of counterpart risk.

Lend Directly to Proprietary Principal

To identify the final end user of any product, one typically looks for the person whose need is the greatest and who is paying the most for it. The securities lending business is no exception to this rule. The proprietary borrowers will tell institutions that they will pay more to borrow securities, borrow from them as a matter of priority, and borrow for longer periods. If this sounds too good to be true, it often is.

The larger proprietary borrowers are frequently able to borrow at rates comparable to those of the principal intermediaries. They effectively eliminate the intermediaries' spread by keeping it for themselves rather than giving it to the institutions. Should an institution wish to gain spread by dealing directly with a proprietary borrower, it will have to fight for every basis point—and know what is a fair market price. This means being an expert and having a number of counterparts, or executing exclusives only after concluding an extensive bidding process.

Choose Some Combination of the Above

An institution is unlikely to hear any combination strategy advice too often. Very few, if any, organizations active in the lending business have all route options available, and fewer still are likely to recommend other options over their own. This is the kind of argument to expect from an experienced lender who has learned over time that a combination approach makes sense, or a representative of a professional counterpart that is taking a realistic long-term perspective, or a specialist consultant.

There are many more marketing strategies that may be adopted to encourage an institution to follow a particular route. When confronted by what seem like logical arguments, many of them contradictory, institutions are not surprisingly bemused, and some fail to make any decision for fear of making the wrong one. Many institutions are led down a particular path by marketing professionals who could just as readily argue in favor of a competing route.

The challenge for an institution is to distinguish between good marketing and good common sense. An examination of one's organizational and portfolio characteristics prior to exploring possible routes will be helpful in selecting the appropriate route, but being prepared for marketing arguments and understanding the pros and cons of each approach is the best form of preparation.

ADVANTAGES AND DISADVANTAGES

There are as many arguments to be made in favor of each route to market as there are arguments to be made against. The goal here is to provide some objective perspective on each approach. Prior to making a route-specific analysis, we offer some general observations.

General

The choice of a route to market brings with it the need to consider the institution's organizational and portfolio characteristics and, above all, the extent to which it wishes to get involved in this peripheral activity. An institution needs to determine whether it is going to embrace the business fully and set up a desk with all the resources that that requires, or take a more passive role and appoint an agent or exclusive principal to reduce the burden of involvement.

The advantages of the former approach are primarily the degree of control and customization combined with retention of all the revenue. However, these benefits are not without cost. Establishing a desk and equipping it to be an efficient market participant is neither cheap nor speedy. An inefficient desk will not generate the revenue that an experienced desk might from the same portfolio. Keeping all of a smaller revenue stream may well be a less attractive proposition than taking the lion's share of a larger revenue pool, particularly when one factors in the cost of establishing the desk in the first place.

The advantages of the latter approach are that the cost of entry is reduced and that the portfolio is being lent by an experienced desk. While it is true that the selected counterpart will take some share of the revenue, the total revenue accruing to the lender may increase. Notwithstanding the revenue sharing issue, the main disadvantage of this approach is the potential sacrifice in terms of control and customization.

While it is possible to negotiate with the agent or principal counterpart the exact type of service that you would like, it is unlikely that you will be able to achieve lending nirvana. One has always to remember, however, that nothing is forever and one could always choose to reassess the options available at a future date.

Route-Specific

Do Not Go to the Market

There are two main forms of inactivity to assess—not lending at all, or choosing not to lend selected portfolios or parts of selected portfolios (e.g., those in particular countries). If you choose not to lend, the main disadvantage is that you may be forgoing revenue. The amount of revenue that you forgo depends on the merit of the portfolios concerned.

The opportunity cost of not lending is equivalent to the potential lending revenue forgone minus a financial estimation of the effort and risk required to generate that revenue. If the opportunity cost is a significant positive number, then the decision not to lend might not be the right one. If, on the other hand, that cost is a small positive or even negative amount, then the decision not to lend is justified.

Use Your Global/Domestic Custodian as Agent

The main advantage of using a custodian is administrative ease. You deal with an entity that you know and trust. Custodians may provide some enhanced security by means of indemnification. There is no need to set up a desk, and the level of management involvement and resources required is minimized.

This is the convenient and conservative way to lend, but convenience does not come without a price or conservatism without missing opportunity. The share of the revenue given to custodians varies from account to account, with a typical range of 20% to 40%. The question the institution must answer is whether this represents value.

Custody lending is conservative or, to put it another way, least common denominator lending. Banks will be banks, and should an institution hanker to be on the leading edge or prefer a customized program, using a custodian is unlikely to be the optimal route.

Some custodians have been so successful at marketing their securities lending programs that some of their customers have become victims of their bank's success. Small and large portfolios alike may be missing revenue opportunities by virtue of the way that the bank allocates loans. Both might lend more securities and generate higher revenues if they were to leave the massive custodial pool and find another route. This might involve appointing another custodian with a smaller pool, or taking another route altogether.

Custodians will make much of their cash reinvestment capabilities. Yet did not certain custodians experience reinvestment problems in 1995?

When you choose this route to market, you are putting all your eggs in one basket: selecting a single organization to be custodian, securities lender, and cash manager. What is the likelihood that one firm is superior at all disciplines?

Appoint Third-Party Specialist as Agent

Using a third-party specialist is the first step away from the custodial route. The principal advantage for the customer is that securities lending-focused organizations and personnel ought to lend effectively.

One reason we see increased use of this choice may be that specialists are newer operations without a lending backlog. As they become successful, however, specialists' customers may suffer the same lack of attention that custodial customers complain about. One consideration is that, as every custodian trots out its agency lending programs, the customer may simply move to another custodian, although the assets remain immobile, unless loaned. There may be situations where regional or product specialization mean that this is nevertheless the right decision.

The unbundling of this product is a double-edged sword. Separating lending from custody brings with it operational disadvantages if the technology is not adequate. Being able to appoint an independent third party to reinvest cash (as some specialists do) allows a further degree of specialization.

Taking this route is something like getting a tailor-made suit rather than one off-the-rack. Finding a good tailor takes some time, and a store-bought option can fit just as well. Using your custodian may be a compromise, but for many it works.

Select Intermediary as Principal

Lenders wishing to receive gross lending fees revenues could choose to deal with an intermediary as principal. The potential gross revenue increase is the main advantage of selecting this route. There are costs, however. This route is essentially only for those for whom the fixed costs of starting a business are less than the variable costs of paying an agent to do it.

Perhaps the major disadvantage of this choice is that you need to establish a business with a desk capable of dealing with the securities lending professionals. A lender's counterpart is rewarded no longer by getting a percentage of the earnings from a portfolio, but now by borrowing securities at the lowest cost. There is, moreover, a potentially combative relationship to be managed. Lenders taking this route need personnel who can extract "fair value" from lendable assets.

Lend Directly to Proprietary Principal

When proprietary principals have similar credit quality as the principal intermediary group, lending directly presupposes that lenders retain even more of the lending fees because they are closer to the market. Taking this route entails only marginally higher fixed costs, because there are likely to be more counterparts. Little else changes, unless the proprietary borrowers are themselves "hedge funds." Dealing with these counterparts requires a sophisticated approach to risk management. The process almost inevitably means, for most lenders, having a principal relationship with various "prime brokers." This is the same as having a relationship with a principal intermediary as lenders have no contractual relationship with the hedge funds themselves.

Some Combination of the Above

Most lenders will find the optimal solution via some combination of the routes described. This can be accomplished in one of two ways. Lenders can make entire portfolios available for loan to both agents and principals on some kind of "first come, first served" basis. Perhaps a better alternative is to segment the lendable inventory. Lend some segments of the portfolio through a custodian, some through an agent, and some on an exclusive or panel basis to selected principals.

COUNTERPART SELECTION CRITERIA

Many lenders are now recognizing securities lending as a standalone business and no longer as a peripheral activity. They are demanding access to relevant business information on which to base securities lending decisions. There is a practical need to know one's counterparts and to understand both their capabilities and requirements.

Exhibit 3.1 identifies some of the key information that a lender should use to select a counterpart.

EXHIBIT 3.1 Key Information a Lender Should Use to Select a Counterpart

Financial Strength
Understand the legal entity that is your counterpart, its relationship with affiliates, and any parental guarantees.
- Credit ratings—Short- and long-term
- Profitability
- Balance sheet size
- Regulatory capital

Commitment
- Personnel involved in management, marketing, desk negotiation, operations, and administration
- Number and locations of desks around the globe capable of servicing local customers (demand and supply)

Experience
- How long has counterpart been in the business?
- How experienced are its key personnel?

Geographic Focus
- Location of global head
- Does geographic demand or distribution capability correlate with your inventory?

Size of Program
- Is counterpart a niche player with a small book of specials?
- Is it a bulge-bracket borrower with massive borrowing or distribution capabilities?
- Will an organization of your size be significant to this counterpart, or will you get lost in the crowd?

EXHIBIT 3.1   (Continued)

Collateral Flexibility
- Will counterpart be able to give you what you require, without constantly trying to get you to accept what you do not want?
- If it is an intermediary, is it taking what the market wants to give?

Legal and Regulatory Framework
- Who regulates the counterpart?
- Which legal framework does it favor?
- Are its personnel registered?

Technological and Operational Capabilities
- Which system does a counterpart use?
- Will it supply you with any technological support, excluding the "auto-fax"?
- How will you communicate with each other?
- What reporting will you receive?

Route-Specific
All Intermediaries—Distribution Capability:
- How capable are they of wholesale distribution?
- How many borrowers do they have?
- Where are they located?
- Which market sectors do they occupy?

Agent Intermediaries
Allocation Algorithms:
- How do the formulas work?
- Under what circumstances, if any, will the algorithms be overridden?
- How will the agent prioritize any guaranteed accounts?

Indemnification
If the agent provides indemnification, which of the following exposures are covered?
- All financial loss
- Borrower default
- Collateral default
- Consequential damages
- How much, in terms of the percentage of revenue forgone, does indemnification "cost"?

Transparency
- Disclosed or undisclosed?

Can a lender receive online information about:
- Loaned securities (in aggregate and per borrowing principal)?
- Collateral portfolios (as above)?

Can a lender direct its portfolio to a select group of borrowers?

EXHIBIT 3.1   (Continued)

Collateral and Reinvestment Policy
- Is the agent capable of managing a wide variety of collateral?
- Does it have a triparty/escrow capability?
- Is it a capable cash manager?
- Can a lender stipulate its own cash reinvestment guidelines?

Custody
- Does a lending agent insist that assets be moved to a designated custodian?

Principal Intermediaries—Demand Drivers

What percentage of demand is driven by:
- "The Street"?
- Proprietary traders?
- Prime broker customers?

Proprietary Principals—Trading Strategy

What percentage of demand is driven by the following trading strategy?
- "Naked" shorts?
- "Pairs" trading?
- Convertible bond arbitrage?
- Fail coverage?
- Index arbitrage?
- Market-making?
- Risk arbitrage?
- Warrant arbitrage?
- Other?

SAMPLE PORTFOLIOS

No two portfolios, even when controlled by the same organization, exhibit identical characteristics. The simplified portfolios we describe are designed to show that the route to market varies by portfolio as well as by organization. Lenders may need to adopt a flexible approach— they may need to have multiple routes available to them in order to do full justice to their inventory.

Small, Active, and Diversified Fund

Characteristics of a small, active, and diversified fund could be:

Portfolio size	$250 million
Average size of individual holdings	$250,000
Investment stance	Actively managed
Geographic/sectoral diversification	Global equities and bonds
Tax position/jurisdiction	U.S. pension fund
Lendable "specials" or "GC"	10% "specials" and 90% "GC"

This portfolio is almost certainly unlendable on a direct basis. Apart from anything else, the individual holding size is just too small and unstable. As part of a custodial or perhaps a third-party agency pool, some percentage of the 100 lines of specials might be lent. It would probably be imprudent to lend more than 50% of any holding. On a lender/agent split of 60/40, at an average fee of 50 basis points (bps), this route might generate $37,500 per year for the pension fund. This is about a 1½bps contribution. If this is an organization's sole fund, the lending case is probably marginal.

Medium, Passive, and Geographically Focused Fund

Characteristics of a medium, passive, and geographically focused fund could be:

Portfolio size	$500 million
Average size of individual holdings	$10 million
Investment stance	Passively managed
Geographic/sectoral diversification	German equities
Tax position/jurisdiction	U.S. pension fund
Lendable "specials" or "GC"	>90% "specials" (seasonal)

This portfolio would set any agent or principal to do cartwheels. Assuming an 85% dividend entitlement and an average 3% dividend yield on the securities held, the lender could expect gross revenue estimates on this portfolio to be in the region of $2.5 million. This represents a 50bps contribution. Even if the lender/agent split were 80/20, the "cost" of the agency route would be $500,000.

Some may believe this is too expensive. A direct route, perhaps even a guaranteed exclusive with a well-rated principal counterpart, might make more sense.

Large, Passive, and Regional Portfolio

Characteristics of a large, passive, and regional portfolio could be:

Portfolio size	$1 billion
Average size of individual holdings	$5 million

Investment stance	Passively managed
Geographic/sectoral diversification	Far Eastern (ex-Japan) equities
Tax position/jurisdiction	U.S. mutual fund
Lendable "specials" or "GC"	25% "specials" and 75% "GC"

This is another attractive portfolio from a securities lending standpoint, although there are some operational challenges that need to be overcome. Any lender's first priority is investment performance, and the lending of securities should not impede that objective. Fails, buy-ins, and recalls are to be avoided if at all possible.

If a 25% buffer were considered appropriate, given the passive nature of the portfolio, and fees averaged 75bps, gross lending income could be about $1.5 million. This represents a 15bps contribution.

It is advisable to deal with a regional expert, be it agent or principal. An agency "cost" of $375,000 based on a lender/agent split of 75/25 might be entirely reasonable, but only if the agent is an expert.

MAINTAINING PERFORMANCE

Just as an institution evaluates its suppliers of custody and asset management services, so it should, we would contend, evaluate the lending performance of its chosen route and counterpart/counterparties. Having expended considerable effort making the original selection, it is essential to allocate some resources to checking whether that choice is as appropriate today as when it was first made.

Exhibit 3.2 provides recommendations for doing so.

EXHIBIT 3.2   Suggestions for Maintaining Performance

Keep Up To Date
- Obtain regular updates of market developments
- Use independent advisors where appropriate
- Make your counterparts understand that you are the customer
- Benchmark lending performance relative to peers

Organization: Should your organizational characteristics change, finding a new route may be necessary.

Portfolio: Portfolios change over time. Check to ensure that these changes do not require a change of route.

Counterparts: Just as your organization changes, so do securities lending counterparts.
- Are they still suitable?
- Are others now more so?

THE WAY FORWARD

What to do now?

Nonlenders

Adopting a logical approach to the lending decision will save time, money, and frustration. Lending is not for everyone.

Examine your organizational and portfolio characteristics before approaching counterparts. When gathering information from the market, do so in a structured manner so that results do not add more confusion than they resolve.

Active Lenders

To ensure that your lending performance remains optimal, you should regularly revisit the lending route decision. Conduct this process with as open a mind as you approached the initial lending decision. Despite what many counterparts may tell you, the barriers to changing routes are less daunting than they would have you believe.

CONCLUSIONS

Navigation is not straightforward. There are often many routes to a particular destination, and it is not always easy to find the best one. It is also difficult to determine what is meant by "the best." Does it mean "the quickest," "the easiest," or "the most profitable"?

Finding the best route to the securities lending market can be as difficult as embarking on an arduous journey. There are no maps, and along the way various vendors will attempt to lure you down their favored path.

The approach we have outlined in this chapter can be adapted to suit any institution's particular circumstances. Should the approach be adopted, it will enable an institution to achieve a better result quicker. The key thing to remember is that while there are many possible routes to take, you should set the pace, and embark on this journey only if you believe it to be worth your while.

We would suggest that institutions focus on the lending decision first and the route second. In reality, lenders are likely to be attracted to the lending decision because of the persuasive powers of a particular route proponent. We would advise taking a step backward to consider in the first place whether participation is really appropriate, and what other routes are available. We would not discourage lenders from calling on the services of an independent specialist's assistance in this endeavor. Then again, we would say that, wouldn't we?

CHAPTER 4

Evaluating Lending Options

Anthony A. Nazzaro
Principal
A.A. Nazzaro Associates

We are fortunate to participate in an ever-growing and vibrant industry amid what might be considered a mature market. The vibrancy of securities lending today can be directly attributed to the proliferation of the hedge fund industry. As hedge funds have multiplied, so have the strategies that spawn the need for pools of securities. Both domestic and foreign securities are in demand and necessary in order to employ the most popular basic strategies such as short selling and the hedging of long positions.

Although there has been a significant evolution in the participant group of lenders through consolidation, there has also been an extension of the playing field in other directions. There are fewer large custodian banks than 10 years ago when more large banks dominated the landscape. Today, the big custodians have become bigger and the regional banks have either disappeared or outsourced the securities lending activity to their larger counterparts. Interestingly, despite this cannibalization, there are some new twists. Large banks are offering third-party agency lending services for assets they do not hold. This is a dramatic departure from a decade ago. Third-party lender/agents have emerged as a greater force as the consolidation of large banks sometimes leaves certain clients unattended in the wake of such mergers. This creates an opportunity for new players to emerge and existing players to reinvent themselves.

Even with the dramatic evolution within the framework of the securities lending industry, the most interesting change has come about through technology. The advent of the Internet and its ability to transmit large amounts of data within seconds has created new avenues to this market that did not previously exist. The basic avenues and choices remain intact for the same principal reasons but now we have an innovative approach which offers another alternative to market. The main entrant that utilizes this approach is eSecLending (see Chapter 5). The eSecLending model is important to the configuration of lending options available to the principal lender.

The options described in this chapter are the more traditional methods and simply a primer, but the advent of new ideas through today's technology and "eBay" culture provide the lender with a variation of the theme that is both unique and opportune.

A fund seeking to enter the securities lending market has a number of options from which to choose. In this chapter, we shall attempt to identify and review the various types of programs available to the current or prospective institutional lender. We shall look at each of these programs in some detail and assess them upon their merits.

The following are the primary types of lending programs:

- Master trust/custody bank participatory program
- Broker/dealer managed program
- In-house managed program
- Outside manager/third-party lender program

Because it is the responsibility of the fund to decide which type of program best fits its needs as a lender, there will be a particular emphasis upon reviewing a set of criteria enabling the fund to evaluate itself as well as its lending options. It is important for the fund/lender to assess its own status and review its profile in order to determine which of the above types of management may be best suited for its securities lending program.

Exhibit 4.1 provides a list of some of the factors and variables that we consider and reference as we explore the four primary lending programs.

THE MASTER TRUST/CUSTODY PARTICIPATORY PROGRAM

The master trust/custody participatory program is by far the largest and most widely chosen option among current participants in the securities lending market, and with good reason. The master trustee bank has custody of the fund/client's assets and provides easy entry into this marketplace. The bank is in the best position to know the client's assets, lend the assets, mark to market the loans, coordinate the purchase and sale activity of other managers of the portfolio, monitor corporate actions, and basically handle all of the operational needs of a lending program for its clients.

Securities lending, by its nature, is an operational activity because it essentially involves the movement of securities and the monitoring of collateral. The bank program is the most widely chosen because it is the best choice from a logistical perspective. Most importantly, the bank has the systems and the personnel with knowledge and expertise in securities lending.

EXHIBIT 4.1   Fund Profile

Type of fund:
> Public/private pension fund
> Nonprofit endowment or foundation
> State or municipality
> Mutual fund
> Insurance company

Size of lendable assets:
> Less than $250 million
> $250 million to $1 billion
> $1 billion to $3 billion
> $3 billion to $5 billion
> Greater than $5 billion

Asset allocation ($ value of lendable assets by type of security):
> U.S. government securities
> Domestic equities
> Corporate bonds
> Foreign fixed income
> Foreign equities

Custodial relationship

In-house management of assets or outside

Personnel available:
> Degree of knowledge and understanding in securities lending
> Overall experience and level of comfort in this activity

Degree of control or oversight desired:
> Management of short-term investment fund
> Investment guidelines
> Approved borrowers and limits
> Reporting requirements

Many funds, in their profiles, do not have any expertise in this area and look to their custodians to provide it. The main caveat here is to avoid becoming too passive. The fund that participates in the bank program has an important fiduciary responsibility which it cannot delegate entirely to the bank. The fund must know and understand the terms of the agency agreement which is the controlling document authorizing the bank to lend the fund's assets. The agency agreement delineates the responsibilities of the custodian, and the guidelines and rules under which the program will operate. The fund/client should be aware of any risks under the program and the limits of its liability and exposure.

Since the bank program is the dominant and most logical choice, why are there other options to consider? Two factors have kept securities lending from being the exclusive domain of the banks. The first factor has to do with sheer size. A very large master trust bank may have as many as 100 to 200 participant clients with aggregate lendable assets exceeding $200 billion. If a typical institutional client, responding to the earlier profile, has lendable assets of $200 million to $300 million, there is a significant dilution effect when pooled with lendable assets of this magnitude.

To illustrate this point with a simple example, let us assume borrower XYZ wishes to borrow 50,000 shares of IBM. Our hypothetical client owns 100,000 shares of IBM. However, the bank may have 5 million shares of IBM available to lend and held by 40 different accounts. Which participant client will get the loan? Loans are automatically allocated within the system in an equitable manner based upon ownership, demand, size, and position in the queue. The point is that the relatively small fund/clients may realize only a minimal incremental return from their participation in this program. The large portfolio of lendable assets of the bank are attractive to borrowers, but there is a law of diminishing returns applicable to the participant. In the aggregate, the bank program may be very large, well managed and successful, but the individual participant is part of a large pool of assets and a long list of clients.

The second factor to be considered is the fee-split. Banks offer a great deal to their participant clients since the bank essentially does everything and offers the client a turnkey program. Also, many banks offer some limited form of indemnification against certain types of losses (i.e., borrower default). In return, the bank expects to be compensated accordingly, and this is reflected in a generous fee split. Today, due to increasing competition, many banks are willing to negotiate their fee in the client's favor. The size and attractiveness of the client's portfolio will dictate the leverage a particular client may have in the negotiation of a fee-split arrangement. In the final analysis, the bank program remains a prudent choice and a wise route to securities lending for many institutions.

THE BROKER-DEALER MANAGED PROGRAM

A second option for participating in securities lending is a contractual arrangement with a major brokerage firm for the lending of the portfolio. This normally involves a custodial relationship with the brokerage firm whereby the firm has custody of all or part of the assets of the fund.

Some brokerage firms are willing to pay a guaranteed fee to the fund for the exclusive rights to the securities lending revenue of the portfolio. The fee may be a flat fee or a small percentage rate based upon the market value of the portfolio. The term of the agreement is usually one year. The major benefit to this approach is the certainty of cash flow or guaranteed income. Also, fluctuations in interest rates or lending demand will have little effect upon the earnings in this type of lending program.

Similar to the banks, brokerage firms offer a turnkey operation with qualified personnel running the program and little active involvement by the client. The major drawback is the concentration of credit exposure to one broker-dealer if the dealer is acting as principal as opposed to being an agent. The fund is essentially lending its assets to one borrower. The key considerations should be the size of the portfolio being allocated to the broker-dealer, the supervision of collateral, that is, marks to the market, and the creditworthiness of the broker-dealer.

Some lenders have contractual arrangements with broker-dealers to manage their lending in only a specific segment of the lending market such as foreign equities. This limited arrangement enables the lender to utilize the strength and expertise of certain brokerage firms while maintaining diversification and control over the rest of its program.

THE IN-HOUSE MANAGED PROGRAM

The third securities lending option is the in-house program. This type of program is ideally suited for funds with large portfolios of assets and an in-house staff of investment professionals with expertise and experience. Examples of this type of profile would be mutual funds and insurance companies. These institutions may have $10 billion or more in lendable securities, manage their own assets, possess strong personnel and systems capabilities, combined with overall market savvy.

The in-house managed program gives the lender ultimate control with full supervision of its lending policies and investment guidelines. In addition, there is no dilution of assets or sharing of income as previously described. Beyond the initial cost of systems, the primary expenses are the salaries of the lending personnel, office overhead, and the bank transaction fees generated by the lending activity.

The securities lending revenues generated by large, in-house programs that are well managed are the highest in the industry. However, along with the benefits of full control and supervision come the full responsibility and commitment necessary to remain competitive in the business. The program cannot be managed as a sideline or ancillary activity. The in-house program requires a full commitment to all facets of the operation, including the maintenance of proper levels of loan collateral, credit analysis of borrowers and investments, implementation of sound lending policies, investment guidelines, and internal reporting to senior management. This last point is especially important. Oversight by senior management is critical to a successful in-house program. The group responsible for the lending and investment activity should be part of a well-defined reporting structure within the organization. As stated earlier, if the in-house program is well managed, the rewards are great.

THE OUTSIDE MANAGER/THIRD-PARTY LENDER PROGRAM

The fourth option is the independent or outside manager, sometimes referred to as a third-party lender. The securities lending manager is not the principal/lender and not the custodian bank, but an independent third party, hence the name. This mode of lending is a hybrid of the bank and in-house programs, and attempts to provide the best attributes of both. The outside manager seeks to provide the expertise of the bank program, but without its portfolio dilution, while maintaining the control and profitability of the in-house program.

For the fund that is not large enough to command a standalone in-house program, but has an attractive portfolio and seeks to maximize its lending potential, the independent manager provides an alternative. Outside managers seek to provide the relatively small client/fund with enhanced portfolio visibility and greater loan opportunities. This is a reasonable expectation given the fact that the manager may have only a limited number of clients. In addition, the fund can dictate specifically tailored investment guidelines, a segregated investment portfolio, approved borrowers, reporting detail and frequency, and an overall high level of supervision.

A good manager with strong client communication and participation can simulate an in-house program, although this requires a much more active and involved fund. The profile of the fund/lender using an outside manager is generally one who has an in-depth knowledge and understanding of securities lending, experience, and a willingness to be involved in the activity. Typically, the custodian bank still plays an integral role in this mode since all activity and instructions must flow through the custodian. This can provide the lender with another layer of reporting and supervision over the lending program. Also, fee splits are more negotiable and heavily weighted in favor of the lender.

A drawback to the outside manager route may be the overall size of the manager's base of lendable assets. Whereas the bank managed program may be too large, the outside manager program may be too small, resulting in an inability to compete effectively. One must find a manager that strikes the right balance in terms of the number of clients, size of lendable assets, and compatibility since the relationship takes on partnership-like qualities. This can be a very rewarding route to securities lending given the right combination of fund and manager.

CONCLUSION

The menu of securities lending options available to the prospective lender is varied and diverse. The analysis of options begins at home with a solid assessment of the individual fund's profile, including its characteristics and goals. A thorough review may act as a helpful guide in finding the perfect match. Although the purpose of this chapter was to introduce and describe the various modes of securities lending, an evaluation of these options will require a more in-depth study not only of each category but also of the individual entities within each type of category. Within each peer group there are better banks, stronger brokerage firms, and more competent managers.

The single most important issue to keep in mind is that all types of funds, within the purview of the prudent man rule standard, have a heavy fiduciary responsibility to learn and understand as much as possible about their securities lending program under any type of management.

CHAPTER 5

The Auction Process and Its Role in the Securities Lending Markets

Daniel E. Kiefer
Opportunistic Portfolio Manager
CalPERS

Judith G. Mabry
Senior Vice President
eSecLending

There has always been a certain element of excitement about the concept of auctions. The tempo, the enthusiasm, and the thrill of bidding up the price of an object, are only surpassed by the satisfying thud of the gavel signaling the end of the process and the distribution of the goods to the happy winning parties.

The variety of auctions in existence today run the gamut from the traditional open outcry, "English" style auction described above, to the high-tech electronic online auctions selling everything from apples to zebras, to the more mundane "silent auctions" popular at every fundraiser across the country. Those that lie in between offer a wide variety of styles, bidding processes, anonymity, and success.

History tells us that auctions began their life back with the Babylonians, in about 500 BCE. The Romans also used auctions to liquidate property and to sell off the spoils of war.

From these ancient beginnings, the concept of "price discovery" through an auction process was born. Letting the marketplace determine the "best price" for an object or service has gained in popularity over the years, and has become a method of choice for everyone from electrical grid operators in England, to the U.S. Treasury, to the famous fine arts auction houses of Sotheby's and Christies, to the everyday bidder on eBay, to the smaller independent financial service companies offering a variety of auction services.

What is common to each of the auction providers is that they provide a platform for buyers and sellers of all sizes and shapes to come together to strike a deal. Whether we attend an open-outcry charity auction, or sit in the comfort of our home office to participate in an online auction, each auction provides the opportunity for buyers and sellers to agree on a price for a particular object or service.

AUCTIONS IN THE SECURITIES LENDING MARKETS

Most people in the financial services markets are aware of the trillions of dollars worth of government securities the U.S. Treasury auctions off every year. The markets have come to recognize that an auction is an efficient and orderly means of determining the best price for selling a series of securities. In the *initial public offering* (IPO) markets, auctions have also gained attention recently with the online auction held by Google for its IPO. Slowly we are seeing more and more "auction-style" trading coming into play across the financial markets.

It is not surprising, then, that the securities lending markets have also picked up on this auction theme. Traditionally securities lending has been an over-the-counter, informal market conducted over the telephone. Borrowers located securities by calling around to various lenders or their agents, and directly negotiated loans with the lenders when they felt the price was right for them. But the markets move quickly, and determining the "right" price can be subject to many variables—such as how many counterparts you contacted, timing of your calls, size and shape of stock available, rebates or fees, type of collateral, credit worthiness of counterparty, etc. Borrowing and lending securities through an auction process is one way of bringing buyers and sellers together in a common setting to determine the "market" price for such transactions. Variables can be captured and controlled, and the flow of information can be disseminated widely.

"TRADITIONAL" LENDING STYLES

As the securities lending markets developed over the years, so has the concept of the "traditional" style of lending. In order to understand and appreciate the auction process as it applies to securities lending, it is important to view it in the context of the broader styles of lending.

There are a number of different styles and methods of lending in existence today—a custodian may manage a lending program, a third-party lender may manage programs, or the beneficial owner of the securities themselves may manage its own lending program. Loans can be executed on a *stock-by-stock basis*, as a *basket of securities* or on an *exclusive principal basis* with the rights to borrow securities sold to one borrower. These different styles work differently for each type of portfolio, and for each class of securities.

In a "traditional" custodial and third-party agency-lending program, either the custodian or a specialist third-party agent manages the program. Generally, stocks are lent on a stock-by-stock basis or as a basket. There is a "fair and equitable" allocation among participants via a queuing mechanism, with the custodian or third-party agent acting in an "agency," rather than "principal" capacity. Price is driven by supply and demand, and the operational and administrative elements of the program are usually handled through the lender's custodian. This "traditional" type of lending has been in existence for more than 20 years and has served the market in a reliable and consistent manner.

A "direct lending" program is one managed by the institution that owns or manages the portfolio. There are usually multiple borrowing relationships with the broker/dealer community, and business is usually done on a "principal," rather than "agency" basis. The manager of this program usually has full-scale operational capabilities in order to administer the program. Price is determined by supply and demand.

In an "exclusive principal" arrangement, a borrower purchases the exclusive right to borrow securities from a portfolio for a fixed period of time, usually for a fixed price. This effectively removes the portfolio from the borrowing community and grants the purchaser the sole right to borrow securities from the portfolio. These programs may be managed by a third-party lender or they may be arranged directly between the beneficial owner (lender) and a select borrower(s). These types of exclusive arrangements have been in existence for many years but have gained in popularity over the last five years or so as technology has assisted in the process.

THE AUCTION AS AN ALTERNATIVE TO THE STATUS QUO

All three types of lenders—the custodial lender, the third-party lender, and the "direct" lender, have used the auction process in some shape or form over the years. Such auctions may be arranged on a stock-by-stock basis, with a basket or subset of a portfolio, or on the entire portfolio. Auctions may be run by independent third-party specialists, custodians, or even by the beneficial owner of the portfolio.

The auction process serves as a means to distribute portfolio information to the borrowers and provides a method of determining the best price for either a single security or a portfolio of securities.

Single-Stock Auctions

There are a number of single-stock auction programs today that support securities lending activities. Most are done on a single-stock basis—whereby the results and delivery of securities are almost immediate. There are at least two major lending institutions running online, single-stock auction programs have proven very interesting to many borrowers. These types of single-stock auctions serve a very viable purpose particularly when the securities on auction are in high demand (i.e., "special"). They provide a mechanism whereby securities are simultaneously offered to borrowers around the globe. This competitive bidding environment promotes transparency and price discovery, ultimately leading to higher returns to lenders. Administration and delivery of securities "won" at auction would likely follow a traditional agency-lending model, with the individual loans collateralized and administered by the custodian or third-party lending agent.

Exclusive Principal Auctions

There is continued growth in the area of exclusive principal lending arrangements offered through the auction process. The more sophisticated providers offer and display their programs via the Internet. Others may create an auction structure through a setup using a fax or telephone.

In an online auction, an entire portfolio or portions of a portfolio may be displayed and ultimately auctioned via a secure Internet connection accessible to a select preapproved universe of borrowers. Prospective borrowers, equipped with a password, may access the auction information well in advance of the auction date in order to evaluate the holdings and formulate their bids. Bidding takes place during a specific time frame, on either an open or blind basis. The manager of the lending and auction program is responsible for setting up the framework of the auction, including determining the most efficient way to break down the portfolio into attractive and manageable pieces or "lots." This is a critical step in that the assets are often awarded to multiple borrowers, leading to a more specialized and refined approach to an exclusive principal deal. With a portfolio segmented on a country-by-country basis, or by asset class, prospective borrowers may selectively bid on those assets of most interest to them. The process, while sophisticated and complex, often results in greater income to the lender.

Using an online auction process to distribute portfolio information and actually run the auction has proven to be a successful means of arranging exclusive principal deals amongst multiple principal borrowers.

There has been a steady growth of both lenders and borrowers in the United States and Europe who have taken advantage of exclusive principal programs arranged via an online auction process. Lenders view these types of programs as an attractive, solid source of guaranteed revenue, often with a higher risk-adjusted return than that received from a more traditional lending program. From the borrowers' perspective, these types of auctions provide an opportunity to lock up specific supply for a fixed period of time, thus creating a competitive advantage in the supply and demand chain.

The key to a successful auction is not only the setup and management of the auction itself, but the maintenance of the program once the auction is completed and the lending commences. Securities lending managers running these types of exclusive principal lending programs via on-line auctions must be positioned to provide the third-party administrative and operational support necessary to manage such a program.

FACTORS DRIVING THE MOVEMENT AND ACCEPTANCE OF THE AUCTION PROCESS TO SECURITIES LENDING

The acceptance of the auction process as a viable mechanism for managing a securities lending program is largely a byproduct of three concurrent forces coming together simultaneously. As the old adage says, "timing is everything." The three instrumental forces creating this success were:

1. Advances in technology
2. Focus by lenders on return-enhancement strategies
3. Pursuit by borrowers of the growing hedge fund marketplace

The interaction of these three forces impacted both lenders and borrowers, and drove the acceptance of the "auction model" as a viable alternative to "traditional" securities lending program structures. The exclusive principal lending process, in particular, has embraced the auction model and successfully expanded this business.

As discussed earlier, principal or exclusive programs have been in existence for many years. These exclusive relationships were often the result of a broker-dealer pursuing a large lender with a guaranteed offer that was higher than what the lender was receiving from their existing agency relationship. The term "exclusive" was appropriate for this type of broker-dealer/lender relationship as it resulted in the lendable assets being removed from circulation for a specific time period and made available exclusively to one broker-dealer. These early exclusive relationships led to a more competitive exclusive environment as lenders started shopping their portfolios around among a small group of counterparties (usually three to five major borrowers). Most of the early participants in these exclusive relationships were sophisticated pension or mutual fund lenders who were experienced with direct lending and had the capacity to manage the operational side of the relationship.

Advances in Technology

Advances in technology have enabled lenders lacking the back-office operational lending expertise to pursue exclusive lending relationships without the operational overhead committed by these early pioneers. Lenders who were reluctant to move from their traditional custodial agency program due to potential operational complications were able to migrate to a hybrid model that incorporated the exclusive relationship as part of their existing lending equation. Technology also enabled lenders to expand the list of acceptable exclusive counterparties due to the reduction in operational risk ushered in by automation.

The marriage of technology and lending helped move securities lending from an operationally intensive "back office" function to a more automated process. With such advancements, operational risks were reduced drastically, allowing for more innovation and higher transaction volume. Advances in technology also eliminated many of the inherent advantages of the custodial agent, which in turn helped promote competition and thus facilitated the movement towards an exclusive lending environment. These advantages included greater operational flexibility given their access to a large lendable asset base to cover sell fails, and use of existing in-house corporate action and income collection systems to monitor securities lending operations.

Focus on Enhancement of Returns

The second factor that drove the acceptance of the auction-based exclusive lending approach was the lender's focus on enhancing returns. When securities lending shifted from being a "back-office" operational function to a "front-office" revenue enhancement product, the key risk went from "operational risk" to "return maximization." As the market has grown, it has become evident that the lack of transparency in the lending process does not support the maximization of revenues.

With the responsibility for the lending operations slowly being taken over by the front office, a total rate of return mentality towards securities lending was starting to develop. Questions arose as to the role of securities lending within the portfolio management process. These questions include the following

- How do you extract the most value out of a securities lending program?
- What is the best and most efficient route to market?
- What are the risk/return trade-offs available within securities lending?
- What price should I be paid for exclusive access to my asset base?
- What is an appropriate benchmark?

With any other asset base these questions are readily answerable. However, securities lending had a somewhat nontransparent process historically dominated by a few large custodial agents. These variables drove the need for alternatives to the traditional lending styles of the past. The alternative needed to generate a solution that offered price transparency and price discovery, while affording a greater degree of flexibility in disseminating information, was the auction process. This combined demand for price discovery and price transparency was a driving force in the growth and development of the auction process for securities lending.

The auction process provided transparency, gave better information to the lender on the value of their lendable asset base and provided a solution to the price discovery dilemma. A potential exclusive borrower could be compared on an equivalent basis to other borrowers. Additionally, agent estimates could be utilized in the auction process as well as historical results to compare alternatives. Winners of the auction were easily identified and a clear mechanism for awarding business was created. The auction process also extracted value from the market since the most efficient borrower or borrowers were often those with large and successful prime brokerage franchises.

Growth in Hedge Funds

The third factor that drove the acceptance of the auction based exclusive approach was the exponential growth in the hedge fund marketplace creating additional demand for stock lending. Currently there are over 6,000 hedge funds running close to $900 billion in assets with an additional $100 billion in capital inflows occurring yearly. This growth in hedge fund activity has driven the bottom line of many broker dealers either through their own proprietary trading desks or through revenue generated from their prime brokerage activities.

The securities lending market, once driven by the need to cover market fails, has evolved into a market driven by a variety of hedge fund strategies. In order to differentiate themselves with their prime brokerage clients, broker dealers sought out additional exclusive lending supply. The broker dealer could use this supply to win business from other broker dealers and guarantee their hedge fund clientele access to key "specials" when they arose.

This exclusive supply could now be conveniently sourced through the auction process. With some major lenders utilizing the auction model as their sole means of placing assets out to bid, the auction process and available assets are too big to ignore. Through the auction process, a borrower has the ability to target their lending supply by asset type, country and lender. No longer does the borrower have to rely on the traditional agency model to secure the majority of their borrowing capacity. With the advent of the auction process, the borrower can actively participate in locking up portfolios that have been historically lent through an agency-only approach. This participation by borrowers has driven pricing and utilization levels up, which has simultaneously driven the movement to push more assets out via this format. A mutually beneficial cycle developed for those borrowers and lenders open to this new style of lending.

GROWTH OF AUCTIONS IN RECENT YEARS

Both North American and European entities are designing and promoting auctions as an innovative way to distribute and price securities lending transactions. As discussed earlier, the auction process has been utilized by a number of organizations to facilitate the placement of exclusive assets over the last few years. One of the more innovative and early pioneers utilizing the auction model to place exclusive assets was the California Public Employees Retirement System—better known as CalPERS. CalPERS is the largest public pension fund in North America with approximately $177 billion in assets. CalPERS provides retirement and health benefits to more than 1.4 million public employees, retirees, and their families and more than 2,500 employers. The CalPERS case study offers a glimpse into the evolution and success of one of the first auction-based approaches to gain critical mass within the securities lending field.

CalPERS Case Study

Historically, in an effort to earn additional income from their existing portfolios, CalPERS utilized a traditional custodial and third-party-agency lending structure to manage their securities lending program. All cash collateral was reinvested through lending agents in compliance with CalPERS' internal guidelines. Fee splits were static and rarely renegotiated. The program was viewed as a back office/administrative function, with management focus devoted primarily to compliance monitoring and cash reinvestment risks.

Recognizing the potential for substantially greater income from an actively managed, customized securities lending approach, CalPERS co-developed an auction-based model and entered into a relationship in the fall of 2000 with United Asset Management (UAM). That effort came to be known as eSecLending. eSecLending developed an online, web-based system as a means to disseminate relevant program information and as the central site to gather bids from approved principal borrowers on auction day. The initial objectives of the CalPERS actively managed program included:

- Increase program control through active management
- Initiate direct lending to principal borrowers on a guaranteed basis
- Utilize the auction process as a price discovery mechanism
- Create a transparent allocation process for the placement of securities lending assets
- Utilize the power of the Internet to facilitate communications between lender and borrower
- Unbundle administration, lending and reinvestment activities
- Obtain meaningful benchmarking and performance attribution

Initial CalPERS auctions were tremendously successful and immediately increased program returns through exclusive principal bids, without increasing risk exposure. Prior to utilizing the auction process, CalPERS earned 6% more than the RMA Industry Averages. Since 2000, CalPERS earned an average of 87% more than RMA industry averages during the three full calendar years since utilizing the auction process. The increased price transparency of the auction format allowed CalPERS to realize the true value of its lendable asset base. By increasing the number of counter-parties and creating portfolio subsets to match borrower needs, CalPERS extracted more value from its existing asset base. This was further proof that securities lending was not a back-office function, but rather a pow-erful investment management tool. In addition, the increase in competi-tion and new business enabled CalPERS to negotiate and substantially reduce its securities lending fees paid to its service providers.

For the four years 2000–2004, CalPERS has auctioned off $365 bil-lion in assets through 14 separate auctions. From the inception of the auction-based approach, 16 different principal borrowers have been awarded assets, with those assets usually being held for a term of one year. Interest by counterparties in the auction process has grown since the first auction. Also, since the introduction of the auction process, the secu-rities lending program has moved out on its risk return frontier, and new and more efficient processes have been created to further enhance pro-gram revenue. Exhibit 5.1 demonstrates the success of CalPERS program.

One unique aspect of an exclusive based auction approach is the increase in utilization levels of CalPERS' assets and the reduction of non-economic loans made from an intrinsic standpoint. Since an exclusive

EXHIBIT 5.1 CalPERS Annual Income versus RMA Industry Averages (Calendar Years 2000–2004)

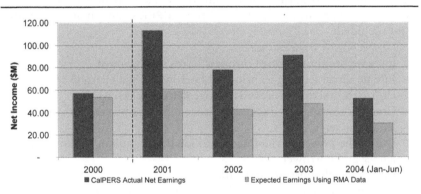

Note: CalPERS earned:

- 6% more than the RMA Industry Averages in 2000, prior to utilizing eSecLend-ing
- An average of 87% more than RMA during the 3 full calendar years since uti-lizing eSecLending
- Only $3.21 million more than RMA in 2000, prior to utilizing eSecLending
- Annually an average of $43.84 million more than RMA during the last 3 full calendar years (2001–2004)

buyer pays for the exclusive right to borrow from a pool of assets, it is in the borrowers' best interest to maximize the potential return from that borrowing base. For CalPERS, this incentive for the borrower to fully reap all the economic advantages from the asset pool dramatically increased utilization levels, which in turn increased the cash collateral balances, thus resulting in higher reinvestment returns. In addition, since the exclusive borrowers were not incentivized to make uneconomic loans in order to boost returns on the cash reinvestment side, CalPERS' overall program interests were aligned with its borrowing base. This is in contrast to a traditional agency-only model in which the agent receives a split from a combination of the intrinsic (or loan-side return) and the cash reinvestment earnings component. So, in essence, the agent is being paid to take reinvestment risk on behalf of the clients with no downside exposure to themselves. This arrangement misaligns the interests of the lender with those of the agent. In summary, the traditional agent may be encouraged to put on noneconomic loans (on behalf of the lender) in order to make additional fees on the cash reinvest side. This conflict of interest is absent with an independent auction-based model.

Currently, CalPERS' program consists of 13 principals, 1 custodial agent, and 3 third-party agents. The program has $25 billion in cash collateral, with $21 billion being managed by three external firms, and $4 billion being actively managed internally. The program generates approximately 80% of its revenue from the intrinsic or loan side with the remaining 20% coming from the cash reinvestment side. CalPERS' securities lending program has generated close to $700 million dollars in securities lending earnings since inception, with the majority of that balance coming since the introduction of the auction format (see Exhibit 5.2).

EXHIBIT 5.2 Net Program Earnings from Inception to Fiscal Year-End June 2004 ($m)

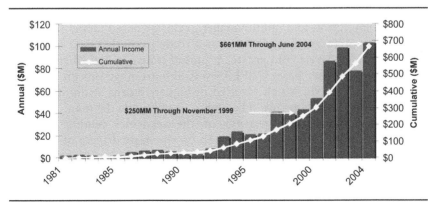

It is important to note that the goal of the CalPERS auction-based approach is not to focus on year over year revenue fluctuations, but to focus on increasing revenue over what would have been generated through alternative routes to market. Comparing program revenue on a year-to-year basis fails to appropriately account for changes in asset values, asset composition, market arbitrage opportunities and changes in international tax withholding rates, which influence the value of CalPERS' lendable asset base. As with any other asset class, the goal for CalPERS' securities lending program is to maximize returns for a given level of risk.

The CalPERS case study clearly demonstrates that the auction format as a route to market has added significant value to CalPERS and is an efficient, transparent route to market for other lenders attempting to add incremental return to their investment portfolios through the use of exclusive principal lending programs.

PROS AND CONS OF THE AUCTION PROCESS IN THE SECURITIES LENDING MARKETS

All innovation, by nature, has both positive and negative side affects. The auction process applied to the securities lending market is no exception. We will use the CalPERS case study to identify many of the positives of using an auction-based approach in the securities lending market. Following the positive examples identified in the case study, we will look at the negative aspects of using an auction-based approach.

The auction model has allowed CalPERS to efficiently migrate from a traditional agency-only based approach to a multimanager model. CalPERS' historical use of an agency-only approach in securities lending was driven by the lack of demands it placed on the organization. As discussed earlier, with the combination of technological innovation and the drive to increase returns across all product sets, the stage was set for a simplified migration to a multimanager/exclusive based model.

The use of an auction platform as a route to market gave CalPERS greater price discovery and greater program transparency when awarding its lendable asset base. CalPERS was able to move out on the risk/return frontier curve, which resulted in higher returns without materially increasing its risk profile. The ability to unbundle the loan, reinvestment and administrative portion of the securities lending process allowed CalPERS to focus its attention on the basic drivers of risk and return. This increased focus lead to reduced fees, more efficient placement of lendable assets and a more streamlined administrative process. The unbundling of the securities lending process also focused CalPERS' attention on the main risk elements within each subsegment of securities lending. As a result, CalPERS put in place additional measures to minimize operational, cash reinvestment, and counterparty risk.

The guaranteed pricing received from entering into an exclusive principal relationship was superior to an agency estimate from both a fiduciary and business standpoint. The auction approach allowed CalPERS to sub-divide assets geographically, by asset type and by size. This subdivision of assets matched the needs of the borrower with the interest of the lender, providing a more level playing field for all participants.

No longer did an exclusive borrower have a competitive advantage based on geographic proximity or a superior marketing team. The auction approach gave all qualified borrowers equal access to large exclusive pools of assets that were formerly unavailable. Under the auction model, the market determined the best price while simultaneously allocating assets to the most suitable party. The auction as a route to market provided a new choice to both lender and borrower.

The CalPERS case study identifies many of the positives of using an auction-based approach as a route to market. However, we have also seen through the CalPERS case study that a portion of CalPERS' assets still reside in an agency-style lending setting. Just as a Swiss Army knife has many tools to do a variety of tasks, so must a modern-day securities lending program have access to a variety of routes to market in order to attain the maximum level of return.

The securities lending process is not a "one-size-fits-all" model. In some cases it makes sense to utilize an agency model or the spot market to place assets while other times it makes sense to auction or place assets out for term. For example, newly created portfolios with no asset management history are initially well suited for an agency-based approach. Once those assets are "seasoned" an auction approach can be used. In addition, portfolios in transition either as a result of a change in management style, size or potential elimination are not well suited from an exclusive placement. Other portfolios that have a low lending value are not well suited to an auction. If any bids are received, they probably will represent only the low intrinsic value of the portfolio and will fail to account for the potential value of a "special" occurring within the portfolio.

An agency model most likely captures more value for lenders when the present value is low and the future value is uncertain. Uncertainty, whether it is in the asset composition, portfolio management style or longevity of the portfolio, minimizes the value received from an auction. If a lender reduces the amount of uncertainty present in a portfolio, the value of the portfolio will increase. Typically, the more uncertainty surrounding a portfolio the more valuable a traditional agency-only approach is to managing the lending of the portfolio.

One area not addressed by the CalPERS case study was the subject of critical portfolio size needed to have an effective auction. In order to auction or place assets on an exclusive basis the lender must give the borrower access to securities with value—that value is derived either by size and/or composition of the asset base being auctioned. Critical mass for a Korean or Taiwanese portfolio, which has a large amount of interest, will be smaller than a general collateral portfolio of government securities. Typically, a borrower writes trade tickets for the assets employed in one-million-dollar increments; anything less starts cutting into the margin of the borrower in the form of higher transaction costs. The borrower must be able to cover transaction costs and meet return on capital requirements for the asset base being utilized. A portfolio highly concentrated and populated with general collateral must be larger than a portfolio of emerging market specials.

The last major negative of using an auction based format to place assets is the challenge of getting internal "buy in" for the process in an organization that has a history of an agency-only approach. As discussed earlier, securities lending has traditionally been a back office function. Back office functions do not lend themselves to new approaches given the risks of process interruptions and operational failures. Most back office personnel are not compensated by how much income they generate; they are motivated to keep processes simple and straightforward. Additionally, the one-on-one business relationships that have developed between the agency lender and the back office can be threatened under a new approach. So the acceptance of a new approach would involve the willingness of an organization to adopt a new route to market, sell the new route to market to upper management and have the ability to stand firm as old entrenched business relationships are reduced in size and scope—not a simple task. Entropy is a powerful inertia to overcome in any organization. Without the right incentive structure in place, it becomes even more difficult to create beneficial change. One of the biggest negatives against adopting an auction process has to do with the ability of an organization to overcome the status quo and risk changing a structure that is not broken—but is not maximizing potential return.

MANAGING THE AUCTION PROCESS

There are many steps to consider when preparing for a securities lending auction. These will vary depending on the type of auction—single-stock/basket or exclusive principal auction. The four main steps are:

1. *Pre-Auction*: Gathering and disseminating asset information to pre-approved pool of borrowers
2. *Auction*: Conducting the actual auction
3. *Post-Auction*: Selection of the winning bidder(s)
4. *Implementation and Administrative Management*: Managing the day-to-day securities lending activities once the program has been awarded and implemented.

Pre-Auction

Determining how to best present information for an auction is dependent on how the auction is structured and what medium is used for distribution of the information (Internet, telephone, etc.). In a single-stock auction, for example, providing the size and individual security description is fairly straightforward. Other variables, such as term length, reserve price, dividend requirements, and the like must also be made available to prospective bidders.

In an exclusive principal deal there are a number of additional variables to be considered. The holdings (assets) must be organized in a manner that is marketable, attractive to lenders, and reasonable from a lending perspective. Assets may be grouped as a single portfolio, or they may be divided into various sublots, depending on the appetite of the borrowing community. These lots are tailored to best match the unique assets of the lender with the ever-changing demands of the borrowers. Once the auction structure is determined, the holdings must then be disseminated to the prospective bidders so that they may review the assets and formulate their bid(s).

In an exclusive principal auction there is often a fixed period of time (which may be hours or days) during which the potential bidders may view the assets, evaluate their options, and formulate their bids.

For credit purposes, all potential borrowers should be precleared from both a credit, legal and suitability standpoint. Lenders should provide a preapproved list of acceptable borrowers to help smooth out the process. Ideally, all legal documentation should be put in place prior to auction day. This allows the eventual "winner(s)" to commence borrowing within a much shorter timeframe, and allows the lender to commence earning revenues more quickly.

Finally, for security reasons, entry to all Internet-based sites for on-line auctions—whether single stock auctions or exclusive principal auctions—should be password protected and subject to strict documentation requirements.

Auction

At the appointed day and hour when the auction is open for bidding, the manager of the auction process must oversee the activity. Common questions that must be addressed include:

- Are all passwords and IDs in hand to allow access to auction information?
- Are bidders following the protocol set up for this particular auction?
- Is there sufficient time for all bidders to place their bids?
- Is there sufficient demand for the assets?
- Is the auction meeting the expectations of the lender?

Post-Auction—Selecting the Winning Bidder

Depending on the type and structure of the auction, the highest paying bidder may not necessarily be the winning bidder. This is particularly true in an exclusive principal arrangement, when the lender must take into consideration the various combinations of bids to achieve their optimum return. In an auction with multiple lots, the individual lots may by themselves be attractive, but not as attractive as a combination bid that may have been posted. Lenders may choose to spread their lending around to a wide variety of borrowers in order to manage their credit and/or concentration risk. In the end, the final decision should reside with the lender.

What the borrowers achieve from this process, however, is a level playing field that provides an opportunity to view a pool of assets, evaluate them, and determine their bids based on an equal status with all other bidders.

Implementation and Administrative Management of the Program Following the Auction

The time spent preparing for a securities lending auction, and the actual bidding process on auction day, can be measured in terms of hours or days. The bigger and often overlooked factor following any auction is the actual day-to-day management of the lending activity once the auction settles—which may be measured in terms of months or even years. The provider of these services must be prepared to address operational, credit, reputational, and reinvestment risks.

In a single-stock auction, often the custodian or third-party agent running the auction will settle the lending transaction(s) in their normal, day-to-day fashion. Specialized administrative follow-up is not usually an issue.

In an exclusive lending program, however, the day-to-day administration of the program following the auction is a critical factor, and one that is often managed by a specialist securities lending manager, who functions as the lender's "back office." This party must perform all the day-to-day loan and return activity inherent in any lending program, but with the added necessity of having electronic feeds to all the borrowers and connections with the lender's custodians as well as all the investment managers.

When the borrowers commence their borrowing, they must follow the operational protocol outlined in the program setup. This includes receiving in automated feeds of daily availability, notification of recalls and returns, entering new loan activity, handling all dividend and corporate action processing, and, finally, monthly reporting and billing. It is important to find a securities lending manager with sufficient experience, infrastructure and personnel to handle a multiple principal lending program on a third-party basis.

The auction is the means to an end from a revenue standpoint—but the day-to-day follow-up is critical to the operational success of the program.

In a typical third-party lending program the securities lending manager takes on the role of managing the day-to-day details of the lending activity on behalf of the lender. Although the lender has a principal relationship with the borrower, most lenders do not want to be actively involved in the day-to-day details of initiating new loans, recalls, returns, marking to market, reconciliations, dividend and corporate action tracking, and monitoring of fails—this is generally the role of the securities lending manager (often referred to as the "administrative agent").

The administrative agent has many relationships to manage—receiving in the individual availability files from custodians for each portfolio; sending these files out to the winning borrowers; interacting with the various investment managers on sales and new purchases; and managing the availability of assets based on the auction rules. The agent must interface with many different parties on a daily basis, and reconcile with each at the end of each day. Additionally, the administrative agent may also be hired to manage the cash collateral on behalf of the lender, which leads to an additional set of relationships including credit, legal and reporting requirements. Exhibit 5.3 shows daily business flows.

Because there is no queuing process in an exclusive principal arrangement, the utilization levels are usually much higher, leading to higher cash balances to be reinvested. However, outstanding loan balances must be monitored in order to insure appropriate collateralization levels and counterparty exposure limits. Likewise, if minimum guaranteed balances were offered through the auction, the administrative agent must be able to monitor and manage these guarantees.

Because most exclusive principal auctions are tailored to meet the needs of the individual lender and their individual portfolios, the rules

EXHIBIT 5.3   Daily Business Flows

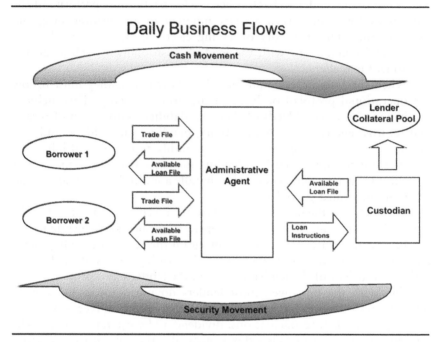

and guidelines that must be followed are often unique to a particular auction. This means that compliance, legal and credit oversight must be adapted for each program.

An experienced third-party administrative agent makes the transition from developing and running a securities lending auction, handling all the legal and credit documentation prior to commencing the program, to setting up the operational infrastructure to managing the day-to-day lending activities effectively and efficiently. Keep in mind, however, the auction results are only as good as the supporting infrastructure provided by an experienced administrative agent.

CONCLUSION

The three forces driving the acceptance of the auction process in the securities lending market—the continued advances in technology, the lenders' focus on return-enhancement strategies, and the continued growth of the hedge fund market—continue to shape the strategies involved in securities lending and encourage the use of auctions for securities lending programs.

The role of the auction process in the securities lending markets has become firmly entrenched in recent times. Auctions have proven successful from the lender's and the borrower's perspective, bringing greater efficiencies and improved price transparency and discovery. Lenders have been able to utilize auctions to maximize returns, generate more focused utilization, and expand their programs to a greater number of providers—while maintaining the same level of risk.

Borrowers have taken advantage of the opportunities offered by the auction process to selectively channel their demands into exclusive principal borrowing relationships that add valuable supply to their supply/demand chain.

The role of the administrative agent, and their ability to manage the resulting exclusive principal deals arranged via auction, has added a "turn-key" approach to the overall process and given the reluctant lender the ability to outsource an exclusive-based securities lending program.

Going forward, we expect a higher volume of securities placed using auctions—utilizing a variety of structures, timetables and pricing mechanisms. The growing number of participants and the depth of its success have validated the auction process. We are confident that the market will continue to embrace this rapidly growing mechanism for the distribution and administration of exclusive principal lending programs.

CHAPTER 6

The Fundamentals of Fixed Income Securities

Frank J. Fabozzi, Ph.D., CFA
Frederick Frank Adjunct Professor of Finance
School of Management
Yale University

A participant in the securities lending business should understand the characteristics of the collateral. The *collateral* can be classified as either equity securities or fixed income securities. In the latter category is a wide range of products with varying risk characteristics. The purpose of this chapter is threefold. First, we describe the basic features of fixed income securities. Second, we look at the risk characteristics of these securities, which is essential to understand how the value of the collateral can change. Moreover, it is these same risks that must be recognized when there is reinvestment of cash collateral. Finally, we look at the issues associated with valuing fixed income securities. While the preference is to mark a position to market based on reliable prices provided by one or more dealers (as set forth in transaction agreement), it may become necessary for complex fixed income securities that are not actively traded—or due to special circumstances in which reliable dealer prices cannot be obtained for a valuation model to get a price for marking a position (i.e., "mark to model"). Disputes in securities finance transactions that require the posting of additional cash revolve around the issue of the fair value of the security used as collateral.

FEATURES OF FIXED INCOME SECURITIES

The features of a fixed income security affect its value and how the security's price changes when interest rates change.

The Maturity of a Bond

The *term to maturity* of a bond is the number of years over which the issuer has promised to meet the conditions of the obligation. The maturity of a bond refers to the date that the debt ceases to exist, at which time the issuer redeems the bond by paying the amount borrowed. The maturity date of a bond is always identified when describing a bond. For example, a description of a bond might state "due 12/1/2020."

The practice in the bond market, however, is to refer to the "term to maturity" of a bond as simply its "maturity" or "term." As we explain below, there may be provisions in the indenture that allow either the issuer or bondholder to alter a bond's term to maturity.

There are three reasons why the term to maturity of a bond is important. The most obvious is that it indicates the time period over which the bondholder can expect to receive the coupon payments and the number of years before the principal is paid in full. The second reason is that the yield on a bond depends on it. Finally, the price of a bond will fluctuate over its life as yields in the market change. The price volatility of a bond is dependent on its maturity. More specifically, with all other factors constant, the longer the maturity of a bond, the greater the price volatility resulting from a change in market yields.

Par Value

The *par value* of a bond is the amount that the issuer agrees to repay the bondholder at the maturity date. This amount is also referred to as the *principal*, *face value*, *redemption value*, or *maturity value*. Bonds can have any par value.

Because bonds can have a different par value, the practice is to quote the price of a bond as a percentage of its par value. The par value is taken to be 100, which means 100% of par value. So, for example, if a bond has a par value of $1,000 and the issue is selling for $900, this bond would be said to be selling at 90. If a bond with a par value of $5,000 is selling for $5,500, the bond is said to be selling for 110.

Coupon Rate

The *coupon rate* is the interest rate that the issuer agrees to pay each year. The annual amount of the interest payment made to owners during the term of the bond is called the *coupon*. The coupon is determined by multiplying the coupon rate by the par value of the bond. For example, a bond with an 8% coupon rate and a principal of $1,000 pays annual interest of $80.

When describing a bond issue, the coupon rate is indicated along with the maturity date. For example, the expression "6s of 12/1/2020" means a bond with a 6% coupon rate maturing on 12/1/2020.

In the United States, the usual practice is for the issuer to pay the coupon in two semiannual installments. Mortgage-backed securities and asset-backed securities typically pay interest monthly. For bonds issued in some markets outside the United States, coupon payments are made only once per year.

In addition to indicating the coupon payments that the investor should expect to receive over the term of the bond, the coupon rate also indicates the degree to which the bond's price will be affected by changes in interest rates. All other factors constant, the higher the coupon rate, the less the price will change in response to a change in interest rates. Consequently, the coupon rate and the term to maturity have opposite effects on a bond's price volatility.

Zero-Coupon Bonds

Not all bonds make periodic coupon payments. Bonds that are not contracted to make periodic coupon payments are called *zero-coupon bonds*. The holder of a zero-coupon bond realizes interest by buying the bond substantially below its par value. Interest then is paid at the maturity date, with the interest being the difference between the par value and the price paid for the bond. So, for example, if an investor purchases a zero-coupon bond for 70, the interest is 30. This is the difference between the par value (100) and the price paid (70).

Floating-Rate Securities

The coupon rate on a bond need not be fixed over the bond's life. *Floating-rate securities*, also called *variable rate securities*, have coupon payments that reset periodically according to some *reference rate*. The typical formula for the coupon rate at the dates when the coupon rate is reset is:

Reference rate + Index spread

The *index spread*, often referred to as simply spread, is the additional amount that the issuer agrees to pay above the reference rate. For example, suppose that the reference rate is the 1-month London interbank offered rate (LIBOR). Suppose that the index spread is 100 basis points. Then the coupon reset formula is:

$$1\text{-month LIBOR} + 100 \text{ basis points}$$

So, if 1-month LIBOR on the coupon reset date is 5%, the coupon rate is reset for that period at 6% (5% plus 100 basis points).

The reference rate for most floating-rate securities is an interest rate or an interest rate index. There are some issues where this is not the case. Instead, the reference rate is some financial index such as the return on the Standard & Poor's 500 or a nonfinancial index such as the price of a commodity. Through financial engineering, issuers have been able to structure floating-rate securities with almost any reference rate. These securities are called *structured notes*.

A floating-rate security may have a restriction on the maximum coupon rate that will be paid at a reset date. The maximum coupon rate is called a *cap*. For example, suppose for our hypothetical floating-rate security whose coupon rate formula is 1-month LIBOR plus 100 basis points, there is a cap of 11%. If 1-month LIBOR is 10.5% at a coupon reset date, then the coupon rate formula would give a value of 11.5%. However, the cap restricts the coupon rate to 11%. Thus, for our hypothetical security, once 1-month LIBOR exceeds 10%, the coupon rate is capped out at 11%.

Because a cap restricts the coupon rate from increasing, a cap is an unattractive feature for the investor. In contrast, there could be a minimum coupon rate specified for a floating-rate security. The minimum coupon rate is called a *floor*. If the coupon reset formula produces a coupon rate that is below the floor, the floor is paid instead. Thus, a floor is an attractive feature for the investor.

Inverse Floaters

Typically, the coupon rate formula on floating-rate securities is such that the coupon rate increases when the reference rate increases and decreases as the reference rate decreases. There are issues whose coupon rate moves in the opposite direction from the change in the reference rate. Such issues are called *inverse floaters* or *reverse floaters*. A general formula for an inverse floater is:

$$K - L \times (\text{Reference rate})$$

For example, suppose that for a particular inverse floater K is 12% and L is 1. Then the coupon reset formula would be:

$$12\% - \text{Reference rate}$$

Suppose that the reference rate is 1-month LIBOR, then the coupon reset formula would be:

$$12\% - \text{1-month LIBOR}$$

If in some month 1-month LIBOR at the coupon reset date is 5%, the coupon rate for the period is 7%. If in the next month 1-month LIBOR declines to 4.5%, the coupon rate increases to 7.5%.

Notice that if 1-month LIBOR exceeded 12%, then the coupon reset formula would produce a negative coupon rate. To prevent this, there is a floor imposed on the coupon rate. Typically, the floor is zero. While not explicitly stated, there is a cap on the floater. This occurs if 1-month LIBOR is zero. In that unlikely event, the maximum coupon rate is 12% for our hypothetical security. In general, it will be the value of K in the general coupon reset formula for a floating-rate security.

Suppose instead that the coupon reset formula for an inverse floater whose reference rate is 1-month LIBOR is as follows:

$$28\% - 3 \times (\text{1-month LIBOR})$$

If 1-month LIBOR at a reset date is 5%, then the coupon rate for that month is 13%. If in the next month 1-month LIBOR declines to 4%, the coupon rate is 16%. Thus, a decline in 1-month LIBOR of 100 basis points increases the coupon rate by 300 basis points. This is because the value for LIBOR in the inverse floater formula is 3. Thus, for each one basis point change in 1-month LIBOR the coupon rate changes by 3 basis points.

Provisions for Paying Off Bonds

Most bonds are *term bonds*; that is, they run for a term of years and then become due and payable. Any amount of the liability that has not been paid off prior to maturity must be paid off at that time. The term may be long or short. Term bonds may be retired by payment at final maturity or retired prior to maturity if provided for in the indenture.

Many issues have a call provision allowing the issuer an option to buy back all or part of the issue prior to the stated maturity date. Some issues specify that the issuer must retire a predetermined amount of the issue periodically. Various types of call provisions are discussed in this section.

An issuer generally wants the right to retire a bond issue prior to the stated maturity date because it recognizes that at some time in the future the general level of interest rates may fall sufficiently below the issue's coupon rate so that redeeming the issue and replacing it with another issue with a lower coupon rate would be beneficial. This right is a disadvantage to the bondholder since proceeds received must be reinvested at a lower interest rate. As a result, an issuer who wants to include this right as part of a bond offering must compensate the bondholder when the issue is sold by offering a higher yield, or equivalently, accepting a lower price than if the right is not included.

The right of the issuer to retire the issue prior to the stated maturity date is referred to as a *call option*. If an issuer exercises this right, the issuer is said to "call the bond." The price the issuer must pay to retire the issue is referred to as the *call price*. Typically, there is not one call price but a *call schedule* that sets forth a call price based on when the issuer can exercise the call option. When a bond is issued, typically the issuer may not call the bond for a number of years. That is, the issue is said to have a *deferred call*. The date at which the bond may first be called is referred to as the *first call date*. Generally, the call schedule is such that the call price at the first call date is a premium over the par value and scaled down to the par value over time. The date at which the issue is first callable at par value is referred to as the *first par call date*.

If a bond issue does not have any protection against early call, then it is said to be a currently callable issue. But most new bond issues, even if currently callable, usually have some restrictions against certain types of early redemption. The most common restriction is that prohibiting the *refunding* of the bonds for a certain number of years. Bonds that are noncallable for the issue's life are more common than bonds that are nonrefundable for life but otherwise callable.

Many investors are confused by the term noncallable and nonrefundable. Call protection is much more absolute than refunding protection. While there may be certain exceptions to absolute or complete call protection in some cases (such as sinking funds and the redemption of debt under certain mandatory provisions), it still provides greater assurance against premature and unwanted redemption than does refunding protection. Refunding prohibition merely prevents redemption only from certain sources, namely the proceeds of other debt issues sold at a lower cost of money. The bondholder is only protected if interest rates decline, and the borrower can obtain lower-cost money to pay off the debt.

Options Granted to Bondholders

Many securities contain an option that grants either the issuer or the investor the right to alter the cash flow of the security. Such an option is referred to as an *embedded option*—it is embedded within the security as opposed to being a stand alone option. A callable bond is the most common example of a bond with an embedded option. A callable bond is one in which the issuer has the right to alter the maturity date of the bond. There may be a provision that allows the bondholder to alter the maturity. This occurs if the bond is putable or convertible.

An issue with a *put provision* included in the indenture grants the bondholder the right to sell the issue back to the issuer at a specified price on designated dates. The specified price is called the *put price*.

A *convertible bond* is an issue giving the bondholder the right to exchange the bond for a specified number of shares of common stock. Such a feature allows the bondholder to take advantage of favorable movements in the price of the issuer's common stock. An *exchangeable bond* allows the bondholder to exchange the issue for a specified number of common stock shares of a corporation different from the issuer of the bond. The number of shares of common stock that the bondholder receives from converting is called the *conversion ratio*. The conversion privilege may extend for all or only some portion of the security's life, and the stated conversion ratio may change over time. Almost all convertible issues are callable by the issuer. Some convertible bonds are putable. Put options can be classified as "hard" puts and "soft" puts. A *hard put* is one in which the convertible security must be redeemed by the issuer only for cash. In the case of a *soft put*, the issuer has the option to redeem the convertible security for cash, common stock, subordinated notes, or a combination of the three.

Currency Denomination

The payments that the issuer of a bond makes to the bondholder can be in any currency. For bonds issued in the United States, the issuer typically makes both coupon payments and principal repayments in U.S. dollars. However, there is nothing that forces the issuer to make payments in this way. The indenture can specify that the issuer can make payments in some other specified currency. Some issues grant either the issuer or the bondholder the right to select the currency in which a payment will be paid. This option effectively gives the party with the right to choose the currency the opportunity to benefit from a favorable exchange rate movement.

RISKS ASSOCIATED WITH INVESTING IN FIXED INCOME SECURITIES

A lender of securities who accepts a fixed income security as collateral, must understand its risk characteristics. In this section we describe the different types of risk that an investor in fixed income securities is exposed to: (1) interest rate risk, (2) call or timing risk, (3) credit risk, (4) liquidity risk, (5) exchange rate or currency risk, and (6) volatility risk.

Interest Rate Risk

The price of a fixed income security moves in the opposite direction to the change in interest rates: as interest rates rise (fall), the price of a fixed income security will fall (rise). Exhibit 6.1 illustrates this property for four hypothetical bonds, where the bond prices are shown assuming a par value of $100.

The risk that interest rates will rise and that the price of the security will fall is called *interest rate risk*. The degree of interest rate risk for any security depends on various characteristics of the security such as coupon and maturity, and options embedded in the security.

Properties of Option-Free Bonds

Exhibit 6.2 uses the four hypothetical bonds in Exhibit 6.1 to show the percentage change in each bond's price for various changes in yield, assuming that the initial yield for all four bonds is 6%. An examination of Exhibit 6.2 reveals several properties concerning the price volatility of an option-free bond.

> *Property 1:* Although the prices of all option-free bonds move in the opposite direction from the change in yield, the percentage price change is not the same for all bonds.

> *Property 2:* For small changes in yield, the percentage price change for a given bond is roughly the same, whether the yield increases or decreases.

EXHIBIT 6.1   Price/Yield Relationship for Four Hypothetical Bonds

Yield (%)	6%/5-year	6%/20-year	9%/5-year	9%/20-year
		Price ($)		
4.00	108.9826	127.3555	122.4565	168.3887
5.00	104.3760	112.5514	117.5041	150.2056
5.50	102.1600	106.0195	115.1201	142.1367
5.90	100.4276	101.1651	113.2556	136.1193
5.99	100.0427	100.1157	112.8412	134.8159
6.00	100.0000	100.0000	112.7953	134.6722
6.01	99.9574	99.8845	112.7494	134.5287
6.10	99.5746	98.8535	112.3373	133.2472
6.50	97.8944	94.4479	110.5280	127.7605
7.00	95.8417	89.3225	108.3166	121.3551
8.00	91.8891	80.2072	104.0554	109.8964

EXHIBIT 6.2 Instantaneous Percentage Price Change for Four Hypothetical Bonds (Initial yield for all four bonds is 6%.)

New Yield (%)	Percent Price Change			
	6%/5-year	6%/20-year	9%/5-year	9%/20-year
4.00	8.98	27.36	8.57	25.04
5.00	4.38	12.55	4.17	11.53
5.50	2.16	6.02	2.06	5.54
5.90	0.43	1.17	0.41	1.07
5.99	0.04	0.12	0.04	0.11
6.01	−0.04	−0.12	−0.04	−0.11
6.10	−0.43	−1.15	−0.41	−1.06
6.50	−2.11	−5.55	−2.01	−5.13
7.00	−4.16	−10.68	−3.97	−9.89
8.00	−8.11	−19.79	−7.75	−18.40

Property 3: For large changes in yield, the percentage price change is not the same for an increase in yield as it is for a decrease in yield.

Property 4: For a given large change in basis points, the percentage price increase is greater than the percentage price decrease.

Characteristics of a Bond that Affect its Price Volatility

There are two characteristics of an option-free bond that determine its price volatility: coupon and term to maturity.

Characteristic 1: For a given term to maturity and initial yield, the lower the coupon rate the greater the price volatility of a bond.

Characteristic 2: For a given coupon rate and initial yield, the longer the term to maturity, the greater the price volatility.

These properties can be verified by examining Exhibit 6.2.

Duration as a Measure of Interest Rate Risk

The most obvious way to measure a bond's price sensitivity to changes in interest rates is to change rates by a small number of basis points and calculate how the security's value will change. The name popularly used to refer to the approximate percentage price change is *duration*. It can be demonstrated that the following formula gives the approximate percentage price change for a 100 basis point change in yield:

$$\frac{\text{Value if rates fall} - \text{Value if rates rise}}{2(\text{Initial value})(\text{Change in yield in decimal form})}$$

where "Value if rates fall" is the estimated value of the security if the yield falls by a small number of basis points; "Value if rates rise" is the estimated value of the security if the yield rises by the same number of basis points; "Initial value" is the current price; and "Change in yield in decimal form" is the number of basis points by which the yield is changed to obtain the values in the numerator.

To illustrate the duration calculation, consider the following option-free bond: a 6% coupon, 5-year bond trading at par to yield 6%. The initial value is 100. Suppose the yield is changed by 50 basis points. Thus, the change in yield in decimal form is 0.005. If the yield is decreased to 5.5%, the value of this bond would be 102.1600 (see Exhibit 6.1). If the yield is increased to 6.5%, the value of this bond would be 97.8944 (see Exhibit 6.1). Substituting these values into the duration formula

$$\text{Duration} = \frac{102.1600 - 97.8944}{2(100)(0.005)} = 4.27$$

The duration of a security can be interpreted as the approximate percentage change in the price for a 100 basis point change in yield. Thus a bond with a duration of 4.8 will change by approximately 4.8% for a 100 basis point change in yield. For a 50 basis point yield change, the bond's price will change by approximately 2.4%; for a 25 basis point yield change, 1.2%, and so on.

It is important to understand that the two values used in the numerator of the formulas are obtained from a valuation model. Consequently, *the resulting measure of the price sensitivity of a security to interest rates changes is only as good as the valuation model employed to obtain the estimated value of the security.* We discuss valuation models later in this chapter.

Dollar Duration

Duration is related to percentage price change. However, for two bonds with the same duration, the dollar price change will not be the same if they differ in coupon, maturity, or yield. For example, consider two bonds, W and X. Suppose that both bonds have a duration of 5, but that W is trading at par while X is trading at 90. A 100 basis point change for both bonds will change the price by approximately 5%. This means a price change of $5 (5% times $100) for W and a price change of $4.5 (5% times $90) for V.

The dollar price volatility of a bond can be measured by multiplying modified duration by the dollar price and the number of basis points (in decimal form) and is called the *dollar duration*.

Modified Duration versus Effective Duration

A popular form of duration that is used by practitioners is *modified duration*. Modified duration is the approximate percentage change in a bond's price for a 100 basis point yield change assuming that the bond's cash flow does *not* change when the yield changes. What this means is that in calculating the values used in the numerator of the duration formula, the cash flow used to calculate the initial value is assumed. Therefore, the change in the bond's value when the yield changed by a small number of basis points is due solely to discounting at the new yield level.

The assumption that the cash flow will not change when the yield changes makes sense for option-free bonds such as noncallable Treasury securities. This is because the payments made by the U.S. Department of the Treasury to holders of its obligations does not change when yields change. However, the same can not be said for callable and putable bonds and mortgage-backed securities. For these securities, a change in yield will alter the expected cash flow.

The price/yield relationship for callable bonds and mortgage passthrough securities is different from that of an option-free bond. As yields in the market decline, the likelihood that yields will decline further so that the issuer or homeowner will benefit from calling the bond or refinancing a mortgage increases. As a result, when rates decline, while the price of a callable bond or mortgage passthrough security will rise, it will not increase by as much as an otherwise option-free bond. For example, suppose the market yield is such that an option-free bond would be selling for 109. Suppose instead that it is callable at 104. Investors would not pay 109. If they did and the bond is called, investors would receive 104 (the call price) for a bond they purchased for 109. For a range of yields there will be price compression—that is, there is limited price appreciation as yields decline. Because of this characteristic, callable bonds are said to have *negative convexity*.

Negative convexity means that the price appreciation will be less than the price depreciation for a large change in yield of a given number of basis points. For a bond that is option-free the price appreciation will be greater than the price depreciation for a large change in yield (Property 4). A bond with this characteristic is said to exhibit positive convexity. The price changes resulting from bonds exhibiting positive convexity and negative convexity can be expressed as follows:

	Absolute value of percentage price change for:	
Change in interest rates	Positive convexity	Negative convexity
−100 basis points	X%	less than Y%
+100 basis points	less than X%	Y%

A valuation model should take into account how yield changes affect cash flow. Thus, when the values used in the numerator are obtained from these valuation models, the resulting duration takes into account both the discounting at different interest rates and how the cash flow can change. When duration is calculated in this manner, it is referred to as *effective duration.*

The difference between modified duration and effective duration for fixed income securities with an embedded option can be quite dramatic. For example, a callable bond could have a modified duration of 6 but an effective duration of only 2. For certain collateralized mortgage obligations, the modified duration could be 7 and the effective duration 20! Thus, using modified duration as a measure of the price sensitivity of a security to yield changes would be misleading. The more appropriate measure for a security with an embedded option is effective duration.

Call or Timing Risk

From the investor's perspective, there are three disadvantages of the call provision. First, the cash-flow pattern of a callable bond is not known with certainty. Second, because the issuer will call the bonds when interest rates have dropped, the investor is exposed to reinvestment risk. That is, the investor will have to reinvest the proceeds received when the bond is called at relatively lower interest rates. Finally, the capital appreciation potential of a bond will be reduced. That is, callable bonds exhibit negative convexity. Collectively, these risks are referred to as *call risk* or *timing risk.*

These risks also exist with mortgage-backed securities and asset-backed securities whose cash flow may depend on the level of interest rates. In the case of mortgage-backed securities, the cash flow depends on prepayments of principal made by the homeowners in the pool of mortgages that serves as collateral for the security. The timing risk in this case is called *prepayment risk.*

CREDIT RISK

Credit risk encompasses three types of risk: default risk, credit spread risk, and downgrade risk. We describe each type below.

Default Risk

Default risk is the risk that the issuer will fail to satisfy the terms of the obligation with respect to the timely payment of interest and repayment of the amount borrowed. To gauge the default risk, investors rely on analysis performed by nationally recognized statistical rating organizations that perform credit analysis of issues and issuers and express their conclusions in the form of a *credit rating*. For long-term debt obligations, a credit rating is a forward-looking assessment of the probability of default and the relative magnitude of the loss should a default occur. For short-term debt obligations, a credit rating is a forward-looking assessment of the probability of default.

The nationally recognized statistical rating organization, or more popularly referred to as "rating agencies" are Moody's Investors Service, Standard & Poor's Corporation, and Fitch Ratings. While a credit rating for a specific debt issue, market participants typically refer to the creditworthiness of the issuing entity in terms of the credit rating of its debt.

The rating systems of the rating agencies use similar symbols. Separate categories are used by each rating agency for short-term debt (with original maturity of 12 months or less) and long-term debt (over one year original maturity). Exhibit 6.3 shows the long-term debt ratings. In all rating systems the term "high grade" means low credit risk, or conversely, high probability of future payments. The highest-grade bonds are designated by Moody's by the letters Aaa, and by the others as AAA. The next highest grade is Aa (Moody's), and by the others as AA; for the third grade all rating agencies use A. The next three grades are Baa (Moody's) or BBB, Ba (Moody's) or BB, and B, respectively. There are also C grades. S&P and Fitch use plus or minus signs to provide a narrower credit quality breakdown within each class. Moody's uses 1, 2, or 3 for the same purpose. Bonds rated triple A (AAA or Aaa) are said to be "prime"; double A (AA or Aa) are of high quality; single A issues are called "upper medium grade"; and triple B are "medium grade." Lower-rated bonds are said to have "speculative" elements or be" distinctly speculative."

Bond issues that are assigned a rating in the top four categories are referred to as *investment-grade bonds*. Bond issues that carry a rating below the top four categories are referred to as *noninvestment grade bonds* or more popularly as *high-yield bonds* or *junk bonds*. Thus, the

EXHIBIT 6.3   Summary of Long-Term Bond Rating Systems and Symbols

Fitch	Moody's	S&P	Summary Description
Investment Grade			
AAA	Aaa	AAA	Gilt edged, prime, maximum safety, lowest risk, and when sovereign borrower considered "default-free"
AA+	Aa1	AA+	
AA	Aa2	AA	High-grade, high-credit quality
AA-	Aa3	AA-	
A+	A1	A+	
A	A2	A	Upper-medium grade
A-	A3	A-	
BBB+	Baa1	BBB+	
BBB	Baa2	BBB	Lower-medium grade
BBB-	Baa3	BBB-	
Speculative Grade			
BB+	Ba1	BB+	
BB	Ba2	BB	Low grade; speculative
BB-	Ba3	BB-	
B+	B1		
B	B	B	Highly speculative
B-	B3		
Predominantly Speculative, Substantial Risk or in Default			
CCC+		CCC+	
CCC	Caa	CCC	Substantial risk, in poor standing
CC	Ca	CC	May be in default, very speculative
C	C	C	Extremely speculative
		CI	Income bonds—no interest being paid
DDD			
DD			Default
D		D	

bond market can be divided into two sectors: the investment grade sector and the noninvestment grade sector. Distressed debt is a subcategory of noninvestment grade bonds. These bonds may be in bankruptcy proceedings, may be in default of coupon payments, or may be in some other form of distress.

Credit Spread Risk

The credit spread is the excess premium over the government or risk-free rate required by the market for taking on a certain assumed credit exposure. *Credit spread risk* is the loss or underperformance of an issue or issues due to an increase in the credit spread. As explained earlier, duration is a measure of the change in the value of a bond when interest rates change. and a useful way of thinking of duration is that it is the approximate percentage change in the value of a bond for a 100 basis point change in "interest rates." The interest rate that is assumed to change is the Treasury or benchmark rate. For credit-risky bonds, the yield is equal to the Treasury or benchmark rate plus the credit spread. A measure of how a credit risky bond's price will change if the credit spread sought by the market changes is called *spread duration*. For example, a spread duration of 2 for a credit-risky bond means that for a 100 basis point increase in the credit spread (holding the Treasury or benchmark rate constant), the bond's price will change by approximately 2%.

Downgrade Risk

Once a credit rating is assigned to a debt obligation, a rating agency monitors the credit quality of the issuer and can reassign a different credit rating. An improvement in the credit quality of an issue or issuer is rewarded with a better credit rating, referred to as an *upgrade*; a deterioration in the credit rating of an issue or issuer is penalized by the assignment of an inferior credit rating, referred to as a *downgrade*. The actual or anticipated downgrading of an issue or issuer increases the credit spread and results in a decline in the price of the issue or the issuer's bonds. This risk is referred to as *downgrade risk* and is closely related to credit spread risk.

To help market participants gauge downgrade risk, the rating agencies periodically publish, in the form of a table, information about how issues that they have rated change over time. This table is called a *rating migration table* or *rating transition table*. A rating migration table is available for different lengths of time.

A rating agency may announce in advance that it is reviewing a particular credit rating, and may go further and state that the review is a precursor to a possible downgrade. This announcement is referred to as putting the issue under *credit watch*. The outcome of a credit watch is in most cases likely to be a rating downgrade, however the review may re-affirm the current rating or possibly upgrade it. During the credit watch phase the rating agency advises investors to use the current rating with caution.

Occasionally the ability of an issuer to make interest and principal payments changes seriously and unexpectedly because of an unforeseen event. This can include any number of idiosyncratic events that are specific to the corporation or to an industry, including a natural or industrial accident, a regulatory change, a takeover or corporate restructuring or even corporate fraud. This risk is referred to generically as *event risk* and results in a downgrading of the issuer by the rating agencies. Because the price of the entity's securities typically change dramatically or jump in price, this risk is sometimes referred to as *jump risk*.

Liquidity Risk

For an individual security, liquidity risk involves the ease with which an issue can be sold at or near its value. The primary measure of liquidity is the size of the spread between the bid price and the offered price quoted by a dealer. The greater the dealer spread, the greater the liquidity risk.

Exchange Rate or Currency Risk

An investor who owns a bond whose payments are denominated in a foreign currency does not know what the cash flows will be in his local currency. The cash flows in the investor's local currency are dependent on the exchange rate at the time the payments are received. The risk of depreciation of the foreign currency relative to the local currency, resulting in a reduction in the cash flows in the local currency, is referred to as *exchange rate risk* or *currency risk*.

In addition to the change in the exchange rate, an investor is exposed to the interest rate risk in the local market. For example, if a U.S. investor purchases German government bonds denominated in euros, the proceeds received from that bond if it is sold prior to maturity will depend on the level of interest rates in the German bond market, in addition to the exchange rate.

Volatility Risk

As will be explained in the next section, the price of a bond with an embedded option depends on the level of interest rates and factors that influence the value of the embedded option. One of the factors is the expected volatility of interest rates. Specifically, the value of an option rises when expected interest rate volatility increases. In the case of a callable bond or mortgage-backed security, since the investor has granted an option to the borrower, the price of the security falls because the investor has given away a more valuable option. The risk that a change in expected volatility will adversely affect the price of a security is called *volatility risk*.

VALUING FIXED INCOME SECURITIES

Valuation is the process of determining the fair value of a financial asset. The fundamental principle of valuation is that the value of any financial asset is the present value of the expected cash flow. This principle applies regardless of the financial asset. Here we explain the general principles of fixed income valuation highlighting the complications involved with the process. It is because of these complications that there can be significant differences in the value assigned to a complex security with one or more embedded options.

Estimating Cash Flow

Cash flow is simply the cash that is expected to be received each period from an investment. In the case of a fixed income security, it does not make any difference whether the cash flow is interest income or repayment of principal.

The cash flow for only a few types of fixed income securities are simple to project. Noncallable Treasury securities have a known cash flow. For a Treasury coupon security, the cash flow is the coupon interest payments every six months up to the maturity date and the principal payment at the maturity date. So, for example, the cash flow per $100 of par value for a 7%, 10-year Treasury security is the following: $3.5 (7%/2 × $100) every six months for the next 20 6-month periods and $100 20 6-month periods from now. In fact, for any fixed income security in which neither the issuer nor the investor can alter the repayment of the principal before its contractual due date, the cash flow can easily be determined assuming that the issuer does not default.

It is difficult to estimate the cash flow for a fixed income security where (1) either the issuer or the investor has the option to change the contractual due date of the repayment of the principal or (2) the coupon payment is reset periodically based on a formula that depends on some value or values for reference rates, prices, or exchange rates. Callable bonds, putable bonds, and mortgage-backed securities are examples of the former; floating-rate securities and structured notes are examples of the latter.

A key factor determining whether either the issuer of the security or the investor would exercise an option is the level of interest rates in the future relative to the security's coupon rate. Specifically, for a callable bond, if the prevailing market rate at which the issuer can call an issue is sufficiently below the issue's coupon rate to justify the costs associated with refunding the issue, the issuer is likely to call the issue. Similarly, for a mortgage loan, if the prevailing refinancing rate available in the mortgage market is sufficiently below the loan's rate so that there will be savings by refinancing after considering the associated refinancing costs, then the homeowner has an incentive to refinance. For a putable bond, if the rate on comparable securities rises such that the value of the putable bond falls below the value at which it must be repurchased by the issuer, then the investor will put the issue.

What this means is that to properly estimate the cash flow of a fixed income security it is necessary to incorporate into the analysis how interest rates can change in the future and how such changes affect the cash flow. This is done in valuation models by introducing a parameter that reflects the expected volatility of interest rates.

Discounting the Cash Flow

Once the cash flow for a fixed income security is estimated, the next step is to determine the appropriate interest rate. To do so, the investor must address the following three questions:

1. What is the minimum interest rate the investor should require?
2. How much more than the minimum interest rate should the investor require?
3. Should the investor use the same interest rate for each estimated cash flow or a unique interest rate for each estimated cash flow?

The minimum interest rate that an investor should require is the yield available in the marketplace on a default-free cash flow or some other benchmark. In the United States, this is often the yield on a U.S. Treasury security. The premium over the yield on a Treasury security that the investor should require should reflect the risks associated with realizing the estimated cash flow. Many market participants have increasingly come to use the swaps rate as the benchmark.

The traditional practice in valuation has been to discount every cash flow of a fixed income security by the same interest rate (or discount rate). For example, consider three hypothetical 10-year U.S. Treasury securities: a 12% coupon bond, an 8% coupon bond, and a zero-coupon bond. Since the cash flow of all three securities is viewed as default free, the traditional practice is to use the same discount rate to calculate the present value of all three securities and the same discount for the cash flow for each period.

The fundamental flaw of the traditional approach is that it views each security as the same package of cash flows. For example, consider a 10-year U.S. Treasury bond with an 8% coupon rate. The cash flow per $100 of par value would be 19 payments of $4 every six months and $104 20 six-month period from now. The traditional practice would discount every cash flow using the same interest rate.

The proper way to view a 10-year, 8% coupon bond is as a package of zero-coupon instruments. Each cash flow should be considered a zero-coupon instrument whose maturity value is the amount of the cash flow and whose maturity date is the date of the cash flow. Thus, a 10-year, 8% coupon bond should be viewed as 20 zero-coupon instruments.

By viewing any financial asset in this way, a consistent valuation framework can be developed. For example, under the traditional approach to the valuation of fixed income securities, a 10-year, zero-coupon bond would be viewed as the same financial asset as a 10-year, 8% coupon bond. Viewing a financial asset as a package of zero-coupon instruments means that these two bonds would be viewed as different packages of zero-coupon instruments and valued accordingly. When the swaps market is used as the benchmark, the swaps curve is used to value a package of zero-coupon instruments.

Valuation Models

The purpose of a valuation model is to provide a theoretical value for a security. Such models are often used for marking to market securities that are infrequently traded.

Valuation models incorporate the general principles that we discussed above. There are assumptions that underlie all valuation models. Some assumptions can have quite a dramatic impact on the theoretical value generated by the model. Consequently, the user of a valuation model is subject to *modeling risk*. To manage modeling risk, the sensitivity of a valuation model should be stressed tested with respect to the underlying assumptions. One particularly important assumption is the expected yield volatility.

There are two valuation models that are commonly used—the binomial model and the Monte Carlo simulation model. A description of these models is beyond the scope of this chapter.[1] The *binomial model* is

---

[1] For an explanation of these valuation models, see Frank J. Fabozzi, *Valuation of Fixed Income Securities and Derivatives* (New Hope, PA: Frank J. Fabozzi Associates, 1995).

used to value nonmortgage-backed products. The Monte Carlo simulation model is used to value mortgage-backed securities.

SUMMARY

In this chapter we looked at the basic features of fixed income securities, the risk characteristics of these securities, and the issues associated with valuing fixed income securities.

We emphasized one particularly important risk, interest rate risk. This is the risk that the value of a fixed income security will decline when interest rates rise. The characteristics of a security that affect its interest rate risk are coupon and term to maturity. Duration is a measure of interest rate risk. Modified duration is an inferior measure for securities with an embedded option. Instead, effective duration should be used and is a byproduct of a valuation model.

Valuing a fixed income security requires that the expected cash flow be projected and appropriate interest rates be used to discount the cash flow. It is not a simple task to project cash flow or determine the appropriate discount rate for securities with embedded options. Valuation models are used to determine the theoretical value. However, these models are dependent on the underlying assumptions.

CHAPTER 7

Managing Liquidity Risks in Cash-Based Lending Programs

Ed Blount
Executive Director
The ASTEC Consulting Group

Aaron J. Gerdeman
Director, Product Management
The ASTEC Consulting Group

Since 1980, the cash-based securities lending program has evolved to become the prevalent form of collateral management model in the United States. By 2005, U.S.-domiciled insurers, pension funds, mutual funds, and corporate treasurers had securities valued at more than $1.25 trillion on loan. This evolution has not come without difficulties. In the 1990s, securities lenders found that a rising interest rate environment suddenly depressed the value of their cash collateral investments, in some cases to the point of loss, when lenders were unexpectedly required to return cash deposits to borrowers. A few lenders sustained losses that exceeded the income they had earned over the course of several years, although in several cases agent lenders absorbed the damages in order to protect their franchises.

The authors thank Kenneth Martin for contributing to the development of the exhibits during his tenure at ASTEC Consulting Group.

Most of the postcrisis auditors focused on the derivative investments that cash managers had selected for their reinvestment pools. Only a few observers noticed that several lenders, holding the same investments in their own pools, were able to escape the difficulties of their peers by deploying the cash from new loans to repay redeeming borrowers. There was no need to liquidate their pool holdings at the time of greatest loss of value for their derivative holdings. That early form of liquidity management was introduced to the market and forged in the crucible of absolute pandemonium.

In more recent years, as the U.S. model has continued to evolve structurally, lenders outside the United States have started to evaluate the additional income opportunities that are available through cash-based securities lending. Based on market experience, most experienced lenders agree that controlling liquidity risk is the most important consideration when lending securities against cash collateral. In anticipation of any such program expansion, program managers and boards of directors should query the cash managers assigned to handling borrowers' collateral, with particular focus on the asymmetric effects that borrower needs and market forces have on the liquidity needs of their lending programs. Simply stated, borrowers will follow considerably different patterns of collateral creation and redemption, resulting mainly from the disparity of their responses to changing market conditions and their own trading strategies. Those differences can lead to tragic consequences for unwary lenders and their cash managers. Risk management begins with an assessment of the asset classes that dominate their lender's program.

ASSET CLASS CONSIDERATIONS

As a general rule, controlling liquidity risk is more important when lending fixed income securities against cash, if the collateral is to be reinvested in instruments that bear a nondiversifiable exposure to market risk. The fixed value of the cash collateral "peg" is the source of this heightened exposure to liquidity risk in the cash-based lending program. Conversely, when lending against noncash collateral, that is, in the form of other securities, especially those sharing some of the characteristics of those which have been lent, there is a tendency for changes in rates to have similar effects on both sides of the transaction. That can create significant pressures on the liquidity of the cash collateral pool in ways that we will describe below.

More situations can arise to impose unmanageable liquidity demands on cash collateral pools derived from fixed income loans because the conditions that prompt borrowers to return the former and large volumes can develop not only from changes in the level of interest rates, which control borrower rebates, but also from changes in the shape of the yield curve itself. The latter affects the value of both the bonds on loan and those instruments in which the cash collateral has been reinvested. In addition, fixed income securities are generally lent on larger tickets than equities, giving rise to the possibility of a magnified effect. Furthermore, the effects of rate changes on fixed income lending programs are relatively more direct and abrupt, since equities are generally less responsive to changes in interest rates than are fixed income securities. The price of a fixed income security is directly affected by the prevailing interest rates in the relevant market, as well as the time left to the redemption of that security. The closer one gets to the redemption date, the less sensitive to price of the bond in response to interest rate changes. This has a material influence on the planning model used by the cash manager for the securities lending program.

In this section, we will examine a set of market scenarios that illustrate how changing market conditions can have a greater effect on the lending program for fixed income securities than for equities; and we will also examine an historical market condition which led to liquidity stresses that were managed efficiently by a major institutional lender at the end of calendar 2004.

Market Scenarios

Changing conditions can affect the liquidity requirements of lending programs for equities and fixed income securities to considerably different degrees. The primary factors to be considered are (1) rising interest rates and (2) shifts in the shape of the short and long-term yield curves from positive to flat or negative. These rate and shape factors are important because portfolio managers and hedge funds with short positions in fixed income securities will respond to changing market conditions by adapting their trading strategies and modifying their need for securities loans. This has a consequential affect on their relationship managers at financing prime brokers, who will in turn change their rebate expectations in dealings with lenders of widely held fixed income securities. As noted above, those expectations are more sensitive for loans of fixed income securities than for equities.

To anticipate sudden, unmanageable demands for redemption of cash collateral, lenders must understand the circumstances under which the borrowers would adopt wholesale changes in their own trading strategies. The most challenging circumstances involved those market conditions in which interest rates rise coincident with a positive shift in the yield curve, while the most benign are those where rates fall and the yield curve moves negative. There are a number of intervening situations, for which the volume and value effects are outlined in Exhibit 7.1. Similarly, the immediate stresses from cash flow and income effects are outlined in Exhibit 7.2. While the dynamics of these two tables are related, the eventual damage to portfolio values (Exhibit 7.1) can be mitigated by skillful management of cash flows (Exhibit 7.2), a circumstance typified in the mid-1990s example given in the opening paragraphs.

We can see from the scenarios set out in the two exhibits that the stresses would be greatest when there is a rise in rates and a steepening of the yield curve. Fortunately, this is a normal situation. Usually, as rates rise the curve flattens. The market has seen this effect in U.S. dollar interest rates in the recent past when the Fed Funds rate was continuously rising: March 1988 to July 1989; April 1994 to May 1995; and July 1999 to December 2000. Nevertheless, when rates are generally rising, as in each of these periods, the income of lenders comes under pressure and liquidity pressures associated with demands for the return of cash collateral becomes greater. These effects are more pronounced for those directional borrowers who have gone short of the long end of the curve than for those arbitraging (most commonly short of the long end while being at the same time long of the short end). A rise in short-term rates, coincident with a flattening yield curve, could add to a lender's difficulties if cash collateral had been invested in longer maturities and/or in more illiquid instruments.

Loan Distribution

In addition to the effect of changing market conditions, there are considerable differences in the characteristics of loans for different asset classes and market sectors. These can also create unmanageable liquidity stresses, resulting from unanticipated demands for return of cash collateral. In 2004, ASTEC Consulting's survey of financing market participants found that the volatility and size of loans, relative to volatility factors, can vary greatly based on an analysis of proprietary historical data:

1. Loans of non-U.S. fixed income securities were more volatile than loans of non-U.S. equities, although volatility was similar for U.S. securities. ASTEC found that the former displayed a 22.1% coefficient of variation versus 12.7% for the latter.
2. Transaction tickets involving non-U.S. fixed income securities were about 10 times larger than those for loans of non-U.S. equities though the former may be subject to a certain amount of aggregation.

EXHIBIT 7.1 Scenario Analysis: Volume and Value Effects

Scenario	Real or Derived Position of True Borrower in Underlying Transaction	Lending Volume	Return Volume	Collateral Value	Reinvested Pool Asset Value
Uncomfortable					
1. Rise in rates and yield curve goes positive					
	a. Sold bonds	▼	▲	▼	▼
	b. Sold bonds bought STIR	—	—	—	—
2. Rise in rates, no change in yield curve					
	a. Sold bonds	▼	▲	▼	▼
	b. Sold bonds bought STIR	▼	▲	▼	▼
Sub-optimal					
3. Yield curve goes positive, no change in rates					
	a. Sold bonds	▼	▲	▼	▼
	b. Sold bonds bought STIR	—	—	—	—
4. Rise in rates and yield curve goes negative					
	a. Sold bonds	—	—	—	—
	b. Sold bonds bought STIR	—	—	—	—
Benign					
5. Fall in rates and yield curve goes positive					
	a. Sold bonds	—	—	—	—
	b. Sold bonds bought STIR	—	—	—	—
6. Yield curve goes negative, no change in rates					
	a. Sold bonds	▲	▼	▲	▲
	b. Sold bonds bought STIR	—	—	—	—
Positive					
7. Fall in rates and yield curve goes negative					
	a. Sold bonds	▲	▼	▲	▲
	b. Sold bonds bought STIR	—	—	—	—
8. Fall in rates, no change in yield curve					
	a. Sold bonds	▲	▼	▲	▲
	b. Sold bonds bought STIR	▲	▼	▲	▲

Key for Exhibits 7.1 and 7.2

▲ up
↑ drifting higher
— no change
▼ down
↓ drifting lower
STIR means short-term interest rate products.
By *true borrower*, we mean the prime broker's client.

EXHIBIT 7.2   Scenario Analysis: Cash Flow and Income Effects

Scenario	Real or Derived Position of True Borrower in Underlying Transaction	Rebate Rate	Reinvestment Income	Lender's Overall Income
Uncomfortable				
1. Rise in rates and yield curve goes positive				
	a. Sold bonds	▲	▼	▼
	b. Sold bonds bought STIR	—	—	—
2. Rise in rates, no change in yield curve				
	a. Sold bonds	▲	▼	▼ but <1a
	b. Sold bonds bought STIR	↑	↑	▼ but <2a
Sub-optimal				
3. Yield curve goes positive, no change in rates				
	a. Sold bonds	—	▼	▼ but <2a
	b. Sold bonds bought STIR	—	—	—
4. Rise in rates and yield curve goes negative				
	a. Sold bonds	—	—	↓
	b. Sold bonds bought STIR	—	—	↓ but <4a
Benign				
5. Fall in rates and yield curve goes positive				
	a. Sold bonds	—	—	↑
	b. Sold bonds bought STIR	—	—	↑ but <5a
6. Yield curve goes negative, no change in rates				
	a. Sold bonds	—	▲	▲ but <8a & 8b
	b. Sold bonds bought STIR	—	—	—
Positive				
7. Fall in rates and yield curve goes negative				
	a. Sold bonds	▼	▲	▲ > 8a
	b. Sold bonds bought STIR	—	—	—
8. Fall in rates, no change in yield curve				
	a. Sold bonds	▼	▲	▲
	b. Sold bonds bought STIR	↓	↓	▲ but <8a

3. Loans of non-U.S. equities were open on average three times longer than were loans of non-U.S. fixed income securities.
4. The average nondollar, noncash equity loan was about $2.5 to $3 million, while the average sovereign, fixed-income securities loan ticket was about $20 to $30 million.

Clearly, these loan transaction dynamics must be taken into account with the composition of their own loan portfolio by cash managers when planning for their strategic liquidity requirements. Furthermore, the dispersion and volatility of borrowers' balances over time must be weighed using a conventional value-at-risk methodology, in order to determine the likelihood of an unexpected surge in redemption demand. If possible, the VaR for an individual portfolio of borrowers should be examined within the context of measured volatility for the same borrowers acting as counterparties to other lenders and the volatility of the entire loan market as a composite. This larger perspective will be useful in helping cash managers understand whether their historical experience is a reasonable basis for projecting future demands for redemption by borrowers acting within a very complex market environment.

CONTROLLING VALUE AT RISK FOR POOL LIQUIDITY

The concept of *value at risk* (VaR), which is used widely to estimate the market and credit risks of trading portfolios, can also be used to describe the liquidity risks of securities lending programs. With knowledge of the borrowing and returning patterns of each securities borrower, lenders can better manage their program expectations and policies. For example, if a fund places a large portion of its loans with a broker who has a history of making large and sudden returns, then to manage for a potential liquidity crunch that lender might consider options such as:

- Reinvesting a larger percentage of the cash collateral offered by that more-volatile borrower in very short term instruments, averaging down the weighted maturity of the pool, while paying a lower rebate to the borrower in order to make up for the lower spreads resulting from the lower yield on collateral
- Keeping easy-to-lend assets in reserve should the need to generate new loan balances arise

Established risk measurement techniques can assist lenders in anticipating changes in exposure resulting from volatility in borrower returns.

Since liquidity risks in securities lending are specific to the abrupt decline in loan balances (increases are not a problem, except to the extent that lending 100% of easy-to-lend assets will preclude the possibility of generating new loans to escape a liquidity crunch), VaR is an ideal risk measurement because it focuses on losses while ignoring the volatility of gains.

Without going into the technical detail that would be outside the scope of this chapter, VaR can be defined as follows: VaR is a statistical method that forecasts the magnitude of a negative change to some value (e.g., a portfolio of assets) that likely will not be exceeded within a certain amount of time. In other words, today's VaR (say, $1,000,000) tells you that if your portfolio declines in value today that the decline probably (say, with 95% likelihood) will be less than the VaR amount. VaR models are used in this way by managers of portfolios of all kinds of liquid assets, bank regulators across the globe, and even securities lenders to measure the market risks and credit risks in their portfolios. Some beneficial owners might be accustomed to seeing VaR statistics on monthly or quarterly reports produced by their lending agent banks. Those VaR statistics relate to the volatility of the price of the assets that form the principal of the loan (such as volatile equities) as well as the relatively low-risk assets in which the cash collateral is reinvested. By focusing on the volatility of cash redemptions made by borrowers, one can extend the traditional application of VaR to liquidity risks in securities lending.

To illustrate the use of VaR to measure liquidity risk, consider the following hypothetical example of two brokerages borrowing from a single beneficial owner. To analyze the brokerages' patterns of cash deposits and redemptions, first calculate the net change in each borrower's collateral balances from day to day. Plotting the frequency distribution of historical fluctuations in collateral balances over a sufficient time period, such as one year, reveals trends in the shifting size of the relationship between lender and borrower. In Exhibit 7.3, we see that Borrower ABC has on a few occasions increased its borrowings by 50% or more but has never redeemed more than half of its collateral on one day. As would be expected, on most days the net change in collateral/loan balances is less than 5% up or down. In Exhibit 7.4, we see that Borrower XYZ also tends to keep its balances with the lender within ±5% of the prior day's amount. However, this borrower exhibits significantly more volatility in its cash redemptions (and deposits). In fact, on several days the lender was required to return large portions of Borrower XYZ's collateral. VaR provides a simple way of summarizing this analysis in one number that can be used by the lender to prepare for sudden redemptions of a certain size.

This historical VaR analysis tells us that Borrower ABC has a 95% collateral redemption VaR of 13%; that is, the lender knows that Borrower ABC usually (95% of the time) either increases loan balances or

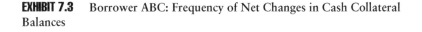

EXHIBIT 7.3   Borrower ABC: Frequency of Net Changes in Cash Collateral Balances

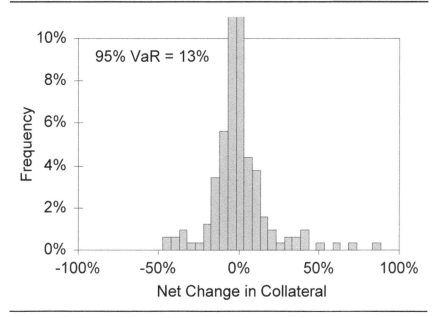

Note: This exhibit shows, for a hypothetical example, the relative size and frequency of collateral withdrawals made by each borrower. Collateral redemption VaR was calculated for the 95% confidence interval. The collateral VaR is an estimate of the probability of large collateral redemptions (negative changes in total loan balances) over the previous 15 months.

redeems no more than 13% of its cash collateral. Either way, this suggests that the lender's relationship with Borrower ABC is fairly stable and therefore has low liquidity risk.

Conversely, Borrower XYZ has a 95% collateral redemption VaR of 52%; that is, the lender knows that Borrower XYZ usually (95% of the time) either increases loan balances or redeems up to 52% of its cash collateral. This indicates a high frequency of negative net changes in collateral balances that necessitates the lender selling off cash collateral reinvestments or generating new loans to raise the cash. Thus, Borrower XYZ has higher liquidity risk.

Such an analysis of the size and frequency of collateral redemptions made by borrowers' yields information important to understanding and managing liquidity risks in securities lending. It cannot indicate the reason for a borrower's relative stability or volatility, which in the case of prime brokerages could derive from the mix of trading strategies employed by its

EXHIBIT 7.4   Borrower XYZ: Frequency of Net Changes in Cash Collateral
Balances

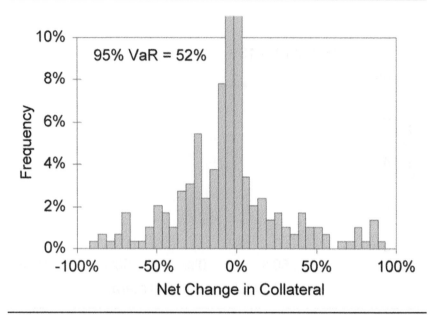

Note: This exhibit shows, for a hypothetical example, the relative size and frequency
of collateral withdrawals made by each borrower. Collateral redemption VaR was
calculated for the 95% confidence interval. The collateral VaR is an estimate of the
probability of large collateral redemptions (negative changes in total loan balances)
over the previous 15 months.

hedge fund clients, but it does describe the effects of such influences. As
we will see in the following case study, large, unexpected returns of cash
collateral are a part of the business of lending. Knowing the extent to
which a particular borrower tends to rebate significant portions of his collateral, whether to a specific lender or to a representative group of lenders,
assists beneficial owners in their management of liquidity risks by measuring the size of the risk and identifying the sources of the risk.

CASE STUDY

A case study illustrates the reality of liquidity risks in securities lending
and the benefits of proper management of those risks. In December
2004, several million dollars worth of a handful of stocks were on loan

to a major prime broker from a large mutual fund complex. The institutional lender acting as an agent for the beneficial owner expected these loans to remain open until nearly the close of the month, but the broker completely returned his positions in these equities on a single day about a week before Christmas.

This sudden return of the borrower's loans triggered the redemption of more than half of the broker's cash collateral deposits (all of which had been reinvested, of course), representing at the time a major portion in the lender's total loan balances because the lender had reallocated positions away from low-margin borrowers and shifted a high portion of its loan portfolio to this one broker. Fortunately, the lending agent's ability to generate sufficient redeployment liquidity helped this event pass without incurring losses. No comment was made about the damage to the relationship between the fund complex and the first broker-dealer.

This successful aversion of investment loss was possible because instead of dumping collateral investments before maturity, the lending agent was able to redeploy a large block of securities to a second prime broker. Faced with the unexpected block redemption, the agent had evaluated its stable of borrowers and assets in reserve to promote the best match, locating securities that which would not only be initially attractive to a creditworthy broker-borrower; but also a sufficiently good fit to the broker's customer, a large hedge fund, to remain in a loaned-out position for several weeks. Still, this happy conclusion might not have been possible, especially during the year-ending period when securities firms sometimes unwind positions in order to "window-dress" their balance sheets, if the lender's agent had not developed a set of insightful relationships with broker-dealers as well as with their hedge fund customers' strategies. Relying on these insights, the agent made enough new loans to generate the cash needed to deliver the necessary collateral to the redeeming broker without collapsing its collateral pool.

As is often true in capital markets, a prior investment in relationships facilitated the core investment process, as the lender benefited from its agent's ability to solve the need for liquidity through the latter's relationship with the second borrower and the insight that both the agent and the broker had of the hedge-fund's strategic needs.

COUNTERPARTY TRADING STRATEGIES

We have described above the exposure that lenders bear to the asset class of the instruments provided to their borrowers. In the examples and scenarios described, the risks from those exposures are magnified by the influence of changing market conditions on the value of the assets held in short positions of the trader-borrower. As we have seen, fixed income loan balances tend to have greater sensitivity to changes in interest rates than do comparable values generated in loans of equity securities. However, the manner in which the trader-borrowers use these assets is also quite significant for risk management, as shown in the case study and described below.

If trader-borrowers manage their loans to satisfy the requirements of their trading strategies nd if market conditions are the greatest influence on the traders' strategies, then lenders must be cognizant of the borrowers' underlying strategies and in particular their resulting sensitivity to changes in market conditions. However, the underlying strategy (or "style", as the term is used by analysts) of the trader-borrower can be even more significant for liquidity risk management than the asset class employed in the implementation of that strategy. For example, trading strategies employing large volumes of assets in long-short positions, such as those typical in statistical arbitrage funds, can lead to dramatic shifts in the cash collateral balances of lenders who cultivate relationships with these borrowers. Once the target yield for a paired long-short position is attained, the trader often closes out the borrowed position and subsequently redirects trading capital into another position. This closeout/redirection can be quite precipitous, particularly for the lenders' cash manager.

Although the assets in arbitrage funds may be relatively easy to borrow and on-lend in the securities financing markets, the rapid withdrawal of a large percentage of the cash pool's deposits may also come at an awkward time for the lender. If the next implementation of the trader-borrowers' follow-up strategy is directed through another prime broker, the lenders agent may be attempting to redistribute the returned the securities into a saturated market. By contrast with the high-volume, but highly-volatile balances of lenders dealing with arbitrage funds, those lenders who deal with fundamental short sellers may have relatively stable and enduring balances, since the positions created by these strategies often endure for months or even years.

If the lender is aware of the anticipated stability of these balances, and consequently lower liquidity risk, the borrowers' cash may be invested in a pool with far more aggressive instruments, at the same time that the cash pool may be structured in a portfolio with a far longer duration and *weighted average maturity* (WAM).

Despite the liquidity advantage that accrues to lenders dealing with fundamental short-sellers, some lenders may be reluctant to lend to traders whose perceived interests and pessimistic viewpoints are at odds with the optimism of the original long-side portfolio manager. Ironically, the eventual reversal of the fundamental short sellers' position, effected by a purchase and return of securities with a consequential demand for redemption of cash balances, usually comes when the market price of the security borrowed has declined sufficiently to offer a capital gain to the short seller. This can create liquidity exposure to the lenders' cash manager, especially if the redemption was unanticipated, but coincidentally the repurchase of securities will prevent further erosion of the market price for the security being returned to the portfolio of the original long side investor, usually cushioning the price fall.

The above examples rely on only two of the more than two dozen recognized strategies employed by short-sellers in contemporary markets. Each short-sellers' strategy creates trading patterns which vary the resulting value and volume of their borrowing needs in harmony with the direction, volatility, and predictability of market conditions. The complexities of the trading strategies means that the year-to-year, even quarter-to-quarter demands of an arbitrage or fundamental short sellers can change dramatically as markets change. Ultimately, each short-sellers' strategy also creates distribution and redemption footprints, i.e., liquidity patterns, in the cash pools of their lenders, which in itself creates a consequential need for their lenders' cash managers to reinvest the collateral into instruments with less-correlated value and volume vectors.

CONCLUSION

In the mid-1990s, cash managers working for securities lenders suffered losses as a result of the derivative assets selected for their investment pools. In the future, it is likely that lenders' losses will also be a function of derivative investments, although the loss is more likely to be a derivative function of unexpected liquidity demands, resulting from the investment demands of borrowers strategies, not of cash managers' pool asset values. In effect, the modern derivative exposure will be to changes in the trading strategies of the ultimate borrower, i.e., the hedge fund or proprietary trading desk. Therefore, the lender's ultimate exposure to loss in a modern securities lending program results less from the counterparty's credit profile, although that remains important, than from the market risk which results from the counterparty's trading strategies.

CHAPTER 8

Quantifying Risks in Securities Lending Transactions

Mark C. Faulkner
Managing Director
Spitalfields Advisors

The securities lending industry, over recent years, has been striving to establish a set of agreed standards for the conduct of its business. These standards embrace topics from legal documentation through to margins imposed on the various transaction types. Indeed, the "performance benchmarking" initiative being conducted by the Robert Morris Associates is a good example of this.

But how appropriate are some of these standards? Have they been developed in the light of experience and analysis—or, have they grown up untried and untested? Are standards appropriate or misleading? Do they provide a, perhaps false, sense of security? Is undue comfort being drawn from the knowledge that if one program fails then there will be others in the same position?

One of the problems of hiding behind standards is that either we fail to think logically about a problem or, alternatively, we find ourselves unable to operate in non-standard situations. Take margining, for example. When accepting cash as collateral against an S&P equity, we know what the standard margins are. If, however, someone wanted to offer European equities as collateral, how would or should we respond? Many lenders, aside from applicable regulatory constraints, would or could not entertain this transaction. For others, a decision to trade would depend on the answer to a few questions, particularly: "What am I going to get paid for this?" and "What is the margin?"

Even when furnished with these answers, the lender may still not have all the information necessary to decide whether to accept or decline the business. This is because there still is one important question unanswered: "What is the risk in the trade?"—how much risk is this lender prepared to accept? The answer should, in theory, be different for each lending institution or entity. Here we have the nub of the problem with standard setting. While the conditions and terms of business may be standard, the relative attraction of any transaction *should vary between* lenders. Where a lender may be comfortable with loans on a 5% margin yielding 20 basis points, another may accept a lesser margin in return for a better fee. Which of the two lenders is the more, or less prudent? In the absence of appropriate and flexible analytics, it is very difficult to say.

In this chapter, we show how an analytical framework can be constructed to help lenders make decisions on the appropriateness of collateral arrangements and understand how they could amend proposed programs to reflect their particular risk/reward tolerance. We will treat cash collateral as just another security type. We are assuming away any cash reinvestment risks/rewards at this stage so as we can focus on the business of the collateralized lending of securities, not that of playing the money-market yield and credit curves.

WHAT DO WE WANT TO UNDERSTAND FROM THE ANALYSIS?

Before bringing together any analysis we need to decide what questions we want answered. Broadly, there are two levels within a lending program that institutions should consider. First, loans are transacted with individual borrowers, even if via a custodian or third-party lending agent (unless that "agent" is acting as principal). The whole program constitutes the aggregation of these individual relationships. It is important to understand, for each borrower, the risks that any default might bring. Secondly, at the total program level the lender will want to understand how these individual risks relate to each other. The lender might also want to quantify the value of its indemnities, or the implied costs to the program of risks being taken. The latter measure would then allow for true risk/return comparisons to be made between programs.

There is the possibility of a profit under the widely used OSLA Agreement (when a lender buys back their "lost" assets at a price lower than the "reference" price). However, one can generally assume that borrower default will only bring a loss, or at best a "break-even" situation to a lender. Any excess collateral is returned to the liquidator, whereas a lender suffers the collateral shortfall, ranking pari passu with other creditors.

Given this situation, the type of questions a lender might ask in relation to each individual borrower include:

1. What is the chance of borrower default?
2. What are the chances of me losing money on default?
3. How much money should we expect to lose on default?
4. How will the answers to 2 and 3 above change if we alter:
   - The counterpart?
   - The margin?
   - The concentration and scope of my lending and collateral arrangements?
   - My reaction time post default?
   - Market liquidity?
   - Asset volatility?
5. Would hedging currency or asset exposure on default reduce my risks?

Looking at the program as a whole the questions we would want to answer include:

1. What is the long-term cost of my program in terms of expected losses?
2. With which borrowers do the bulk of these costs lie?
3. Is there a likelihood of several borrowers defaulting simultaneously?
4. How would changing borrowers affect the costs?
5. What are my risk-adjusted net returns on this business?

ESTABLISHING THE RISKS

Apart from operational risks our main concern arises on the default of a borrower. On default, we are in the scenario that, to make good our pre-default position we need to sell our collateral and buy-back the loaned securities.

First though, we need to get access to that collateral. What stops us? It could be our own ability to react. Just imagine you hear that Megabank International has defaulted—what do you do now? What if the stock lending manager is away on holiday? How long before you can confirm the true position? Are you confident that your legal documents would give you immediate access to the collateral or could there be some delays here, for example, U.S. Treasuries pledged by primary dealers?

While you ponder your position, of course, financial markets are moving. If Megabank International defaulted it is highly likely that financial conditions could be very volatile indeed. The longer the delay, the more likely that the relationship between our collateral and the lost portfolio will have moved adversely.

Once we get hold of our collateral we need to liquidate and repurchase the lost portfolio. This may be straightforward if we are dealing with highly liquid portfolios. In practice this may not be the case. Factors influencing this process include:

- Volatility of markets
- Liquidity of portfolios
- Concentration of portfolios
- Correlation between collateral and lent portfolios

Given this environment what are the key characteristics that we may wish to incorporate in our analytical framework?

Credit Risk

This should reflect not simply the possibility of an individual borrower defaulting, but the possibility of linked defaults.

Reaction and Legal Risk

This should reflect the delay in being able to start liquidating our collateral.

Liquidity Risk

Our collateral and loan portfolios will have probably been valued on the basis that we can repurchase our loan portfolio at market prices. In practice this is unlikely to prove the case and needs to be reflected. The less liquid, more concentrated and more volatile our portfolios, the more expensive will be our switching process, the more our margin is consumed or extinguished.

Mismatch Risk

If our lent and collateral portfolios were identical then we would be exposed to no market risk. In practice, of course, our lent and collateral portfolios are very different. Mismatch risk is a quantification of the difference between these two portfolios.

BUILDING AN ANALYTICAL FRAMEWORK

In constructing our analysis, one of the main assumptions is that we can compare two portfolios and draw a picture showing the statistical distribution of the difference in the value of these two portfolios at some future date. This is not to say that we can predict the future—merely that we can attribute some probability to certain projected scenarios.

Conventionally analysts assume that price changes conform to the lognormal distribution when drawing such pictures. In this case the two portfolios are the collateral and the lent portfolios. If we assume that we have a £5m margin of collateral over lent securities and we were to look at the constituents of our two portfolios then we could draw the type of picture shown in Exhibit 8.1. As you will see we expect the difference to be around £5m, but there is possibility that the difference in the portfolios could be anything from a loss of £3m to a profit of £14m.

Exhibit 8.1 is drawn in the light of specific collateral and lent portfolio over a known time horizon. To draw it we have had to make assumptions about the volatility and correlation of markets and securities, as well as, the distribution we assume. If we vary any of these inputs we will get different results.

Consider Exhibit 8.2. Where the vertical axis is the same as Exhibit 8.1. You will notice that, although the spread of outcomes is centred in the same place as Exhibit 8.1 the distribution is much broader and flatter. There is now a greater likelihood of high profits or losses. What could have led to these two exhibits being so different? In practice there are several reasons.

EXHIBIT 8.1   Difference in Collateral over Lent Portfolios in *n* Days (Version 1)

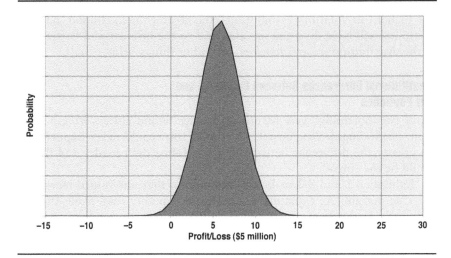

EXHIBIT 8.2   Difference in Collateral over Lent Portfolios (Version 2)

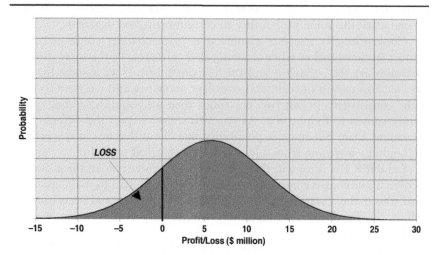

Time

The longer our reaction time assumption, the greater the likelihood that the portfolios have diverged in value and so the broader and flatter will be the distribution (all other things being equal).

Asset Volatility Assumptions

The higher our volatility assumptions, the greater the likelihood that the portfolios will have diverged in value and so the broader and flatter will be the distribution (*ceteris paribus*—all other things being equal).

Constitutional Differences Between Collateral and Lent Portfolios

If our two portfolios were identical then we would always have a £5m profit (excluding dealing costs). Of course, this would never happen but the greater the difference between our portfolios the broader and flatter would be the spread.

Exhibits 8.1 and 8.2 make the assumption that our valued margin is our true margin. As explained earlier, poor liquidity may make this an unrealistic assumption. To circumvent this we need to apply an adjustment to capture the likely market impact of dealing in the collateral and lent securities. These "haircuts" applied to any asset will reflect a number of factors including:

◼ *The value of that security held in the portfolio*
The larger the position, the greater should be the applied haircut.

◼ *The average daily volume of the security*
The lower the daily volume, the greater should be the applied haircut.

◼ *The volatility of the security*
The higher the volatility, the greater should be the applied haircut.

The effect of these haircuts will be to shift the distributions in Exhibits 8.1 and 8.2 to the left, thus increasing the likelihood of the collateral being inadequate on default.

DECIPHERING THE ANALYSIS

Having drawn these charts how can we now interpret the results? The gray-shaded area of Exhibit 8.3 represents loss-making outcomes should the borrower default. The white area represents all break-even outcomes and can be ignored for the purposes of this analysis.

What statements can we make in the light of Exhibit 8.3? The two important points would be the probability of loss and the expected value of loss. The probability of losing money, on default, is represented by the size of the shaded area (in this case 20%). This last statement is a value-at-risk (VAR) analysis.

EXHIBIT 8.3   Probability Distribution of Loss-Making Outcomes

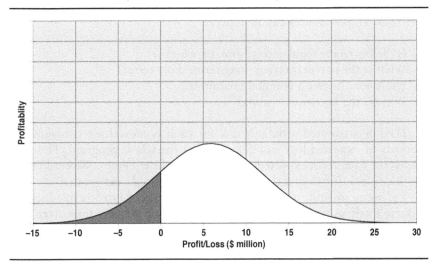

This kind of statement is very common within the banking industry where there is a need to understand capital at risk. However, there are other, possibly more appropriate or intuitive ways to cut the analysis.

One of these could be to calculate the long-term expected loss of a program. We know that default will not lead to profit—only loss, or at best break-even. If we could calculate the expected loss then we could adjust the returns we are currently earning on the program to give the risk-adjusted return.

Calculating the expected loss is slightly more complicated. The red shaded area resembles a put option payoff. Indeed, we can use an adaptation of an option-pricing formula to calculate the expected loss. In this case the expected loss is around £2.75 million.

In summary, *if this borrower defaulted* and with our current assumptions about time, volatility etc. there is a 20% probability that we will lose money and our expected loss will be £2.75 million.

TOTAL PROGRAM RISK

Having calculated the expected loss on default for each borrower we now need to bring these together to quantify the risks attached the program as a whole. To do this we need to apply default probabilities to the expected losses. Where they exist, data from rating companies such as S&P and Moody's can be used.

Often, however, the borrower has no formal parental guarantee or rating. In these cases we need to attribute our own rating scale. Commonly, this can be achieved by attributing scores for defined features of a borrower. These features can include:

- Is the borrower regulated (yes/no, by whom)?
- What is the parental rating (long-term, short-term)?
- Has the borrower a parental guarantee?
- What is the borrower's rating?

Having attributed a default risk for each borrower we can sum the products of expected loss and defaults over the whole program. This will give us the long-term expected annual loss of the program. We could then use this to adjust our gross returns to "risk-adjusted" net returns.

For some institutions quantifying this "expected loss" is insufficient. It doesn't tell us anything about the distribution of outcomes over any one period. Take a simple example. One program could incur a small number of losses through default over a 10-year period, say £100,000 per annum.

Another program could incur no losses for 9 years out of 10 but a £1,000,000 in the other year. Both programs have the same expected annualized adjustment, but the distribution is very different and may be of importance.

Our second example arises when defaults are correlated. The higher the default correlation the more lumpy will be the default experience.

DATA INPUT AND SENSITIVITY ANALYSIS

So far we have made only passing reference to the data used to drive the analysis. We have blithely mentioned volatility, correlation, default probabilities and the like. Whatever data we use, the aim is to try to capture some property of financial markets, instruments, or institutions.

By using historic data, we are effectively implying that future asset class relationships or default experience will be similar to those we have observed in the past. Is this fair?

Remember that the expected loss figures are calculated assuming default. What kind of turmoil will financial markets be in if Megabank International defaulted?

Making the assumption that markets will behave as they have done over the recent past is not intuitive. They will probably be much more volatile; but there is not enough experience for us to quantify this with any certainty. Instead, we may want to adjust our historic data.

For example, we could examine the risks assuming volatility is a multiple of our historic input. In our analysis we have used 10-year historic data to drive the base analysis.

This is not because we think that 10-year is any better a guide to what will happen in the future than one or five-year data.

However, it has some advantages. It reduces the effect where the analysis varies sharply because of changes in data input rather than changes in the program itself. Take, for example, a sharp movement in financial markets. This will have a greater effect on one-year volatility than 10-year volatility figures. The calculated risk in a program will also suddenly jump. But has the prospective risk really changed? Most probably, it has not. More important would have been the question—"did the lender understand the risks it was bearing under that more volatile financial environment?" This can be more easily understood by adjusting stable long-term data.

What else may we want to adjust to understand the potential risks of our program?

Residual Volatility

We make an assumption about how individual securities move relative to markets. This affects the risk of the program directly and indirectly through the haircut applied to asset values.

Liquidity

If we assume lower liquidity then this, too, increases the haircuts that we need to make to the asset classes.

Default

Because of the paucity of default data and the cyclical nature of this risk, it is important to have the facility to adjust the historic data and understand the long-term costs on the program.

Of course, one of the benefits of such a model is that we can use it to do "What if?" scenarios and test the impact that changes in these factors have on the answers to our original questions.

CONCLUSION

We have outlined an approach that can be used by participants in the securities lending business to understand and quantify the relative risks inherent in different programmes. By using an analytical framework, program managers can decide if the terms being offered are commensurate with their own ability to bear risk—or the rewards they demand for bearing that risk. We subscribe to the old adage that "if you can't measure it you can't manage it." We believe that it is possible to measure the risk in securities lending and know that risk can be managed more efficiently than at present.

It is well past the time that this kind of analysis, fairly commonplace in many other financial markets, be made available to institutional lenders of securities. Our approach is to take proven statistical techniques and approaches to the particular environment in which institutions lend. The outcome is a better understanding of where risks lie and their size. Armed with this information, lenders can make decisions about policy that are consistent with their own appetite, not just established standards.

CHAPTER 9

Risk, Return, and Performance Measurement in Securities Lending

Peter Economou, CFA
Senior Vice President
Securities Finance, State Street

With the ongoing evolution and growth of the securities finance marketplace worldwide, it has become increasingly clear that securities lending is indeed an investment management business that is subject to the same market forces—and market expectations—as any other investment management function.

In the broader financial market, indexes such as the Standard & Poor's 500 or the Dow Jones Industrial Average provide information about market valuations and price volatility. Changes in an index over specified periods can be used as a benchmark for investor portfolios that have a similar composition, illustrating whether the portfolios have over- or underperformed. However, as modern portfolio theory has taught us, return is meaningless unless it is considered in the context of the associated risk. In light of this, prudent investors combine a measure of risk (e.g., the standard deviation of the historical returns of an index) with the degree of historical return in order to make intelligent asset allocation decisions about the future.

Jeffrey W. Trencher, CFA, Glenn Horner, CFA, F.R.M., and Karen Witham, all of State Street Securities Finance, contributed to this chapter.

Within the securities lending industry, the goal historically has been to evaluate performance by developing a set of benchmarks through the gathering and ranking of static performance measures. However, benchmarking alone presents a distorted picture. For benchmarks to be meaningful, the underlying investment or structure must be achievable or replicable. For securities lending, this is highly problematic because very few clients have identical holdings, assets on loan, or collateral reinvestment guidelines. In addition, the pricing of loans is not transparent as there is no publicly quoted market.

Traditionally, performance reporting has focused on the drivers of spread income, including:

- Collateral portfolio yield
- Rebate statistics
- Spread statistics for noncash transactions
- Spread and on-loan balances by loan type
- Period to period comparisons
- Earnings comparisons versus program averages

While standard performance reporting provides important statistics, it typically fails to address the issue of risk—so crucial questions are often left unanswered:

- How much risk is the plan taking to generate the level of returns it is receiving?
- Is the plan being adequately compensated for the level of risk being taken?
- How does the risk/return dynamic compare with that of the plan's underlying asset allocation activity?
- What alternative management strategies could be employed that would result in increased returns for the same level of risk or a lower level of risk for the same return?

Reporting performance on a risk-adjusted basis can provide the participant with the information necessary to answer these and other questions. Risk-adjusted rates of return are standard in the investment management world and applying them to the measurement of securities lending makes demonstrable sense.

SECURITIES LOAN TRANSACTION SUMMARY

The securities lending transaction begins with the loan of securities to counterparts against the receipt of collateral generally valued at 102%–

105% of the market value of the loaned securities. Acceptable collateral can include both cash and noncash (other marketable securities) instruments and the loan-to-collateral values should be monitored on a daily basis, with adjustments made as needed to maintain the acceptable percentage value.

The posting of cash collateral generally requires the payment of a rebate or interest charge to the borrower for its use. The level of the rebate rate is related to the demand for the on-loan security relative to its available supply. When noncash collateral is involved, the borrower pays a fee, which generally approximates the difference between the cash rebate that would have been paid relative to the overnight repurchase agreement rate. The income earned by the plan sponsor and lending agent is the difference, or spread, between the rebate rate paid to the borrower and the yield on the reinvestment of the cash collateral. This income is split between the two at a predetermined rate.

Risk in a securities lending transaction emanates from its two major components. These components are the lending of securities to counterparts against the receipt of collateral and the subsequent reinvestment of the collateral received. The lending component's risks include loan and securities collateral market risk, including liquidity risk, and borrower default risk. The reinvestment component risks include: interest rate risk and floating rate security spread risk, issuer credit migration and default risk, counterpart default risk, and reinvestment pool liquidity. Of course there are a number of less quantifiable risks associated with technological, operational, and legal issues. These clearly need to be managed but are difficult to model.

Lending Risks

The first major risk element of the securities lending transaction arises from the exposure of the ultimate lender and agent to the various borrowing counterparts. This exposure results from the risk that a borrower may not return the loaned securities and that the collateral may be insufficient to fully fund the purchase of replacement securities.

In analyzing this risk, it is important to note that a collateral insufficiency results in a loss only if the borrower is financially unable to meet its contractual obligations. Specifically, loss occurs if the borrower fails to continue to provide additional collateral on a daily basis as required or fails to return the borrowed securities when required and the subsequent repurchase of the loaned securities occurs at a loss. The standard loan agreement entered into with borrowing counterparts should enable the immediate termination of open loan transactions if certain events of default occur.

Maintenance of a positive net collateral position, one in which aggregate collateral value exceeds aggregate loan value, is key. The adequacy of collateral is a function of the price behavior of the underlying securities coupled with the length of time elapsed between the default and the purchase of replacement securities (the holding period). Measuring this risk requires that the price relationships between all securities' positions are captured, both loan and collateral, in the context of an assumed replacement period.

In addition to the length of time elapsed between the last mark-to-market collateral adjustment and the securities repurchase, the size of the transactions relative to trading activity and general availability of the individual securities in question affects replacement cost. One method of accounting for this is by lengthening the risk measurement period to a level that more accurately reflects the increased replacement risk engendered by having to repurchase relatively concentrated positions.

One challenge in constructing a risk-adjusted performance model is the treatment of the relationship between price volatility/collateral adequacy and default. While there may be a relationship between general market volatility and the incidence of default, it is not possible to make a definitive statement about the relationship between market volatility and collateral adequacy given the wide range of loan collateral combinations possible in securities lending. In addition, risk assumed in securities lending is likely to be a relatively small component of the overall risk assumed by the borrower across its numerous business lines. This permits us to make the simplifying assumption that default and the probability distribution of market outcomes (collateral adequacy) are independent events.

This can be summarized as follows:

$$E = LV - C$$

where E is exposure, LV is loan value, and C is collateral.

In the event of default, the potential loss on a cash loan can be calculated at any confidence level by:

$$PL = (LV - LVaR) - C$$

where PL is potential loss and $LVaR$ is the value at risk on the loaned securities.

For a noncash loan the potential loss would be:

$$PL = LV - C - IVaR$$

where $IVaR$ is the integrated value at risk of the loaned securities and collateral. In such case the loaned securities would be viewed as short positions and the collateral would be viewed as long positions. However, this must be viewed in conjunction with the probability of default over the contractual term of the loan (typically overnight given the right to recall).

It should be noted that most lending agents offer indemnification against broker default, an accommodation or request that is priced as part of the income sharing arrangement. Clearly a function of the credit quality of the agent providing it, such an arrangement can serve to mitigate the counterpart-related risks.

Reinvestment Risk

In the context of securities lending, the market risk portion of collateral reinvestment risk, or asset/liability risk, refers to the risk to cash flow and, secondarily, the collateral pool market value engendered by market fluctuations. The risk to spread income arises from the funding of cash positions on generally an overnight or short-term basis and the subsequent investment of these proceeds into securities of slightly longer term. This is known as duration mismatching. The risk-to-market value, or collateral pool market value (*net asset value* or NAV), is a function of the impact to overall portfolio value of changes in underlying market interest rates, changes in market spread levels for floating rate securities, and portfolio duration and convexity.

The analysis is somewhat complicated by the fact that the collateral pools are operated on a stable value basis, and increases or decreases in portfolio value are unrealized as long as program participation continues and prices are maintained at least at a 0.9950 level. However, a decrease in market value ultimately translates into an opportunity cost with respect to future spread income. This cost is equivalent to the present value of cash flows foregone by receiving a below-market rate of interest. If a probabilistic estimate of the change to market value possible in the current market environment can be derived, it is possible to estimate the risk to cash flow.

The analysis can be enhanced by broadening the portfolio concept to include the rate and term structure of the loans. In this construct, all securities in the reinvestment pools could be treated as long positions and the term and rate structure of the loan transactions could be treated as short positions. From this, it is possible to calculate an integrated portfolio value that more accurately measures net risk.

An additional aspect of market risk that must be quantified is termed spread duration. This is the risk that the market spread to a benchmark rate for a floating-rate security may change, resulting in both an effect to

NAV and reduced opportunity cost for spread income. In addition to the risk to cash flow engendered by interest rate and spread movements, changes to portfolio asset values resulting from credit migration and default/recovery need to be considered. Specifically, this refers to the change in the value of an underlying asset caused by a change in debt rating and, in an extreme case, by the default of an issuer. Clearly, events such as these affect portfolio NAV but it is the impact to cash flow of such changes that is of concern. An issue that has been downgraded commands a greater yield, but this only benefits the post-downgrade acquirer. Owners of a downgraded security receive a less-than-optimal return, resulting in reduced spread income relative to that which could have been achieved by holding a comparably rated issue.

The task of establishing and integrating credit outcomes into the model is conceptually challenging due to their relatively infrequent occurrence coupled with the short-term nature of the market exposure. A distribution of combined market and credit outcomes must be created over at least a one-year time horizon and mathematically scaled to match the market-risk exposure cycle.

Maintaining sufficient liquidity to meet loan returns (the return of cash collateral to the borrowers upon the return of the loaned securities) is an important part of the reinvestment management process. Generally, liquidity is maintained through the use of overnight reverse repurchase agreements or other short-term money market investments. The former are overnight loans made to securities brokers/dealers and banks that are collateralized by securities such as corporate bonds and asset-backed or U.S. government securities. An analysis of these transactions would be similar to that employed in the lending side of the transaction, where market and counterpart credit risk are focal.

Styles of Lending

To identify clearly the components of risk associated with securities lending, the client must understand the agent's style of lending. An understanding of the component risks inherent in an agent's style provides lenders with important knowledge related to answering the ever-present question: Is the return worth the risk?

To begin formulating an answer to that critical question, it helps to recognize five distinct theoretical lending styles, ranging from the most conservative to the most aggressive on the risk/return spectrum:

- Natural spread
- Short-duration mismatch
- Long-duration mismatch

■ Credit mismatch
■ Portfolio leverage

A lending program using a *natural spread* approach, so-called because it is designed to earn only the natural, or demand, spread, makes loans secured by cash and invests in overnight repurchase agreements (repo) deliverable to the agent's custodian. In this style the lender is willing to ignore the incremental investment spread. This style generally works better for classes of lendable assets in which large natural spreads are normally available.

In a *short-duration mismatch* approach, a program creates investment spread by investing primarily in money market and other short- and intermediate-term securities. These markets are very deep and efficient, allowing portfolios to generate a return between LIMEAN and LIBOR. The duration of the collateral portfolio is typically between 30 and 90 days, although the interest sensitivity gap between the collateral investments and the loans is usually somewhat shorter, given the variable occurrence of term loans. Lenders using this style create an investment spread to augment the natural or inherent spread on the loaned security.

A *long-duration mismatch* style reinvests cash in cash collateral portfolios with a duration longer than 90 days. This style seeks to create more income by increasing the investment spread through the purchase of securities with longer final maturities. While the credit profile of the portfolio may be similar to that used in the short duration mismatch, the longer duration mismatch creates more income over time, depending upon the interest rate environment. Most importantly, however, a long duration mismatch also creates a higher probability for volatile short-term earnings and net asset values.

The *credit mismatch* approach attempts to achieve higher returns by accepting collateral of lower credit quality than the loaned security. An investment spread can be earned through this mismatch. This can be done by either investing directly into instruments of lower credit quality or by investing in repo secured by lower quality securities. Often the securities borrower and the repo counterparty are the same and the loan and the collateral investment are negotiated at the same time. Those who use this style in isolation often refer to it as a perfectly matched portfolio, as there is no interest rate risk. The credit risk on repo transactions can also be mitigated by taking additional margin and by having a repo counterparty with a strong credit rating. However, investing with weaker counterparties or directly in lower-rated investments increases the probability of default. If the transactions are not collateralized or more volatile collateral is taken, the likelihood and potential degree of losses in the event of default are increased. Generally, the earnings stream achieved from this strategy can be more stable, but losses in the extreme may be greater.

All securities lending that seeks to earn incremental income above the natural spread in a transaction employs some leverage. *Portfolio leverage*, however, is a more aggressive style of lending where the collateral is invested using techniques typically associated with hedge funds. These strategies include index arbitrage in which the collateral is invested in long or short positions in equities while simultaneously off-setting the position with short or long holdings in options or futures. These strategies are generally intended to be market neutral. This approach attempts to capture the price differences between the market for stocks and the market for futures or options. This style can create significantly higher income for hedgers and arbitrageurs, but there is some argument as to whether this is truly a securities lending function.

Each style of lending has a direct impact upon both the related collateral management and loan-allocation process and hence a direct impact on both income and risk. A program with a very aggressive reinvestment strategy using split-rated commercial paper, below-investment grade debt instruments and repo collateral, or perhaps with a portfolio duration of 180 days or longer, will have the potential for a significantly higher yield than most others. Acceptance of this risk level (which includes credit risk, unmatched duration risk and, in a rising-rate environment, amortized cost accounting risk) may well increase the frequency and enhance the profitability of lending opportunities for participants. Other lenders may decide that the cost of the elevated returns is too high, but they can only make an informed decision when their performance measurement tools reflect and account for these various levels of risk.

MODELING THE RISKS RELATIVE TO PERFORMANCE

The challenge in modeling the risks discussed above centers on developing a quantitative construct that can be applied in a consistent manner to disparate activities and form the basis for meaningful comparisons. The statistically based value-at-risk (VaR) approach is gaining increasing acceptance as one such sound risk measurement model.

Value-at-risk represents an estimate of the largest gain or loss that a portfolio of securities is likely to experience within a defined time horizon and at a given confidence level. Value-at-risk measurements calculate the individual price volatility of each security in the portfolio and the relationship of its expected price movement (magnitude and direction) to the expected price movements of the other positions in the portfolio. The result is a blended risk measure with total portfolio risk almost always lower, and potentially markedly lower, than the sum of the individual position risks. The VaR analysis can be used to predict the overall volatility of the portfolio and to position the portfolio in a manner consistent with the risk profile of the investor.

The VaR model includes variance-covariance methods as well as simulation-based techniques. The variance-covariance methods rely on the price relationship history contained in the correlation matrix to estimate VaR. They have the advantage of being readily scalable to different holding periods or confidence levels but require assumptions about normality of returns and are not suited for portfolios that have a preponderance of securities or structures that exhibit nonlinear price behavior. The simulation-based techniques—such as historical or Monte Carlo—have the advantage of handling variables that do not exhibit normality, such as credit migration, or securities with imbedded optionality that lack the flexibility of the variance-covariance approach noted above. In the case of Monte Carlo simulations, the underlying assumptions that are used in constructing the simulated distribution will clearly affect the results produced.

For example, a measure of VaR can be taken by applying the following general variance-covariance formula:

$$((Z\sigma_{S1}\text{Pos.}_{S1})^2 + (Z\sigma_{S2}\text{Pos.}_{S2})^2 + \ldots + (Z\sigma_{Sn}\text{Pos.}_{Sn})^2 + 2\rho_{I1I2}(Z\sigma_{S1}\text{Pos.}_{S1})$$
$$(Z\sigma_{S2}\text{Pos.}_{S2}) + 2\rho_{I1I3}(Z\sigma_{S1}\text{Pos.}_{S1})(Z\sigma_{S3}\text{Pos.}_{S3}) + \ldots + 2\rho_{Fn-1Fn}$$
$$(Z\sigma_{Sn-1}\text{Pos.}_{Sn-1})(Z\sigma_{Sn}\text{Pos.}_{Sn}))^{1/2}$$

where:

Z	= The standard normal variable or the number of standard deviations that correspond to the desired level of confidence
$Z\sigma_{S1}\text{Pos.}_{S1}$	= The value-at-risk of security number 1
$Z\sigma_{S2}\,\text{Pos.}_{S2}$	= The value-at-risk of security number 2
$Z\sigma_{Sn}\,\text{Pos.}_{Sn}$	= The value-at-risk of the final security
ρ_{I1I2}	= The correlation between interest rate node for security 1 and interest rate node for security 2
ρ_{I1I3}	= The correlation between interest rate node for security 1 and interest rate node for security 3

An ideal model would allow for the use of multiple techniques depending upon the properties of the particular risk(s) being measured. The integration and evaluation of market and credit risks requires the analysis of the joint market-credit distribution. Changes in credit factors may be assumed to be independent of changes in market factors to be able to simplify this model. It should be noted that methodology decisions need to be consistent with program attributes and balance model appropriateness with data availability, processing, and general technology issues.

In linking these risk measures to their associated returns, one workable option would be to use a Sharpe-type measure. The Sharpe ratio is calculated as the differential or excess return relative to the risk-free rate divided by its risk given as the standard deviation of returns. It assumes that investments can be ranked solely in terms of the mean and standard deviation of excess returns.[1]

The assumption of comparability is powerful because it can be used to evaluate the risk-adjusted returns generated by each quantifiable program component and alternative program parameters, such as reinvestment pool options, alternative security types available for loan, and specific borrowers or subsets of borrowers. However, one must use caution in relying too generally on such quantitative methods, as the distribution of various forms of risk are not equivalent. It is easy to assume a lognormal distribution for market risks; however, credit risks are significantly skewed. Therefore, in the interior of the distribution market risks may appear greater, but in the extremes credit risks may be greater. For instance, market exposures may result in greater volatility of earnings under most conditions; however, one significant credit default can be substantially more damaging to the program.

However, with these known caveats, the ability to perform a risk-adjusted return comparison between the securities lending activity and that of the participant's underlying investment portfolio can provide powerful insight. From this, for example, it can be quantitatively determined if securities lending efficiently adds value to the plan's overall risk/return profile.

While the value at risk approach can add significant value to an assessment of risk-adjusted returns, it is important to note that predictive models based on historical observations cannot account for or protect one from exceptional events. Quantitative results should be used as a tool and should not replace sound business judgment.

NEW TRENDS IN BENCHMARKING

Early in this chapter, we noted that benchmarking alone could present a distorted picture, as in securities lending very few clients have identical program parameters that would allow for an "apples to apples" comparison of key performance elements: percent on loan; gross, reinvestment, and demand spread; and risk-adjusted returns. The markets have evolved

---

[1] See William F. Sharpe, "The Sharpe Ratio," *Journal of Portfolio Management* 20 (Fall 1994): 49–58.

to the point where it is generally acknowledged that all of these components are crucial to evaluating a program, and that no one element can or should be analyzed in a vacuum or used as the sole benchmark. However, this understanding does not diminish lenders' desire to have some way of assessing their securities lending program's performance in relation to the programs of their peers.

Independent firms are leveraging the latest technologies and working with lenders and agents to gather, analyze and publish data that will help create further benchmarking-related tools and resources. These independent firms typically provide program data at different levels that can include program, portfolio, asset class, security and transaction levels. The data can be analyzed to dissect pricing and asset utilization as well as obtain a relatively accurate peer comparison.

One such firm has noted that a benchmark must meet several requirements, including: It must be representative of the industry, credible in scale and coverage, "granular" enough to enable action to be taken, easy for non-practitioners to understand, actionable by practitioners, frequent enough to take seasonality into account, divisible into applicable peer groups, and independent and explicit. A benchmark must also meet several important measurement and communication criteria as well, including frequency, presentation mode, and format.[2]

CONCLUSIONS

Concerns expressed regarding the benchmarking approach have focused more on the potential lack of uniformity using various quantitative methods and less on its conceptual validity. There is no disagreement that different models and their underlying assumptions will yield different results. These issues exist in the mainstream investment process as well, and they are not unique to securities lending.

Focusing exclusively on returns may incur an unwanted and even unknown level of risk, creating a false sense of security about a particular lending program and possibly creating incentives for an agent or collateral manager to take undesirable risk. Data from benchmarks are elements in a much larger equation that needs to include risk as a measurable component. Only when measurements include the reinvestment or collateral side of a securities lending transaction can the beneficial owner develop the necessary insight into how returns are created and what level of risk is incurred. Armed with this knowledge, lenders can set measurement criteria

---

[2] RMA Committee on Securities Lending, "Focusing on the Trend Toward Sophisticated Information Demands," *Securities Lending Update*, December 2004.

for both risk and return and exercise control throughout the lending cycle, including the reinvestment of collateral. The first step in exercising this control is by ensuring compatibility between the agent's style—the manner in which the agent, acting on behalf of the lender, takes risk and creates returns—and the lender's objectives.

As to the issue of whether the return is appropriate to the level of risk taken, no one answer exists. Appropriateness depends on the particular risk/return profile of the participant. The role of a risk-adjusted performance construct is to provide the quantitative tools to enable the decision-making process. By establishing a baseline and framework through which changes to the risk/return profile can be portrayed and interpreted, appropriate management decisions can be made. The risk-adjusted performance construct does not replace established risk management practices; rather, it complements and strengthens them. The tool set developed should be used both to report and to proactively manage the process.

Risk-adjusted performance measurement—combining financial results with clear, quantifiable and correlated measurements of risk—provides necessary insight to clients, consultants, and agents alike. What it boils down to is this: if two investment managers operate under identical guidelines and restrictions to generate identical returns, the manager who incurs less risk is a superior performer. Applied to the securities lending industry, this principle gives industry participants a useful and more accurate instrument for evaluating investment performance.

GLOSSARY OF TERMS

Above-the-line Spread   See *Collateral Reinvestment Spread*

Asset/Liability Management   A risk-management technique designed to earn a surplus return on assets beyond the cost of liabilities. Takes into consideration interest rates, earning power, and degree of willingness to take on debt. In securities lending transactions the objective of the asset-liability management process is to ensure that reinvestment securities purchased with cash collateral (an asset of the lender) earn an adequate yield and cover the cost (the rebate rate) of the security loans (a liability of the lender) that finance the purchase of the reinvestment securities.

Asset/Liability Mismatch   The process of maintaining assets and liabilities with different durations in an attempt to optimize return. In securities lending transactions, securities loans (liabilities of the lender) are typically overnight instruments while the reinvestment securities (assets of the lender) have various durations, depending on the condition of the yield curve at the time of purchase.

Below-the-Line Spread   See *Funding Spread*

Collateral Reinvestment Risk   The potential that investments purchased with cash collateral will provide insufficient return to satisfy rebate payments owed to the borrower on the cash collateral and/or that investments purchased with cash collateral will decrease in value to an extent that there is insufficient value to return the cash collateral owed to the borrower at the end of the term of the loan. The collateral reinvestment risk is comprised of interest rate risk, credit risk, and spread risk. Also known as *reinvestment risk*.

Collateral Reinvestment Spread   Weighted average collateral portfolio yield less the weighted average risk-free rate. This represents a measure of the excess return generated by the investment process. This is also referred to as asset spread, investment spread, "above the line" spread or collateral spread.

Collateral Yield   The annual rate of return on a collateral portfolio, expressed as a percentage. Also called the *reinvestment yield*.

Combined Spread   The difference between the yield generated by the cash collateral and the rebate paid on the securities loans (or, the in case of loans versus noncash collateral, the premium). It is comprised of the demand spread and the reinvestment spread. Also referred to as *gross spread*, *integrated* or *total spread*.

Credit Migration Risk   The chance that a change in the credit quality of a security issuer will impact the value of securities it has issued or that a change in the credit quality of a structured security will impact its value.

Credit Risk   The potential for a decline in asset value brought about by the inability, or perceived inability, of a security issuer or borrower to meet its financial obligations. Credit risk is comprised of migration risk and default risk. It is present on both the lending side (borrower credit risk) and the collateral reinvestment side (reinvestment security issuer credit risk) of a securities lending transaction.

Default Risk   The possibility that a bond issuer will default by failing to repay principal and interest in a timely manner or the possibility that a security borrower will default by failing to maintain appropriate collateral margin or by failing to return the borrowed securities when required. Default risk is a component of credit risk.

Funding Spread   For loans versus cash collateral, it is the weighted average risk-free rate less the weighted average rebate rate. For loans versus non-cash collateral, it is equal to the premium paid by the borrower, less any premium related to the riskiness of the collateral. It represents a measure of the demand value of the loaned security and is also referred to as the *demand spread*, the *intrinsic spread*, the *intrinsic value*, the *natural spread*, or the *"below the line" spread*.

Interest Rate Risk   The possibility of a reduction in the value of a security or loan resulting from a change in interest rates levels.

Legal Risk   The possibility of loss because of the unexpected application of a law or regulation or because of the lack of enforceability of the provision(s) of an agreement.

Liquidity Risk   The risk that arises from the difficulty of selling an asset. An investment may sometimes need to be sold quickly. An insufficient secondary market may prevent the liquidation or limit the funds that can be generated from the asset. Some assets are highly liquid and have low liquidity risk (such as U.S. Treasuries), while other assets are highly illiquid and have high liquidity risk (such as a house).

Market Risk   Risk that is common to an entire class of assets or liabilities. The value of investments may decline over a given time period simply because of economic changes or other events that impact large portions of the market. Asset allocation and diversification can protect against market risk because different portions of the market tend to under perform at different times.

Migration Risk   The chance that a change in the credit quality of a security issuer will impact the value of the securities it has issued. Migration risk is a component of credit risk.

Net Asset Value   The dollar value of a single commingled fund share, based on the value of the underlying assets of the fund minus its liabilities, divided by the number of shares outstanding. Calculated at the end of each business day.

Net Asset Value Risk   Uncertainty related to the future net asset value (NAV) of a portfolio. In the securities lending context, NAV risk is driven by borrower default risk, credit spread risk, interest rate risk, issuer default risk, credit migration risk and liquidity risk.

Operational Risk   The risk that deficiencies in information systems or internal controls could result in an unexpected loss.

Reinvestment Yield   The annual rate of return on a collateral portfolio, expressed as a percentage. Also called *collateral yield.*

Repurchase Agreement (Repo)   A financing arrangement in which the holder of securities sells them to a lender under an agreement to repurchase them on a specified date at an agreed-to price.

Return-to-Variability Ratio   Represents average return relative to volatility of returns. Can be viewed as a measure of risk-adjusted return.

Reverse Repurchasing Agreement (Reverse Repo)   A contract with a counterparty to buy and subsequently resell securities at a specified date and price; the other side of a repo.

Risk-Adjusted Performance   The return on your lending activity based on the risks you took to earn that income. Also called risk-adjusted return.

Risk-Free Rate   A theoretical interest rate that would be returned on an investment that was completely free of risk. The very short-term government securities are usually used as proxies for the risk-free rate, since they are virtually risk-free. In securities lending transactions the overnight U.S. Government repo rate and the EONIA are used as close approximations of the risk-free rate for loans versus USD collateral and loans versus euro collateral, respectively. The risk-free rate serves as the breakpoint, which segments the total spread/income earned on a securities lending transaction into the portion of spread/income attributable to the demand for the loaned securities and the portion attributable to the reinvestment process.

Spread Income   Equal to the reinvestment return minus the rebate paid to the borrower, or in the case of loans versus noncash collateral, the premium. Also known as spread return.

Spread Risk   The risk of a contraction or widening of spread due to the business cycle.

Spread Variability Risk   Uncertainty of the consistency of future spreads or earnings.

Total Spread   The difference between the yield generated by the cash collateral and the rebate paid on the securities loans (or, the in case of loans versus noncash collateral, the premium). It is comprised of the funding spread and the collateral reinvestment spread. Also referred to as gross spread, integrated spread or combined spread.

Value-at-Risk (VaR)   A technique which uses the statistical analysis of historical market trends and volatilities to estimate the likelihood that a given portfolio's losses will exceed a certain amount over a particular time horizon.

CHAPTER 10

Developing Effective Guidelines for Managing Legal Risks— U.S. Guidelines

Charles E. Dropkin, JD
Partner
Proskauer Rose LLP

Securities lending, whether viewed as a means of generating incremental income to reduce custody expense or as a means of leveraging a portfolio to generate cash for investment, is a highly regulated activity. Securities owners (such as custody and trust customers of banks, public funds, pension funds subject to the Employee Retirement Income Security Act of 1974 [ERISA], insurance companies and mutual funds), lending agents, and broker-dealers (as borrowers) are each subject to a host of legal concerns and regulatory oversight. In this chapter, we will (1) identify certain key legal and regulatory issues applicable to lenders, lending agents and borrowers which must be understood and followed as part of any effective compliance program and (2) discuss contractual measures available for reducing insolvency risk.

LENDER REGULATIONS

Different categories of lenders are subject to different regulations. ERISA lenders, for instance, must be cognizant of potential prohibited transactions which could result from lending securities to a borrower who provided (or whose affiliate provided) financial, advisory or other services to the plan. To facilitate lending by plans, the Department of Labor in 1985 promulgated a safe harbor.

Prohibited Transaction Class Exemption 81-6 (PTCE 81-6) allows lending of securities by employee benefit plans subject to ERISA, under prescribed circumstances, to domestic banks and registered broker-dealers who are "parties-in-interest" with respect to such plans. Because the definitional reach of a "party-in-interest" in Section 3(14) of ERISA is so broad, it is very difficult to be sure that a counterparty is not a party-in-interest. In order to safeguard against the unintentional violation of ERISA, which could give rise to pecuniary penalties in the form of an excise tax on the borrower and strict liability for any losses on the plan fiduciary, an ERISA lender should ensure compliance with PTCE 81-6, as well as general ERISA standards of prudence and diversification of cash collateral investments.

The primary condition of PTCE 81-6 is that neither the borrower nor an affiliate of the borrower has discretionary authority or control with respect to the investment of the plan assets involved in the transaction, or renders investment advice with respect to those assets. In addition, the plan must receive from the borrower (either by physical delivery or by book entry in a securities depository) by the close of the lending fiduciary's business on the day in which the securities lent are delivered to the borrower, collateral (consisting of cash, securities issued or guaranteed by the United States government or its agencies or instrumentalities, or irrevocable bank letters of credit issued by a person other than the borrower or an affiliate thereof, or any combination thereof) having, as of the close of business on the preceding business day, a market value, or in the case of letters of credit a stated amount, equal to not less than 100% of the then market value of the securities lent. Prior to the making of any loan, the borrower must have furnished the lending fiduciary with its most recent available audited statement of the borrower's financial condition, its most recent available unaudited statement of its financial condition (if more recent than such audited statement), and a representation that, at the time the loan is negotiated, there has been no material adverse change in its financial condition since the date of the most recent financial statement furnished to the plan that has not been disclosed to the lending fiduciary.

The loan must be evidenced by a written loan agreement, the terms of which are at least as favorable to the plan as an arm's-length transaction with an unrelated party would be. The plan must receive a reasonable fee that is related to the value of the borrowed securities and the duration of the loan, or has the opportunity to derive compensation through the investment of cash collateral. Where the plan has that opportunity, the plan may pay a loan rebate or similar fee to the borrower, if such fee is not greater than the plan would pay in a comparable transaction with an unrelated party. The plan must also receive the equivalent of all distributions ("in lieu of" payments) made to the holders of the borrowed securities during the term of the loan, including, but not limited to, cash dividends, interest payments, shares of stock as a result of stock splits and rights to purchase additional securities. Marks-to-market must be made daily, and loans must be terminable on demand.

The Master Securities Loan Agreement (2000 version) promulgated by The Bond Market Association (the BMA model documentation), which has become a market benchmark (although it is not universally used by lending agents), provides, in the first instance, that the lender shall notify the borrower in respect of any loan where the subject securities have been obtained, directly or indirectly, from or using the assets of any plan. Once the lender so notifies the borrower, the parties are required to conduct the loan in accordance with PTCE 81-6 (unless reliance is made upon another exemption) and, throughout the loan, the borrower is deemed to represent that neither it nor an affiliate has any discretionary authority or control with respect to the investment of the assets involved in the loan or renders investment advice with respect to such assets. The lender has a continuing obligation to notify the borrower of those persons who have such discretionary authority or control or render such investment advice.

The Department of Labor has under consideration a new PTCE which would amend, combine and replace PTCE 81-6 and PTCE 82-63 (dealing with lending compensation)[1] with a new exemption which would, among other things, expand eligible borrowers to include foreign broker-dealers and foreign banks and allow ERISA plans to accept additional forms of collateral including the currency of the United Kingdom, Euros, securities issued or guaranteed by the Government of the United Kingdom or one of its agencies or instrumentalities, sovereign debt of a member country of the European Monetary Union that is denominated in Euros, or irrevocable letters of credit issued by a foreign bank (other than the borrower) which has an investment grade rating. Enhanced collateral requirements would be made applicable to loans of other than U.S. securities between U.S. parties. The proposal has not yet been adopted.

---

[1] Under PTCE 82-63, plans may compensate the fiduciary managing the lending of securities by plans to parties-in-interest provided: (i) the loan itself is not a prohibited transaction, (ii) the lending agent is authorized to engage in securities lending transactions on behalf of the plan, (iii) the compensation is reasonable and is paid in accordance with the terms of a written instrument and (iv) the securities lending arrangement is subject to the prior written authorization of a plan fiduciary who is independent of the lending agent, and the authorization is terminable on not more than five days' notice, without penalty to the plan.

Insurance companies and public funds must determine as a threshold matter, under state law, the extent to which securities lending is a recognized practice, either regulated as an investment or as a loan, and any applicable restrictions thereon, including with respect to cash collateral investment and (in the case of insurance companies) eligibility of securities out on loan for required minimum capital purposes.

The extent to which mutual funds may lend securities will depend, in the first instance, upon applicable provisions in the governing prospectus and constituent documents. Typically, reflective of SEC no-action letters and Section 6(c) orders under the Investment Company Act of 1940 (which governs both open and closed-end mutual funds), a mutual fund will not have more than one-third of its portfolio out on loan at any one time. Potential investors in mutual funds should review a fund's prospectus carefully, since the proceeds of cash received as collateral in a securities loan may be invested in instruments of a type and risk profile different than that of other fund holdings.

AGENT REGULATIONS

Lending agents, such as banks, are independently regulated in securities lending activities. In 1985, the Federal Financial Institutions Examinations Council (FFIEC) issued a statement on bank activities in securities lending which has been adopted by both the Office of the Comptroller of the Currency (OCC), the regulator of national banks, and the Board of Governors of the Federal Reserve System (FRB), the regulator of state member banks and bank holding companies. The Statement provides guidelines under which bank activities as a lender and as an agent are to be conducted. Those guidelines require the following:

1. The bank's recordkeeping system should produce daily reports showing securities available for lending and those out on loan, as well as the material terms of each loan.
2. Collateral is to be marked to market daily. A collateral margin greater than 100% of loan value should be set on the basis of price volatility, and lent securities should not be released unless collateral is sent simultaneously.
3. A management committee should approve each borrower after independent credit review. Management should establish individual credit limits for each borrower.
4. Lending should be effected under written contracts with the owner of the securities and with the borrower, outlining the bank's responsibilities and fees.

5. If the bank indemnifies lenders, written opinions of its counsel and accountants should be obtained as to legality and proper accounting treatment.
6. Loans and indemnities should be reported on the bank's call report.

Under present risk-based capital guidelines of the OCC and the FRB, banks generally may indemnify customers in securities lending transactions, and incur no risk-based capital charge, if the indemnification is limited to no more than the difference between the market value of the securities lent and the market value of the collateral received, and any reinvestment risk associated with cash collateral is borne solely by the customer. Where an agent bank seeks to indemnify a customer against both borrower default risk and cash collateral reinvestment risk, the FRB has allowed a bank, based on VAR (value at risk) modeling, to determine an unsecured loan equivalent amount for each counterparty, which amount is then assigned the risk weight appropriate to such counterparty.

A lending agent bank with discretion to invest cash collateral on behalf of a customer will be treated as a fiduciary. Lending agent banks, when dealing with mutual fund customers, should be careful to limit investment discretion to avoid characterization as an investment adviser to the fund, which would require separate approval by the fund's directors.

BORROWER REGULATIONS

Broker-dealers are subject to rules and regulations of both the Securities and Exchange Commission (SEC) and the FRB.

The customer protection rules under the Securities Exchange Act of 1934, as amended (Exchange Act), and particularly Rule 15c3-3 thereunder relating to possession and control of customer securities, contain specific provisions relating to the contents of a written securities lending agreement. In brief, any loan of securities must be evidenced by a written agreement that at a minimum:

1. sets forth in a separate schedule or schedules the basis of compensation for any loan, and generally the rights and liabilities of the parties as to the borrowed securities;
2. provides that the lender will be given a schedule of the securities actually borrowed at the time of the borrowing of the securities;
3. specifies that the broker or dealer (A) must provide to the lender, upon the execution of the agreement or by the close of the business day of the loan if the loan occurs subsequent to the execution of the agree-

ment, collateral, consisting exclusively of cash or United States Treasury bills and Treasury notes or an irrevocable letter of credit issued by a bank as defined in the Exchange Act or such other collateral as the Commission designates as permissible by order as necessary or appropriate in the public interest and consistent with the protection of investors after giving consideration to the collateral's liquidity, volatility, market depth and location, and the issuer's creditworthiness[2] which fully secures the loan of the securities, and (B) must mark the loan to the market not less than daily and, in the event that the market value of all the outstanding securities loaned at the close of trading at the end of the business day exceeds 100% of the collateral then held by the lender, the borrowing broker or dealer must provide additional collateral to the lender by the close of the next business day as necessary to equal, together with the collateral then held by the lender, not less than 100% of the market value of the securities loaned; and

4. contains a prominent notice that the provisions of the Securities Investor Protection Act of 1970 (SIPA) may not protect the lender with respect to the securities loan transaction and that, therefore, the collateral delivered to the lender may constitute the only source of satisfaction of the broker's or dealer's obligation in the event the broker or dealer fails to return the securities. If securities provided as collateral include those permissible under the SEC order expanding the categories of acceptable collateral, the notice in the written agreement with the customer must state that some of the securities being provided as collateral may not be guaranteed by the United States.

Regulation T, one of the margin rules which deals with extensions of credit by and to brokers and dealers, provides that "without regard to the other provisions of this part, a creditor [broker/dealer] may borrow or lend securities for the purpose of making delivery of the securities in the case of short sales, failure to receive securities required to be delivered, or

---

[2] Acceptable collateral has been expanded by SEC order to include: government securities, including certain securities of certain federal agencies, designated multilateral development banks, mortgage-backed securities, negotiable certificates of deposit and bankers acceptances issued by "banks," as defined in the Exchange Act, foreign sovereign debt securities rated in one of the top two rating categories or, if not in the top two categories, in the top four categories if securing a borrowing of non-equity securities from the same jurisdiction, Euros, British pounds, Swiss francs, Canadian dollars or Japanese yen and non-governmental debt securities rated in one of the top two rating categories if they trade flat and are not in default in payments of principal or interest. If the collateral of any of the above is denominated in a different currency than the securities borrowed, the collateral must include a percentage above the minimum collateralization requirement of the rule.

other similar situations." This language does not require that the delivery for which securities are borrowed must be on a transaction which the borrower has himself made, either as agent or principal; one may borrow in order to relend to another for the latter to make such a delivery. However, the borrowing must be related to an actual delivery in connection with a specific transaction that has occurred or is in immediate prospect.[3] A broker/dealer may not borrow securities merely to enable it or another broker to have the securities "on hand" or to anticipate some need that may or may not arise in the future. A borrower, however, who reasonably anticipates a short sale may borrow securities up to one standard settlement cycle in advance of the trade date. Borrowers may "lock up" a supply of lendable securities for potential future use by paying an up-front commitment fee to reserve particular securities anticipated to be needed for a future borrowing. Regulation T is not violated by such a "lock-up" since the broker-dealer would not be committed to borrowing the securities, but merely would be assured that the securities would be available, if and when needed for a permissible borrowing purpose.

The staff of the FRB has tended to read the borrowing purpose requirement of "other similar transactions" narrowly in the context of bona fide arbitrage. Thus, borrowing equity securities for the purpose of becoming a registered owner to participate in a dividend reinvestment plan has been held to be an impermissible purpose and not "bona fide arbitrage." But borrowing a convertible security and immediately converting it to make delivery on a short sale was permissible where effected as part of a bona fide arbitrage (and where the broker had received assurance that the conversion process would be completed in time to make actual delivery on the short sale). The FRB continues to resist changing its stance on borrowing U.S. securities to take advantage of dividend reinvestment.

---

[3] In a recent liquidation under SIPA, a major clearing broker, acting in an intermediary capacity in so-called "chain" or "conduit" lending, sustained material losses. Chain lending involves a series of borrows and loans where the ultimate borrower has the permitted purpose. In this case, the chain lending was used to perpetrate a fraudulent scheme by the original lender to manipulate the price of the loaned securities in the market. The lenders in the chain were effectively distributing, through multiple back-to-back loans, large amounts of what turned out to be illiquid securities. As the (manipulated) securities prices continued to rise, margin calls were required to be made, with the ultimate effect of passing more and more collateral up the chain to the original lender. The scheme collapsed when the price of the securities could no longer be supported after the events of September 11 and the original lender absconded with the collateral. Lenders down the chain could not or would not return any of the collateral securing the loans to their counterparties, and the loaned securities could not be liquidated.

In addition, the securities lending provision of Regulation T now permits "exempted borrowers," which are essentially broker-dealers which deal primarily with the public and not only other broker-dealers, to lend securities without a permitted purpose, and for borrowers to borrow securities from exempted borrowers without a permitted purpose. Further, securities may be loaned to foreign borrowers for any lawful purpose in the country of the borrower. In this regard, a foreign security not listed on NASDAQ or a U.S. national securities exchange is not "U.S. traded" solely because American Depository Receipts on the foreign security are traded in the United States.

Transactions involving "non-equity securities" may now be effected through a "good faith account" established under Regulation T, which removes loans of such securities from the permitted purpose requirements now applicable only to loans of equity securities. Transactions in U.S. government securities, formerly outside the securities lending provisions of Regulation T through the availability of a government securities account, are now included in the good faith account.

Regulation T no longer prescribes the scope of collateral which can be pledged, but transactions with "customers" are still subject to the acceptable collateral provisions of SEC Rule 15c3-3 as described above.

The SEC recently adopted Regulation SHO to curb naked short selling and resulting abuses by requiring, among other things, that short sellers in all equity securities "locate" securities to borrow before selling. Additional delivery requirements are imposed on broker-dealers for securities in which a substantial number of fails to deliver have occurred.

The anti-money laundering provisions of the USA Patriot Act, particularly the regulations requiring financial institutions, including banks and broker-dealers, to adopt customer identification programs (CIPs), have implications for securities lending activities when a lender is acting in an agency capacity on behalf of a number of ultimate lenders. In these instances, the borrower must determine whether it is reasonable to rely on representations in the written agreement that the lending agent has verified the identities of the lenders through the agent's own CIP or whether the borrower must treat each lender as its own customer and perform due diligence on each.

STRENGTHENING REMEDIES THROUGH DOCUMENTATION

Failure to comply with applicable legal provisions relevant to the conduct of securities lending can subject participants both to civil and, in some cases, criminal sanctions. Compliance, however, with such provisions, while legally mandated, will not protect a lender against the most significant transactional risk it faces, namely, counterparty insolvency. A well drafted securities lending agreement, however, can be of benefit in seeking to mitigate this risk.

When a broker faces bankruptcy, a lender or agent is usually not taken completely by surprise. The broker may have informed it of financial difficulties, the lender may have deduced it on its own or based on action of the SEC or a national securities exchange, or the lender may have heard rumors in the marketplace.

Ideally, the lender would like to terminate the loan and regain possession of the loaned securities before the broker enters bankruptcy. It can do so in one of two different ways. First, the lender may call the loan. If a broker has borrowed U.S. government securities, it is required under most securities loan agreements to return the loaned securities the same day it receives the call notice or the next business day. However, if the bank has loaned foreign securities or U.S. equity securities, the agreements typically permit the borrower up to the normal settlement period to return them. Obviously, as the settlement period for return of loaned securities increases, the risk that the broker may file for bankruptcy or be the subject of an involuntary proceeding during that interval is heightened.

Before it calls a loan in advance of an expected termination date, the lender must determine the amount of the damages that the broker likely will seek to assess against the lender for early termination. Similarly, the lender must analyze the cost of liquidating any cash collateral it had received from the broker that may have been invested in term instruments. It may be that the total of these costs is higher than the discounted cost to the lender of the risk of a bankruptcy filing by the borrower.

A second way for a lender to obtain the loaned securities is to exercise a buy-in by foreclosing on the collateral and applying the proceeds to the purchase of equivalent securities. Depending on the applicable loan contract, prior notice to a borrower (and an opportunity to cure) may be required. However, as a threshold matter, a lender can foreclose on collateral only if an event of default has occurred under the applicable contract. A lender must be especially careful in determining whether an event of default actually has occurred before it acts—if it improperly forecloses on collateral and triggers a chain reaction in the market in which other lenders foreclose on the broker, resulting in the broker's financial collapse, the broker stands a good chance of winning a suit against the lender and being awarded significant damages. There are a number of standard defaults that should be contained in loan documentation with the broker to allow the lender to foreclose on the broker.

For instance, the agreement should contain a default for breach of the broker's covenants to provide timely financial statements to the lender and reports with the appropriate regulatory agencies. The broker should covenant to give notice to the lender of any material adverse change in connection with its business or financial condition. It also should be obligated to notify the lender of any stock exchange, Securities Investor Protection Corporation (SIPC), SEC or National Association of Securities Dealers investigation, complaint or proceeding, or any similar action by a state regulatory body. And the broker should covenant to provide the lender with all tax receipts related to any withholding on payments made by it to a lender in respect of borrowed foreign securities (including "in lieu of" payments).

The securities lending agreement should contain a cross default to any other debt upon which the broker is or becomes obligated, including debt owed to the lender in any different capacity. The lender should also insist on defaults related to any breach of representations by the broker, including the Regulation T representation (as applicable) under which the borrower has agreed to use the borrowed securities only for limited purposes, as described above. Finally, the documentation should allow the lender to call a default upon the broker's failure to remit its "in lieu of" payment or failure to respond to requests for additional required collateral. Requiring a broker to furnish adequate assurance of its ability to perform whenever a lender deems itself insecure is also a desirable contractual protection for a lender.

Supplementing the BMA model documentation to provide enhanced reporting and covenant obligations and broader default coverage can be quite helpful to lenders, but this is often heavily negotiated and resolved based on the relative bargaining power of the parties.

Once a broker has defaulted, the terms of the agreement it has entered into with the lender will either permit the lender to terminate the loan on notice to the broker or will terminate the loan automatically. If the lender gives notice to the broker, it is able to exercise its rights within a reasonable period thereafter. It can foreclose on its collateral and buy-in securities immediately after a securities loan automatically terminates.

To avoid claims that the lender has waived a particular default, the default upon which the lender relies to foreclose on collateral should occur at some time reasonably near the time at which it acts. Very often a lender will not be able to call a loan or realize on collateral and buy-in securities before a broker files for bankruptcy. Under the U.S. Bankruptcy Code, a "securities contract" is defined to include a loan of security. A "security" is defined to include, inter alia, notes, bonds, debentures, collateral trust certificates, transferable shares, limited partnership interests, and other interests commonly known as "securities." While ordinarily the right of a securities lender, upon the default of a broker-dealer as borrower, would not preclude the lender from immediately exercising contractual remedies, liquidating collateral and applying proceeds thereof to the buy-in of equivalent replacement securities, the applicable provisions of SIPA would override this lender protection in the event of the liquidation of a registered broker-dealer. In the past, the trustee appointed pursuant to SIPA typically, as one of its first acts, would request the bankruptcy court to issue an order staying a securities lender (or repo participant) from immediately exercising available contractual remedies. It may be that until a lender is served with a copy of that order or has knowledge or notice of it, the lender is entitled to liquidate a broker's collateral without violating the court order. If a lender were to so act, though, it is likely that it would be challenged by the SIPA trustee and that challenge would have to be resolved by the courts. How the courts would decide the issue is far from certain.

By letter dated October 30, 1990, the Deputy General Counsel of SIPC stated that, in the future, SIPC would not seek to stay the exercise by a financial institution of its contractual right to utilize cash collateral to cause the liquidation of a securities lending contract with a broker-dealer under liquidation. The SIPC letter, however, intentionally did not address securities loans collateralized by securities and, accordingly, SIPC retains the option to seek to stay liquidation thereof. During the period of an imposed stay a lender may suffer losses if the market moves against it. A lender is unable effectively to hedge its exposure since it cannot predict with confidence when the stay will be lifted. This "stay" risk is also troubling for banks who have indemnified their customers against loss from broker default since the agent banks, upon the insolvency of the broker (which is a normal default under the applicable securities lending contracts), will promptly have to perform upon the indemnity at the time when they are stayed from liquidating the collateral to fund the buy-in. The SIPC letter, as an expression of policy, is subject to change or withdrawal at any time.

There are a number of steps that lenders could take to minimize the damage from an injunction prohibiting close-outs. Lenders could expand the scope of defaults contained in their securities lending agreements to increase their ability to call a default and foreclose on their collateral before any bankruptcy filing takes place. Along these lines, lenders may seek to increase the number of automatic loan termination provisions contained in the agreements and decrease the ability of brokers to cure defaults during grace periods.

Perhaps the best course of action for lenders to take is to try to avoid the SIPA risk. To do so, lenders can contract with entities that are not eligible for SIPA protection. The contra-party in a securities loan could be the parent of a broker-dealer, or a government securities affiliate of a broker-dealer that is not subject to SIPA, perhaps with a parent company guarantee. Alternatively, lenders could request letters of credit to secure their borrowers' obligations. Because they should not be included in the broker's bankruptcy estate, there is virtually no risk that payment under a letter of credit would be enjoined. A clean draft typically would be honored the day it was presented or the next day. Where a lender accepts a letter of credit as collateral, it should be careful not to allow the broker to initiate amendments without prior consent of the lender or to sanction a course of conduct whereby the issuing bank, upon request of the account party, amends the letter of credit and then sends a confirmation to the beneficiary. As is its right, the lender should insist that the issuing bank obtain its prior express written approval for any changes to the terms or amount of the credit.

Finally, to shift the stay risk to customers, agent banks may refrain from offering indemnification. If a bank acts prudently during the course of its relationship with the broker, it should not be held liable for any ensuing losses suffered by its customers due to broker defaults.

CHAPTER 11

Tax Issues Associated with Securities Lending

Richard J. Shapiro
Tax Partner
Ernst & Young LLP

The typical securities lending transaction involves the owner of securities lending the securities to a broker and the broker using these borrowed securities to cover short sales or fail sales where a third-party seller has failed to deliver securities to the broker on the settlement date. Additionally, securities lending is utilized in connection with certain arbitrage or derivative trading strategies. This chapter focuses on the Federal income tax consequences of securities lending transactions.

GENERAL TERMS AND PRINCIPLES

Before delving into the technical and sometimes arcane world of the Internal Revenue Code (the "Code"), Treasury Regulations ("Regulations"), case law and the like, it may be helpful to review some of the terms and general principles that will be repeated throughout the chapter.

Securities Loan

A securities loan is a transaction in which the beneficial owner of securities (the securities lender) loans the securities to another party (the securities borrower). The securities borrower is obligated to return identical securities to the securities lender at some time in the future. Typically, the securities borrower will dispose of the securities (e.g., in connection

179

with a short sale) and then purchase the identical securities in the market to replace the lender's securities.

Generally, the securities borrower provides collateral for the loan in the form of cash, a letter of credit, Treasury obligations, or other securities at least equal in value to the securities loaned. The collateral is generally marked to market on a daily basis and is increased or decreased as necessary. During the term of the loan, cash collateral is typically invested for the benefit (and the risk) of the securities lender. The income generated from the invested cash is returned to the securities borrower; however, a percentage of the income is paid as consideration to the lender for the securities loan. If the collateral is a letter of credit, or government or other securities, then the securities borrower will pay a predetermined fee to the securities lender. If an intermediary is involved (e.g., a broker or a bank) then the fee is split between the intermediary and the securities lender. These fees paid by the borrower to the lender for the use of the securities are known as "borrow fees" when the fee is based on the value of the securities, whereas when the borrower posts cash collateral, the lender's fee ("embedded fee") is the income earned from investing the cash less an agreed upon percentage of the income which is rebated to the borrower ("rebate").

Dividends or interest on the loaned securities are paid to the registered owner of the securities during the period of the loan. However, an equal amount, known as a "substitute payment" or an "in lieu of payment," is required to be paid by the securities borrower to the securities lender.

At the end of the term of the loan, the securities are returned to the securities lender and the collateral is returned to the securities borrower. The lender may terminate the loan upon notice, typically of not more than five business days.

Short Sales

Securities are sold that are not owned by the seller. The short seller is required to return the borrowed securities as well as pay to the lender all dividends/interest and other distributions made with respect to the loaned securities. A corporate lender of stock is not entitled to the dividends received deduction.[1]

Fail Sales

Securities are loaned to a broker in order to cover sales of stock by sellers who own the shares they are selling but whose certificates are either lost or have yet to be delivered to the broker. Under the lender's agreement with the broker, the borrowed securities as well as dividends and other distributions made with respect to the loaned securities are the

---

[1] Rev. Rul. 60-177, 1960-1 C.B. 9. *See* note 26, *infra*.

lender's property. A fail sale is taxed in the same manner as a short sale, so that a corporate lender of stock in connection with a fail sale is not entitled to the dividends received deduction.[2]

Repurchase Agreement

A repurchase agreement ("repo") is a secured financing agreement. The vast similarities between repos and securities lending transactions necessitate a detailed description of a repo transaction and a comparison of the transactions. A repo is a financing transaction in which an owner of securities (the "seller")[3] sells the securities (typically, U.S. government obligations) to another party (the "purchaser")[4] and simultaneously agrees to repurchase the securities from the purchaser at a fixed future date (the "repurchase date") at the original sales price plus a specified interest rate ("repo margin"). In effect, money is temporarily exchanged for a security which, upon its subsequent return, will require repayment of the funds plus interest. By contrast, a securities loan involves the exchange of a security for a contract right to repurchase the same security.

A repo transaction when viewed from the perspective of the purchaser is commonly referred to as a "reverse repo." The duration of a repo may vary from one day to the maturity date of the underlying security ("repo to maturity"). At the repurchase date, repos are often "rolled over" or renewed until the maturity date of the security. In fact, it is this flexibility of term which has made repurchase agreements a favorite among many financial officers for investing corporate funds on a temporary basis. Additionally, tax-exempt organizations and regulated investment companies ("RICs") have been frequent lenders of securities as a means of obtaining additional income.

In many respects, repos and securities loans are substantially alike. In both transactions the recipient of the securities forwards funds to the counterparty until both positions are reversed at the date stipulated in the agreement. In each transaction the economic benefits and risks of ownership are retained by the securities owner. Further, collateral is posted by the borrower in a securities loan as well as the seller in a repo. Also, the securities borrower and the repo purchaser (under common industry practice) may freely dispose the subject securities.

The following example illustrates the substantial similarities between the repo and the securities loan. Corporation S ("S") needs to cover a short sale with certain governmental securities. To obtain the needed securities, S enters into an agreement with an owner ("O") of the required

---

[2] *Id.*

[3] The seller can also be called the "debtor" or the "repoing party."

[4] The purchaser is also known as the "creditor" or the "reverse repoing party."

securities. Under the agreement, O will transfer the securities to S in return for cash. At a specified date in the future, S will return the securities to O and the cash will be returned to S.

Economically, the transaction described has the effect of a secured loan, in that O obtains cash and transfers securities as collateral. However, the same result could be achieved by structuring the transaction as either a repo or a securities loan.

If the transaction is in the form of a securities loan, then O would be referred to as a securities lender and S would be the securities borrower. Pursuant to the securities loan agreement, O would loan the securities to S and S would provide O with cash collateral. During the term of the loan, O would receive income from the investment of the collateral and S would be required to pay O an amount equivalent to the interest coupon on the securities. At the end of the term of the loan, S would return the same (or identical) securities to O. Effectively, O would be compensated for allowing S to use the securities, to the extent the income earned from the invested collateral exceeds the rebate to S.

On the other hand, if the transaction were structured as a repo, then O, as the repoing party (or seller-debtor), would purport to sell the securities to S, the reverse repoing party (or buyer-creditor), thus giving S the use of the securities and O the use of the cash. During the period of the agreement S would be required to pay an amount equivalent to the coupon interest on the securities to O. At the end of the term S would purport to resell the securities to O at an enhanced price. Effectively, S would be compensated for allowing O to use the cash, to the extent that the "resale" price exceeded the "sale" price.

In light of these similarities, it is often difficult to rationalize the differing tax treatments that apply to these two transactions.

CURRENT TAX TREATMENT (DOMESTIC)

Securities Lending Transactions

The current tax treatment governing securities lending is based, in part, on Section 1058 of the Code and the proposed regulations issued under that provision of the Code. Although Section 1058 of the Code is a relatively recent development, enacted in 1978,[5] the analysis behind its gen-

---

[5] *See* Senate Finance Committee Report on P.L. 95-345 (1978) (the "Committee Report"); S. Rep. No. 762, 95th Cong., 2d Sess. 3, *reprinted in* 1978 U.S. Code Cong. & Admin. News 1286, which made Code Section 1058 applicable to amounts received after December 31, 1976 regardless of the taxpayer's year-end.

eral principles and thus the basic foundation for the current tax treatment of securities lending transactions can be traced back to 1926 with the U.S. Supreme Court's decision in *Provost v. U.S.*[6] In that case, the Supreme Court described a stock loan in the following manner:

> When the transaction is thus completed, neither the lender nor the borrower retains any interest in the stock that is the subject matter of the transaction and that has passed to and become the property of the purchaser. Neither the borrower nor the lender has the status of a stockholder of the corporation whose stock was dealt in, nor any legal relationship to it. Unlike the pledgee of stock, who must have specific stock available for the obligor on payment of his loan, the borrower of stock has no interest in the stock nor the right to demand it from any other. For that reason he can be neither a pledgee, trustee nor bailee for the lender, and he is not the one "with whom stock has been deposited as collateral security for money loaned." For the incidents of ownership, the lender has substituted the personal obligation, wholly contractual, of the borrower to restore him, on demand, to the economic position in which he would have been, as the owner of the stock, had the loan transaction had not been entered into.[7]

Section 1058 and Proposed Treasury Regulations

Section 1058 of the Code and the proposed regulations issued with respect to that section provide for an exception to the general recognition principles of Section 1001 of the Code[8] where certain requirements are satisfied. Taxpayers who enter into a "qualifying" lending agreement pursuant to the provisions of Section 1058 of the Code can receive non-recognition treatment with respect to the gain or loss realized on the transfer of the securities. The lender will not recognize gain or loss on the exchange of the securities for the obligation of the borrower, nor will the

---

[6] 269 US 443 (1926). In *Provost v. U.S.*, the Supreme Court examined the appropriateness of imposing a stamp tax on a "loan" and "return" transaction as a taxable exchange. *Id. Also, see* GCM 36948 (1976), which, citing *Provost*, held that the transfer of securities in a securities "loan" was a disposition and not a loan for Federal income tax purposes. However, if securities not differing materially in kind or extent were delivered, the disposition might be non-taxable under then existing law. GCM 36948 (1976).

[7] 269 US 443 (1926).

[8] Generally, the gain or loss realized on an exchange of property is recognized unless specifically exempted from the recognition provisions of Section 1001 of the Code and the Regulations issued thereunder. IRC §1001(c).

lender recognize gain or loss on the exchange of the rights under the loan agreement in return for securities identical to the securities transferred.[9]

Qualified Loans

To qualify for non-recognition treatment, a lending agreement must satisfy the three requirements specifically enumerated in Section 1058(b) of the Code and any requirements as prescribed by regulations. First, the agreement must provide that the borrower is required to return to the lender securities identical to those lent to the borrower.[10] For purposes of Section 1058, the term "securities" is defined in Section 1236(c) of the Code, and includes shares of stock in any corporation, certificates of stock or interest in any corporation, notes, bonds, debentures, other evidences of indebtedness, or any evidences of an interest in or right to subscribe to or purchase any of the foregoing.[11] "Identical securities" are securities of the same class and issue as the securities lent to the borrower.[12] However, if the agreement permits the borrower to return equivalent securities in the event of a reorganization, recapitalization or merger of the issuer of the securities during the term of the loan, this requirement will be deemed satisfied.[13]

The second requirement mandates that the agreement must require the borrower to make payments to the lender equivalent to all interest, dividends, and other distributions which the owner of the securities is entitled to for the period during which the securities are borrowed.[14]

The third requirement specifically enumerated in the Code is that the agreement can not reduce the risk of loss or opportunity for gain of the transferor of the securities in the securities transferred.[15]

Section 1058(b)(4) of the Code grants the Internal Revenue Service ("Service") the authority to prescribe additional requirements through regulations. The proposed regulations require the agreement to be in writ-

---

[9] IRC §1058(a); Prop. Treas. Reg. §1.1058-1(a).
[10] IRC §1058(b)(1); Prop. Treas. Reg. §1.1058-1(b)(1). The significance of the return of "identical" securities is rooted in general recognition provisions of Section §1001 of the Code and Treasury Regulation §1.1001-1 which indicate that where there is material difference in the property exchanged the taxpayer must recognize the gain or loss on the exchange. Similarly, in Revenue Ruling 57-451, the Service utilized Sections 421 and 1036 of the Code to provide for non-recognition treatment where the stock of the same corporation is exchanged. Rev. Rul. 57-451, 1957-2 C.B. 295. *See* GCM 36948, *supra*, note 6.
[11] Prop. Treas. Reg. §1.1058-1(b)(1).
[12] *Id.*
[13] *Id. See* Special Rule for Mergers, Recapitalizations and Reorganizations, infra.
[14] IRC §1058(b)(2); Prop. Treas. Reg. §1.1058-1(b)(2).
[15] IRC §1058(b)(3); Prop. Treas. Reg. §1.1058-1(b)(3).

ing and require that the lender be allowed to terminate the loan upon notice of not more than 5 business days.[16]

If these requirements are met the lending transaction "qualifies" for Section 1058 non-recognition treatment. The proposed regulations provide the following illustration of these rules.[17]

> *Example*: A owns 1,000 shares of XYZ stock. A instructs A's broker, B, to sell the XYZ stock. B sells to C. After the sale, B learns that A will not be able to deliver to B certificates representing the 1,000 shares in time for B to deliver them to C on the settlement date. B effects the delivery by borrowing stock from a third party, D. D is a non-exempt organization having a large position in XYZ stock. This borrowing is evidenced by a written agreement with the following terms:
>
> 1. D will transfer to B certificates representing 1,000 shares of XYZ common stock.
> 2. B will pay D an amount equivalent to any dividends or other distributions paid on the XYZ stock during the period of the loan.
> 3. Regardless of any increases or decreases in the market value of XYZ common stock, B will transfer to D 1,000 shares of the XYZ common stock of the same issue as that of the XYZ common stock transferred from D to B.
> 4. B agrees that upon notice of 5 business days, B will return identical securities to D.[18]

The example concludes that the agreement between B and D satisfies the requirements of Proposed Treasury Regulation Section 1.1058-1. The agreement is in writing. It requires the borrower, B, to return to the lender, D, identical securities and to pay to D amounts equivalent to any dividends or other distributions paid on the stock during the period of the loan. It does not reduce D's risk of loss or opportunity for gain because, regardless of the fluctuations in the market value of XYZ common stock, B is obligated to return 1,000 shares of XYZ common stock.[19]

Collateral Consequences

Where the taxpayers enter into a qualifying loan agreement pursuant to Section 1058 of the Code, the parties receive non-recognition treatment

---

[16] Prop. Treas. Reg. §1.1058-1(b).
[17] Prop. Treas. Reg. §1.1058-2, Ex.(1).
[18] *Id.*
[19] *Id.*

on the qualifying transaction. In addition, the lender's basis and holding period in the lent stock are impacted.

Basis

Consistent with other non-recognition provisions of the Code, the lender's basis in the identical securities returned by the borrower will be the same as the lender's basis in the securities lent to the borrower.[20] In other words, the lender will have a substituted basis in the exchanged securities to preserve the gain or loss inherent in the securities. Similarly, the lender's basis in the contractual obligation received from the borrower in exchange for the lender's securities will be equal to the lender's basis in the securities exchanged.[21]

Although the proposed regulations are silent as to the treatment of original issue discount ("OID"), it appears that in transactions where the loaned security is an OID obligation, any OID accruing during the time that the bonds are lent out under a loan arrangement is not included in the lender's basis when the bonds are returned.[22] The treatment of the in lieu of payment in connection with OID obligations is unclear.

Holding Period

The lender's holding period is determined under Treasury Regulation Section 1.1223-2.[23] Accordingly, the holding period in the hands of the lender of the securities received by the lender from the borrower at the termination of the agreement includes both the period for which the lender held the securities which were transferred to the borrower *and* the period between the transfer of the securities from the lender to the borrower and the return of the securities to the lender.[24]

Treatment of Payments to Lender

A payment made by the borrower in lieu of interest, dividends, or any other distribution is treated by the lender as a fee for the temporary use

---

[20] Prop. Treas. Reg. §1.1058-1(c)(1).

[21] Prop. Treas. Reg. §1.1058-1(c)(2).

[22] *See* American Bar Association Section of Taxation, Committee on Financial Transactions, Securities Loans Task Force, Report on Securities Lending Transactions Governed by Section 1058 (April 22, 1991); Rev. Rul. 74-482, 1974-2 C.B. 267.

[23] Prop. Treas. Reg. §1.1058-1(g). The Committee Report indicates that where the lender does not recognize gain or loss under Section 1058 of the Code, then upon the borrower's transfer of the securities in satisfaction of the contractual obligation, the lender will have a tacked holding period in the securities which are returned.

[24] Treas. Reg. §1.1223-2(a).

of property.[25] The payment does not retain the character of the income that is being replaced (i.e., interest or dividend), because the lender holds a contractual obligation, and not the security itself. Thus, for example, a payment received by a lender in lieu of a dividend is treated as ordinary income and not as a dividend for purposes of the corporate dividends received deduction.[26] It is also not entitled to the reduced tax rate for "qualified dividends."[27] Similarly, where the obligation lent is a tax-exempt security, the lender has ordinary income, not tax-exempt income.[28] Generally, the Service requires information reporting with respect to substitute dividend and interest payments.[29]

Special Rules for Regulated Investment Companies and Tax-Exempt Entities

As a result of the special rules for regulated investment companies ("RICs") and tax-exempt entities, these potential lenders are not discouraged from engaging in securities lending. Under the Committee Report, payments received on security loans which satisfy certain requirements

---

[25] Prop. Treas. Reg. §1.1058-1(d).

[26] *Id. See* Rev. Rul. 60-177, 1961-1 C.B. 9, in which the Service held that an amount equal to a cash dividend paid to a lender in a short sale transaction is not a dividend for purposes of the corporate dividends received deduction because the lender is no longer considered the shareholder for purposes of IRC §316. *See also* PLR 8828003 which applies the disallowance of the dividends received deduction of Revenue Ruling 60-177 to both the lender and borrower in the "fail sale" context. The Service reasoned that the purchaser was not entitled to the dividends received deduction on the loaned stock because the purchaser was not the owner of the stock on the ex-dividend date. Additionally, the seller was not entitled to the dividends received deduction, either, because the seller was required to make an in lieu, or substitute, payment to the buyer. *Id.*

[27] Conference Report on HR2, the Jobs and Growth Tax Relief Reconciliation Act of 2003, Sec. 302.

[28] Rev. Rul. 80-135, 1980-1 C.B. 402. *See* note 59, *infra*, which discusses the elimination of the tax-exempt status on payments received in a repo transaction where the underlying security is a U.S. government security. *See* Rev. Rul. 79-108, 1979-1 C.B. 466, which disallowed an exclusion from gross income under Section 103 of the Code where municipal obligations are issued solely to derive an arbitrage profit.

[29] Treas. Reg. §1.6045-2(a). Information reporting was generally not required in the case of substitute dividend payments made to a broker on behalf of individuals for taxable years beginning before January 1, 2003. Reporting for substitute payments to individuals on or after January 1, 2003 is now required. TD 9103, 68 Fed. Reg. 74847 (2003). Additionally, such reporting requirements are not imposed upon substitute payments made to tax-exempt organizations, individual retirement plans and certain U.S. and foreign governmental organizations. Treas. Reg. §1.6045-2(b).

can retain their interest or dividend character for certain purposes.[30] With regard to RICs, the income received from substitute payments is characterized the same as the income from the underlying securities for purposes of the RIC diversification requirements.[31] For example, RICs are able to satisfy the gross income test of Section 851(b)(2)[32] of the Code because the substitute payments are considered interest or dividend income depending on the underlying security. However, where such payments are passed through to the shareholders of these lending RICs, the payments would not be treated as dividends for purposes of the dividends received deduction.[33]

Special rules also apply in the case of amounts received by tax-exempt organizations.[34] Income from substitute payments ("payments made with respect to securities loans") will not be taken into account in computing

---

[30] S. Rep. No. 762, 95th Cong., 2d Sess. 1978, 1978-2 C.B. 357.

[31] *Id. See* PLR 9030048 for illustration of the RICs ability to use its securities loans to satisfy its asset diversification requirements, which is one of the prerequisites to the special tax treatment of RICs.

[32] The gross income test is another requirement for RIC tax treatment. If a RIC fails either the asset diversification or gross income test, the entity may lose the pass through nature of a RIC and become a taxable entity. Thus, the ability for the securities loan assets and income to qualify under these tests is essential to the ability of the RIC to be able to utilize secured loan transactions as a means of generating additional income.

[33] Committee Report, 1978-2 C.B. 357. This limitation on the characterization of the payments as dividends for purposes of the dividends received deduction is consistent with the general treatment of securities loan transactions, as seen in note 26, *supra*. As such, the special rules regarding the retention of the character of the underlying payment provides RICs with the ability to engage in securities lending transactions without violating the requirements for RIC status under the Code, but does not provide RIC shareholders with a benefit not afforded to other securities lenders.

[34] The proposed regulations provide that "*except as otherwise provided in section 512(a)(5)*, a payment of amounts required to be paid by the borrower . . . shall be treated by the lender as a fee for the temporary use of property." Prop. Treas. Reg. §1.1058-1(d) (emphasis added). The legislative history of Section 512 of the Code indicates that "Congress did not intend for ordinary or routine investment activities of a section 501(a) organization in connection with its securities portfolio to be treated as the conduct of a trade or business for purpose of section 513." Rev. Rul. 78-88, 1978-1 C.B. 163. "Taxing such income is inconsistent with the generally tax-free treatment accorded to exempt organizations' income from investment activities." S. Rep. No. 94-1172, 94th Cong., 2d Sess. 3,4 (1976). However, this exclusion from taxation does not extend to organizations which hold the securities in the ordinary course of their trade or business or hold such securities as inventory. *Id.*

unrelated business taxable income ("UBTI")[35] in the hands of a tax-exempt lender,[36] provided that the agreement with regard to the loaned securities satisfies certain requirements.[37] Further, income received by a tax-exempt lender in connection with a qualified loan agreement is not taxable to the lender as debt financed property[38] nor as acquisition indebtedness.[39] Payments made with respect to securities loans are deemed to be derived from the securities loaned and not from collateral security or the investment of collateral security from the loans.[40]

---

[35] "Unrelated business taxable income" is defined pursuant to Sections 512 and 513 of the Code as income derived by any organization through any trade or business the conduct of which is not substantially related to the exercise or performance of its tax exempt functions. Section 511 of the Code imposes income tax on a tax-exempt entity's UBTI. IRC §511(a).

[36] Section 512(a) of the Code through its reference to the modifications in subsection (b) excludes "payments with respect to securities loans" from the definition of UBTI. IRC §512(a). Section 512(a)(5) of the Code defines payment with respect of securities as all amount received in respect of a security ... including, (i) amounts in respect of dividends, interest or other distributions; (ii) fees computed by reference to the period beginning with the transfer of securities by the owner and ending with transfer of identical securities back to the transferor . . . ; (iii) income from collateral security for such a loan; and (iv) income from the investment of collateral security. IRC §512(a)(5).

[37] Section 512 of the Code requires provisions similar to Section 1058 of the Code to establish a "qualified loan" for purposes of receiving non-recognition treatment. IRC §512. For example, Section 512 of the Code requires that the transferor be able to terminate the loan upon notice of not more than five days. IRC §512(a)(5)(B). This is the same requirement as under the Proposed Regulations under Section 1058 of the Code.

[38] S. Rep. No. 762 at 1294, in which the Committee agreed with Service's position in Revenue Ruling 78-88 that the income earned by an exempt organization which lends securities ... pursuant to a typical securities lending transaction is not taxable as debt financed income. P.L. 95-345. However, if an exempt organization incurs indebtedness to purchase loaned securities, any income from the securities would be considered debt financed income and subject to taxation as UBTI under Sections 512 and 514 of the Code. *Id.*

[39] IRC §514(c)(8)(C). As discussed in note 35, *supra*, tax-exempt organizations are taxed on their UBTI. The significance of debt financed property and acquisition indebtedness, for our purposes, is simply that the Code subjects the tax-exempt entities to tax on these purchases or investments if the transactions meet the technical definition set forth in the Code. As such, the exemption from tax on these transactions, when entered into pursuant to a qualified loan arrangement, does not discourage tax-exempt entities from becoming lenders in such transactions.

[40] IRC §514(c)(8)(A). Additionally, any deductions which are directly connected with collateral security for such loan, or with the investment of collateral security, are deemed to be deductions which are directly connected with the securities loaned. IRC §514(c)(8)(B).

Transactions Collateralized by Cash

In transactions where the loan is collateralized by cash, the cash is usually invested for the account and at the risk of the securities lender. The income from the invested capital is returned to the securities borrower, a rebate, except that a percentage of the income or return on the invested collateral is paid to the securities lender as a fee. If the loan is collateralized by other securities, the borrow fee is a predetermined amount for the use of the securities paid to the securities lender. Although not specifically addressed in Section 1058 of the Code or in the proposed regulations, the borrow fee should also be characterized as a "fee" for the temporary use of property and, as such, should constitute ordinary income to the lender.

Special Rule for Mergers, Recapitalizations, and Reorganizations

In the case of a merger, recapitalization, or reorganization of the issuer of securities lent pursuant to Section 1058, the loan transaction is deemed terminated immediately prior to the merger, recapitalization, or reorganization and a second Section 1058 transaction is deemed entered into immediately following the merger, recapitalization, or reorganization on terms identical to the original Section 1058 transaction.[41] Thus, the borrower of the securities is deemed to have returned the securities to the lender immediately prior to the merger, recapitalization, or reorganization and immediately thereafter the lender and borrower are deemed to have entered into a second Section 1058 loan transaction, on terms identical to the original Section 1058 loan transaction.[42] However, this special rule does not apply in the case where the lender ultimately is repaid with securities identical to the securities originally transferred.[43]

The proposed regulations illustrate these rules with the same facts from the example noted above,[44] with the following additions:

> *Example:* 1. Upon D's transfer to B of the certificates representing the 1,000 shares of XYZ common stock, B will transfer to D, cash equal to the market value of the XYZ common stock on the business day pre-

---

[41] Prop. Treas. Reg. §1.1058-1(f)

[42] *Id.* This rule permits the parties in securities lending transactions to continue to engage in their transactions without amending, or closing and re-entering into, agreements due to internal changes in the corporation of the stock or securities of which are underlying the lending arrangement. Additionally, the rule is consistent with the treatment accorded to such tax-free reorganizations.

[43] *Id.*

[44] *See* note 17, *supra.*

ceding the transfer, as collateral for the stock. The collateral will be increased or decreased daily to reflect increases or decreases in the market value of the XYZ stock during the period of the loan.

2. B agrees that upon notice of five (5) business days, B will return to D 1,000 shares of XYZ common stock, or the equivalent thereof in the event of reorganization, recapitalization or merger of XYZ during the term of the loan. Upon delivery of the stock to D, D will return the cash collateral to B. [45]

According to the proposed regulation, the agreement between B and D satisfies the requirements for a qualified loan agreement. If XYZ merged into another corporation and B returns an equivalent amount of stock in the resulting corporation, the qualified loan agreement is deemed terminated immediately before the merger. Thus, D is deemed to be the owner of the XYZ common stock at the time of the merger. D does not recognize gain or loss upon the transfer of the XYZ common stock to B or upon the return of the stock of the resulting corporation to D.[46]

Failure to Comply with Requirements

If a transfer of securities is intended to comply with these rules but the contractual obligation does not satisfy the requirements of a qualified loan agreement, gain or loss is recognized upon the initial transfer of the securities in accordance with the rules of Section 1001 of the Code.[47] For example, if the agreement provided that the lender must give notice in excess of five business days to terminate the agreement, the agreement would not satisfy the contractual requirements of Proposed Treasury Regulation Section 1.1058-1(b)(3), and gain or loss would be recognized upon the initial transfer. The holding period in the hands of the lender of the securities transferred to the borrower terminates on the day the securities are transferred to the borrower, and the holding period in the hands of the borrower of the property transferred to it begins on the date that the securities are delivered pursuant to the transfer loan agreement.[48]

---

[45] Prop. Treas. Reg. §1.1058-2, Ex. (2).

[46] *Id.*

[47] Prop. Treas. Reg. §1.1058-1(e)(1). Whether a secured loan transaction which fails to qualify under Section 1058 of the Code will produce a taxable gain or loss is uncertain. Although Section 1001 of the Code is a general recognition provision, there are several exceptions which could give a secured loan which failed to satisfy Section 1058 of the Code non-recognition treatment. *See* notes 6 and 10, *supra. See also* M. Feder, "Securities Lending Transactions: Tax Considerations in Domestic and Cross-Border Transactions," 3 *Journal of Taxation of Financial Products* (Winter 2002).

[48] Prop. Treas. Reg. §1.1223-2(b)(1).

Whereas, if the agreement satisfies the requirements of Section 1058 of the Code but the borrower fails to return to the lender the requisite identical securities or otherwise defaults under the agreement, gain or loss is recognized on the day the borrower fails to return identical securities as required by the agreement, or otherwise defaults.[49] In this case, the holding period in the hands of the lender, of the securities transferred to the borrower, terminates on the day the borrower fails to return the identical securities, and, similarly, the holding period in the hands of the borrower begins on the day the borrower fails to deliver or otherwise defaults.[50]

Application of the Wash Sale Rules

Finally, it is important to note that Section 1091 of the Code and the related regulations thereunder apply the wash sale rules[51] to losses recognized as the result of the failure to comply with Section 1058. In other words, the application of the wash sale rules may prevent the recognition of a loss that would otherwise be recognized under Section 1058.[52] A similar non-recognition provision is applicable to short sales, which can prevent a taxpayer from recognizing a loss on its short position.[53]

Repurchase Agreements

The key element in determining the tax treatment of a repo transaction is whether a sale or a secured loan has occurred. If, based upon the particular facts and circumstances, a sale of securities has indeed taken place, gain

---

[49] Prop. Treas. Reg. §1.1058-1(e)(2).

[50] Prop. Treas. Reg. §1.1223-2(b)(2).

[51] In general, the wash sale rules disallow losses which lack economic substance because the taxpayer has not truly "disposed" of the interest in the security. Under Section 1091 of the Code, a loss is disallowed if within 30 days before or after the sale or disposition of the stock or security, the taxpayer has acquired by purchase or exchange or has entered into a contract or option to acquire substantially identical stock or securities. IRC §1091(a). Also, the wash sale rule will not fail to apply to a contract or option to acquire or sell stock or securities solely by reason of the fact that the contract or option settles in (or could be settled in) cash or property other than such stock or securities. IRC §1091(f).

[52] Prop. Treas. Reg. §1.1223-2(b)(2).

[53] The wash sale rule, described in note 51, *supra*, applies to short sales. A closing of a short sale or entering into a short sale, depending on the facts, can be deemed a sale date for purposes of applying the wash sale rule. Also, a realized loss on a short sale is deferred if, during the period beginning 30 days before and ending 30 days after the date of the closing, the taxpayer has either sold substantially identical stock or securities or entered to another short sale transaction on substantially identical stock or securities. IRC §1091(e).

or loss will be recognized by both the seller and the purchaser.[54] Alternatively, if the transaction is deemed a securities loan, gain or loss may not be recognized on either the transfer or the return of the securities.[55] The factors to which the courts and the Service have looked in characterizing the transaction as either a loan or a sale include the intent of the parties, which party exercised control over the securities, which party bore the risk of loss, whether the seller was contractually obligated to pay interest to the buyer, and whether the seller had the right to repurchase the securities.[56]

The typical repo transacted in today's capital markets is treated by the Service and the courts as a loan collateralized by the underlying securities. If the repo is treated as a loan the seller is considered to have retained the benefits and burdens of ownership, and, as such, the seller will recognize gain or loss only upon the ultimate disposition (or "sale") of the securities underlying the repurchase agreement.[57] No gain or loss is recognized by either the seller upon the initial transfer of the securities to the purchaser, nor by the purchaser upon returning the securities to the seller. Although not formally ruled upon by the Service, loan characterization should be equally appropriate where different certificates (although identical securities) are returned upon repurchase. With the purchaser being insulated from the risk of market fluctuation of the repoed securities, the phrase "sale and repurchase" is not to be construed literally, as a true sale does not occur.

With respect to the contractual interest payments or "repo margin," the purchaser includes this amount in gross income (sourced based upon

---

[54] IRC §1001. However, there are several provisions which disallow losses, including but not limited to the wash sale rules under Section 1091 of the Code and the straddle rules under Section 1092 of the Code. The purpose of these provisions is to defer tax losses until taxpayers are truly out of the position, or have reduced the investment in the loss position, and to prevent creation of tax losses which have not economically occurred.

[55] IRC §1058. *See Section 1058* discussion, *supra.*

[56] *See Citizen's National Bank of Waco v. U.S.,* 551 F.2d 832 (Ct. Cl. 1977), 1977-1 U.S.T.C. 9298; Rev. Rul. 74-2, 1974-1 C.B. 24. *See also* Rev. Rul. 77-59, 1977-1 C.B. 196, in which, a REIT's purchase agreement involving U.S. Treasuries were treated as a loan; Rev. Rul. 60-177, 1960-1 C.B. 9, in which, the Service held that substitute payments received by the lender were not dividends for certain federal tax purposes because the lender did not retain ownership of the stock; Rev. Rul. 57-451, 1957-2 C.B. 295, where the Service ruled that a shareholder who loaned securities to satisfy a broker's short sale obligation had transferred all incidents of ownership; and W. Chip, "Are Repos Really Loans," *Tax Analysts, Tax Notes Today* (March 13, 2002) *available in* Lexis at 2002 TNT, 98-28, Fedtax, TNT.

[57] *See* Rev. Rul. 79-108, 1979-1 C.B. 75; Rev. Rul. 77-59, 1977-1 C.B. 196; Rev. Rul. 74-27, 1974-1 C.B. 24.

the seller's residence)[58] and is taxed at the ordinary rates, while the seller incurs otherwise deductible interest expense.[59] If the repoed securities are tax-exempt, however, the seller's interest expense is lost under the federal tax provision which disallows such expenses when incurred to purchase or carry tax-exempt securities.[60] Also, if interest payments are payable on the underlying securities, the purchaser is liable to pay the seller any substitute payments during the life of the repo.

One type of repo where a logical argument can be made for sale (rather than loan) treatment under certain circumstances is the "repo to maturity." Since the term of the repo coincides with the maturity date of the collateral and the repurchase price equals the proceeds of the collateral, the seller is not in a position to profit from or lose on the market fluctuation of the security.[61] Indeed, several court cases have denied the seller's interest deduction relating to Treasury bill repos to maturity.[62]

CROSS-BORDER SECURITIES LENDING

Background

Cross-border securities lending transactions involve a broader set of issues not significant or relevant in a purely domestic setting. For example, in a cross-border transaction the characterization of payments made or received is significant because of the interrelationship of the withholding at source, characterization, and sourcing rules. The United States ("U.S."), as a taxing authority, had been particularly concerned for years

---

[58] *See* IRC §861. The sourcing of gross income has significant tax consequences in cross-border (or international) transactions, discussed later in the chapter.

[59] In *Nebraska Dept. of Revenue v. Loewenstein,* the Supreme Court held that the "interest income earned from repurchase agreements involving federal securities is not interest on 'obligations of the U.S. Government,'" but rather interest on loans to a private party. 115 S.Ct. 557 (1994). As such, the state of Nebraska was able to tax the interest income. *Id.*

[60] IRC §265(a)(2).

[61] Commentators were concerned that Treasury Regulation 1.1058-1(e) could be used to treat a repo to maturity as a failed Section 1058 transaction and, thus, a sale. *See e.g.*, Lee Sheppard, "On the Border: IRS Contemplates Narrow Mission of Section 1058," 49 *Tax Notes* (August 27, 1990), p. 1083. Indeed, the Service held the positions that such repos should be treated as sales because the beneficial ownership shift to the borrower. *Id.*

[62] *See U.S. v. Wexler,* 31 F.3d 117, 94-2 U.S.T.C. 50,361 (3d Cir. 1994); *U.S. v. Charles Agee Atkins and William S. Hack,* 869 F.2d 135, 89-1 U.S.T.C. 9195 (2d Cir. 1989); *Steven R. Sheldon and Ellen G. Sheldon v. Comm'r,* 94 T.C. 738 (1990), *citing, Goldstein v. Comm'r,* 44 T.C. 284 (1965), *affd.,* 364 F.2d 734 (2d Cir. 1966).

prior to the issuance of regulations, with the "inbound stock loan" transaction and the potential ability of foreign investors to avoid foreign withholding tax through such exchanges.[63] The example below illustrates one of those revenue concerns.

Securities Loans

Inbound Stock Loan Example

A foreign investor (L) owns shares in XYZ Corporation, a publicly traded U.S. company. L lends the XYZ stock to a U.S. broker-dealer (B), with the right to terminate the loan upon five-days' notice to B. B sells the XYZ stock to a U.S. investor (P). P pays B cash for the XYZ stock and B uses the cash as collateral. The collateral is marked to market daily to ensure that the cash collateral equals the fair market value of the stock on that day. If the XYZ corporation pays a dividend, B is required to make a payment to L equal to the dividends that L would have received if L still owned the XYZ stock (substitute dividend payments). L makes payments to B of $X as a rebate reflecting a percentage of the interest earned on the cash collateral. Upon termination, B gives L identical, but not the actual original, shares of the XYZ stock and L returns the cash collateral to B. If L merely held the stock of XYZ corporation, the U.S. government would collect a 30% withholding tax (assuming no lower treaty rate is applicable) on the dividends received by L, the foreign investor. In contrast, under the loan transaction, unless the substitute dividend payments are subject to the 30% withholding tax (assuming no lower treaty rate is applicable), the U.S. government may not collect any tax on the transaction.[64]

Out Bound Concern

Additionally, the Service had been concerned that U.S. lenders of U.S. securities could use the substitute payments paid by foreign borrowers to increase the U.S. lender's foreign tax credit by claiming that the substitute payments are foreign source income.[65]

---

[63] "The Service is concerned that foreign lenders of U.S. securities are attempting to convert U.S. source dividend and interest income into substitute payments to avoid U.S. withholding tax" by claiming that substitute payments are exempt from withholding tax as "industrial or commercial profits" or "other income" under income tax treaties. "ABA Members Say Cross-Border Regs Exceed Legislative Authority," 92 *Tax Analysts, Tax Notes Today* (April 23, 1992), *available in* Lexis as 92 TNT 87-38, Fedtax, TNT.

[64] Adapted from David P. Hariton, "Withholding on Cross-Border Stock Loans and Other Equity Derivatives," *Taxes* (December 1994), pp. 1050-1051.

[65] 92 *Tax Analysts, Tax Notes Today* (April 23, 1992), *available in* Lexis as 92 TNT 87-38, Fedtax, TNT.

Withholding at Source

Nonresident alien individuals, foreign corporations, foreign partnerships and foreign fiduciaries are subject to U.S. withholding at source.[66] The U.S. government requires withholding at source at a 30% rate (or lower treaty rate)[67] on "fixed or determinable annual or periodical" ("FDAP") income from sources within the United States that is not effectively connected with the conduct of a U. S. trade or business.[68] Where the U.S. has a treaty with a foreign country, the withholding rate under the treaty varies according to the type of income and from treaty to treaty.

FDAP income includes, in part, interest, dividends, rent, compensation and remunerations.[69] Capital gains (other than certain pension distributions and certain gains from the sale or exchange of patents, trademarks, copyrights)[70] and "portfolio interest"[71] are exempt from withholding. Portfolio interest is interest (including OID) paid on portfolio debt investment obligations issued after July 18, 1984 meeting certain requirements intended to ensure that U.S. persons are not avoiding U.S. taxation with respect to those instruments. For example, interest on bearer instruments "targeted at foreign markets"[72] is considered portfolio interest and, thus, is exempt from withholding. Interest on registered obligations can be exempt from withholding, provided that the withholding agent is in receipt of a statement documenting that the beneficial owner is not a U.S. person.[73] Additionally, no withholding is required on interest from deposits[74] which are not effectively connected with the conduct of a trade or business.

The question of withholding is important for borrowers and lenders alike. For U.S. tax purposes, every person having the control, receipt, custody, disposal, or payment of any item of income subject to withholding at source of any nonresident alien, foreign partnership, or foreign corpo-

---

[66] Foreign taxpayers are required to file an appropriate Form W-8 or substitute form indicating their nonresident or foreign status.

[67] *See* Treas. Reg. Sec. 1.1441-6.

[68] IRC §871(a)(1).

[69] IRC §871(a)(1)(A).

[70] IRC §871(a)(1).

[71] IRC §871(h)(2).

[72] "Targeted at foreign markets" for purposes of the portfolio interest exemption means that there are arrangements to ensure that the obligation will be sold or resold only to nonresident aliens, the interest on the obligation is payable outside of the U.S. and the face of the obligation states that a U.S. person holding such obligation will be subject to the requirements of the U.S. law. IRC §871(h)(2)(A).

[73] IRC §871(h)(2)(B).

[74] IRC §871(i). For purposes of this section, deposits mean the amounts deposited with U.S. banks, savings and loan associations, or similar institutions, and certain deposits with insurance companies.

ration has the obligation to withhold.[75] Any person required to deduct and withhold tax is liable for such tax.[76]

As noted above, treaties often provide for reduced rate of tax withholding on various types of payments, such as dividends and interest. Treaties generally do not explicitly provide for a reduced rate of withholding for substitute payments in lieu of dividends or interest or for related securities lending payments. However, other provisions of treaties, such as "industrial or commercial profit," "business profit," or "other income" provisions may serve to eliminate or reduce withholding.[77] This is the case both as to U.S. withholding tax and withholding on the part of other countries at source under their income tax treaties with the U. S. and with other countries.

Income Sourcing

Whether U.S. withholding is required on a payment depends on whether the payment is from U.S. sources. In the context of securities lending, there are potentially at least six alternative approaches available in determining the source of such income and payments: (i) the location or place of use of loaned securities; (ii) the place where the lending activity occurs; (iii) the source of the underlying securities' income; (iv) the residence of the borrower; (v) the residence of the lender; or (vi) some combination of the above.[78]

The Code and the Regulations provide sourcing rules which are dependent on the nature of an income item. For example, the source of interest income is generally determined by reference to the residence of the debtor.[79] Thus, interest on obligations of noncorporate residents and

---

[75] IRC §1441(a).

[76] IRC §1461.

[77] An example of an "industrial or commercial" or "business profits" provision is the following excerpt from Article 7 of the U.S.–U.K. treaty indicating that the income is exempt unless conducted through a permanent establishment. "The business profits of an enterprise of a Contracting State shall be taxable only in the State unless the enterprise carries on business in the other Contracting State through a permanent establishment situated therein." An example of an "other income" provision is contained in Article 22 of the U.S.–U.K. treaty indicating that the income that is not otherwise addressed is exempt. "Items of income beneficially owned by a resident of a resident of a Contracting State, wherever arising, not dealt with in the foregoing Articles of this Convention (other than income paid out of trusts or the estates of deceased persons in the course of administration) shall be taxable only in that State."

[78] See New York State Bar Association Tax Section, "Report on Proposed Regulations on Certain Payment Made Pursuant to Securities Lending Transactions" (July, 1992); ABA Section of Taxation Financial Transactions Committee Subcommittee on Securities Investors and Broker/Dealers, Securities Loans Task Force, "ABA Committee Reports on Securities Lending Transactions" (April, 1991).

[79] IRC §861(a)(1).

domestic corporations generally constitutes domestic U.S. source income, while interest paid by foreign residents is foreign source income. The source of dividend income generally depends on the nationality or place of incorporation of the corporate payer.[80] Thus, dividend distributions by U.S. corporations are domestic U.S. source income, while dividends of foreign corporations are foreign source income. Rents and royalty income are sourced at the location, or place of use, of the leased or licensed property.[81] Gain from the sale of personal property is generally determined by the seller's residence,[82] except in the case of inventory property which is sourced where title to the goods pass.[83] Income from "notional principal contracts" is generally residence based.[84]

Substitute Payments

In January 1992, the Internal Revenue Service issued proposed regulations[85] relating to the source, character, and income tax treaty implications of substitute interest and dividend payments made pursuant to cross-border

---

[80] IRC §861(a)(2).

[81] IRC §861(a)(4).

[82] IRC §865(a). As such, income from the sale of personal property by a U.S. "resident" is sourced to the U.S. A U.S. resident is defined as an individual who is a citizen or resident alien, who does not have a tax home outside the U.S., or non-resident alien with a U.S. tax home. IRC §865(g). Additionally, a domestic corporation, partnership or trust is a U.S. resident for purposes of these sourcing rules. IRC §7701(a)(30).

[83] IRC §861(a)(6); Treas. Reg. §1.861-7(a).

[84] Treas. Reg. §1.863-7(b). A notional principal contract is a financial instrument that provides for the payment of amounts by one party to another at specified intervals calculated by reference to a specified index upon a notional principal amount in exchange for specified consideration or a promise to pay similar amounts. Treas. Reg. §1.863-7(a). To determine if a security loan could constitute a notional principal contract, commentators have applied Treasury Regulation Section 1.446-3, which defines a "notional principal amount" to include "any specified amount of property that, when multiplied by a specified index, measures a party's rights or obligations under the contract." Since the lent stock could be argued to constitute an amount of property which measures the lender's rights and the borrower's obligation under the loan agreement, a stock loan could be viewed as a notional principal contract, provided that the transaction is treated as "sale" of the stock, rather than a "loan." If the agreement is considered a loan then it would be excluded from the definition of notional principal amount which excludes any amount which is "borrowed or loaned between the parties as part of the contract." Hariton, *supra*, p. 1055. Note that the notional principal contract provision does not apply to transactions relating to the treatment of certain nonfunctional currency transactions pursuant to Section 988 of the Code. Treas. Reg. §1.863-7(a).

[85] INTL – 106-89, 57 Fed. Reg. 860 (1992).

securities lending transactions. With limited changes, these were substantially adopted in final Substitute Payment Regulations[86] in October 1997.

The Substitute Payment Regulations apply to substitute payments made under a securities lending transaction described in Section 1058 or a substantially similar transaction,[87] generally effective for payments made after November 13, 1997. They also apply to substitute payments received by a transferor in a sale-repurchase transaction.[88] A "substitute payment" is a payment made to the transferor of a security in a securities lending transaction (or sale-repurchase transaction) of an amount equivalent to a dividend or interest payment that the owner of the transferred security is entitled to receive during the term of the transaction.[89] By their terms, the Substitute Payment Regulations explicitly do not address the treatment of fees or interest paid to the transferee in such transactions (for example, the interest component of a sale-repurchase agreement).[90] The Substitute Payment Regulations do not change existing law that substitute dividend payments are not eligible for the dividends received deduction[91] and that substitute interest payments received on state and local bonds are not eligible for exclusion from income.[92]

The Substitute Payment Regulations source substitute interest and dividend payments made pursuant to a securities lending (or sale-repurchase) transaction by reference to the underlying interest or dividend payment. This applies for all purposes of the Internal Revenue Code and regardless of whether the recipient of the income is a U.S. or foreign person (including, for example, for foreign tax credit purposes). The source of dividend income

---

[86] TD 8735, 62 Fed. Reg. 53498 (1997). The final Substitute Payment Regulations issued under IRC Sections 861, 864, 871, 881 and 894 are referred to as the "Substitute Payment Regulations."

[87] Many commentators believe that the term "substantially similar transactions" is intended to extend these provisions to transactions that are similar to Section 1058 lending transactions but which fail to satisfy one or more of the technical requirements of Section 1058. See "New York State Bar Association Tax Section: Report on Proposed Regulations on Certain Payments Made Pursuant to Securities Lending Transactions ("NYSBA"), reprinted in *Tax Analyst, Tax Notes Today* (July 24, 1992).

[88] *See* discussion, *infra*.

[89] Treas. Reg. Sec. 1.861-2(a)(7); 1.861-3(a)(6).

[90] Preamble to TD 8735, *supra*.

[91] Rev. Rul. 60-177, 1960-1 C.B. 9. The Service denied the dividends received deduction to the recipient of the substitute dividend on the basis that there can only be one true owner of the shares and, as such, the shares should not be able to produce the benefit for more than one party. *See also* note 26, *supra*.

[92] Rev. Rul. 80-135, 1980-1 C.B. 18. In Revenue Ruling 80-135, the Service denied lenders the tax-exempt nature underlying the substitute payment. The Service relied on the Supreme Court decision in *Provost*, 268 U.S. 443 (1926), which held that because title passes to the buyer of a security loaned in a short sale transaction, the result is that the lender is not in receipt of interest on the loaned tax-exempt bond. *Id. See also* note 28, *supra*.

generally depends on the nationality or place of incorporation of the corporate payor.[93] Thus, dividend distributions by U.S. corporations are U.S.-source income, while dividends paid by foreign corporations generally are foreign-source income, unless a test relating to effectively connected income is met. Similarly, the source of interest income is generally determined by reference to the residence of the debtor.[94] Accordingly, interest on obligations of noncorporate residents and domestic corporations is generally U.S. source income, while interest paid by foreign corporations is foreign-source income.

Under the Substitute Payment Regulations, a substitute payment is characterized under a "transparency rule"—i.e., in the same manner as the underlying dividend or interest payment, but *only* with respect to *foreign* taxpayers and only for limited purposes,[95] such as withholding, treaties and effectively connected U.S. trade or business income. Substitute payments received by U.S. persons are not recharacterized as interest or dividends for any purposes.

Substitute payments to a foreign person with respect to stock and securities that would otherwise (but for the securities lending transaction) give rise to foreign source effectively connected income retain that character as dividend or interest income for purposes of determining whether the income is effectively connected with a U.S. trade or business.[96] This transparency approach does not apply to characterize the U.S. source income of U.S. trades or businesses of foreign taxpayers. Thus, U.S. source effectively connected income of foreign taxpayers and U.S. source income of U.S. taxpayers will be treated the same.

A substitute payment received by a foreign person that is treated as U.S. source income that is not effectively connected with a U.S. trade or business is characterized as a U.S. source interest or dividend payment for the withholding tax under Sections 871(a) and 881 of the Code[97] and tax treaty purposes.[98]

---

[93] *See* IRC Sec. 861(a)(2).

[94] *See* IRC Sec. 861(a)(1).

[95] *See* Treas. Reg. §1.864-5(b)(2)(ii), 1.871-7(b)(2), 1.881-2(b)(2), 1.894-1(c).

[96] *See* Treas. Reg. §1.864-5(b)(2)(iii).

[97] *See* Treas. Reg. §1.871-7(b)(2) and 1.881-2(b)(2).

[98] *See* Treas. Reg. §1.894-1. The Preamble to the Substitute Payment Regulations notes that the IRS and Treasury believed that, in the absence of a transparency rule, may taxpayers would use securities lending transactions in order to avoid tax under tax treaties or under the Code. A transparency approach provides uniform results for economically similar investments. Nonetheless, it has been suggested that many treaties do not contain clear references to U.S. tax law definitions. In those cases, substitute dividend payments, for example, might not be covered by the dividend article of a particular treaty; substitute payments might then be exempt from U.S. withholding tax under a "business profits" or "other income" article of such treaty. *See* L.Z. Swartz, "ABCs of Cross Border Derivatives," 2 *Journal of Taxation of Financial Products* (Spring 2001).

Substitute payments on portfolio debt[99] are characterized as portfolio interest if appropriate documentation is provided[100] and no exception from portfolio debt treatment applies. For example, the Preamble to the Substitute Payment Regulations notes that if a bank lends securities in a transaction that the facts and circumstances indicate is in substance an extension of credit under a loan agreement in the ordinary course of the bank's trade or business, the substitute payments may be characterized as interest that does not qualify as portfolio interest under Section 881(c)(3)(A).

The characterization rules apply to payments received by a foreign person from either U.S. persons or foreign persons. Thus, a U.S. source substitute dividend payment received by a foreign person is characterized as a dividend payment subject to withholding tax, regardless of whether the payment is made by a U.S. person or a foreign person.

One significant issue not addressed in the Substitute Payment Regulations is the potential for excessive withholding at source on multiple back-to-back securities lending and sale-repurchase transactions. This is covered in Notice 97-66.[101] Under the Notice, the U.S. withholding tax to be imposed with respect to a foreign-to-foreign payment equals the underlying dividend multiplied by a rate equal to the excess of (1) the U.S. withholding tax rate that would apply to U.S. source dividends paid by a U.S. person directly to the recipient of the substitute payment over (2) the U.S. withholding tax rate that would apply to U.S. source dividends paid by a U.S. person directly to the payor of the substitute payment. This amount may be reduced or eliminated to the extent that the total U.S. tax actually withheld on the underlying dividend and previous substitute payments is greater than the U.S. withholding that would have been imposed on U.S. dividends paid by a U.S. person directly to the payor of the substitute payment. However, to the extent that a foreign-to-foreign securities loan or sale-repurchase transaction would reduce the overall U.S. withholding tax, an incremental amount of U.S. withholding tax is imposed on the substitute payment. The recipient of a substitute payment may not disregard the form of its transaction to reduce the U.S. withholding tax. Thus, a foreign-to-foreign payment is not entitled to a refund or tax credit against any other U.S. tax liability.[102]

---

[99] IRC §871(h); §881(h).

[100] *See* Treas. Reg. Sec. §1.871-14(c).

[101] 1997-2 C.B. 328.

[102] *See* R. Shapiro and R. Lorence, "New Regs. On Securities Lending, Withholding on Payments to Foreign Persons: Will One Year's Preparation Be Enough," 9 *Journal of International Taxation* 14 (February 1998).

Borrow Fees

Neither the Proposed Section 1058 nor Substitute Payment Regulations address the source and characterization of fees paid to a lender of securities. This has led to many U.S. borrowers treating the fees paid to lenders as neither dividends nor interest but as some unspecified type of FDAP income (for example, rent),[103] subject to 30% U.S. withholding tax unless an exception from withholding applies. Many foreign lenders claim exemption from, or reduction of, the U. S. withholding tax on such fees based on "business profits," "industrial or commercial profits," or "other income" provisions of the U.S. income tax treaty with the jurisdiction where the lender resides.[104] On the income side, the receipt of loan fees would be ordinary taxable income, not taxable to an exempt organization.

In one private letter ruling, the Service has held that borrow fees paid to a securities lender constituted income derived from the active conduct of an insurance business and therefore "industrial and commercial profits" under the terms of the applicable treaty. This may indicate that the Service might, in the absence of a tax treaty, view borrow fees as constituting U.S source FDAP income that is otherwise subject to withholding. It also suggests that borrow fees are not properly treated as interest.[105]

Income on Collateral

Rebates are generally treated as interest for tax purposes since the fees compensate the borrower for the lender's use of the borrower's cash collateral during the securities loan period. Interest is generally sourced to the U.S. if it is paid on interest bearing obligations of U.S. noncorporate residents or domestic U.S. corporations.[106] If the securities lending arrangement is treated as an interest bearing obligation, rebates might be viewed as U.S. source interest income to a foreign borrower. Under that theory, exemption from the 30% withholding tax would likely be available under an applicable

---

[103] *See* J. Hardin, "Cross-Border Securities Lending and the Withholding Tax: The Ambiguity Continues," *Tax Notes Today* (June 12, 2000) *available in* Lexis at 2000 TNT, 113-84, Fedtax, TNT.

[104] It is important to note that the purpose of borrow fees is quite different from the purpose of substitute payments. 92 *Tax Analyst, Tax Notes Today* (April 23, 1992). Where substitute payments merely reimburse the lender for the income lost due to the lending arrangement, borrow fees are compensatory, a fee for permitting the borrower to use the lender's property. Additionally, the borrow fees do not bear the causal relationship to the underlying security as does the substitute payment. As such, characterizing borrow fees as ordinary compensatory income does not raise the same concerns caused by the characterization of substitute payments as compensatory. *See also* M. Feder, *supra*; L.Z. Swartz, *supra*.

[105] PLR 8822061, *see* M. Feder, *supra*.

[106] IRC §861.

treaty or the portfolio interest rules.[107] Alternatively, a rebate might be treated as a fee and, thus, taxed as some type of FDAP income, subject to 30% U.S. withholding tax unless a treaty exemption applies.

CFC Income

The objective of Subpart F[108] of the Code is to minimize the tax-deferral benefits enjoyed by the shareholders of controlled foreign corporations ("CFCs")[109] on foreign sourced income that is not repatriated to the United States. This provision taxes U.S. shareholders on certain income, generally passive in nature, earned by the foreign corporation.[110] Currently, Subpart F income includes all income with respect to debt securities subject to Section 1058 of the Code, as well as payments in lieu of dividends from equity securities lending transactions pursuant to Section 1058.[111]

Repurchase Agreements

The Substitute Payment Regulations apply to certain "sale-repurchase" transactions. For purposes of the Substitute Payment Regulations, a sale-repurchase transaction is described as "an agreement under which a person transfers a security in exchange for cash and simultaneously agrees to receive substantially identical securities from the transferee in the future in exchange for cash."[112] The regulations do not apply to sale-repurchase transactions that are secured loans, where the transferee holds the security as collateral for the loan and must deliver identical securities back to the transferor when the loan is repaid.[113]

---

[107] IRC §871; §881. *See* "Withholding at Source," *supra*.

[108] Subpart F (IRC §951-§964 of the Code) is the mechanism by which the U.S. government taxes income earned by foreign corporations which is attributable to investments made by "U.S. shareholders." For purposes of Subpart F, a U.S. shareholder is defined as a U.S. person who owns 10% or more of the total combined voting power of all classes of voting stock of the foreign corporation. IRC §951(b).

[109] Defined in Section 957 of the Code, a CFC is a foreign corporation in which U.S. shareholders own more than 50% of the total combined voting power and value of all classes of stock. IRC §957(a).

[110] A CFC is subject to U.S. taxation on income which is effectively connected to the conduct of a U.S. trade or business. IRC §882. Additionally, a CFC is subject to tax on its FDAP income. IRC §881. Thus, a CFC with no income producing connections with the U.S. will not be subject to U.S. taxation. The U.S. shareholders of a CFC, on the other hand, are taxed on the shareholders' share of the CFC's Subpart F income. IRC §951.

[111] *See* Treas. Reg. §1.954-2(h)(2)(i)(H) and §954(c)(i)(G).

[112] Treas. Reg. §1.861-2(a)(7); 1.861-3(a)(6).

[113] A. Kramer, *Financial Products: Taxation, Regulation and Design, Third Edition*, Sec. 41.08 (2004).

The Substitute Payment Regulations clarify that substitute payments made in a sale-repurchase transaction are sourced and characterized in the same manner that substitute payments are sourced and characterized in securities lending transactions.[114]

---

[114] Preamble to TD 8735, *supra.*

CHAPTER 12

Accounting Treatment of Loans of Securities

Susan C. Peters
Chief Executive Officer
eSecLending

The purpose of this chapter is to provide guidance regarding the recording and financial treatment of loaned securities.

The primary accounting literature on securities lending is Statement of Financial Accounting Standard 140 (SFAS 140). The basic concept in determining the accounting treatment for the securities lending transaction is control. If the lender in effect retains control of the securities lent, the lender treats the transaction as a financing and keeps the securities lent on the books notwithstanding that title to the loaned securities passes to the borrower. Control also includes "effective" control (SFAS 140 paragraph 9c), which, for example, would include an arrangement where the lender could recall the lent security from the borrower on short notice. The majority of securities lending agreements today contain provisions whereby the lender retains "effective control" of the security. If in reviewing the terms of the securities lending arrangement it is determined that the lender does give up effective control of the security, then the transaction should be recorded as a sale.

A lender would be viewed for accounting purposes as having ceded control of the asset to a borrower, within the meaning of paragraph 9c, only under circumstances where (1) the transferred asset is no longer available to the transferor's creditors, (2) the borrower receives the asset free and clear of the rights of others, *and* (3) the lender does not retain recall or buy-in rights. Most lending contracts provide for a right of recall such that the lender may recall the asset at any time from the borrower. Moreover, in the event that the borrower fails to return the asset, the lender has the right to seize the collateral, liquidate it if necessary, and apply the proceeds towards the purchase of replacement securities. Therefore, notwithstanding that the lender actually transfers the security from its account to the borrower's account, the lender may continue to treat the transferred security as an asset provided that the contract allows for recall and a possible buy-in of the loaned security if it is not returned.

While the security lent is not removed from the accounting records, the security is moved by the custodian from the lender's account to an account designated by the borrower. Thus, the securities on loan is a reconciling item between the custodial records and the accounting records. Typically, the custodian notes that the security is on loan on its books and records while maintaining it on the lender's balance sheet as an asset.

RECORDING THE RECEIPT AND INVESTMENT OF COLLATERAL

As with the recording of the securities lending transaction, the concept of effective control also applies to the accounting treatment of collateral.

Cash Collateral

Receipt of Cash Collateral

Cash collateral is the most common form of collateral in the United States. If the lender receives cash as collateral, the lender clearly has control over the collateral. SFAS 140 requires that cash collateral is removed from the balance sheet of the payer and is recognized as an asset by the recipient. It should not be recorded as collateral; rather, it should be noted as either proceeds of sale or a borrowing. When the lender has control over the collateral SFAS 140 (paragraph 15) requires the collateral to be recorded on the lender's balance sheet. If the lender reinvests the collateral, the security purchased is included in investments, with a liability for the amount of cash collateral received reflecting the obligation to return the collateral to the borrower upon termination of the loan.

Investment of Cash Collateral

When the lender receives cash as collateral, the lender reinvests the collateral, typically in some form of short-term money market instruments or a money market fund collective investment vehicle. If the lender is subject to investment restrictions, the security purchased with the cash collateral

must comply with those investment restrictions. When the loan is negotiated, the lender and borrower typically agree upon a rebate payable to
the borrower that is intended to cover the borrower's cost of funds. In a
traditional lending program, higher rebates are payable for less desirable
securities. Put another way, the more desirable the securities are to the
borrower, the lower the rebate. The lender then rebates a portion of the
income earned on the reinvestment back to the borrower. The amount of
the rebate is usually negotiated in advance at a specified percentage of the
amount of the collateral. Factors that may be considered in determining
the amount of the rebate include: demand for the security, availability of
the security, and unusual corporate action activities.

In an auction style of lending,[1] where cash is the form of collateral,
the lender receives two sources of revenue: an agreed fee, expressed
either as a fixed amount or in basis points calculated with respect to the
portfolio to which the borrower has exclusive access, and the proceeds
from the investment of the cash collateral. The rebate to the borrower is
fixed at an agreed amount, negotiated during the auction process.

The revenue derived from loan-by-loan securities lending, where
cash is the form of collateral, is diagrammed in Exhibit 12.1. Portfolio
auction revenue is diagrammed in Exhibit 12.2. The lender also assumes
the risk associated with the investment of cash collateral (i.e., the lender
earns a lower amount of income from the reinvestment than the rebate
he has to pay to the borrower, or, the cash, once invested, declines in
value due to a shift in interest rates, or a principal loss).

EXHIBIT 12.1   Cash Collateral Reinvestment

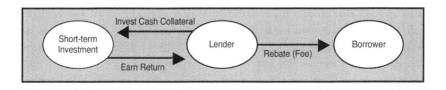

EXHIBIT 12.2   Cash Collateral Reinvestment in an Auction Environment

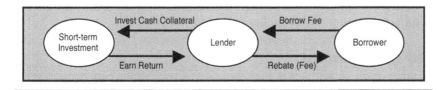

---

[1] The auction style of lending is discussed in Chapter 5.

Securities as Collateral

Receipt of Securities as Collateral

Loan transactions, in which a lender receives securities as collateral, are generally treated as off-balance-sheet transactions. Securities used for collateral are usually limited to U.S. Government securities, high-grade corporate debt, or sovereign debt, but may also include equities or other securities. In a typical loan, whether derived through a loan-by-loan agency model or through an auction process, the securities held as collateral are not placed on the balance sheet of the lender because the holder of that collateral does not have the right to further encumber that security or sell or pledge it. The one exception to off-balance sheet treatment would be if the holder had the ability to pledge or sell the security in the absence of a default by the borrower. In this case, the holder of the collateral would be deemed to have effective control over the collateral and would be required to record the collateral on the balance sheet.

Fees for Securities Collateral

If the lender did not have effective control of the securities collateral, the lender is not able to earn a return. Thus, instead of the lender paying a rebate to the borrower, the borrower will be required to pay the lender a fee.

Mark to Market

The securities lending agreement will specify the percentage that the market value of the collateral must be relative to the market value of the security on loan (collateral/security on loan). The percentage typically varies depending on the type, volatility, and availability of the security. Both the securities on loan and the collateral (i.e., if noncash) are marked to market each day to ensure that the collateral still complies with the percentage called for in the agreement. If, for example, there has been an increase in the market value of the security on loan (or decrease in the value of the noncash collateral), additional collateral will be delivered (typically on a one day lag basis) to the lender.

For registered investment companies, the Securities and Exchange Commission (SEC) requires that the collateral is no less than 100% (with industry standard ranging from 102% to 105%).

Other Types of Collateral

Another type of collateral may be a letter of credit. Since the lender would not be deemed to have control of an asset, the letter of credit would be treated as an off-balance sheet item.

CORPORATE ACTIONS

With a securities lending transaction, legal title of the security passes from the lender to the borrower. Most securities lending agreements specify that the lender retains the right to all dividends, interest, and other corporate actions (e.g., stock splits) on the loaned security (i.e., as if the lender still retained possession of the security). The borrower will receive the distributions and is required to make an "in lieu" payment to the lender (or in the case of a stock split, return the post split number of shares). Provisions should also be made for situations where the issuer has a voluntary corporate action (e.g., a tender offer) and a decision needs to be made on the course of action desired by the lender.

Proxies

Since legal title has passed from the lender to the borrower, the lender gives up the right to vote on any proxies. The SEC has issued a series of guidelines related to securities lending and *Guideline #6* requires the registered investment company to be entitled to exercise voting rights over the loaned securities if there is a material event. Thus, registered investment companies must have the ability to recall any security on loan to vote on a material event proxy.

Tax Considerations

While the lender is entitled to an equivalent of all dividends and interest on the security, the payments received may change the tax characteristics of the payment. This is because the payments received are generally considered payments "in lieu" of the dividends and interest. For example, if a tax-exempt bond is lent out, the payment received from the borrower may not retain its tax-exempt character. Similarly, a payment in-lieu of dividends may not qualify for the dividends received deduction.

SUMMARY FINANCIAL REPORTING OF SECURITIES LENDING BY INVESTMENT COMPANIES

Investment companies are required to follow the guidance contained in SFAS 140, the *AICPA Audit and Accounting Guide—Audits of Investment Companies* (hereafter, AICPA Audit Guide) and SEC Regulation S-X (registered investment companies only). Following is a summary of the appropriate financial reporting for investment companies.

Schedule of Investments

Securities lent should be included in the schedule of investments. Investment companies may either present a full listing of portfolio securities or a condensed schedule. For registered investment companies, industry practice has been to disclose the securities that are on loan by including a footnote indicating that the security (or portion thereof) is on loan. The footnote typically states "All or a portion of this security is on loan."

Balance Sheet

Investments

SFAS 140 (paragraph 15(a)) requires the following "reclassify that asset and report that asset in its statement of financial position separately (for example, as security pledged to creditors) from other assets not so encumbered." It would be difficult for an investment company to report securities on loan as a separate balance sheet line item; this is because investment companies include a schedule of investments that is required to agree with the balance sheet. Thus, in order to comply with this requirement investment companies would be required to report two separate schedules of investments, which would not be meaningful disclosure. Investment companies disclose the value of securities on loan parenthetically on the investments line item adopted (see Paragraph 7.78 of the AICPA Audit Guide). This combined with the footnoting of the securities on loan on the Schedule of Investments is deemed to meet the SFAS 140 requirements.

Collateral Received

If the investment company receives cash collateral, the reinvestment of the collateral should be included in the investments balance sheet line item. If noncash collateral is received (and the investment company does not have the right to sell or pledge) then the collateral is not recorded on the balance sheet, unless the recipient takes title to the asset and has effective control over the asset.

Collateral Liability

If the collateral is recorded as an asset on the balance sheet, there will be a corresponding liability for the amount that is required to be returned to the borrower. SEC Regulation S-X Article 6-04.11 requires the line item to be called "Deposits for securities loaned." Article 6-04.11 also requires the registered investment company to "indicate the nature of the collateral received as security for the loan, including the amount of any cash received."

Statement of Operations

Securities Lending Income

Lenders may earn income in several ways. The more typical arrangements include:

1. If collateral is securities, the lender receives a fee.
2. If collateral is cash, the lender invests the collateral and pays a rebate to the borrower.
3. The lender receives a fixed payment (usually spread equally over the period of the contract).

In all three cases, investment companies report the net amount received as "Securities Lending Income." If not material, securities lending income can be classified with "Other Income." Some investment companies include securities lending income in investment income, with parenthetical disclosure of the amount of securities lending income.

A securities lending arrangement may be structured such that the income from securities lending arrangements is used to offset the custody charges. SEC Regulation S-X 6-07(g) does not permit this netting for financial reporting purposes.

Footnotes

There should be an accounting policy footnote that describes the practice of securities lending (for example, the accounting, income recognition, counterparty risk and collateral requirements). Also, there should be disclosure of the gross dollar amount of securities on loan and the market value of the collateral. Regulation S-X Article 6-04.11 also requires the registered investment company to "indicate the nature of the collateral received as security for the loan, including the amount of any cash received".

SFAS 140 Paragraph 17 requires the following footnote disclosure related to collateral:

- Policy for requiring collateral or other security
- If the entity has pledged any of its assets as collateral that are not reclassified and separately reported in the statement of financial position pursuant to paragraph 15(a), the carrying amount and classification of those assets as of the date of the latest statement of financial position presented
- If the entity has accepted collateral that it is permitted by contract or custom to sell or repledge, the fair value as of the date of each statement of financial position presented of that collateral and of the por-

tion of that collateral that it has sold or repledged, and information about the sources and uses of that collateral

Other Items of Interest to Mutual Funds

The securities lending activities should be described in the mutual fund's prospectus and are limited by the SEC's guidelines. There is no statutory prohibition against the lending of a mutual fund's portfolio securities. If a mutual fund engages in securities lending activities, it should comply with certain SEC guidelines which dictate that general principles of fiduciary responsibility are followed with respect to the management and control of a mutual fund's assets.

DIFFERENCES RELATED TO GOVERNMENTAL ENTITIES

Governmental entities are required to follow the guidance from the Governmental Accounting Standards Board (GASB). In 1995, GASB issued this guidance in *Governmental Accounting Statement No. 28 Accounting and Financial Reporting for Securities Lending Transactions* (GAS 28).

The majority of the accounting and reporting requirements of SFAS 140 are consistent with GAS 28. However, GAS 28 does contain several differences and additional disclosures. Following is a summary of the more significant differences.

Accounting Differences

Expenses

GAS 28 (paragraph 8) requires that securities lending expenses (e.g., rebates and agent fees) should be reported as an expense. Investment companies typically net expenses with interest revenue (see AICPA Audit Guide paragraph 7.83).

Pooling of Investments

GAS 28 (paragraph 9) provides that if a governmental entity pools its investments the entity should report its pro rata share of the securities lending transaction related accounting entries (balance sheet and income statement). Investment companies typically do not pool their investments with other funds in this manner.

Disclosure Differences

GAS 28 contains the following additional footnote disclosures:

- The source of legal or contractual authorization for the use of securities lending transactions and any significant violations of those provisions that occurred during the period.

- Governmental entities also should disclose in the notes to the financial statements a general description of their securities lending transactions during the period, including the types of securities lent, the types of collateral received, whether the government has the ability to pledge or sell collateral securities without a borrower default, the amount by which the value of the collateral provided is required to exceed the value of the underlying securities, any restrictions on the amount of the loans that can be made, and any loss indemnification provided to the entity by its securities lending agents. The entity also should disclose the carrying amount and fair market values of underlying securities at the balance sheet date.

- Governmental entities should disclose whether the maturities of the investments made with cash collateral generally match the maturities of their securities loans, as well as the extent of such matching at the balance sheet date.

- The amount of credit risk, if any, related to the securities lending transactions at the balance sheet date should be disclosed. Credit risk is calculated as the aggregate of the lender's exposures to individual borrowers or on individual loans, depending on whether individual loans to the same borrower can be aggregated for purposes of offset in the event of default. A lender has exposure if the amount a borrower owes the lender exceeds the amount the lender owes the borrower. If the governmental lender has no credit risk, that fact should be stated, and disclosure of the net amounts owed to the borrowers is not required.

- Governmental entities should disclose the amount of any losses on their securities lending transactions during the period resulting from the default of a borrower or lending agent and amounts recovered from prior-period losses, if not separately displayed in the operating statement.

- Disclosures required by Statement 3 should be made for securities lending collateral that is reported in the balance sheet and for the underlying securities. Therefore, the carrying amounts and fair market value of these investments should be disclosed by type of investment, as required by paragraph 68 of Statement 3.

  a. Collateral that is reported in the balance sheet should be classified by category of custodial credit risk as defined in paragraph 68 of Statement 3, unless it has been invested in a securities lending collateral investment pool or another type of investment that is not classified, as provided in paragraph 69 of that Statement.

  b. Underlying securities should not be classified by category of custodial credit risk if the collateral for those loans is reported in the balance sheet.

c. Underlying securities should be classified by category of custodial credit risk if the collateral for those loans is not reported in the balance sheet. The categories in which the underlying securities are classified should be based on the type of collateral and the custodial arrangements for the collateral securities.

DIFFERENCES RELATED TO NONGOVERNMENTAL ENTITIES

Nongovernmental entities are not required to follow the accounting and disclosure requirements of the AICPA, SEC and GASB discussed above. Only the accounting and disclosure requirements of SFAS 140 discussed above apply to nongovernmental entities.

The one disclosure difference compared to mutual funds is that industry practice for mutual funds is to disclose the value of securities on loan parenthetically; nongovernmental entities will more likely follow the SFAS 140 requirement to show the amount of securities on loan as a separate balance sheet line item.

SUMMARY OF SECURITIES LENDING ACCOUNTING TREATMENT

SFAS 140 is the primary accounting literature for non-governmental entities. Investment companies are also required to follow the AICPA Audit guide. Governmental entities are required to follow GASB 28. The securities lending accounting and reporting treatment contained in SFAS 140 and GASB 28 are in substance very similar (except as noted in Exhibit 12.3). Exhibit 12.3 summarizes the accounting treatment for governmental and nongovernmental entities.

ACCOUNTING GUIDANCE

Under the hierarchy of GAAP, statements of the Financial Accounting Standards Board (FASB) are the highest. Following FASB is the AICPA, including the AICPA Audit and Accounting Guides. Entities that are registered with the Securities and Exchange Commission (SEC) or are governmental entities also have to comply with the regulations of the SEC or the Governmental Accounting Standards Board (GASB), respectively. Industry whitepapers are considered the lowest level and generally are not considered authoritative literature. Exhibit 12.4 provides a summary of the key securities lending accounting literature available today.

EXHIBIT 12.3 Accounting Treatment Differences between Governmental and Nongovernmental Entities

Item	Nongovernmental Entities Accounting Treatment	Governmental Entities Accounting Treatment
Balance Sheet		
Loaned securities	Report as asset. Separate line item disclosure is required on the balance sheet (registered investment companies disclose parenthetically on the investments line item). Also, for registered investment companies that present a schedule of investments, asterisk those securities that are on loan.	Report as asset.
Cash collateral	Report as asset. Report reinvestment of cash in the investments line item. Report obligation to return collateral to the borrower as a liability. Industry practice for registered investment companies is to footnote in the Schedule of Investments the securities that were purchased with the cash collateral.	Report as asset. Report reinvestment of cash in the investments line item. Report obligation to return collateral to the borrower as a liability.
Securities collateral	Do not report as asset, unless the lender has the right to sell or repledge the securities. If lender does have the right to sell or repledge the securities, then report as assets. Disclose securities collateral not reported as assets in footnotes.	Do not report as asset, unless the lender has the right to sell or repledge the securities. If lender does have the right to sell or repledge the securities, then report as assets. Disclose loaned securities collateralized by securities not reported as assets in custodial risk statement.

215

EXHIBIT 12.3 (Continued)

Item	Nongovernmental Entities Accounting Treatment	Governmental Entities Accounting Treatment
Balance Sheet		
Tri-party collateral	Do not report as asset. Disclose securities collateral held in connection with tri-party arrangements in footnotes.	Do not report as asset. Disclose loaned securities collateralized by assets held in connection with tri-party arrangements in custodial risk statement.
Letters of credit	Do not report as asset. Disclose letters of credit in footnotes.	Do not report as asset. Disclose loaned securities collateralized by letters of credit in custodial risk statement.
Income Statement		
Income from investment of cash collateral	Report as income.	Report as income.
Rebate Fees paid by the lender to the borrower (i.e., Cash Collateral)	Net the rebate fees against income.	Report as expense.
Fees paid by the borrower to the lender (i.e., securities collateral)	Report as income.	Report as income.
Fees Paid by the lender to an agent	Net the agent fees against income.	Report as expense.

EXHIBIT 12.4   Summary of the Key Securities Lending Accounting Literature Available Today

---

FASB

SFAS 140: Accounting for Transfers and Servicing of Financial Assets and Extinguishments of Liabilities, a replacement of FASB Statement 125 (September 2000)

AICPA

AICPA—Audit and Accounting Guide—Audits of Investment Companies (May 2003)

SEC

Article 6 of Regulation S-X provides guidance on the form and content of financial statements of registered investment companies. Regulation S-X 6-04.11 provides some guidance relative to securities lending.

The SEC has issued nine guidelines related to registered investment companies involvement with lending securities.

SEC Division of Investment Management Dear CFO Letter (November 7, 1997).

GASB

Statement No. 28 of the Governmental Accounting Standards Board—Accounting and Financial Reporting for Securities Lending Transactions (May 1995). *Note:* GAS 28 has been updated by GAS 31 and 34.

Investment Company Institute (ICI)

ICI White Paper—Securities Lending for Mutual Funds (October 1998). *Note:* This white paper was issued after SFAS 125, but before SFAS 140 (and has not been updated).

Bond Financing via the Repo Market

CHAPTER 13

Repurchase and Reverse Repurchase Agreements

Frank J. Fabozzi, Ph.D., CFA
Frederick Frank Adjunct Professor of Finance
School of Management
Yale University

Steven V. Mann, Ph.D.
Professor of Finance
Moore School of Management
University of South Carolina

One of the largest segments of the money markets worldwide is the market in repurchase agreements or repos. A most efficient mechanism by which to finance bond positions, repo transactions enable market makers to take long and short positions in a flexible manner, buying and selling according to customer demand on a relatively small capital base. In addition, repos are used extensively to facilitate hedging and speculation. Repo is also a flexible and relatively safe investment opportunity for short-term investors. The ability to execute repo is particularly important to firms in less-developed countries that might not have access to a deposit base. Moreover, in countries where no repo market exists, funding is in the form of unsecured lines of credit from the banking system that is restrictive for some market participants. A liquid repo market is often cited as a key ingredient of a liquid bond market. In the United States, repo is a well-established money market instrument and is developing in a similar way in Europe and Asia.

A repurchase agreement or "repo" is the sale of a security with a commitment by the seller to buy the same security back from the purchaser at a specified price at a designated future date. For example, a dealer who owns a 10-year U.S. Treasury note might agree to sell this security (the "seller") to a mutual fund (the "buyer") for cash today while simultaneously agreeing to buy the same 10-year note back at a certain date in the future (or in some cases on demand) for a predetermined price. The price at which the seller must subsequently repurchase the security is called the *repurchase price* and the date that the security must be repurchased is called the *repurchase date*. Simply put, a repurchase agreement is a collateralized loan where the collateral is the security that is sold and subsequently repurchased. One party (the "seller") is borrowing money and providing collateral for the loan; the other party (the "buyer") is lending money and accepting a security as collateral for the loan. To the borrower, the advantage of a repurchase agreement is that the short-term borrowing rate is lower than the cost of bank financing, as we will see shortly. To the lender, the repo market offers an attractive yield on a short-term secured transaction that is highly liquid. This latter aspect is the focus of this chapter.

THE BASICS

Suppose that on October 22, 2003 a government securities dealer purchases a 4.25% coupon on-the-run 10-year note that matures on August 15, 2013. The face amount of the position is $1 million and the note's full price (i.e., flat price plus accrued interest) is $1,007,384.51. Furthermore, suppose the dealer wants to hold the position until the end of the next business day which is Thursday, October 23, 2003. Where does the dealer obtain the funds to finance this position?

Of course, the dealer can finance the position with its own funds or by borrowing from a bank. Typically, though, the dealer uses a repo to obtain financing. In the repo market, the dealer can use the purchased Treasury note as collateral for a loan. The term of the loan and the interest rate a dealer agrees to pay are specified. The interest rate is called the *repo rate*. When the term of a repo is one day, it is called an *overnight repo*. Conversely, a loan for more than one day is called a *term repo*. The transaction is referred to as a repurchase agreement because it calls for the security's sale and its repurchase at a future date. Both the sale price and the purchase price are specified in the agreement. The difference between the purchase (repurchase) price and the sale price is the loan's dollar interest cost.

Let us return now to the dealer who needs to finance the Treasury note that it purchased and plans to hold overnight. We illustrate this transaction using Bloomberg's Repo/Reverse Repo Analysis (RRRA) that appears in Exhibit 13.1. The settlement date is the day that the collateral must be delivered and the money lent to initiate the transaction. Likewise, the termination date of the repo agreement is October 23, 2003 and appears in the lower left-hand side of the screen. At this point we need to ask, who is the dealer's counterparty (i.e., the lender of funds). Suppose that one of the dealer's customers has excess funds in the amount of $1,007,384.51 labeled "SETTLEMENT MONEY" in Exhibit 13.1 and is the amount of money loaned in the repo agreement.[1] Thus, on October 22, 2003, the dealer would agree to deliver ("sell") $1,007,384.51 worth of 10-year U.S. Treasury notes to the customer and buy the same 10-year notes back for an amount determined by the repo rate the next business day on October 23, 2003.[2]

EXHIBIT 13.1   Bloomberg Repo/Reverse Repo Analysis Screen

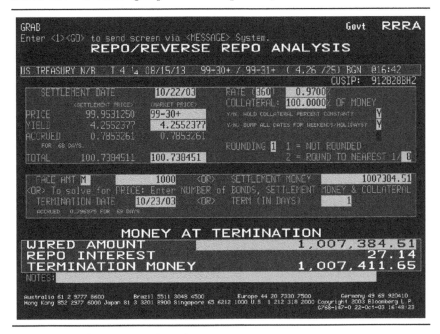

Source: Bloomberg Financial Markets

---

[1] For example, the customer might be a municipality with tax receipts that it has just collected and no immediate need to disburse the funds.

[2] We assume in this illustration that the borrower provides collateral that is equal in value to the money that is loaned. In practice, lenders usually require borrowers to provide collateral in excess of the value of money that is loaned. We illustrate how this is accomplished when we discuss repo margins in this chapter.

Suppose the repo rate in this transaction is 0.97%, which is shown in the upper right-hand corner of the screen. Then, as will be explained, the dealer would agree to deliver the 10-year Treasury notes for $1,007,411.65 the next day. The $27.14 difference between the "sale" price of $1,007,384.51 and the repurchase price of $1,007,411.65 is the dollar interest on the financing.

Repo Interest

The following formula is used to calculate the dollar interest on a repo transaction:

Dollar interest = (Dollar principal) × (Repo rate) × (Repo term/360)

In our illustration, using a repo rate of 0.97% and a repo term of one day, the dollar interest is $27.11 as shown below:

$$\$1,007,384.51 \times 0.0097 \times (1/360) = \$27.14$$

This calculation agrees with repo interest as calculated in the lower right-hand corner in Exhibit 13.1.

The advantage to the dealer of using the repo market for borrowing on a short-term basis is that the rate is lower than the cost of bank financing for reasons explained shortly. From the customer's perspective (i.e., the lender), the repo market offers an attractive yield on a short-term secured transaction that is highly liquid.

Reverse Repo and Market Jargon

In the illustration presented above, the dealer is using the repo market to obtain financing for a long position. The repo market can correspondingly be used to borrow securities. Securities are routinely borrowed for a number of reasons including opening a short position, the need to deliver securities against the exercise of a derivative contract, and the need to cover a failed transaction in the securities settlement system.[3] Many arbitrage strategies involve the borrowing of securities (e.g., convertible bond arbitrage).

Suppose a government dealer established a short position in the 30-year Treasury bond one week ago and must now cover the position—namely, deliver the securities. The dealer accomplishes this task by engaging in a reverse repo. In a reverse repo, the dealer agrees to buy securities at a specified price with a commitment to sell them back at a later date for

---

[3] Technical Committee of The International Organizations of Securities Commissions, "Securities Lending Transactions: Market Development and Implications," July 1999.

another specified price.[4] In this case, the dealer is making a collateralized loan to its customer. The customer is lending securities and borrowing funds obtained from the collateralized loan to create leverage.

There is a great deal of Wall Street jargon surrounding repo transactions. In order to decipher the terminology, remember that one party is lending money and accepting a security as collateral for the loan; the other party is borrowing money and providing collateral to borrow the money. By convention, whether the transaction is called a repo or a reverse repo is determined by viewing the transaction from the *dealer's* perspective. If the dealer is borrowing money from a customer and providing securities as collateral, the transaction is called a repo. If the dealer is borrowing securities (which serve as collateral) and lends money to a customer, the transaction is called a reverse repo.

When someone lends securities in order to receive cash (i.e., borrow money), that party is said to be "reversing out" securities. Correspondingly, a party that lends money with the security as collateral for the loan is said to be "reversing in" securities.

The expressions "to repo securities" and "to do repo" are also commonly used. The former means that someone is going to finance securities using the securities as collateral; the latter means that the party is going to invest in a repo as a money market instrument.

Lastly, the expressions "selling collateral" and "buying collateral" are used to describe a party financing a security with a repo on the one hand, and lending on the basis of collateral on the other.

Types of Collateral

While in our illustration, we use a Treasury security as collateral, the collateral in a repo is not limited to government securities. Money market instruments, federal agency securities, and mortgage-backed securities are also used. In some specialized markets, even whole loans are used as collateral.

Upon occasion, the lender of securities in a repo may need the securities for another delivery. To insure this flexibility, the lender of securities may reserve the right to substitute collateral when the repo is negotiated. If permitted to do so, the lender of securities delivers other securities of equal market value in exchange for the original collateral.

Documentation

Most repo market participants in the United States use the Master Repurchase Agreement published by Bond Market Association. In

---

[4] Of course, the dealer eventually would have to buy the 30-year bonds in the market in order to cover its short position.

Europe, the Global Master Repurchase Agreement, published by the Bond Market Association (formerly, the Public Securities Association) and the International Securities Market Association, has become widely accepted. The full agreement may be downloaded from www.isma.org.

CREDIT RISKS

Just as in any borrowing/lending agreement, both parties in a repo transaction are exposed to credit risk. This is true even though there may be high-quality collateral underlying the repo transaction. Consider our initial example in Exhibit 13.1 where the dealer uses U.S. Treasuries as collateral to borrow funds. Let us examine under which circumstances each counterparty is exposed to credit risk.

Suppose the dealer (i.e., the borrower) defaults such that the Treasuries are not repurchased on the repurchase date. The investor gains control over the collateral and retains any income owed to the borrower. The risk is that Treasury yields have risen subsequent to the repo transaction such that the market value of collateral is worth less than the unpaid repurchase price. Conversely, suppose the investor (i.e., the lender) defaults such that the investor fails to deliver the Treasuries on the repurchase date. The risk is that Treasury yields have fallen over the agreement's life such that the dealer now holds an amount of dollars worth less then the market value of collateral. In this instance, the investor is liable for any excess of the price paid by the dealer for replacement securities over the repurchase price.

Repo Margin
While both parties are exposed to credit risk in a repo transaction, the lender of funds is usually in the more vulnerable position. Accordingly, the repo is structured to reduce the lender's credit risk. Specifically, the amount lent should be less than the market value of the security used as collateral, thereby providing the lender some cushion should the collateral's market value decline. The amount by which the market value of the security used as collateral exceeds the value of the loan is called *repo margin* or "haircut." Repo margins vary from transaction to transaction and are negotiated between the counterparties based on factors such as the following: term of the repo agreement, quality of the collateral, creditworthiness of the counterparties, and the availability of the collateral. Minimum repo margins are set differently across firms and are based on models and/or guidelines created by their credit departments. Repo margin is generally between 1% and 3%. For borrowers of lower credit worthiness and/or when less liquid securities are used as collateral, the repo margin can be 10% or more.

   To illustrate the role of the haircut in a repurchase agreement, let us once again return to the government securities dealer that purchases a 4.25% coupon, 10-year Treasury note and needs financing overnight. The face amount of the position is $1 million and the note's full price is $1,007,540.76. As before, we will use Bloomberg's RRRA screen to illustrate the transaction in Exhibit 13.2.

   When a haircut is included, the amount the customer is willing to lend is reduced by a given percentage of the security's market value. In this case, the collateral is 102% of the amount being lent. This percentage appears in the box labeled "COLLATERAL" in the upper right-hand corner of the screen. Accordingly, to determine the amount being lent, we divide the notes' full price of $1,007,540.76 by 1.02 to obtain $987,785.06 which is labeled "SETTLEMENT MONEY" located on the right-hand side of the screen. Suppose the repo rate in this transaction is 0.97%. Then, the dealer would agree to deliver the 10-year Treasury notes for $987,785.06 and repurchase the same securities for $987,811.67 the next day. The $26.62 difference between the "sale" price of $987,785.06 and the repurchase price of $987,811,67 is the dollar interest on the financing. Using a repo rate of 0.97% and a repo term of 1 day, the dollar interest is calculated as shown:

EXHIBIT 13.2   Bloomberg Repo/Reverse Repo Analysis Screen

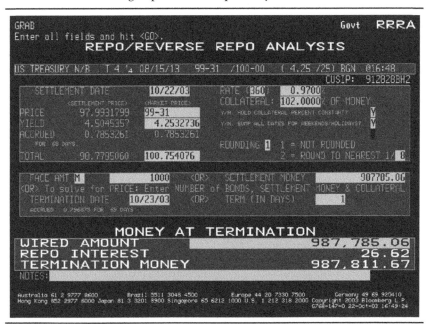

Source: Bloomberg Financial Markets

$$\$987{,}7875.06 \times 0.0097 \times (1/360) = \$26.62$$

This calculation agrees with the repo interest as calculated in the lower right-hand corner of Exhibit 13.2.

Marking the Collateral to Market

Another practice to limit credit risk is to mark the collateral to market on a regular basis. Marking a position to market means simply recording the position's value at its market value. When the market value changes by a certain percentage, the repo position is adjusted accordingly. The decline in market value below a specified amount results in a margin deficit. [Paragraph 4(a) of the Master Repurchase Agreement gives the "Seller" (the dealer/borrower in our example) the option to remedy the margin deficit by either providing additional cash or by transferring "additional Securities reasonably acceptable to Buyer." The Buyer in our example is the investor/lender.] Conversely, suppose instead that the market value rises above the amount required by margin. This circumstance results in a margin excess. If this occurs, Paragraph 4(b) states the "Buyer" will remedy the excess by either transferring cash equal to the amount of the excess or returning a portion of the collateral ("purchased securities") to the "Seller."

Because the Master Repurchase Agreement covers all transactions where a party is on one side of the transaction, the discussion of margin maintenance in Paragraph 4 is couched in terms of "the aggregate Market Value of all Purchased Securities in which a particular party hereto is acting as Buyer" and "the aggregate Buyer's Margin Account for all such Transactions." Thus, maintenance margin is not viewed from an individual transaction or security perspective. However, Paragraph 4(f) permits the "Buyer" and "Seller" to agree to override this provision so as to apply the margin maintenance requirement to a single transaction.

The price used to mark positions to market is defined in Paragraph 2(j)—the definition of "Market Value." The price is one "obtained from a generally recognized source agreed to by the parties or the most recent closing bid quotation from such a source." For complex securities that do not trade frequently, there is considerable difficulty in obtaining a price at which to mark a position to market.

Delivery of the Collateral

One concern in structuring a repurchase agreement is delivery of the collateral to the lender. The most obvious procedure is for the borrower to actually deliver the collateral to the lender or to the cash lender's clearing agent. If this procedure is followed, the collateral is said to be "delivered out" or "delivery versus payment." At the end of the repo term, the lender returns collateral to the borrower in exchange for the repurchase price (i.e., the amount borrowed plus interest).

The drawback of this procedure is that it may be too expensive, particularly for short-term repos (e.g., overnight) owing to the costs associated with delivering the collateral. Indeed, the cost of delivery is factored into the repo rate of the transaction in that if delivery is required this translates into a lower repo rate paid by the borrower. If delivery of collateral is not required, an otherwise higher repo rate is paid. The risk to the lender of not taking actual possession of the collateral is that the borrower may sell the security or use the same security as collateral for a repo with another counterparty.

As an alternative to delivering out the collateral, the lender may agree to allow the borrower to hold the security in a segregated customer account. The lender still must bear the risk that the borrower may use the collateral fraudulently by offering it as collateral for another repo transaction. If the borrower of the cash does not deliver out the collateral, but instead holds it, then the transaction is called a *hold-in-custody repo* (HIC repo).[5] Despite the credit risk associated with a HIC repo, it is used in some transactions when the collateral is difficult to deliver (e.g., whole loans) or the transaction amount is relatively small and the lender of funds is comfortable with the borrower's reputation.

Investors participating in a HIC repo must ensure: (1) they transact only with dealers of good credit quality since an HIC repo may be perceived as an unsecured transaction and (2) the investor (i.e., the lender of cash) receives a higher rate in order to compensate them for the higher credit risk involved. In the U.S. market, there have been cases where dealer firms that went into bankruptcy and defaulted on loans were found to have pledged the same collateral for multiple HIC transactions.

Another method for handling the collateral is for the borrower to deliver the collateral to the lender's custodial account at the borrower's clearing bank. The custodian then has possession of the collateral that it holds on the lender's behalf. This method reduces the cost of delivery because it is merely a transfer within the borrower's clearing bank. If, for example, a dealer enters into an overnight repo with Customer A, the next day the collateral is transferred back to the dealer. The dealer can then enter into a repo with Customer B for, say, five days without having to redeliver the collateral. The clearing bank simply establishes a custodian account for Customer B and holds the collateral in that account. In this type of repo transaction, the clearing bank is an agent to both parties. This specialized type of repo arrangement is called a *tri-party repo*. For

---

[5] Other terms include *segregation repo* and *safekeeping repo*.

some regulated financial institutions (e.g., federally chartered credit unions), this is the only type of repo arrangement permitted.

Paragraph 8 ("Segregation of Purchased Securities") of the Master Repurchase Agreement contains the language pertaining to the possession of collateral. This paragraph also contains special disclosure provisions when the "Seller" retains custody of the collateral.

Paragraph 11 ("Events of Default") details the events that will trigger a default of one of the counterparties and the options available to the non-defaulting party. If the borrower files for bankruptcy, the U.S. bankruptcy code affords the lender of funds in a qualified repo transaction a special status. It does so by exempting certain types of repos from the stay provisions of the bankruptcy law. This means that the lender of funds can immediately liquidate the collateral to obtain cash. Paragraph 19 ("Intent") of the Master Repurchase Agreement is included for this purpose.

DETERMINANTS OF THE REPO RATE

Just as there is no single interest rate, there is not one repo rate. The repo rate varies from transaction to transaction depending on a number of factors: quality of the collateral, term of the repo, delivery requirement, availability of the collateral, and the prevailing federal funds rate. Panel A of Exhibit 13.3 presents a Bloomberg screen (MMR) that contains repo and reverse repo rates for maturities of 1 day, 1 week, 2 weeks, 3 weeks, 1 month, 2 months, and 3 months using U.S. Treasuries as collateral in Panel A. Panel B presents repo and reverse repo rates with agency securities as collateral. Note how the rates differ by maturity and type of collateral. For example, the repo rates are higher when agency securities are used as collateral versus governments. Moreover, the rates generally decrease with maturity that mirrors the inverted Treasury yield curve on that date.

Another pattern evident in these data is that repo rates are lower than the reverse repo rates when matched by collateral type and maturity. These repo (reverse repo) rates can viewed as the rates the dealer will borrow (lend) funds. Alternatively, repo (reverse repo) rates are prices at which dealers are willing to buy (sell) collateral. While a dealer firm primarily uses the repo market as a vehicle for financing its inventory and covering short positions, it will also use the repo market to run a "matched book." A dealer runs a matched book by simultaneously entering into a repo and a reverse repo for the same collateral with the same maturity. The dealer does so to capture the spread at which it enters into a repurchase agreement (i.e., an agreement to borrow funds) and a reverse repurchase agreement (i.e., an agreement to lend funds).

EXHIBIT 13.3 Bloomberg Screens Presenting Repo and Reverse Repo Rates for Various Maturities and Collateral
Panel A: U.S. Treasuries

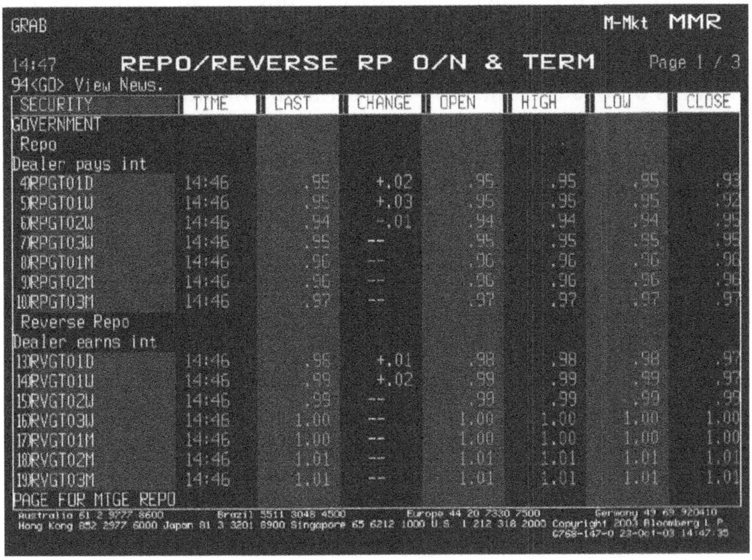
GRAB M-Mkt MMR
14:47 REPO/REVERSE RP O/N & TERM Page 1 / 3
94<GO> View News.

SECURITY	TIME	LAST	CHANGE	OPEN	HIGH	LOW	CLOSE
GOVERNMENT							
Repo							
Dealer pays int							
4)RPGT01D	14:46	.95	+.02	.95	.95	.95	.93
5)RPGT01W	14:46	.95	+.03	.95	.95	.95	.92
6)RPGT02W	14:46	.94	-.01	.94	.94	.94	.95
7)RPGT03W	14:46	.95	--	.95	.95	.95	.95
8)RPGT01M	14:46	.96	--	.96	.96	.96	.96
9)RPGT02M	14:46	.96	--	.96	.96	.96	.96
10)RPGT03M	14:46	.97	--	.97	.97	.97	.97
Reverse Repo							
Dealer earns int							
13)RVGT01D	14:46	.96	+.01	.98	.98	.98	.97
14)RVGT01W	14:46	.99	+.02	.99	.99	.99	.97
15)RVGT02W	14:46	.99	--	.99	.99	.99	.99
16)RVGT03W	14:46	1.00	--	1.00	1.00	1.00	1.00
17)RVGT01M	14:46	1.00	--	1.00	1.00	1.00	1.00
18)RVGT02M	14:46	1.01	--	1.01	1.01	1.01	1.01
19)RVGT03M	14:46	1.01	--	1.01	1.01	1.01	1.01

PAGE FOR MTGE REPO
Australia 61 2 9777 8600 Brazil 5511 3048 4500 Europe 44 20 7330 7500 Germany 49 69 920410
Hong Kong 852 2977 6000 Japan 81 3 3201 8900 Singapore 65 6212 1000 U.S. 1 212 318 2000 Copyright 2003 Bloomberg L.P.
G768-147-0 23-Oct-03 14:47:35

Panel B: Agency Securities

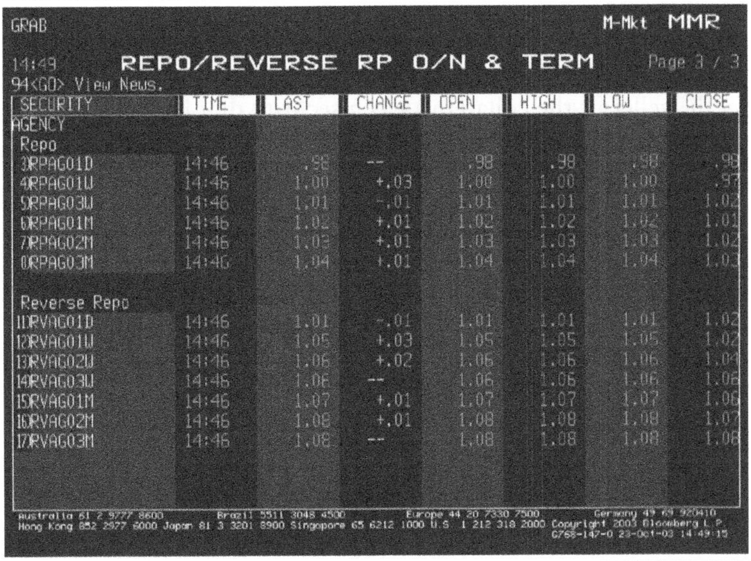
GRAB M-Mkt MMR
14:49 REPO/REVERSE RP O/N & TERM Page 3 / 3
94<GO> View News.

SECURITY	TIME	LAST	CHANGE	OPEN	HIGH	LOW	CLOSE
AGENCY							
Repo							
3)RPAG01D	14:46	.98	--	.98	.98	.98	.98
4)RPAG01W	14:46	1.00	+.03	1.00	1.00	1.00	.97
5)RPAG03W	14:46	1.01	-.01	1.01	1.01	1.01	1.02
6)RPAG01M	14:46	1.02	+.01	1.02	1.02	1.02	1.01
7)RPAG02M	14:46	1.03	+.01	1.03	1.03	1.03	1.02
8)RPAG03M	14:46	1.04	+.01	1.04	1.04	1.04	1.03
Reverse Repo							
11)RVAG01D	14:46	1.01	-.01	1.01	1.01	1.01	1.02
12)RVAG01W	14:46	1.05	+.03	1.05	1.05	1.05	1.02
13)RVAG02W	14:46	1.06	+.02	1.06	1.06	1.06	1.04
14)RVAG03W	14:46	1.06	--	1.06	1.06	1.06	1.06
15)RVAG01M	14:46	1.07	+.01	1.07	1.07	1.07	1.06
16)RVAG02M	14:46	1.08	+.01	1.08	1.08	1.08	1.07
17)RVAG03M	14:46	1.08	--	1.08	1.08	1.08	1.08

Australia 61 2 9777 8600 Brazil 5511 3048 4500 Europe 44 20 7330 7500 Germany 49 69 920410
Hong Kong 852 2977 6000 Japan 81 3 3201 8900 Singapore 65 6212 1000 U.S. 1 212 318 2000 Copyright 2003 Bloomberg L.P.
G768-147-0 23-Oct-03 14:49:15

Source: Bloomberg Financial Markets

For example, suppose that a dealer enters into a term repo for one month with a money market mutual fund and a reverse repo with a corporate credit union for one month for which the collateral is identical. In this arrangement, the dealer is borrowing funds from the money market mutual fund and lending funds to the corporate credit union. From Panel A in Exhibit 13.3, we find that the repo rate for a one-month repurchase agreement is 0.96% and the repo rate for a one-month reverse repurchase agreement is 1.00%. If these two positions are established simultaneously, then the dealer is borrowing at 0.96% and lending at 1%, thereby locking in a spread of 4 basis points.

However, in practice, traders deliberately mismatch their books to take advantage of their expectations about the shape and level of the short-dated yield curve. The term matched book is therefore something of a misnomer in that most matched books are deliberately mismatched for this reason. Traders engage in positions to take advantage of (1) short-term interest rate movements and (2) anticipated demand and supply in the underlying bond.

The delivery requirement for collateral also affects the level of the repo rate. If delivery of the collateral to the lender is required, the repo rate will be lower. Conversely, if the collateral can be deposited with the bank of the borrower, a higher repo rate will be paid. For example, on October 23, 2003, Bloomberg reports that the general collateral rate (repos backed by non-specific collateral) is 0.99% if delivery of the collateral is required. For a tri-party repo discussed earlier, the general collateral rate is 1.02%.

The more difficult it is to obtain the collateral, the lower the repo rate. To understand why this is so, remember that the borrower (or equivalently the seller of the collateral) has a security that lenders of cash want for whatever reason.[6] Such collateral is said to "on special." Collateral that does not share this characteristic is referred to as "general collateral." The party that needs collateral that is "on special" will be willing to lend funds at a lower repo rate in order to obtain the collateral. For example, on October 23, 2003, Bloomberg reports the 10-year Treasury note (3.625% coupon maturing May 15, 2013) was "on special" such that the overnight repo rate was 0%. At the time, the general collateral rate was 1.02%.

There are several factors contributing to the demand for special collateral. They include:

■ Government bond auctions—the bond to be issued is shorted by dealers in anticipation of new supply and due to client demand

---

[6] Perhaps the issue is in great demand to satisfy borrowing needs.

- Outright short selling whether a deliberate position taken based on a trader's expectations or dealers shorting bonds to satisfy client demand
- Hedging including corporate bonds underwriters who short the relevant maturity benchmark government bond that the corporate bond is priced against
- Derivative trading such as basis trading creating a demand for a specific bond
- Buy-back or cancellation of debt at short notice

Financial crises also impact a particular security's "specialness." *Specialness* is defined the spread between the general collateral rate and the repo rate of a particular security. Michael Fleming found that the on-the-run 2-year note, 5-year note, and 30-year bond traded at an increased rate of specialness during the Asian financial crisis of 1998. In other words, the spread between the general collateral rate and the repo rates on these securities increased. Moreover, these spreads returned to more normal levels after the crisis ended.[7]

While these factors determine the repo rate on a particular transaction, the federal funds rate determines the general level of repo rates. The repo rate generally will trade lower than the federal funds rate, because a repo involves collateralized borrowing while a federal funds transaction is unsecured borrowing. Exhibit 13.4 presents a time series plot of the federal funds rate and the overnight repo rate from April 23, 2002 to October 23, 2003. Over this period of time, the overnight repo rate is on average −3.56 basis points below the federal funds rate.[8]

SPECIAL COLLATERAL AND ARBITRAGE

As noted earlier in the chapter, there are a number of investment strategies in which an investor borrows funds to purchase securities. The investor's expectation is that the return earned by investing in the securities purchased with the borrowed funds will exceed the borrowing cost. The use of borrowed funds to obtain greater exposure to an asset than is possible by using only cash is called *leveraging*. In certain circumstances, a borrower of funds via a repo transaction can generate an arbitrage opportunity. This occurs when it is possible to borrow funds at a lower rate than the rate that can be earned by reinvesting those funds.

---

[7] Michael J. Fleming, "The Benchmark U.S. Treasury Market: Recent Performance and Possible Alternatives," *FRBNY Economic Policy Review* (April 2000), pp. 129–145.
[8] Source: Bloomberg.

EXHIBIT 13.4   Bloomberg Screen of Time Series Plot of the Federal Funds Rate and Overnight Repo Rate

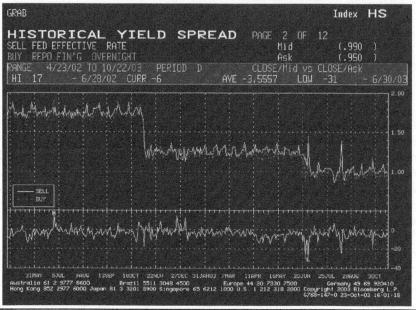

Source: Bloomberg Financial Markets

Such opportunities present themselves when a portfolio includes securities that are "on special" and the manager can reinvest at a rate higher than the repo rate. For example, suppose that a manager has securities that are "on special" in the portfolio, Bond X, that lenders of funds are willing to take as collateral for two weeks charging a repo rate of, say, 3%. Suppose further that the manager can invest the funds in a 2-week Treasury bill (the maturity date being the same as the term of the repo) and earn 4%. Assuming that the repo is properly structured so that there is no credit risk, then the manager has locked in a spread of 100 basis points for two weeks. This is a pure arbitrage and the manager faces no risk. Of course, the manager is exposed to the risk that Bond X may decline in value but this the manager is exposed to this risk anyway as long as the manager intends to hold the security.

The Bank of England has conducted a study examining the relationship between cash prices and repo rates for bonds that have traded special.[9] The results of the study suggest a positive correlation between

---

[9] See the markets section of the *Bank of England's Quarterly Bulletin* in the February 1997 and August 1997 issues.

changes in a bond trading expensive to the yield curve and changes in the degree to which it trades special. This result is not surprising. Traders maintain short positions in bonds which have associated funding costs only if the anticipated fall in the bond is large enough to engender a profit. The causality could run in either direction. For example, suppose a bond is perceived as being expensive relative to the yield curve. This circumstance creates a greater demand for short positions and hence a greater demand for the bonds in the repo market to cover the short positions. Alternatively, suppose a bond goes on special in the repo market for whatever reason. The bond would appreciate in price in the cash market as traders close out their short positions which are now too expensive to maintain. Moreover, traders and investors would try to buy the bond outright since it now would be relatively cheap to finance in the repo market.

PARTICIPANTS IN THE MARKET

The repo market has evolved into one of the largest sectors of the money market because it is used continuously by dealer firms (investment banks and money center banks acting as dealers) to finance positions and cover short positions. Exhibit 13.5 presents the average daily amount outstanding (in billions of dollars) for reverse repurchase/repurchase agreements by U.S. government securities dealers for the period 1981–2002. The primary borrowers of securities include major security dealers and hedge funds. Conversely, the primary lenders of securities include institutional investors with long investment horizons (e.g., insurance companies, pension funds, mutual funds). These institutional investors view securities lending as an additional source of revenue. Alternatively, viewing the repo market as a mechanism to borrow and lend cash, the primary borrowers of cash are the same institutions that also borrow securities namely dealer firms and hedge funds. Lenders of cash include financial institutions, nonfinancial corporations, money market mutual funds, and municipalities.

Another repo market participant is the repo broker. To understand the repo broker's role, suppose that a dealer has shorted $50 million of the current 10-year Treasury note. It will then query its regular customers to determine if it can borrow, via a reverse repo, the 10-year Treasury note it shorted. Suppose that it cannot find a customer willing to do a repo transaction (repo from the customer's perspective, reverse repo from the dealer's perspective). At that point, the dealer will utilize the services of a repo broker who will find the desired collateral and arrange the transaction for a fee.

EXHIBIT 13.5   Average Daily Amount Outstanding (in billions of dollars) for
Reverse Repurchase/Repurchase Agreements

Year	Reverse Repurchase	Repurchase	Total
1981	46.7	65.4	112.1
1982	75.1	95.2	170.3
1983	81.7	102.4	184.1
1984	112.4	132.6	245.0
1985	147.9	172.9	320.8
1986	207.7	244.5	452.2
1987	275.0	292.0	567.0
1988	313.6	309.7	623.3
1989	383.2	398.2	781.4
1990	377.1	413.5	790.5
1991	417.0	496.6	913.6
1992	511.1	628.2	1,139.3
1993	594.1	765.6	1,359.7
1994	651.2	825.9	1,477.1
1995	618.8	821.5	1,440.3
1996	718.1	973.7	1,691.8
1997	883.0	1,159.0	2,042.0
1998	1,111.4	1,414.0	2,525.5
1999	1,070.1	1,361.0	2,431.1
2000	1,093.3	1,439.6	2,532.9
2001	1,311.3	1,786,5	3,097.7
2002	1,615.7	2,172.4	3,788.1

Source: Federal Reserve Bank of New York

REPO/REVERSE TO MATURITY

One important type of repo is a repo/reverse to maturity. A repo/reverse
to maturity is one where the term of the repurchase agreement coincides
with the maturity date of the collateral and the repurchase price equals
the proceeds of the collateral. As before, whether the transaction is a repo
or reverse is viewed from the dealer's perspective. This type of transaction
is driven primarily for accounting/tax reasons. For example, suppose a
dealer has a customer has bond in their portfolio that they would like to
sell but the bond is trading below its carrying value. Furthermore, suppose the customer does have any gains to offset the loss. In this case, the
customer might consider a repo to maturity as an alternative to selling the

bond. By doing so, the customer is using the bonds as collateral for a loan and gains access to funds without selling the bond outright.

BUY/SELL BACK

Another securities lending arrangement that is functionally equivalent to a repurchase agreement is a buy/sell back agreement. A buy/sell back agreement separates a securities lending transaction into separate buy and sell trades that are entered into simultaneously. The security borrower buys the security in question and agrees to return the borrowed security (i.e., sell back) at some future date for an agreed upon forward price. The forward price is usually derived using a repo rate. A buy/sell back agreement differs from a repurchase agreement in that the security borrower receives legal title and beneficial ownership of the securities for the length of the agreement. The security borrower, moreover, retains any accrued interest and coupon payments until the security is returned to the lender. Nevertheless, the price on the termination date reflects the fact that the economic benefits of the coupon interest being transferred back to the seller.

As an illustration, suppose a primary dealer wants to borrow $1 million par value of the on-the-run 3-year note overnight. This security carries a 2.375% coupon and matures on August 15, 2006. This transaction is presented Panels A and B in Exhibit 13.6. On the settlement date of October 27, 2003, the dealer buys the 3-year notes for the current market price of $1,004,531.25 (i.e., the flat price) plus accrued interest of $4,775.82 for a total of $1,009,207.07. This number is located in Panel B on the left-hand side of the screen by "TOTAL" under the heading "AT SETTLEMENT DATE." The termination date of the agreement is the next day October 29, 2003, the dealer sells the notes back to the customer for a price of $1,004,493.35 (the forward price for a $1,000,000 par value position) plus accrued interest of $4,840.35 for a total of $1,009,307.07. This number is located on the bottom right-hand corner of Panel A and is labeled "Termination Money." The interest on the one-day loan is $26.63 using a repo interest rate 0.95% and the calculation appears on the left-hand side of Panel B.

REPO MARKET STRUCTURES

Structured repo instruments have developed in recent years mainly in the U.S. market where repo is widely accepted as a money market instrument. Following the introduction of new repo types it is also possible now to transact them in other liquid markets.

EXHIBIT 13.6   Bloomberg Buy/Sell Back Repo Analysis
Panel A: Details of the Transaction

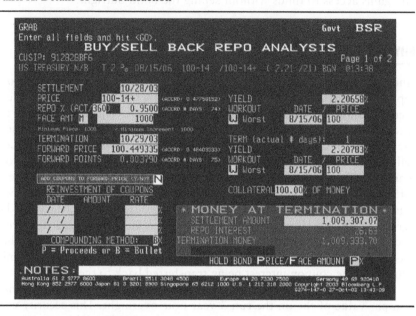

Panel B: Analysis of Funding Cost

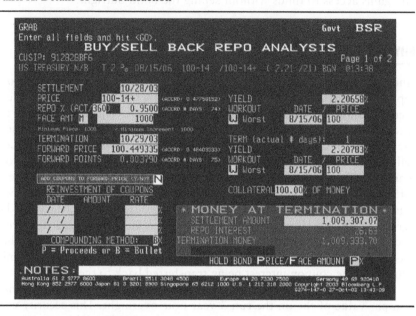

Source: Bloomberg Financial Markets

LIBOR-Financed Treasury Repo

As the name implies, a LIBOR-financed Treasury repurchase agreement differs from a traditional repo in that the repo rate is tied to 3-month LIBOR rather than the overnight Federal Funds rates. The repo rate is reset quarterly according to movements in the level of 3-month LIBOR. Accordingly, unlike a traditional repo, the repo rate over the term of the agreement is uncertain.

General Collateral Financing Repos

General collateral financing (GCF) *repo* is a recent innovation for repurchase agreements secured by general collateral Treasuries. The GCF repo was designed by the Government Securities Clearing Corporation and allows dealer firms to actively participate in the repo market without requiring each trade to be settled individually. Instead, there is a net delivery or receipt of collateral at the end of the trading day. The GCF repo reduces the transaction costs of the general collateral Treasury repo market and increases the liquidity.

Cross-Currency Repo

A cross-currency repo is an agreement in which the cash lent and securities used as collateral are denominated in different currencies say, borrow U.S. dollars with U.K. gilts used as collateral. Of course, fluctuating foreign exchange rates mean that it is likely that the transaction will need to be marked-to-market frequently in order to ensure that cash or securities remain fully collateralized.

Convertible Repo

A *convertible repo* is a repo in which the dealer has the option to convert a fixed-rate term repo to a floating-rate term repo. The dealer's counterparty sells the conversion option and is compensated in the form of a higher repo rate than an otherwise similar conventional repo.

Callable Repo

In a callable repo arrangement, the lender of cash in a term fixed-rate repo has the option to terminate the repo early. In other words, the repo transaction has an embedded interest rate option that benefits the lender of cash if rates rise during the repo's term. If rates rise, the lender may exercise the option to call back the cash and reinvest at a higher rate. For this reason, a callable repo will trade at a lower repo rate than an otherwise similar conventional repo.

Whole Loan Repo

A whole loan repo structure developed in the U.S. market as a response to investor demand for higher yields in a falling interest rate environment. Whole loan repo trades at a higher rate than conventional repo because a lower quality collateral is used in the transaction. There are generally two types: mortgage whole loans and consumer whole loans. Both are unsecuritized loans or interest receivables. The loans can also be credit card payments and other types of consumer loans. Lenders in a whole loan repo are not only exposed to credit risk but prepayment risk as well. This is the risk that the loan package is paid off prior to the maturity date which is often the case with consumer loans. For these reasons, the yield on a whole loan repo is higher than conventional repo collateralized by say U.S. Treasuries, trading at around 20–30 basis points over LIBOR.

Total Return Swap

A total return swap structure, also known as a "total rate of return swap," is economically identical to a repo. The main difference between a total return swap and a repo is that the former is governed by the International Swap Dealers Association (ISDA) agreement as opposed to a repo agreement. This difference is largely due to the way the transaction is reflected on the balance sheet in that a total return swap is recorded as an off-balance sheet transaction. This is one of the main motivations for entering into this type of contract. The transaction works as follows:

1. The institution sells the security at the market price.
2. The institution executes a swap transaction for a fixed term, exchanging the security's total return for an agreed rate on the relevant cash amount.
3. On the swap's maturity date, the institution repurchases the security for the market price.

In theory, each leg of the transaction can be executed separately with different counterparties; in practice, the trade is bundled together and, therefore, is economically identical to a repo.

CHAPTER 14

The European Repo Market

Richard Comotto
ISMA Centre
University of Reading, England

There have been repo markets in some European countries since the nineteenth century, but the modern form of the instrument and a cross-border repo market emerged only in the late 1980s. The initial impetus came from U.S. investment banks seeking to cover short positions in European government bond markets. Since the mid-1990s, however, there has been spectacular growth and development in the European repo market that is increasingly organic, driven by forces such as the creation of the Single Market and the euro. In this chapter, we describe the European repo market that now rivals the U.S. market in size and sophistication.

SIZE, GROWTH, AND COMPOSITION OF THE EUROPEAN REPO MARKET

Since December 2002, the European Repo Council (ERC) of the International Securities Market Association (ISMA) has been conducting semi-annual surveys of the European repo market. The survey asks participating institutions for the value of repo contracts outstanding on their books at close of business on the second Wednesday of June or December. They are also asked to give breakdowns of their business in terms of currency, collateral, maturity, and the like. The firms participating are mainly repo dealers. However, in recent surveys, returns have also been received from automatic repo trading systems (ATS) and tri-party repo agents as well as a group of London-based voice-brokers under the auspices of the Wholesale Market Brokers' Association (WMBA).[1] The ISMA surveys provide the only authoritative picture of the European repo market and a level of detail that is fairly unique in any market survey.

At the last ISMA survey, on June 9, 2004, the outstanding value of repo contracts of the 81 institutions that participated in that survey totalled €4,561 billion.[2] This is a massive number but, even so, it is merely the floor to the actual size of the European market. Given that there are a few hundred institutions in the European repo market, the actual size of the market as a whole must be much higher.[3]

It is worth remembering that the European repo market has grown to its current size largely since the mid-1990s. The triggers for this rapid growth were:

- The reshaping of the international repo market in London in the wake of the opening of a market in U.K. government bond repo
- The reform of Continental European repo markets, particularly in France
- The introduction of better cross-border repo documentation in the form of the 1995 version of the PSA/ISMA Global Master Repurchase Agreement (GMRA)
- The tightening of regulatory capital requirements and the shift out of unsecured lending; the need of banks to contain credit risk and improve their capital efficiency in a more competitive global market
- The general growth and restructuring of financial markets catalysed by the introduction of the euro.

The ISMA survey provides a measure of recent growth in the European repo market by comparing the returns from constant samples of

---

[1] The results of the ISMA surveys are published on the ISMA website www.isma.org/surveys.

[2] The results of the survey on December 8, 2004 are due to be published on March 17, 2005. The next survey is due on June 9, 2005.

[3] The survey number is however inflated by double counting. This problem occurs when two institutions participating in the survey report the same transaction, which is, therefore, counted twice. As most of the participants in the survey are dealers, the problem does not arise in the case of "customer" business. Unfortunately, the survey cannot measure the split between interdealer and customer business because of the different definitions of "customer" used by dealers. Anecdotal evidence suggests that customer business may be about half of the total repo market: in this case, the maximum adjustment that would have to be made for double counting—if all dealers participated in the survey—would be 25%. So, the double-counting problem may not yet be too significant.

institutions that have participated in the surveys at the beginning and end of each 12-month period. The year-on-year growth of such a sample to June 2004 was 19%, most of which occurred over the first six months of 2004. The rate and pattern of growth were similar in the previous year: sample growth was about 17%, virtually all of which took place in the first half of 2003.

Unsurprisingly, most of the cash in repo trading in Europe is euros. This currency accounted for 70.5% of reported outstanding repos in June 2004. There are also sizable markets in pounds sterling (11.8%) and U.S. dollars (10.7%). Japanese yen accounted for 3.5%. The remainder was mainly Swiss francs and Scandinavian currencies.

The overwhelming bulk of collateral (87.4%) took the form of European government bonds. The remainder was largely covered bonds like Pfandbrief and mortgage-backed securities. Equity was relatively insignificant at just 1.8%, but there could be problems here in terms of whether the survey is reaching the areas in some banks where equity repo is traded. There has been considerable interest recently in the use of corporate and asset-backed securities (ABS) as collateral. In terms of scale, however, this segment of the market does not yet appear to be large.

The share of repo collateral held by survey participants which was issued in countries in the eurozone was 69.0%. The largest single share was securities issued in Germany (28.6%). However, whereas German collateral, in the case of government bonds at least, tends to be a specials market, the major sources of general collateral in Europe are Italy (14.3%), reflecting the liquidity of Italian government bonds, and Belgium (4.3%), reflecting both liquidity and ease of settlement through the domestic custodian. Big pools of repo collateral also originate in France (9.3%), the United Kingdom (11.6%) and Spain (5.7%), but these are still largely domestic markets.

With the introduction of the euro, it was expected by many that the repo rates on eurozone government bonds would completely converge. This has not happened. Small spreads persist between the collateral of different governments. These are usually attributed to differences in supply and demand, market liquidity and problems in moving some bonds between national and international central securities depositories.

Considerable interest has been focused on the repo markets of the 10 countries that joined the European Union in 2004, but as yet, these are very small and accounted for only 0.2% of collateral in the survey, most of which was from Hungary and Poland. The residual 9.8% of collateral in the survey was issued mainly in "other OECD countries" (i.e., neither the European Union nor the United States).

It is worth noting that, while the share of the U.S. dollar on the cash side of repo trading was 10.7%, the share of collateral issued in the

United States was much smaller. This suggests cross-currency repo trading (typically, cash in U.S. dollars, collateral in euros). Yet, the reported share of cross-currency repos was very low (1.1% in June 2004). Some of the discrepancy may be accounted for by U.S. dollar-denominated Eurobonds, which are reported in the survey under the country of issue (London or Luxembourg). Another source of error may be the very low response rate to this question (only 24 participants answered this question in the latest survey). However, it would also appear that a lot of cross-currency repo trading is settled through tri-party arrangements which participants have difficulty reporting. Because there is a delay of one day in the reporting of the currency composition of tri-party collateral to counterparties, it is too late for risk management reporting and is therefore often ignored.

Most repo activity in Europe is short-term. Just over 68% of outstanding contracts had a remaining term of one month or less, and almost 40% were for one week or less. Even so, the ISMA survey has shown that the share of longer-term business was larger than previously estimated. Contracts with remaining terms of between 3 and 6 months accounted for 7.3% and over 6 months was 7.0%. The share of forward-forward repos was 5.2%. These are repos with a value date beyond spot and are primarily used for interest rate risk trading. Their share therefore fluctuates with the strength of interest rate expectations.

The flow of business in the repo market is split almost equally between domestic and cross-border transactions (49% and 51%, respectively, in June 2004). Cross-border business was almost equally split between business with counterparties inside and outside the eurozone. The scale of domestic business in the ISMA survey, and of the business crossing into or out of the eurozone, is likely to be largely a reflection of the major role played by London in the European repo market, including that in euros, despite the UK being outside the eurozone.

It is important to note that the ISMA survey only identifies the destination of business, not its sources (this is a problem caused by the increasing use of pan-European repo books).

Moreover, the ISMA survey cannot measure the destination of repo trades, which are transacted anonymously on ATS's such as BrokerTec and Eurex Repo, and settled with a *central clearing counterparty* (CCP). The share of anonymous trading has risen sharply since the survey started and stood at 11.6% in June 2004 (compared to 9% in June 2004).

CCPs provide multilateral netting services for repos and cash transactions in the underlying bonds. In this respect, they are similar in function to futures clearing houses. Multilateral netting means that a member can offset obligations to and from several counterparties who are also members of the CCP, rather than with one other party as in bilateral netting. The principal CCP in Europe is the London Clearing House's (LCH) RepoClear. LCH has recently merged with Clearnet, which is a CCP for French government bonds. The other major clearing house in Europe is Eurex Clearing, but this only nets transactions on Eurex Repo.

CCPs play a key role in repo trading in the European market. It is no coincidence that electronic trading of repo took off following the arrival of the first CCP. They have allowed the large repo dealers to continue to grow their business by mitigating the risk, capital, balance sheet, and operational constraints of expansion. They have also allowed ATS's like BrokerTec and Eurex Repo to offer anonymous trading. Where an ATS is linked to a CCP, the CCP will step into each transaction reported by the ATS to become the seller to the original buyer and the buyer to the original seller. As the CCP will become their counterparty, there is no need for the original buyer and seller to ever know each other's identity. Trading can, therefore, be anonymous both pre- and post-trade.

One survey statistic that needs particularly careful handling is the share of reported outstanding repo contracts taking the form of classic repos (also called *repurchase agreements*) or sell/buy-backs. The share of classic repos was 80.9% in June 2004. Sell/buy-backs documented under agreements such as the TBMA/ISMA or PSA/ISMA GMRA took 11.2% and undocumented sell/buy-backs 7.8%. The share of sell/buy-backs, particularly undocumented transactions, is far lower than anecdotal evidence suggests and it would appear that the survey has a bias towards cross-border transactions in which classic repos would be expected to predominate. If the survey included a greater number of smaller domestic players, particularly in Italy and Spain, the balance would undoubtedly shift towards sell/buy-backs.

The European repo market includes a segment in floating-rate transactions. The main floating rate index is EONIA (Euro Overnight Interbank Average). This is the daily volume-weighted average overnight euro-denominated deposit rate. Floating-rate repos accounted for 6.6% of the survey in June 2004, but were largely concentrated in the French market. Such indices have long been established in France, where there is a substantial money market mutual funds industry, which is a major user of indexed products.

The success of EONIA has prompted much discussion about how appropriate it is to use an unsecured deposit rate—despite being short-term and, therefore, risk-free—as an index in a money market that is shifting so dramatically into secured transactions such as repo. Accordingly, a number of market associations in Europe, in cooperation with ISMA's ERC, have developed an index for the euro-denominated repo market, Eurepo. So far, there has been modest market use of Eurepo, but it is still relatively new.[4]

Unfortunately, one statistic that the ISMA survey has so far been unable to supply—and that is of great interest—is the split in the repo market between specials and general collateral.

INTERDEALER ELECTRONIC TRADING

One of the most significant developments in the repo market in Europe since the late 1990's has been the introduction and growth of interdealer electronic trading on *automatic trading systems* (ATS). Here, we are talking about electronic systems that allow prices on screens to be hit and automatically executed (i.e., not just display screens that require deals to be executed by telephone or systems that require further negotiation). The principal ATSs in the European repo market are BrokerTec, Eurex Repo, and MTS.

BrokerTec was set up by a consortium of investment banks, but subsequently sold to the moneybrokering firm, Icap. It has the largest share of electronic repo trading in Europe and is a significant platform for the electronic trading of European government bonds. Its success owes much to the decision to offer, wherever possible, anonymous trading settled through a CCP.

Eurex Repo has a euro and a Swiss franc platform. The Swiss franc repo platform is well established and dominates that market. It is also significant because it is a fully integrated market with straight-through processing from the trading platform through tri-party facilities to automatic settlement. The platform is also used by the Swiss National Bank for its money market operations and by the Swiss government to issue bonds. The euro platform of Eurex Repo started with German government bonds. It is the newcomer to the electronic repo market and has the smallest share. The euro platform of Eurex Repo offers anonymous trading through a CCP; The Swiss franc platform does not.

MTS originated as the electronic trading system for Italian government bonds, but has since expanded into other European government bonds and high-grade nongovernment bonds as well as repos. While it dominates the electronic trading of European government bonds and the market in repos of Italian government bonds, it plays second fiddle to BrokerTec in other repo markets. Unlike BrokerTec, MTS does not yet offer anonymous trading.

---

[4] More information about Eurepo can be found on www.eurepo.org.

Fortuitously, the ISMA survey was started just as electronic repo trading started to take off in Europe. The share of ATS reached almost 24% of the total value of outstanding contracts in June 2004, compared with 18.0% in June 2003. Note that these data are for the value of outstanding contracts (i.e., a stock figure), not turnover (i.e., a flow figure). Many ATSs prefer to publish turnover figures. Turnover figures give electronic trading a larger market share than they have in terms of the value of outstanding contracts. Turnover is more important to ATSs given that they earn fees on each transaction rather than its value and turnover gives greater weight to the short-term transactions in which ATSs specialize.

The June 2004 survey also showed a significant jump to 11.6% in the share of repo contracts that had been negotiated anonymously on an ATS and settled with a CCP.

The profile of electronic repo trading is quite different from the traditional market. From the data reported directly by ATSs, the bulk of electronic trades was against German and Italian collateral (38.8% and 29.4%, respectively). Other significant shares were held by collateral issued in France (8.6%), "other OECD countries" (7.3%), United Kingdom (3.5%), Belgium (2.9%), Netherlands (2.8%), Spain (1.9%), Greece (1.6%), and Austria (1.0%). In total, collateral issued in EU countries accounted for 92.4% of outstanding repos transacted electronically and collateral issued in eurozone countries for 88.9%. Most of the collateral traded in ATSs is also government bonds (97.4% in June 2004).

The euro was the predominant currency of ATS business, accounting for 89.2%. Sterling accounted for 3.5% and "other currencies" for 7.3%. The latter was predominantly Swiss francs, reflecting the success of the electronic Swiss franc market operated by Eurex Repo.

As expected, the average remaining term to maturity of electronic trading was very short term: 97.1% of outstanding contracts had one month or less remaining to maturity compared to 68.1% in the survey of dealers, and 82.2% had a remaining term to maturity of just one day (82.2%). It is often argued that very short-term repos are most easily automated because of their simplicity and lower risk and there is a greater incentive due to the lower margins on such transactions.

VOICE-BROKERS

To some extent, the rise of electronic trading has been at the expense of traditional voice-brokers at least in terms of market share. (Their business has continued to grow in absolute terms.) As the share of electronic trading has grown, the share of voice-brokers declined, touching 24.8% in June 2004 from 30.7% in June 2003.

In the case of the voice-brokering firms represented in the WMBA data, of the contracts brokered by those firms and still outstanding on the survey date, the proportion between domestic counterparties was 43.1%, higher than the share of domestic business reported in the main survey (37.3%). This would seem to reflect the location of the WMBA voice-brokers in the large London repo market. Of the cross-border business brokered by WMBA members, 23.8% was between counterparties in countries both within the eurozone and 23.4% was between counterparties of which only one was in the eurozone.

The voice-brokered business reported by the WMBA had a much longer average remaining term to maturity than the main survey or the ATSs. Only 8.7% of this business was for one week or less, and 22.5% for one month or less. The most important share of the voice-brokers' repo business was in forward-forward repos (47.7%). This seems to confirm the argument that voice-brokers have a comparative advantage over ATS's in more complex, riskier and higher margin transactions such as long-term and forward-forward repos.

The importance of the euro in voice-brokered repos was lower than in the main survey (60.0%) and the share of the pound sterling much higher (26.3%). Again, this would seem to reflect the location of WMBA voice-brokers in London.

TRI-PARTY REPO

Tri-party repo was introduced into Europe in the early 1990s, but has been slow to take off. That now appears to be happening. In June 2004, 10.9% of total outstanding business was settled through tri-party repo arrangements, largely sustaining the dramatic increase in share seen between December 2003 (11.2%) and June 2003 (6.2%).

However, the growth of European tri-party repo has not happened as many expected, which was that Europe would follow U.S. experience. In fact, European and U.S. tri-party repo are very different products.

In the United States, because tri-party services, at least in bonds, are dominated by two agents, the product offers economies of scale and attracts high-volume, low-margin transactions. This means repos of U.S. Treasuries. More interesting types of collateral are settled by bilateral delivery. In Europe, although there is a dominant tri-party repo agent in the form of Euroclear, it still faces vigorous competition from other agents, notably from Clearstream. This makes European tri-party a more fragmented market and specialist product. Moreover, the lack of major alternative types of collateral means that, in Europe, government bonds are not as low-margin as U.S. Treasuries. European government bond collateral therefore tends to be settled by bilateral delivery (government bonds accounted for only 36.3% of outstanding European tri-party repo contracts). Tri-party is used more as a means of outsourcing the settlement and management of illiquid collateral. The fact that non-government collateral has only a small share of the European repo market is, therefore, a constraint on the potential growth of tri-party repos in Europe. In addition, the fragmentation of settlement systems in Europe makes it difficult, if not impossible, to access some government bonds for tri-party repos.

In the June 2004 ISMA survey, the main tri-party repo agents in Europe were asked to contribute data. Returns were received from Citigroup, Clearstream, Euroclear, JP Morgan Chase, and SegaInterSettle (SIS). The total value of outstanding tri-party repo contracts reported directly by the tri-party agents was €260.6 billion, equivalent to 5.7% of the total value of outstanding repos reported in the survey of dealers. The difference with the 10.9% reported by dealers is likely to be due mainly to double-counting, as the data reported by the tri-party repo agents include only one side of each transaction.

The composition of tri-party repo business was very different from that reported in the survey of dealers. 38.4% was domestic and 60.8% was cross-border with counterparties outside the eurozone. 59.8% was against euro, 11.6% against sterling and 28.1% against U.S. dollars. 60.5% of tri-party contracts were cross-currency. Collateral issued in the European Union accounted for 76.5% and collateral issued in the eurozone for 64.9%. The largest shares of collateral were accounted for by collateral issued in Germany (27.2%), United States (11.1%), United Kingdom (8.6%), France (8.2%), Netherlands (7.7%), and Italy (5.5%). Tri-party tends to be more short term: 76.8% were for one month or less. 87.4% of tri-party was fixed-term: the remainder were open contracts—that is, no fixed maturity date: Either counterparty can terminate the contract with sufficient notice.

DOCUMENTATION AND LEGAL ISSUES

The development of a sound and orderly market in repos in Europe has been crucially facilitated by the growing use of master agreements to document transactions. The use of documentation has in turn been facilitated by the provision of standard master agreements. The initiative for cross-border repos was taken by ISMA, which published a master agreement in 1992 based, initially quite closely, on the master agreement produced for the U.S. Treasury repo market by the Public Securities Association (PSA), but translated into English law, and called the PSA/ISMA Global Master Repurchase Agreement (GMRA).

The value of the GMRA has been much enhanced by the provision and regular maintenance of legal opinions on the legal enforceability of the agreement in various countries, particularly the enforceability of the netting provisions set out in the agreement.

Periodically, it has been necessary to update the GMRA. Valuation difficulties caused by time zone differences that became evident during the Barings crisis in 1994 prompted a revision of the 1992 agreement and the publication of a new version in 1995. Valuation difficulties caused by the illiquidity of collateral markets during the Asian and Russian market crises of 1997 and 1998 respectively led to a second revision in the form of the TBMA/ISMA GMRA in 2000 (by this time, the PSA had changed its name to The Bond Market Association or TBMA).[5] Under the 2000 version, nondefaulting parties now have a range of valuation methods to fall back on, including their own estimation of the fair value of a security in the event of market difficulties. The opportunity was also taken to tidy up the structure of the agreement, to update and clarify certain clauses and to apply lessons learned since 1995. It is unclear how fast the transition is being made from the 1995 to the 2000 GMRA, but it is likely to be well advanced.

In addition to the periodic revision of the GMRA, ISMA has also produced Annexes to the main agreement to allow its application to special repo markets (e.g., repos with an agent, equity repos, repos of net-paying securities) and in different jurisdictions, or in response to exceptional situations (e.g., the introduction of the euro and the disappearance of legacy currencies).[6]

New market crises may necessitate further revisions to the GMRA. In the meantime, a project has been launched to merge the GMRA with the standard master agreement for securities lending (Global Master Securities Lending Agreement or GMSLA published by the International Securities Lending Association or ISLA). There is already some overlap in the GMRA Equity Annex but anyone who has read them will know that merging the main texts is going to be a complex undertaking.

---

[5] Copies of all ISMA master agreements can be downloaded from the ISMA website, www.isma.org.

[6] Copies of the annexes to the GMRA are also downloadable from the ISMA website.

While the GMRA is the clear market standard for cross-border documentation in Europe, there are a number of domestic master agreements. The introduction of the euro also led to an initiative sponsored by bodies such as the European Banking Federation and supported by the European Central Bank to frame a harmonized master agreement that could be used in domestic markets within the eurozone (e.g., French-French transactions, German-German transactions). This is the European Market Agreement. A major innovation in the EMA was the inclusion of securities lending under the agreement and the proposal to include other markets such as FX and derivatives.

Reaction to the EMA has been mixed, particularly at the suggestion that it should be used for cross-border transactions within the eurozone. Many market participants do not welcome the proliferation of agreements and the EMA has undoubtedly raised eyebrows at ISMA and ISDA.

Despite the availability of a number of master agreements, there is still a very large market in Europe in undocumented repos in the form of sell/buy-backs. Increasingly, this is concentrated in domestic markets, particularly since the introduction in 1995 by ISMA of the Buy/Sell-Back Annex that allowed the documentation of sell/buy-backs. The persistence of undocumented sell/buy-backs is difficult to understand given that regulatory capital requirements should favour documented and margined repos.

MARKET ORGANIZATION

The European repo market has undoubtedly benefited from the strong sense of community among dealers and their commitment to the promotion of the marketplace. A central role in representing the market, for example, in discussions with regulators and in developing consensual solutions to market issues, is played by the European Repo Council (ERC). This is a committee of ISMA, originally called the Committee of Reporting Dealers' Repo Sub-Committee. The ERC meets twice a year at various locations across Europe to discuss issues of importance to the European repo market. At its meeting in March, the ERC elects a Steering Committee to represent the Council during the year.

The ERC is the body responsible for maintaining the GMRA. It also manages ISMA's semiannual survey of the European market. The ERC publishes a set of Recommended Repo Trading Guidelines for the European market and a Best Practice Guide to Repo Margining. Each November, the ERC, in cooperation with ACI, the Financial Markets Association, also runs the market's main educational event in the form of the annual Professional Repo Market Course.

CAPITAL REQUIREMENTS

One of the driving forces behind the expansion of the European repo market has been the impact of regulatory capital requirements on unsecured lending. Banks and securities houses in the member countries of the European Union are subject to the requirements outlined at the European level by the Capital Adequacy Directive (CAD), which is in turn based on the Basel Accord of 1988. In some EU countries, the CAD is implemented and elaborated in national legislation, but many countries simply transpose the CAD directly. Under the existing CAD (derived from the 1988 Basel Accord), for a firm with a 20% target return on capital, the benefit of collateral is equivalent to over 30 basis points. With such an incentive, it is easy to understand why liquidity has drained out of the unsecured deposit market and into the repo market.

Under the current Basel Accord and the existing CAD, the capital treatment of repos depends on whether a transaction is booked in a firm's Banking Book or Trading Book. However, the calculation for either book is simple. For example, in the Trading Book, provided that repos are documented and margined, their exposure is calculated as the difference between the market value of collateral and the value of the cash. This is weighted by the counterparty risk weight (e.g., 20% for an OECD bank) and the capital ratio (which is a minimum 8%). The capital requirement for an unsecured transaction is simply the nominal value of the loan weighted by the counterparty risk weight and the capital ratio. However, while relatively simple, Basel I is crude: Risk is weighted on the basis of whether a firm is public or private sector, and whether it is headquartered inside or outside the OECD group of industrialized countries.

Under the new Basel Accord (often called Basel II), which is expected to be implemented in 2007, a much more complex regime will come into force. Basel II aims to make regulatory capital requirements more sensitive to risk and to take explicit account of collateral in mitigating risk. Firms will have a choice of two approaches: Standardized or Internal Ratings-Based (IRB). The Standardized approach is further divided into Simple and Comprehensive, and the IRB approach into Foundation and Advanced. The more advanced the approach adopted by a firm, the more flexibility it is supposed to have and the less prescriptive the regime. However, to progress to more advanced approaches, firms must overcome increasingly high operational hurdles.

The various Basel II approaches overlap each other. The Simple Standardized approach is similar to the current Basel Accord. Both the Simple and Comprehensive Standardized approaches use external credit ratings to weight credit risk rather than the public/private and OECD/

non-OECD classification of Basel I. The Comprehensive Standardized and Foundation IRB approaches apply haircuts to the market valuation of collateral, but the Foundation IRB approach allows firms to calculate their own haircuts. The IRB approaches allow firms to use their own estimates of the four parameters used in the calculation of risk weights: under the Foundation IRB, firms can estimate probabilities of default; under the Advanced IRB, they can also estimate loss given default, exposure at default and effective term to maturity. Collateral will impact the loss given default.

As one of the aims of Basel II is to promote risk mitigation techniques such as collateralisation, in principle, the new regime should be helpful to repo and is likely to accelerate the migration from unsecured lending. Within the repo market, the new regime will change the relative attractiveness of different types of collateral, but its complexity makes it difficult to predict exactly how.

CHAPTER 15

Overview of U.S. Agency Mortgage-Backed Securities

Frank J. Fabozzi, Ph.D., CFA
Frederick Frank Adjunct Professor of Finance
School of Management
Yale University

Mortgage-backed securities (MBS) are securities backed by a pool of mortgage loans. While any type of mortgage loans, residential or commercial, can be used as collateral for an MBS, most are backed by residential mortgages. Within the U.S. MBS sector, the largest sector is for securities issued by Ginnie Mae, Fannie Mae, and Freddie Mac. Ginnie Mae is a U.S. government agency whose obligations are backed by the full faith and credit of the United States. Freddie Mac and Fannie Mae are government-sponsored enterprises. It is typical to refer to the securities issued by these three entities as "agency MBS." The agency MBS sector is the largest sector of the U.S. investment-grade, broad-based bond indexes created by dealer firms (Lehman, Salomon Smith Barney, and Merrill Lynch). In 2005, it was roughly 38% of the broad-based bond indexes.

The securities in the agency MBS sector are mortgage passthrough securities. From agency mortgage passthrough securities, dealers create two derivative products, *collateralized mortgage-backed securities* (CMOs) and *stripped MBS*. A good number of repo transactions occur in the market to finance positions in agency mortgage passthrough securities and bond classes of CMO transactions. In fact, a specialized type of repo agreement where the collateral is an agency mortgage passthrough security has developed. This transaction, called a *dollar roll*, is discussed in the next chapter.

The purpose of this chapter is to provide an overview of agency MBS (agency mortgage passthrough securities, agency CMOs, and agency mortgage strips). While nonagency MBS (including commercial mortgage-backed securities) and asset-backed securities (ABS) are used as collateral in repo transactions, they are not covered in this chapter. The key difference in risk of these securities compared to agency MBS has to do with credit risk. There are varying degrees of liquidity risk between these products and agency MBS, as well as for CMOs relative to agency mortgage passthrough securities. It should be noted that ABS have different degrees of prepayment risk, with those backed by residential mortgages (home equity loans and manufactured-housing loans) having the most prepayment risk in this sector.

MORTGAGES

A mortgage is a loan secured by the collateral of some specified real estate property which obliges the borrower to make a predetermined series of payments. The mortgage gives the lender the right, if the borrower defaults (i.e., fails to make the contractual payments), to "foreclose" on the loan and seize the property in order to ensure that the debt is paid off. The interest rate on the mortgage loan is called the *mortgage rate*.

When the lender makes the loan based on the credit of the borrower and on the collateral for the mortgage, the mortgage is said to be a *conventional mortgage*. The lender also may take out mortgage insurance to guarantee the fulfillment of the borrower's obligations. Some borrowers can qualify for mortgage insurance which is guaranteed by one of three U.S. government agencies: the Federal Housing Administration (FHA), the Veteran's Administration (VA), and the Rural Housing Service (RHS). There are also private mortgage insurers. The cost of mortgage insurance is paid to the guarantor by the mortgage originator, but it is passed along to the borrower in the form of higher mortgage payments.

There are many types of mortgage designs available in the United States. A mortgage design is a specification of the interest rate, term of the mortgage, and the manner in which the borrowed funds are repaid. The most common type is the fixed rate, level-payment, fully amortized mortgage.

The basic idea behind this mortgage design is that the borrower pays interest and repays principal in equal installments over an agreed-upon period of time, called the maturity or term of the mortgage. Thus at the end of the term, the loan has been fully amortized. The frequency of payment is typically monthly, and the prevailing term of the mortgage is 15 to 30 years.

Each monthly mortgage payment is due on the first of each month and consists of:

1. Interest of one-twelfth of the fixed annual interest rate times the amount of the outstanding mortgage balance at the beginning of the previous month
2. A repayment of a portion of the outstanding mortgage balance (principal)

The difference between the monthly mortgage payment and the portion of the payment that represents interest is equal to the amount that is applied to reduce the outstanding mortgage balance. The monthly mortgage payment is designed so that, after the last scheduled monthly payment of the loan is made, the amount of the outstanding mortgage balance is zero (i.e., the mortgage is fully repaid).

To illustrate a fixed rate, level-payment, fully amortized mortgage, consider a 30-year (360-month), $100,000 mortgage with an 8.125% mortgage rate. The monthly mortgage payment would be $742.50. Exhibit 15.1 shows for selected months how each monthly mortgage payment is divided between interest and repayment of principal. At the beginning of month 1, the mortgage balance is $100,000, the amount of the original loan. The mortgage payment for month 1 includes interest on the $100,000 borrowed for the month. Because the interest rate is 8.125%, the monthly interest rate is 0.0067708 (0.08125 divided by 12). Interest for month 1 is, therefore, $677.08 ($100,000 times 0.0067708). The $65.41 difference between the monthly mortgage payment of $742.50 and the interest of $677.08 is the portion of the monthly mortgage payment that represents repayment of principal. This $65.41 in month 1 reduces the mortgage balance.

The mortgage balance at the end of month 1 (beginning of month 2) is then $99,934.59 ($100,000 minus $65.41). The interest for the second monthly mortgage payment is $676.64, the monthly interest rate (0.0066708) times the mortgage balance at the beginning of month 2 ($99,934.59). The difference between the $742.50 monthly mortgage payment and the $676.64 interest is $65.86, representing the amount of the mortgage balance paid off with that monthly mortgage payment. Notice that the last mortgage payment in month 360 is sufficient to pay off the remaining mortgage balance.

As Exhibit 15.1 clearly shows, the portion of the monthly mortgage payment applied to interest declines each month and the portion applied to reducing the mortgage balance increases. The reason for this is that as the mortgage balance is reduced with each monthly mortgage payment, the interest on the mortgage balance declines. Because the monthly mort-

EXHIBIT 15.1   Amortization Schedule for a Fixed Rate, Level-Payment, Fully Amortized Mortgage

Mortgage loan: $100,000
Mortgage rate: 8.125%
Monthly payment: $742.50
Term of loan: 30 years (360 months)

	Beginning of Month Mortgage Balance	Monthly Payment	Monthly Interest	Scheduled Principal Repayment	Ending Mortgage Balance
1	$100,000.00	$742.50	$677.08	$65.41	$99,934.59
2	99,934.59	742.50	676.64	65.86	99,868.73
3	99,868.73	742.50	676.19	66.30	99,802.43
4	99,802.43	742.50	675.75	66.75	99,735.68
25	98,301.53	742.50	665.58	76.91	98,224.62
26	98,224.62	742.50	665.06	77.43	98,147.19
27	98,147.19	742.50	664.54	77.96	98,069.23
74	93,849.98	742.50	635.44	107.05	93,742.93
75	93,742.93	742.50	634.72	107.78	93,635.15
76	93,635.15	742.50	633.99	108.51	93,526.64
141	84,811.77	742.50	574.25	168.25	84,643.52
142	84,643.52	742.50	573.11	169.39	84,474.13
143	84,474.13	742.50	571.96	170.54	84,303.59
184	76,446.29	742.50	517.61	224.89	76,221.40
185	76,221.40	742.50	516.08	226.41	75,994.99
186	75,994.99	742.50	514.55	227.95	75,767.04
233	63,430.19	742.50	429.48	313.02	63,117.17
234	63,117.17	742.50	427.36	315.14	62,802.03
235	62,802.03	742.50	425.22	317.28	62,484.75
289	42,200.92	742.50	285.74	456.76	41,744.15
290	41,744.15	742.50	282.64	459.85	41,284.30
291	41,284.30	742.50	279.53	462.97	40,821.33
321	25,941.42	742.50	175.65	566.85	25,374.57
322	25,374.57	742.50	171.81	570.69	24,803.88
323	24,803.88	742.50	167.94	574.55	24,229.32
358	2,197.66	742.50	14.88	727.62	1,470.05
359	1,470.05	742.50	9.95	732.54	737.50
360	737.50	742.50	4.99	737.50	0.00

gage payment is fixed, an increasingly larger portion of the monthly payment is applied to reduce the principal in each subsequent month.

Our illustration assumes that the homeowner does not pay off any portion of the mortgage balance prior to the scheduled due date. But homeowners do pay off all or part of their mortgage balance prior to the maturity date. Payments made in excess of the scheduled principal repayments are called *prepayments*.

Prepayments occur for one of several reasons. First, homeowners prepay the entire mortgage when they sell their home because of a change of employment that necessitates moving or the purchase of a more expensive home. Second, the borrower may be moved to pay off part of the mortgage balance as market rates fall below the mortgage rate. This is referred to as refinancing a mortgage. Third, in the case of homeowners who cannot meet their mortgage obligations, the property is repossessed and sold. The proceeds of such a sale are used to pay off the mortgage in the case of a conventional mortgage. For an insured mortgage, the insurer will pay off the mortgage balance. Finally, if property is destroyed by fire or if another insured catastrophe occurs, the insurance proceeds are used to pay off the mortgage.

The effect of prepayments is that the amount and timing of the cash flow from a mortgage is not known with certainty. This risk is referred to as *prepayment risk*. For example, all that the investor in a $100,000, 8.125% 30-year FHA-insured mortgage knows is that as long as the loan is outstanding, interest will be received and the principal will be repaid at the scheduled date each month; then at the end of the 30 years, the investor would have received $100,000 in principal payments. What the investor does not know—the uncertainty—is for how long the loan will be outstanding, and, therefore, what the timing of the principal payments will be. This is true for all mortgage loans, not just fixed rate, level-payment, fully amortized mortgages.

MORTGAGE PASSTHROUGH SECURITIES

A mortgage passthrough security is created when one or more holders of mortgages form a collection (pool) of mortgages and sell shares or participation certificates in the pool. A pool may consist of several thousand or only a few mortgages.

Cash Flow

The cash flow of a mortgage passthrough security depends on the cash flow of the underlying mortgages. As we explained for mortgages, the cash flow consists of monthly mortgage payments representing interest, the scheduled repayment of principal, and any prepayments.

Payments are made to security holders each month. However, neither the amount nor the timing of the cash flow from the pool of mortgages is identical to that of the cash flow passed through to investors. The monthly cash flow for a passthrough is less than the monthly cash flow of the underlying mortgages by an amount equal to servicing and other fees. The other fees are those charged by the issuer or guarantor of the passthrough for guaranteeing the issue (discussed later). The coupon rate on a passthrough, called the *passthrough coupon rate*, is less than the mortgage rate on the underlying pool of mortgage loans by an amount equal to the servicing and guaranteeing fees.

The timing of the cash flow is also different. The monthly mortgage payment is due from each mortgagor on the first day of each month, but there is a delay in passing through the corresponding monthly cash flow to the security holders. The length of the delay varies by the type of passthrough security.

WAC and WAM

Not all of the mortgages that are included in a pool of mortgages that are securitized have the same mortgage rate and the same maturity. Consequently, when describing a passthrough security, a weighted average coupon rate and a weighted average maturity are determined. A *weighted average coupon rate*, or WAC, is found by weighting the mortgage rate of each mortgage loan in the pool by the amount of the mortgage outstanding. A *weighted average maturity*, or WAM, is found by weighting the remaining number of months to maturity for each mortgage loan in the pool by the amount of the mortgage outstanding.

Types of Agency Mortgage Passthrough Securities

In the United States, the three major types of passthrough securities are guaranteed by agencies created by the U.S. Congress to increase the supply of capital to the residential mortgage market and to provide support for an active secondary market: Government National Mortgage Association ("Ginnie Mae"), Federal National Mortgage Association ("Fannie Mae"), and Federal Home Loan Mortgage Corporation ("Freddie Mac").

While Fannie Mae and Freddie Mac are commonly referred to as "agencies" of the U.S. government, both are corporate instrumentalities of the U.S. government. That is, they are government sponsored enterprises. Their guarantee does not carry the full faith and credit of the U.S. government. In contrast, Ginnie Mae is a federally related institution because it is part of the Department of Housing and Urban Development. As such, its guarantee carries the full faith and credit of the U.S. government.

Ginnie Mae mortgage-backed securities are guaranteed by the full faith and credit of the United States government with respect to timely payment of both interest and principal. That is, the interest and principal will be paid when due even if the borrowers fail to make their monthly mortgage payment. The security guaranteed by Ginnie Mae is called a *mortgage-backed security* (MBS). Only mortgages insured or guaranteed by either the Federal Housing Administration, the Veterans Administration, or the Farmers Home Administration can be included in a mortgage pool guaranteed by Ginnie Mae.

The mortgage passthrough security issued by Freddie Mac is called a *participation certificate* (PC). Freddie Mac has outstanding passthroughs with one of two types of guarantees. All PCs issued under Freddie Mac's *Gold PC* program are guaranteed with respect to the timely payment of interest and principal. The Gold PC was first issued in the fall of 1990 and is the only type of PC that will be issued by Freddie Mac in the future. The other PCs are guaranteed with respect to the timely payment of interest but the scheduled principal is passed through as it is collected, with Freddie Mac guaranteeing only that the scheduled payment will be made no later than one year after it is due.

The mortgage passthrough securities issued by Fannie Mae are called *mortgage-backed securities* (MBS). These passthroughs are guaranteed with respect to the timely payment of both interest and principal.

There are many seasoned issues of the same agency with the same coupon rate outstanding at any given time. Each issue is backed by a different pool of mortgages. For example, there are many seasoned pools of Ginnie Mae 7s. One issue may be backed by a pool of mortgages all for California properties, while another may be backed by a pool of mortgages for primarily New York homes. Others may be backed by a pool of mortgages on homes in several regions of the country. Which pool is a dealer referring to when it refers to, say, GNMA 7s? They are not referring to any specific pool but they mean a "generic" 7s coupon Ginnie Mae security.

Prepayment Conventions and Cash Flow

In order to value a passthrough security, it is necessary to project its cash flow. The difficulty is that the cash flow is unknown because of prepayments. The only way to project a cash flow is to make some assumption about the prepayment rate over the life of the underlying mortgage pool.

Estimating the cash flow from a passthrough requires making an assumption about future prepayments. Two conventions have been used as a benchmark for prepayment rates—conditional prepayment rate and Public Securities Association prepayment benchmark.

The *conditional prepayment rate* (CPR) assumes that some fraction of the remaining principal in the pool is prepaid each month for the remaining term of the mortgage. The CPR assumed for a pool is based on the characteristics of the pool (including its historical prepayment experience) and the current and expected future economic environment.

The CPR is an annual prepayment rate. To estimate monthly prepayments, the CPR must be converted into a monthly prepayment rate, commonly referred to as the *single-monthly mortality rate* (SMM). A formula can be used to determine the SMM for a given CPR:

$$SMM = 1 - (1 - CPR)^{1/12}$$

Suppose that the CPR used to estimate prepayments is 6%. The corresponding SMM is:

$$SMM = 1 - (1 - 0.06)^{1/12}$$
$$= 1 - (0.94)^{0.08333} = 0.005143$$

An SMM of $w\%$ means that approximately $w\%$ of the remaining mortgage balance at the beginning of the month less the scheduled principal payment will prepay that month. That is:

Prepayment for month t = SMM
$\times$ (Beginning mortgage balance for month t
− Scheduled principal payment for month t)

For example, suppose that an investor owns a passthrough in which the remaining mortgage balance at the beginning of some month is $290 million. Assuming that the SMM is 0.5143% and the scheduled principal payment is $3 million, the estimated prepayment for the month is:

$$0.005143 \times (\$290,000,000 - \$3,000,000) = \$1,476,041$$

The *Public Securities Association (PSA) prepayment benchmark* is expressed as a monthly series of annual prepayment rates.[1] The PSA benchmark assumes that prepayment rates are low for newly originated

---

[1] This benchmark is commonly referred to as a prepayment model, suggesting that it can be used to estimate prepayments. Characterization of this benchmark as a prepayment model is inappropriate.

mortgages and then speed up as the mortgages become seasoned. Specifically, the PSA benchmark assumes the following prepayment rates for 30-year mortgages: (1) a CPR of 0.2% for the first month, increased by 0.2% per year per month for the next 29 months when it reaches 6% per year, and (2) a 6% CPR for the remaining years. This benchmark is referred to as "100% PSA" or simply "100 PSA."

Slower or faster speeds are then referred to as some multiple of PSA. For example, 50 PSA means one-half the CPR of the PSA benchmark prepayment rate; 165 PSA means 1.65 times the CPR of the PSA benchmark prepayment rate; 300 PSA means three times the CPR of the benchmark prepayment rate. A prepayment rate of 0 PSA means that no prepayments are assumed. The CPR is converted to an SMM using the equation above.

Exhibit 15.2 shows the monthly cash flow for a hypothetical passthrough security assuming (1) the underlying mortgages are fixed-rate level-payment, fully amortizing mortgages with a WAC of 8.125% and a WAM of 357 months; (2) a passthrough rate of 7.5%; and (3) a prepayment rate of 165 PSA. The cash flow is broken down into three components: (1) interest (based on the coupon passthrough rate); (2) the regularly scheduled principal repayment; and (3) prepayments based on 165 PSA. The notes to the exhibit explain how the value in the exhibit are obtained.

Extension Risk and Contraction Risk

An investor who owns passthrough securities does not know what the cash flow will be because that depends on prepayments. As we noted earlier, this risk is called prepayment risk.

To understand the significance of prepayment risk, suppose an investor buys a 10% coupon Ginnie Mae at a time when mortgage rates are 10%. Let's consider what will happen to prepayments if mortgage rates decline to, say, 6%. There will be two adverse consequences. First, a basic property of fixed income securities is that the price of an option-free bond will rise. But in the case of a passthrough security, the rise in price will not be as large as that of an option-free bond because a fall in interest rates will give the borrower an incentive to prepay the loan and refinance the debt at a lower rate. This results in the same adverse consequence faced by holders of callable corporate and agency bonds. As in the case of those bonds, the upside price potential of a passthrough security is truncated because of prepayments. The second adverse consequence is that the cash flow must be reinvested at a lower rate. These two adverse consequences when mortgage rates decline is referred to as *contraction risk*.

EXHIBIT 15.2 Monthly Cash Flow for a $400 Million Passthrough with a 7.5% Passthrough Rate, a WAC of 8.125%, and a WAM of 357 Months Assuming 165 PSA

Month	Outstanding Balance	SMM	Mortgage Payment	Net Interest	Scheduled Principal	Prepayment	Total Principal	Cash Flow
1	$400,000,000	0.00111	$2,975,868	$2,500,000	$267,535	$442,389	$709,923	$3,209,923
2	399,290,077	0.00139	2,972,575	2,495,563	269,048	552,847	821,896	3,317,459
3	398,468,181	0.00167	2,968,456	2,490,426	270,495	663,065	933,560	3,423,986
4	397,534,621	0.00195	2,963,513	2,484,591	271,873	772,949	1,044,822	3,529,413
5	396,489,799	0.00223	2,957,747	2,478,061	273,181	882,405	1,155,586	3,633,647
6	395,334,213	0.00251	2,951,160	2,470,839	274,418	991,341	1,265,759	3,736,598
7	394,068,454	0.00279	2,943,755	2,462,928	275,583	1,099,664	1,375,246	3,838,174
8	392,693,208	0.00308	2,935,534	2,454,333	276,674	1,207,280	1,483,954	3,938,287
9	391,209,254	0.00336	2,926,503	2,445,058	277,690	1,314,099	1,591,789	4,036,847
10	389,617,464	0.00365	2,916,666	2,435,109	278,631	1,420,029	1,698,659	4,133,769
11	387,918,805	0.00393	2,906,028	2,424,493	279,494	1,524,979	1,804,473	4,228,965
12	386,114,332	0.00422	2,894,595	2,413,215	280,280	1,628,859	1,909,139	4,322,353
13	384,205,194	0.00451	2,882,375	2,401,282	280,986	1,731,581	2,012,567	4,413,850
14	382,192,626	0.00480	2,869,375	2,388,704	281,613	1,833,058	2,114,670	4,503,374
15	380,077,956	0.00509	2,855,603	2,375,487	282,159	1,933,203	2,215,361	4,590,848
16	377,862,595	0.00538	2,841,068	2,361,641	282,623	2,031,931	2,314,554	4,676,195
17	375,548,041	0.00567	2,825,779	2,347,175	283,006	2,129,159	2,412,164	4,759,339
18	373,135,877	0.00597	2,809,746	2,332,099	283,305	2,224,805	2,508,110	4,840,210
19	370,627,766	0.00626	2,792,980	2,316,424	283,521	2,318,790	2,602,312	4,918,735
20	368,025,455	0.00656	2,775,493	2,300,159	283,654	2,411,036	2,694,690	4,994,849

EXHIBIT 15.2 (Continued)

Month	Outstanding Balance	SMM	Mortgage Payment	Net Interest	Scheduled Principal	Prepayment	Total Principal	Cash Flow
21	$365,330,765	0.00685	$2,757,296	$2,283,317	$283,702	$2,501,466	$2,785,169	$5,068,486
22	362,545,596	0.00715	2,738,402	2,265,910	283,666	2,590,008	2,873,674	5,139,584
23	359,671,922	0.00745	2,718,823	2,247,950	283,545	2,676,588	2,960,133	5,208,083
24	356,711,789	0.00775	2,698,575	2,229,449	283,338	2,761,139	3,044,477	5,273,926
25	353,667,312	0.00805	2,677,670	2,210,421	283,047	2,843,593	3,126,640	5,337,061
26	350,540,672	0.00835	2,656,123	2,190,879	282,671	2,923,885	3,206,556	5,397,435
27	347,334,116	0.00865	2,633,950	2,170,838	282,209	3,001,955	3,284,164	5,455,002
28	344,049,952	0.00865	2,611,167	2,150,312	281,662	2,973,553	3,255,215	5,405,527
29	340,794,737	0.00865	2,588,581	2,129,967	281,116	2,945,400	3,226,516	5,356,483
30	337,568,221	0.00865	2,566,190	2,109,801	280,572	2,917,496	3,198,067	5,307,869
100	170,142,350	0.00865	1,396,958	1,063,390	244,953	1,469,591	1,714,544	2,777,933
101	168,427,806	0.00865	1,384,875	1,052,674	244,478	1,454,765	1,699,243	2,751,916
102	166,728,563	0.00865	1,372,896	1,042,054	244,004	1,440,071	1,684,075	2,726,128
103	165,044,489	0.00865	1,361,020	1,031,528	243,531	1,425,508	1,669,039	2,700,567
104	163,375,450	0.00865	1,349,248	1,021,097	243,060	1,411,075	1,654,134	2,675,231
105	161,721,315	0.00865	1,337,577	1,010,758	242,589	1,396,771	1,639,359	2,650,118
200	56,746,664	0.00865	585,990	354,667	201,767	489,106	690,874	1,045,540
201	56,055,790	0.00865	580,921	350,349	201,377	483,134	684,510	1,034,859
202	55,371,280	0.00865	575,896	346,070	200,986	477,216	678,202	1,024,273

EXHIBIT 15.2 (Continued)

Month	Outstanding Balance	SMM	Mortgage Payment	Net Interest	Scheduled Principal	Prepayment	Total Principal	Cash Flow
203	$54,693,077	0.00865	$570,915	$341,832	$200,597	$471,353	$671,950	$1,013,782
204	54,021,127	0.00865	565,976	337,632	200,208	465,544	665,752	1,003,384
205	53,355,375	0.00865	561,081	333,471	199,820	459,789	659,609	993,080
300	11,758,141	0.00865	245,808	73,488	166,196	100,269	266,465	339,953
301	11,491,677	0.00865	243,682	71,823	165,874	97,967	263,841	335,664
302	11,227,836	0.00865	241,574	70,174	165,552	95,687	261,240	331,414
303	10,966,596	0.00865	239,485	68,541	165,232	93,430	258,662	327,203
304	10,707,934	0.00865	237,413	66,925	164,912	91,196	256,107	323,032
305	10,451,827	0.00865	235,360	65,324	164,592	88,983	253,575	318,899
350	1,235,674	0.00865	159,202	7,723	150,836	9,384	160,220	167,943
351	1,075,454	0.00865	157,825	6,722	150,544	8,000	158,544	165,266
352	916,910	0.00865	156,460	5,731	150,252	6,631	156,883	162,614
353	760,027	0.00865	155,107	4,750	149,961	5,277	155,238	159,988
354	604,789	0.00865	153,765	3,780	149,670	3,937	153,607	157,387
355	451,182	0.00865	152,435	2,820	149,380	2,611	151,991	154,811
356	299,191	0.00865	151,117	1,870	149,091	1,298	150,389	152,259
357	148,802	0.00865	149,809	930	148,802	0	148,802	149,732

EXHIBIT 15.2 (Continued)
Notes:
Column 2: This column gives the outstanding mortgage balance at the beginning of the month. It is equal to the outstanding balance at the beginning of the previous month reduced by the total principal payment in the previous month.

Column 3: This column shows the SMM for 165 PSA. Two things should be noted in this column. First, for month 1, the SMM is for a passthrough that has been seasoned three months. That is, the CPR is 0.8% times 1.65 or 1.32%. This is because the WAM is 357. Second, from month 27 on, the SMM is 0.0865, which corresponds to a CPR of 9.9% (6% times 1.65).

Column 4: The total monthly mortgage payment is shown in this column. Notice that the total monthly mortgage payment declines over time as prepayments reduce the mortgage balance outstanding. There is a formula to determine what the monthly mortgage balance is for each month given prepayments.

Column 5: The monthly interest paid to the passthrough investor is found in this column. This value is determined by multiplying the outstanding mortgage balance at the beginning of the month by the passthrough rate of 7.5% and dividing by 12.

Column 6: This column gives the regularly scheduled principal repayment. This is the difference between the total monthly mortgage payment [the amount shown in column (4)] and the gross coupon interest for the month. The gross coupon interest is 8.125% multiplied by the outstanding mortgage balance at the beginning of the month, then divided by 12.

Column 7: The prepayment for the month is reported in this column. The prepayment is found as follows:

$$\text{SMM} \times (\text{Beginning mortgage balance for month } t$$
$$- \text{Scheduled principal payment for month } t)$$

Column 8: The total principal payment, which is the sum of columns (6) and (7), is shown in this column.

Column 9: The projected monthly cash flow for this passthrough is shown in this last column. The monthly cash flow is the sum of the interest paid to the passthrough investor [column (5)] and the total principal payments for the month [column (8)].

Now let's look at what happens if mortgage rates rise to, say, 15%. The price of the passthrough, like the price of any bond, will decline. But again it declines more because the higher rates tend to slow down the rate of prepayment, in effect increasing the amount invested at the coupon rate, which is lower than the market rate. Prepayments slow down, because homeowners will not refinance or partially prepay their mortgages when mortgage rates are higher than the contract rate of 10%. Of course, this is just the time when investors want prepayments to speed up so that they can reinvest the prepayments at the higher market interest rate. This adverse consequence of rising mortgage rates is called *extension risk.*

Therefore, prepayment risk encompasses contraction risk and extension risk. Prepayment risk makes passthrough securities unattractive for certain financial institutions to hold from an asset/liability perspective. Some institutional investors such as depository institutions are concerned with extension risk and others such as pension funds with contraction risk when they purchase a passthrough security. Is it possible to alter the cash flow of a passthrough so as to reduce the contraction risk and extension risk for institutional investors? This can be done, as we shall see later in this chapter.

Average Life

The yield on mortgage passthrough securities are often compared to Treasury securities. When we speak of comparing a mortgage passthrough security to a comparable Treasury, what does "comparable" mean? The stated maturity of a mortgage passthrough security is an inappropriate measure because of prepayments. Instead, market participants have used two measures: duration and average life. We discussed duration in Chapter 6. The more commonly used measure is the average life.

The *average life* of a mortgage-backed security is the average time to receipt of principal payments (scheduled principal payments and projected prepayments), weighted by the amount of principal expected. Mathematically, the average life is expressed as follows:

$$\text{Average life} = \sum_{t=1}^{T} \frac{\text{Projected principal received at time } t}{12(\text{Total principal})}$$

where T is the number of months.

The average life of a passthrough depends on the PSA prepayment assumption. To see this, the average life is shown below for different prepayment speeds for the passthrough we used to illustrate the cash flow for 165 PSA in Exhibit 15.2:

PSA speed	50	100	165	200	300	400	500	600	700
Average life	15.11	11.66	8.76	7.68	5.63	4.44	3.68	3.16	2.78

COLLATERALIZED MORTGAGE OBLIGATIONS

As we noted, there is prepayment risk associated with investing in a mortgage passthrough security. Some institutional investors are concerned with extension risk and others with contraction risk when they invest in a passthrough. This problem can be mitigated by redirecting the cash flows of mortgage-related products (passthrough securities or a pool of loans) to different bond classes, called *tranches*, so as to create securities that have different exposure to prepayment risk and, therefore, different risk/return patterns than the mortgage-related product from which they were created.

When the cash flows of mortgage-related products are redistributed to different bond classes, the resulting securities are called *collateralized mortgage obligations*. The creation of a CMO cannot eliminate prepayment risk; it can only distribute the various forms of this risk among different classes of bondholders.

Rather than list the different types of tranches that can be created in a CMO structure, we will show how two common types of tranches can be created. This will provide an excellent illustration of financial engineering. We will look at a plain vanilla sequential-pay CMO structure and a structure with planned amortization class bonds.

Sequential-Pay Tranches

A CMO structured so that each class of bond would be retired sequentially is referred to as *sequential-pay CMOs*. To illustrate a sequential-pay CMO, we discuss CMO-1, a hypothetical deal made up to illustrate the basic features of the structure. The collateral for this hypothetical CMO is a hypothetical passthrough with a total par value of $400 million and the following characteristics: (1) The passthrough coupon rate is 7.5%; (2) the weighted average coupon (WAC) is 8.125%; and (3) the weighted average maturity (WAM) is 357 months. This is the same passthrough that we used earlier in this chapter to describe the cash flow of a passthrough based on a 165 PSA assumption.

From this $400 million of collateral, four bond classes or tranches are created. Their characteristics are summarized in Exhibit 15.3. The total par value of the four tranches is equal to the par value of the collateral (i.e., the passthrough security). In this simple structure, the coupon rate is the same for each tranche and also the same as the coupon rate on the collateral. There is no reason why this must be so, and, in fact, typically the coupon rate varies by tranche.

Now remember that a CMO is created by redistributing the cash flow—interest and principal—to the different tranches based on a set of payment rules. The payment rules at the bottom of Exhibit 15.3 describe

EXHIBIT 15.3   CMO-1: A Hypothetical Four-Tranche Sequential-Pay Structure

Tranche	Par Amount ($)	Coupon Rate (%)
A	194,500,000	7.5
B	36,000,000	7.5
C	96,500,000	7.5
D	73,000,000	7.5
Total	400,000,000	

Payment rules:

1. *For payment of periodic coupon interest:* Disburse periodic coupon interest to each tranche on the basis of the amount of principal outstanding at the beginning of the month.

2. *For disbursement of principal payments:* Disburse principal payments to tranche A until it is completely paid off. After tranche A is completely paid off, disburse principal payments to tranche B until it is completely paid off. After tranche B is completely paid off, disburse principal payments to tranche C until it is completely paid off. After tranche C is completely paid off, disburse principal payments to tranche D until it is completely paid off.

how the cash flow from the passthrough (i.e., collateral) is to be distributed to the four tranches. There are separate rules for the payment of the coupon interest and the payment of principal, the principal being the total of the regularly scheduled principal payment and any prepayments.

In CMO-1, each tranche receives periodic coupon interest payments based on the amount of the outstanding balance at the beginning of the month. The disbursement of the principal, however, is made in a special way. A tranche is not entitled to receive principal until the entire principal of the tranche before it has been paid off. More specifically, tranche A receives all the principal payments until the entire principal amount owed to that tranche, $194,500,000, is paid off; then tranche B begins to receive principal and continues to do so until it is paid the entire $36,000,000. Tranche C then receives principal, and when it is paid off, tranche D starts receiving principal payments.

While the priority rules for the disbursement of the principal payments are known, the precise amount of the principal in each period is not. This will depend on the cash flow, and therefore principal payments, of the collateral, which depends on the actual prepayment rate of the collateral. An assumed PSA speed allows the cash flow to be projected. Exhibit 15.2 shows the cash flow (interest, regularly scheduled principal repayment, and prepayments) assuming 165 PSA. Assuming that the collateral does prepay at 165 PSA, the cash flow available to all four tranches of CMO-1 is precisely the cash flow shown in Exhibit 15.2.

To demonstrate how the priority rules for CMO-1 work, Exhibit 15.4 shows the cash flow for selected months assuming the collateral prepays at 165 PSA. For each tranche, the exhibit shows: (1) the balance at the end of the month; (2) the principal paid down (regularly scheduled principal repayment plus prepayments); and (3) interest. In month 1, the cash flow for the collateral consists of principal payment of $709,923 and interest of $2.5 million (0.075 times $400 million divided by 12). The interest payment is distributed to the four tranches based on the amount of the par value outstanding. So, for example, tranche A receives $1,215,625 (0.075 times $194,500,000 divided by 12) of the $2.5 million. The principal, however, is all distributed to tranche A. Therefore, the cash flow for tranche A in month 1 is $1,925,548. The principal balance at the end of month 1 for tranche A is $193,790,076 (the original principal balance of $194,500,000 less the principal payment of $709,923). No principal payment is distributed to the three other tranches because there is still a principal balance outstanding for tranche A. This will be true for months 2 through 80.

After month 81, the principal balance will be zero for tranche A. For the collateral, the cash flow in month 81 is $3,318,521, consisting of a principal payment of $2,032,196 and interest of $1,286,325. At the beginning of month 81 (end of month 80), the principal balance for tranche A is $311,926. Therefore, $311,926 of the $2,032,196 of the principal payment from the collateral is disbursed to tranche A. After this payment is made, no additional principal payments are made to this tranche as the principal balance is zero. The remaining principal payment from the collateral, $1,720,271, is disbursed to tranche B. According to the assumed prepayment speed of 165 PSA, tranche B then begins receiving principal payments in month 81.

Exhibit 15.4 shows that tranche B is fully paid off by month 100, when tranche C now begins to receive principal payments. Tranche C is not fully paid off until month 178, at which time tranche D begins receiving the remaining principal payments. The maturity (i.e., the time until the principal is fully paid off) for these four tranches assuming 165 PSA would be 81 months for tranche A, 100 months for tranche B, 178 months for tranche C, and 357 months for tranche D.

Let us look at what has been accomplished by creating the CMO. First, as shown earlier in this chapter the average life for the passthrough is 8.76 years, assuming a prepayment speed of 165 PSA. Exhibit 15.5 reports the average life of the collateral and the four tranches assuming different prepayment speeds. Notice that the four tranches have average lives that are both shorter and longer than the collateral thereby attracting investors who have a preference for an average life different from that of the collateral.

EXHIBIT 15.4 Monthly Cash Flow for Selected Months for CMO-1 Assuming 165 PSA

Month	Tranche A			Tranche B		
	Balance	Principal	Interest	Balance	Principal	Interest
1	$ 194,500,000	$ 709,923	$1,215,625	$ 36,000,000	$0	$225,000
2	193,790,077	821,896	1,211,188	36,000,000	0	225,000
3	192,968,181	933,560	1,206,051	36,000,000	0	225,000
4	192,034,621	1,044,822	1,200,216	36,000,000	0	225,000
5	190,989,799	1,155,586	1,193,686	36,000,000	0	225,000
6	189,834,213	1,265,759	1,186,464	36,000,000	0	225,000
7	188,568,454	1,375,246	1,178,553	36,000,000	0	225,000
8	187,193,208	1,483,954	1,169,958	36,000,000	0	225,000
9	185,709,254	1,591,789	1,160,683	36,000,000	0	225,000
10	184,117,464	1,698,659	1,150,734	36,000,000	0	225,000
11	182,418,805	1,804,473	1,140,118	36,000,000	0	225,000
12	180,614,332	1,909,139	1,128,840	36,000,000	0	225,000
75	12,893,479	2,143,974	80,584	36,000,000	0	225,000
76	10,749,504	2,124,935	67,184	36,000,000	0	225,000
77	8,624,569	2,106,062	53,904	36,000,000	0	225,000
78	6,518,507	2,087,353	40,741	36,000,000	0	225,000
79	4,431,154	2,068,807	27,695	36,000,000	0	225,000
80	2,362,347	2,050,422	14,765	36,000,000	0	225,000
81	311,926	311,926	1,950	36,000,000	1,720,271	225,000
82	0	0	0	34,279,729	2,014,130	214,248
83	0	0	0	32,265,599	1,996,221	201,660
84	0	0	0	30,269,378	1,978,468	189,184
85	0	0	0	28,290,911	1,960,869	176,818
95	0	0	0	9,449,331	1,793,089	59,058
96	0	0	0	7,656,242	1,777,104	47,852
97	0	0	0	5,879,138	1,761,258	36,745
98	0	0	0	4,117,880	1,745,550	25,737
99	0	0	0	2,372,329	1,729,979	14,827
100	0	0	0	642,350	642,350	4,015
101	0	0	0	0	0	0
102	0	0	0	0	0	0
103	0	0	0	0	0	0
104	0	0	0	0	0	0
105	0	0	0	0	0	0

EXHIBIT 15.4 (Continued)

	Tranche C			Tranche D		
Month	Balance	Principal	Interest	Balance	Principal	Interest
1	$96,500,000	$ 0	$603,125	$ 73,000,000	$0	$456,250
2	96,500,000	0	603,125	73,000,000	0	456,250
3	96,500,000	0	603,125	73,000,000	0	456,250
4	96,500,000	0	603,125	73,000,000	0	456,250
5	96,500,000	0	603,125	73,000,000	0	456,250
6	96,500,000	0	603,125	73,000,000	0	456,250
7	96,500,000	0	603,125	73,000,000	0	456,250
8	96,500,000	0	603,125	73,000,000	0	456,250
9	96,500,000	0	603,125	73,000,000	0	456,250
10	96,500,000	0	603,125	73,000,000	0	456,250
11	96,500,000	0	603,125	73,000,000	0	456,250
12	96,500,000	0	603,125	73,000,000	0	456,250
95	96,500,000	0	603,125	73,000,000	0	456,250
96	96,500,000	0	603,125	73,000,000	0	456,250
97	96,500,000	0	603,125	73,000,000	0	456,250
98	96,500,000	0	603,125	73,000,000	0	456,250
99	96,500,000	0	603,125	73,000,000	0	456,250
100	96,500,000	1,072,194	603,125	73,000,000	0	456,250
101	95,427,806	1,699,243	596,424	73,000,000	0	456,250
102	93,728,563	1,684,075	585,804	73,000,000	0	456,250
103	92,044,489	1,669,039	575,278	73,000,000	0	456,250
104	90,375,450	1,654,134	564,847	73,000,000	0	456,250
105	88,721,315	1,639,359	554,508	73,000,000	0	456,250
175	3,260,287	869,602	20,377	73,000,000	0	456,250
176	2,390,685	861,673	14,942	73,000,000	0	456,250
177	1,529,013	853,813	9,556	73,000,000	0	456,250
178	675,199	675,199	4,220	73,000,000	170,824	456,250
179	0	0	0	72,829,176	838,300	455,182
180	0	0	0	71,990,876	830,646	449,943
181	0	0	0	71,160,230	823,058	444,751
182	0	0	0	70,337,173	815,536	439,607
183	0	0	0	69,521,637	808,081	434,510
184	0	0	0	68,713,556	800,690	429,460
185	0	0	0	67,912,866	793,365	424,455
350	0	0	0	1,235,674	160,220	7,723
351	0	0	0	1,075,454	158,544	6,722
352	0	0	0	916,910	156,883	5,731
353	0	0	0	760,027	155,238	4,750
354	0	0	0	604,789	153,607	3,780
355	0	0	0	451,182	151,991	2,820
356	0	0	0	299,191	150,389	1,870
357	0	0	0	148,802	148,802	930

EXHIBIT 15.5   Average Life for the Collateral and the Four Tranches of CMO-1

Prepayment	Average Life for				
Speed (PSA)	Collateral	Tranche A	Tranche B	Tranche C	Tranche D
50	15.11	7.48	15.98	21.02	27.24
100	11.66	4.90	10.86	15.78	24.58
165	8.76	3.48	7.49	11.19	20.27
200	7.68	3.05	6.42	9.60	18.11
300	5.63	2.32	4.64	6.81	13.36
400	4.44	1.94	3.70	5.31	10.34
500	3.68	1.69	3.12	4.38	8.35
600	3.16	1.51	2.74	3.75	6.96
700	2.78	1.38	2.47	3.30	5.95

A major problem still exists: There is considerable variability of the average life for the tranches. However, there is some protection provided for each tranche against prepayment risk. This is because prioritizing the distribution of principal (i.e., establishing the payment rules for principal) effectively protects the shorter-term tranche A in this structure against extension risk. This protection must come from somewhere. In fact, it comes from the three other tranches. Similarly, tranches C and D provide protection against extension risk for tranches A and B. At the same time, tranches C and D benefit because they are provided protection against contraction risk, the protection coming from tranches A and B.

Accrual Tranches

In many sequential-pay CMO structures, at least one tranche does not receive current interest. Instead, the interest for that tranche would accrue and be added to the principal balance. Such a bond class is commonly referred to as an *accrual tranche* or a *Z bond* (because the bond is similar to a zero-coupon bond). The interest that would have been paid to the accrual tranche is then used to speed up paying down the principal balance of earlier tranches.

For example, suppose that tranche D in CMO-1 is an accrual tranche. The rules for the distribution of the monthly interest and principal would then be as follows:

■ Disburse monthly interest to tranches A, B, and C on the basis of the amount of principal outstanding at the beginning of the month. For tranche Z, accrue the interest based on the principal plus accrued interest in the previous month. The interest for tranche Z is paid to the earlier tranches as a principal paydown.

■ Disburse principal payments to tranche A until it is completely paid off. After tranche A is completely paid off, disburse principal payments to tranche B until it is completely paid off. After tranche B is completely paid off, disburse principal payments to tranche C until it is completely paid off. After tranche C is completely paid off, disburse principal payments to tranche Z until the original principal balance plus accrued interest is completely paid off.

The effect on the average life of the inclusion of a Z-bond is to shorten the average life of the nonaccrual tranches.

Floating-Rate Tranches

A floating-rate tranche can be created from a fixed-rate tranche by creating a floater and an inverse floater combination. Any tranche can be selected from which to create a floating-rate and inverse floating-rate tranche. In fact, these two securities can be created for more than one tranches or for only a portion of one tranche.

For example, suppose in CMO-1 a floater and an inverse floater are created from tranche C. The par value for this tranche is $96.5 million, and we create two tranches that have a combined par value of $96.5 million. The par value of the floating-rate tranche will be some portion of the $96.5 million. There are an infinite number of ways to cut up the $96.5 million between the floater and inverse floater, and final partitioning will be driven by the demands of investors. Unlike a floating-rate note in the corporate bond market whose principal is unchanged over the life of the instrument, the floater's principal balance declines over time as principal payments are made. The principal payments to the floater are determined by the principal payments from the tranche from which the floater is created.

Planned Amortization Class Tranches

Since 1987, CMO transactions were issued wherein some of the tranches have the following characteristic: If prepayments are within a specified range, the cash flow pattern is known. The greater predictability of the cash flow for these tranches, referred to as *planned amortization class* (PAC) bonds, occurs because there is a principal repayment schedule that must be satisfied. PAC bondholders have priority over all other tranches in the CMO structure in receiving principal payments from the underlying collateral. The greater certainty of the cash flow for the PAC bonds comes at the expense of the non-PAC classes, called the *support* or *companion bonds*. It is these bonds that absorb the prepayment risk.

To illustrate how to create a PAC bond, we use as collateral the $400 million passthrough with a coupon rate of 7.5%, an 8.125% WAC, and a WAM of 357 months. The second column of Exhibit 15.6 shows the principal payment (regularly scheduled principal repayment plus prepayments) for selected months assuming a prepayment speed of 90 PSA, and the next column shows the principal payments for selected months assuming that the passthrough prepays at 300 PSA.

The last column of Exhibit 15.6 gives the *minimum* principal payment if the collateral speed is 90 PSA or 300 PSA for months 1 to 349. (After month 349, the outstanding principal balance will be paid off if the prepayment speed is between 90 PSA and 300 PSA.) For example, in the first month, the principal payment would be $508,169.52 if the collateral prepays at 90 PSA and $1,075,931.20 if the collateral prepays at 300 PSA. Thus, the minimum principal payment is $508,169.52, as reported in the last column of Exhibit 15.6. In month 103, the minimum principal payment is also the amount if the prepayment speed is 90 PSA, $1,446,761, compared to $1,458,618.04 for 300 PSA. In month 104, however, a prepayment speed of 300 PSA would produce a principal payment of $1,433,539.23, which is less than the principal payment of $1,440,825.55 assuming 90 PSA. So, $1,433,539.23 is reported in the last column of Exhibit 15.6. In fact, from month 104 on the minimum principal payment is the one that would result assuming a prepayment speed of 300 PSA.

In fact, if the collateral prepays at *any* speed between 90 PSA and 300 PSA, the minimum principal payment would be the amount reported in the last column of Exhibit 15.6. For example, if we had included principal payment figures assuming a prepayment speed of 200 PSA, the minimum principal payment would not change: from month 1 through month 103, the minimum principal payment is that generated from 90 PSA, but from month 104 on, the minimum principal payment is that generated from 300 PSA.

This characteristic of the collateral allows for the creation of a PAC bond, assuming that the collateral prepays over its life at a constant speed between 90 PSA to 300 PSA. A schedule of principal repayments that the PAC bondholders are entitled to receive before any other bond class in the CMO is specified. The monthly schedule of principal repayments is as specified in the last column of Exhibit 15.6, which shows the minimum principal payment. While there is no assurance that the collateral will prepay between these two speeds, a PAC bond can be structured to assume that it will.

EXHIBIT 15.6   Monthly Principal Payment for $400 Million 7.5% Coupon
Passthrough with an 8.125% WAC and a 357 WAM Assuming Prepayment Rates
of 90 PSA and 300 PSA

Month	At 90% PSA	At 300% PSA	Minimum Principal Payment —the PAC Schedule
1	$508,169.52	$1,075,931.20	$508,169.52
2	569,843.43	1,279,412.11	569,843.43
3	631,377.11	1,482,194.45	631,377.11
4	692,741.89	1,683,966.17	692,741.89
5	753,909.12	1,884,414.62	753,909.12
6	814,850.22	2,083,227.31	814,850.22
7	875,536.68	2,280,092.68	875,536.68
8	935,940.10	2,474,700.92	935,940.10
9	996,032.19	2,666,744.77	996,032.19
10	1,055,784.82	2,855,920.32	1,055,784.82
11	1,115,170.01	3,041,927.81	1,115,170.01
12	1,174,160.00	3,224,472.44	1,174,160.00
13	1,232,727.22	3,403,265.17	1,232,727.22
14	1,290,844.32	3,578,023.49	1,290,844.32
101	1,458,719.34	1,510,072.17	1,458,719.34
102	1,452,725.55	1,484,126.59	1,452,725.55
103	1,446,761.00	1,458,618.04	1,446,761.00
104	1,440,825.55	1,433,539.23	1,433,539.23
105	1,434,919.07	1,408,883.01	1,408,883.01
211	949,482.58	213,309.00	213,309.00
212	946,033.34	209,409.09	209,409.09
213	942,601.99	205,577.05	205,577.05
346	618,684.59	13,269.17	13,269.17
347	617,071.58	12,944.51	12,944.51
348	615,468.65	12,626.21	12,626.21
349	613,875.77	12,314.16	3,432.32
350	612,292.88	12,008.25	0
351	610,719.96	11,708.38	0
356	603,003.38	10,295.70	0
357	601,489.39	10,029.78	0

EXHIBIT 15.7   CMO-2: CMO Structure with One PAC Bond and One Support
Bond

Tranche	Par Amount ($)	Coupon Rate (%)
P (PAC)	243,800,000	7.5
S (Support)	156,200,000	7.5
Total	400,000,000	

Payment rules:

1. *For payment of monthly coupon interest:* Disburse periodic coupon interest to
each tranche on the basis of the amount of principal outstanding at the beginning of the month.

2. *For disbursement of monthly principal payments:* Disburse principal payments to tranche P based on its schedule of principal repayments as given in
column (4) of Exhibit 15.6. Tranche P has priority with respect to current and
future principal payments to satisfy the schedule. Any excess principal payments in a month over the amount necessary to satisfy the schedule for tranche
P are paid to tranche S. When tranche S is completely paid off, all principal
payments are to be made to tranche P regardless of the schedule.

Exhibit 15.7 shows a CMO structure, CMO-2, created from the
$400 million, 7.5% coupon passthrough with a WAC of 8.125% and a
WAM of 357 months. There are just two tranches in this structure: a
7.5% coupon PAC bond created assuming 90 to 300 PSA with a par
value of $243.8 million and a support bond with a par value of $156.2
million.

Exhibit 15.8 reports the average life for the PAC bond and the support bond in CMO-2 assuming various *actual* prepayment speeds.
Notice that between 90 PSA and 300 PSA, the average life for the PAC
bond is stable at 7.26 years. However, at slower or faster PSA speeds,
the schedule is broken, and the average life changes, lengthening when
the prepayment speed is less than 90 PSA and shortening when it is
greater than 300 PSA. Even so, there is much greater variability for the
average life of the support bond.

In practice, CMO structures that include a PAC tranche typically do
not have just one PAC tranche. Rather, there are several PAC tranches
created from the same tranche. For example, several PAC tranches that
pay off in sequence can be created with a total par value equal to
$243.8 million, which is the amount of the single PAC bond in CMO-2.
This allows for the creation of PACs with a wide-range of average lives.

EXHIBIT 15.8   Average Life for PAC Bond and Support Bond in CMO-2 Assuming
Various Prepayment Speeds

Prepayment Rate (PSA)	PAC Bond (P)	Support Bond (S)
0	15.97	27.26
50	9.44	24.00
90	7.26	18.56
100	7.26	18.56
150	7.26	12.57
165	7.26	11.16
200	7.26	8.38
250	7.26	5.37
300	7.26	3.13
350	6.56	2.51
400	5.92	2.17
450	5.38	1.94
500	4.93	1.77
700	3.70	1.37

Support Tranches

The support tranches provide prepayment protection for the PAC
tranches. Consequently, support tranches expose investors to the greatest
level of prepayment risk. Because of this, investors must be particularly
careful in assessing the cash flow characteristics of support tranches to
reduce the likelihood of adverse price movement due to prepayments.

The support tranche typically is divided into different tranches. All
the tranche types we have discussed earlier are available, including
sequential-pay support tranches, accrual support tranches, and floating-
rate support tranches. The support tranche can even be partitioned to
create support tranches with a schedule of principal payments. That is,
support tranches that are PAC can be created. In a structure with a PAC
tranche and a support tranche with a PAC schedule of principal payments, the former is called a *PAC I tranche* or *Level I PAC tranche* and
the latter a *PAC II tranche* or *Level II PAC tranche* or a *scheduled
tranche*. While PAC II tranches have greater prepayment protection than
the support tranches without a schedule of principal repayments, the
prepayment protection is less than that provided PAC I tranches.

The support tranche without a principal repayment schedule can be
used to create any type of tranche. In fact, a portion of the non-PAC II
tranche can be given a schedule of principal repayments. This bond class
would be called a *PAC III tranche* or a *Level III tranche*. While it pro-

vides protection against prepayments for the PAC I and PAC II tranches and is therefore subject to considerable prepayment risk, such a tranche has greater protection than the support tranche without a schedule of principal repayments.

STRIPPED MORTGAGE-BACKED SECURITIES

A mortgage passthrough security divides the cash flow from the underlying pool of mortgages on a pro rata basis to the security holders. A stripped mortgage-backed security is created by altering that distribution of principal and interest from a pro rata distribution to an unequal distribution. The result is that the securities created will have a price/yield relationship that is different from the price/yield relationship of the underlying passthrough security.

In the most common type of stripped mortgage-backed securities all the interest is allocated to one class (called the *interest only* or *IO class*) and all the principal to the other class (called the *principal only* or *PO class*). The IO class receives no principal payments.

The PO security is purchased at a substantial discount from par value. The return an investor realizes depends on the speed at which prepayments are made. The faster the prepayments, the higher the investor's return. For example, suppose there is a mortgage pool consisting of only 30-year mortgages, with $400 million in principal, and that investors can purchase POs backed by this mortgage pool for $175 million. The dollar return on this investment will be $225 million. How quickly that dollar return is recovered by PO investors determines the actual return that will be realized. In the extreme case, if all homeowners in the underlying mortgage pool decide to prepay their mortgage loans immediately, PO investors will realize the $225 million immediately. At the other extreme, if all homeowners decide to remain in their homes for 30 years and make no prepayments, the $225 million will be spread out over 30 years, which would result in a lower return for PO investors.

Let's look at how the price of the PO would be expected to change as mortgage rates in the market change. When mortgage rates decline below the coupon rate, prepayments are expected to speed up, accelerating payments to the PO holder. Thus, the cash flow of a PO improves (in the sense that principal repayments are received earlier). The cash flow will be discounted at a lower interest rate because the mortgage rate in the market has declined. The result is that the PO price increases when mortgage rates decline. When mortgage rates rise above the coupon rate, prepayments are expected to slow down. The cash flow deteriorates (in the sense that it takes longer to recover principal repayments). Couple this with a higher discount rate, and the price of a PO falls when mortgage rates rise.

An IO has no par value. In contrast to the PO investor, the IO investor wants prepayments to be slow. The reason is that the IO investor receives interest only on the amount of the principal outstanding. When prepayments are made, less dollar interest will be received as the outstanding principal declines. *In fact, if prepayments are too fast, the IO investor may not recover the amount paid for the IO.*

Let us look at the expected price response of an IO to changes in mortgage rates. If mortgage rates decline below the coupon rate, the prepayments are expected to accelerate. This would result in a deterioration of the expected cash flow for an IO. While the cash flow will be discounted at a lower rate, the net effect typically is a decline in the price of an IO. If mortgage rates rise above the coupon rate, the expected cash flow improves, but the cash flow is discounted at a higher interest rate. The net effect may be either a rise or fall for the IO. Thus, we see an interesting characteristic of an IO: its price tends to move in the same direction as the change in mortgage rates: (1) when mortgage rates fall below the coupon rate and (2) for some range of mortgage rates above the coupon rate.

Both POs and IOs exhibit substantial price volatility when mortgage rates change. The greater price volatility of the IO and PO compared to the passthrough is due to the fact that the combined price volatility of the IO and PO must be equal to the price volatility of the passthrough.

CHAPTER 16

Dollar Rolls

Frank J. Fabozzi, Ph.D., CFA
Frederick Frank Adjunct Professor of Finance
School of Management
Yale University

Steven V. Mann, Ph.D.
Professor of Finance
Moore School of Management
University of South Carolina

A special type of collateralized loan has developed in the *mortgage-backed securities* (MBS) market because of the characteristics of these securities and the need of dealers to borrow these securities to cover short positions. This arrangement is called a *dollar roll* and can be thought of as a specialized form of a reverse repurchase agreement with passthrough securities serving as collateral. A dollar roll is so named because dealers are said to "roll in" securities they borrow and "roll out" securities when returning the securities to the investor.

Dollar rolls resemble repurchase agreements on a number of dimensions. For example, a dollar roll is a collateralized loan that calls for the sale and repurchase of a passthrough security on different settlement dates. However, unlike a repurchase agreement, the dealer who borrows passthrough securities need only return "substantially identical securities." Although we discuss this in more detail shortly, for now, "substantially identical securities" returned by the dealer must match certain criteria such as the coupon rate and security type—that is, issuer (e.g., Ginnie Mae) and mortgage collateral (e.g., 30-year fixed rate).[1] This fea-

---

[1] These are the same general trade parameters that buyer and seller would agree to when trading passthroughs on a to-be-announced (TBA) basis.

ture provides valuable flexibility to dealers for either covering short positions or obtaining passthroughs to collateralize a CMO deal. In order to obtain this flexibility, the dealer provides the security lender (i.e., the investor) provides 100% financing—no overcollateralization or margin required. The financing cost may also be cheaper (sometimes considerably so) because of this flexibility. Lastly, recall that with a repurchase agreement, there is no transfer of security's cash flows. The original owner continues to receive any principal and coupon interest. Not so with a dollar roll, the dealer borrowing the passthrough security keeps the coupon interest and any principal paydown during the length of the agreement.

THE MARKET FOR AGENCY PASSTHROUGHS

In this first part of the chapter we describe the basic features of mortgage passthrough securities that are securities that serve as collateral for a dollar roll. We then provide a sketch of the trading and settlement procedures for these securities that gives rise to a dollar roll in the first place. More details on the types of agency mortgage-backed securities are provided in the previous chapter.

Features of Passthrough Securities

A mortgage passthrough security (henceforth, passthrough) is created when one or more mortgage holders form a collection (pool) of mortgages and sell shares or participation certificates in the pool. The cash flow of a passthrough depends on the cash flow of the underlying mortgages. It consists of monthly mortgage payments representing interest, the scheduled repayment of principal, and any prepayments.

Payments are made to security holders each month. Neither the amount nor the timing, however, of the cash flow from the mortgage pool is identical to that of the cash flow passed through to investors. The monthly cash flow for a passthrough is less than the monthly cash flow of the underlying mortgages by an amount equal to servicing and other fees. The other fees are those charged by the issuer or guarantor of the passthrough for guaranteeing the issue. The coupon rate on a passthrough is less than the mortgage rate on the underlying pool of mortgage loans by an amount equal to the servicing and guaranteeing fees.

The timing of the cash flows is also different. The monthly mortgage payment is due from each mortgagor on the first day of each month. There is then a delay in passing through the corresponding monthly cash to the security holders, which varies by the type of passthrough. Because of prepayments, the cash flow of a passthrough is not known with certainty.

There are three major types of passthroughs guaranteed by the following organizations: Government National Mortgage Association ("Ginnie Mae"), Fannie Mae, and Freddie Mac. These are called *agency passthroughs*. Ginnie Mae passthroughs are backed primarily by Federal Housing Authority (FHA) insured or Veterans Administration (VA) guaranteed mortgage loans. Correspondingly, Fannie Mae and Freddie Mac securitize conforming mortgage loans. A conforming mortgage is one that meets the underwriting standards established by these institutions for being in a mortgage pool underlying a security that they guarantee. In order to qualify as a conforming mortgage, a mortgage loan must meet three underwriting standards which include: (1) a maximum payment-to-income (PTI) ratio; (2) a maximum loan-to-value (LTV) ratio; and (3) a maximum loan amount ($333,700 for a single-family mortgage as of January 2004).

An agency can provide one of two types of guarantees. One type guarantees the timely payment of both interest and principal meaning that the interest and principal will be paid when due, even if any of the mortgagors fail to make their monthly mortgage payments. Passthroughs with this type of guarantee are referred to as *fully modified passthroughs*. The second type guarantees both interest and principal payments but it guarantees the timeliness of the interest payment only. The scheduled principal is passed through as it is collected with a guarantee that the scheduled payment will be made no later than a specified time after it is due. Passthroughs with this of guarantee are called *modified passthroughs*.

Trading and Settlement Procedures for Agency Passthroughs

Agency passthroughs are identified by a pool prefix and pool number provided by the agency. The prefix indicates the type of passthrough. Exhibit 16.1 presents a Bloomberg screen with a pool prefix guide for Freddie Mac Gold PCs (participation certificates). The pool number indicates specific mortgages underlying the passthrough as well as the passthrough's issuer.

The trading and settlement of mortgage-backed securities is governed by rules established by the Bond Market Association. We limit our discussion in this section to agency passthrough securities. Many trades of passthrough securities are derived from mortgage pools that have yet to be specified. As a result, no pool information is available at the time of the trade. Such a trade is denoted as a "TBA" trade which stands for "to be announced." In a TBA trade, the buy and seller agree on the issuer, type of program, coupon rate, face value, the price, and the settlement date. The actual pools underlying the passthrough are not specified. This information is provided by the seller to the buyer before delivery. There are also specified pool trades wherein the actual pool numbers to be delivered are specified.

EXHIBIT 16.1   Bloomberg Screen of the Freddie Mac Pool Prefix Guide

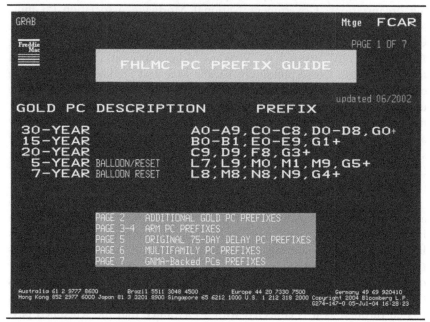

Source: Bloomberg LP

Agency passthroughs usually trade on a forward basis and settlement occurs once month. Each passthrough is assigned a settlement day during the month based on the issuer and type of collateral. For example, for July 2004 passthroughs issued by Fannie Mae or Freddie Mac backed by 30-year mortgages, the settlement date is July 15. The delivery schedule is determined by BMA.

This system of forward settlement is crucial to the MBS market for two reasons. First, forward settlement allows the originators of mortgages to sell passthroughs forward before creating mortgage pools. Accordingly, originators can hedge the mortgage rates at which they are lending. Second, forward settlement also facilitates CMO production as the collateral for CMOs is agency passthroughs. The settlement of CMO deals is usually one month from the pricing date. Thus, issuers of CMOs are active players in the one-month forward market.[2] Moreover, it is the demand for newly minted passthroughs needed for CMO collateral that gives rise to the existence of the dollar roll market.

---

[2] See Andrew Davidson and Anne Ching, "Agency Mortgage-Backed Securities," Chapter 23 in Frank J. Fabozzi (ed.), *The Handbook of Fixed-Income Securities,* 7th ed. (New York: McGraw-Hill, 2005),

DETERMINATION OF THE FINANCING COST

The process for determining the dollar roll's financing cost is not as straightforward as that of a repurchase agreement. The key elements in determining a dollar roll's financing cost *assuming that the dealer is borrowing securities/lending cash* are:

1. Sale price and the repurchase price
2. Amount of the coupon payment
3. Amount of scheduled principal payments
4. Projected prepayments of the security sold to the dealer
5. Attributes of the substantially identical security returned by the dealer
6. Amount of under- or overdelivery permitted

Let us consider each of these elements. The repurchase price is usually less than the sale price in a dollar roll. At first blush, this may seem counterintuitive. After all, as discussed in Chapter 13 on repurchase agreements, the repurchase price is always greater than the sale price where the difference represents repo interest. In a dollar roll, the reason the repurchase price is less than the sales price is because of the second element—the investor surrenders any coupon payments they would have received had they simply held the securities during the length of the dollar roll agreement. Thus, the financing costs of a dollar roll depend on the difference between what the investor gives up in terms of forgone coupon interest and what the investor gives back in the form of a lower repurchase price. Specifically, when the yield curved is positively sloped (i.e., long-term interest rates exceed short-term interest rates), the coupon rates of newly minted passthroughs will exceed short-term collateralized borrowing rates. The greater the slope of the yield curve, the lower the repurchase price must be to offset the forgone coupon interest, other things equal.

The third and fourth elements involve principal payments. There are two types of principal payments: scheduled and prepayments. Scheduled principal payments are predictable and are due to loan amortization. Prepayments occur because the homeowner's option to make principal payments in excess of the scheduled amount (in whole or in part) at any time prior to the mortgage's maturity date usually at no cost. As with the coupon payments, the investor forfeits any principal payments during the length of the agreement. A gain will be realized by the dealer on any principal payments if the security is purchased by the dealer at a discount and a loss if purchased at a premium. Because of prepayments, the principal paydown over the life of the agreement is unknown so the investor's borrowing rate is not known with certainty. This uncertainty represents another difference between dollar rolls and repurchase agreements. In a repurchase agreement, the lender of securities/borrower of funds borrows at a known financing rate. Conversely, with a dollar roll, the financing rate is unknown at the outset of the agreement and can only be projected based on an assumed prepayment rate.

The fifth element is another risk because the effective financing cost depends on the attributes of the substantially identical security that the dealer returns to the lender. Note that this differs from a repurchase agreement in that the security borrower must return securities that are identical to those pledged as collateral. A dealer that borrows mortgage passthroughs will almost never return the identical securities (i.e., passthroughs derived from the same mortgage pools) to the investor. Instead the dealer is only required mortgage passthroughs that met certain criteria. The American Institute of Certified Public Accountants, Statement of Position 90-3 requires substantially identical securities met the following criteria:

1. Be collateralized by similar mortgages;
2. Be issued by the same agency and be a part of the same program;
3. Have the same original stated maturity;
4. Have identical coupon rates;
5. Be priced at similar market yields; and
6. Satisfy delivery requirements, i.e., the aggregate principal amounts of the securities delivered and received back must be within 0.1% of the initial amount delivered.

There are literally hundreds if not thousands of passthrough securities that met these criteria at any given time. However, these passthroughs differ in that they are securitized by different mortgage pools. As a result, even among substantially identical securities, some pools perform worse than others.

The last element is the amount of under- or overdelivery permitted. Specifically, the BMA (Bond Market Association) delivery standards permit under- or overdelivery of up to 0.01%. In a dollar roll agreement, both the investor and the dealer have the option to under- or overdeliver: the investor when delivering the securities at the outset of the transaction and the dealer when returning the securities at the end of the agreement.

ILLUSTRATIONS OF DOLLAR ROLL AGREEMENTS

The decision of whether or not a mortgage-backed securities investor participates in a dollar roll agreement depends on a number of factors.

These factors include the size of the difference between the sale price and the repurchase price (called the drop or the forward drop), prepayment speeds of the collateral underlying the securities, and available reinvestment rates. In this section, we present two illustrations using discount and premium passthroughs highlighting how these factors impact the investor's decision to roll their securities.

Dollar Roll with Discount Passthroughs

Consider some June 2004 production Fannie Mae passthroughs that carry a 5% coupon. and a principal balance of $1,000,000. The payment delay is 54 days and the settlement date is June 14, 2004. Suppose that an investor enters into an agreement with a dealer in which it agrees to sell $1,000,000 par value (i.e., unpaid aggregate balance) of these Fannie Mae 5s at $94^{21}/_{32}$ and repurchase substantially identical securities one month later at $94^9/_{32}$ (the repurchase price).[3] This agreement is illustrated in Exhibit 16.2 using Bloomberg's Dollar Roll Analysis screen. Note that the difference the sales price and the repurchase price is $^{12}/_{32}$ and this is located in the upper-center

EXHIBIT 16.2 Bloomberg Dollar Roll Analysis Screen for a Discount Passthrough

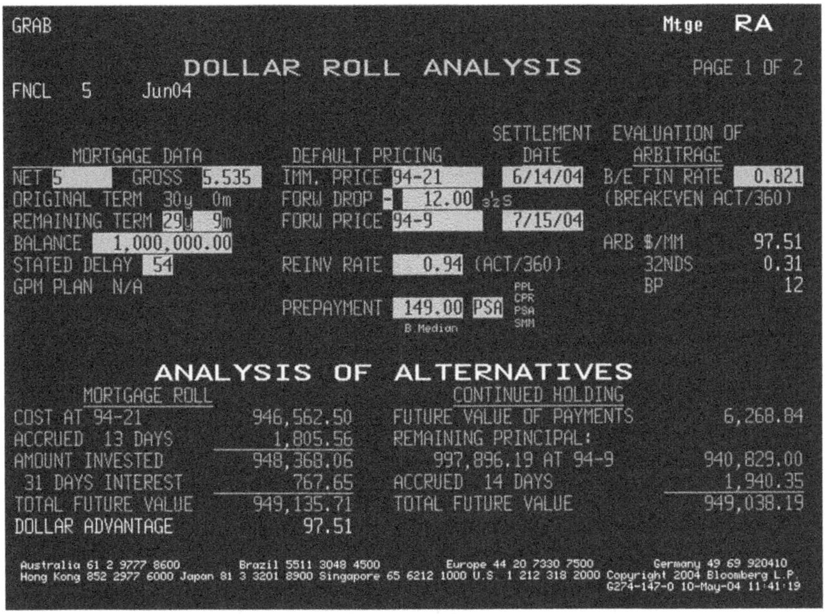

Source: Bloomberg LP

---

[3] In market parlance, a trader would say "buy $1 million of the June/July roll."

portion of the screen labeled as "FORW DROP" (forward drop). The key question that the investor faces is whether she (or he) should roll the passthroughs versus simply holding them over the same time period.

If the investor chooses to roll the passthroughs, she receives the sale price of 94²¹⁄₃₂ or $946,562.50 for a $1,000,000 principal balance on the settlement date of June 14, 2004. In addition, the investor receives 13 days accrued interest of $1,805.56 ($1,000,000 × 5% × (13/360)) because interest starts accruing June 1. The total amount received on the settlement date is $948,368.06. This number is labeled "AMOUNT INVESTED" and is located in the lower left-hand portion of the screen. It is assumed that the proceeds of the dollar roll will be reinvested for the length of the agreement from June 14 to July 15 or 31 days. The default reinvestment rate in Bloomberg is the rate on a repurchase agreement collateralized by Treasury securities over the same period. Accordingly, the assumed reinvestment rate is 0.94% and is labeled "REINV RATE." The reinvestment income generated over the length of the agreement is the repo interest of $767.65 (0.94% × $948,368.06 × (31/360)). The investor will have $949,135.71 at the end of the agreement July 15, 2004. This number must be compared to the number of dollars generated by simply holding the securities over the same period of time.

If the investor holds the passthroughs, she will receive a cash flow on July 25 for the month of June because 54 day stated payment delay. The cash flows consist of coupon interest and principal paydown—both scheduled and prepayments. The breakdown of these cash flows is presented in Exhibit 16.3 which is the second page of Bloomberg's dollar roll analysis. The interest for the month of June is $4,166.67 (5% × $1,000,000 × 1/12). While the scheduled principal payments are known, prepayments must be forecasted using an assumed prepayment rate. We use the Bloomberg Median prepayment assumption of 149 PSA, which is the default. The June principal payments are projected to be $2,103.81. The total cash flow to be received by the investor on July 25 is $6,270.47. We must take the present value of this payment to find how much they will be worth on July 15 (the end of the dollar roll agreement). Using the reinvestment rate of 0.94%, we discount $6,270.47 back 10 days to obtain $6,268.04. Returning to Exhibit 16.2, this number is labeled "FUTURE VALUE OF PAYMENTS" and is located on the lower right side of the screen.

The remaining principal is worth $940,829.00 using the dollar roll repurchase price of 94⁹⁄₃₂. In addition, there will 14 days accrued interest for the month of July of $1,940.35 (5% × $997,896.19 × 14/360). The total number of dollars generated by continuing to hold the passthrough securities on July 15 is $949,038.19. Comparing this number to future value generated by the dollar roll indicates there is a $97.51 gain (labeled DOLLAR ADVANTAGE) per $1 million of principal for rolling the

EXHIBIT 16.3   Bloomberg Dollar Roll Analysis Screen for a Discount Passthrough

```
GRAB                                                        Mtge   RA
                  DOLLAR ROLL ANALYSIS              PAGE 2 OF 2
FNCL   5     Jun04

NET 5           GROSS 5.535
ORIGINAL TERM  30y   0m    STATED DELAY  54      REINV RATE   0.94 ACT
                                                                   360
REMAINING TERM 29y   9m    GPM PLAN N/A          PREPAYMENT  PSA 149.00

         CONTINUED HOLDING OF SECURITY
PAYMENT       PRINCIPAL                   PRINCIPAL    NET CASH    VALUE AS OF
 DATE          BALANCE      INTEREST       PAYMENT       FLOW       7/15/04
7/25/04       997,896.19   4,166.67       2,103.81     6,270.47    6,268.84




Australia 61 2 9777 8600      Brazil 5511 3048 4500      Europe 44 20 7330 7500      Germany 49 69 920410
Hong Kong 852 2977 6000 Japan 81 3 3201 8900 Singapore 65 6212 1000 U.S. 1 212 318 2000 Copyright 2004 Bloomberg L.P.
                                                                   G274-147-0 10-May-04 11:42:40
```

Source: Bloomberg LP

passthroughs. From the investor's perspective, engaging in a dollar roll is tantamount financing the passthroughs using a repurchase agreement. As such, it is possible to compute a breakeven reinvestment rate that would make dollar advantage of rolling the securities equal to zero all else being equal. In this example, the breakeven rate is 0.821% and is located in the top left portion of the screen. If the investor can reinvest at a rate higher than this, When the investor's reinvestment rate is higher than this, there is an advantage to rolling the passthroughs all else equal. In comparing financing costs, it is important that the dollar amount of the cost be compared to the amounts borrowed. Moreover, it is not proper to compare financing costs of other alternatives without recognizing the risks associated with a dollar roll.

Dollar Roll with Premium Passthroughs

Now suppose an investor is contemplating a dollar roll with $1 million Ginnie Mae 30-year 6½ passthroughs at a price of 103⁶/₃₂ for settlement on June 22, 2004. Exhibit 16.4 presents a Bloomberg Dollar Roll Analysis screen with the particulars of the transaction. The drop is ¹¹/₃₂ and the repurchase price on July 22 (the end of the dollar roll agreement) is

EXHIBIT 16.4   Bloomberg Dollar Roll Analysis Screen for a Premium Passthrough

```
GRAB                                                          Mtge   RA
Enter all values and hit <GO>.
              DOLLAR  ROLL  ANALYSIS               PAGE 1 OF 2
GNSF  6'2   Jun04


                                    SETTLEMENT  EVALUATION OF
        MORTGAGE DATA        DEFAULT PRICING    DATE        ARBITRAGE
NET 6'2    GROSS  ?      IMM. PRICE 103-6        6/22/04   B/E FIN RATE   1.710
ORIGINAL TERM  30y  0m   FORW DROP  -  11.00 3½S           (BREAKEVEN ACT/360)
REMAINING TERM 28y  1m   FORW PRICE 102-27       7/22/04
BALANCE   1,000,000.00                                     ARB $/MM      -673.48
STATED DELAY  44         REINV RATE   0.93 (ACT/360)       32NDS          -2.16
GPM PLAN  N/A                                      PPL     BP             -78
                         PREPAYMENT  341.00 PSA   CPR
                                     B.Median      PSA
                                                   SMM

            ANALYSIS  OF  ALTERNATIVES
        MORTGAGE ROLL                   CONTINUED HOLDING
COST AT 103-6          1,031,875.00  FUTURE VALUE OF PAYMENTS    21,147.55
ACCRUED  21 DAYS           3,791.67  REMAINING PRINCIPAL:
AMOUNT INVESTED        1,035,666.67       984,272.94 AT 102-27 1,012,263.20
 30 DAYS INTEREST            802.64  ACCRUED  21 DAYS               3,732.03
TOTAL FUTURE VALUE    1,036,469.31   TOTAL FUTURE VALUE         1,037,142.79
                                     DOLLAR ADVANTAGE              673.48

Australia 61 2 9777 8600      Brazil 5511 3048 4500      Europe 44 20 7330 7500      Germany 49 69 920410
Hong Kong 852 2977 6000 Japan 81 3 3201 8900 Singapore 65 6212 1000 U.S 1 212 318 2000 Copyright 2004 Bloomberg L.P.
                                                               G274-147-0 13-May-04 16:28:45
```

Source: Bloomberg LP.

$102^{27}\!/_{32}$. Using the Bloomberg Median prepayment assumption of 341 PSA, the breakeven reinvestment rate is 1.71%. If the investor uses the one-month repo rate as a proxy for their reinvestment rate of 0.93%, the investor would not to roll the passthroughs. Specifically, using these assumptions, there is a $673.48 (per $1 million) for holding rather than rolling these Ginnie Mae passthroughs.

RISKS IN A DOLLAR ROLL FROM THE INVESTOR'S PERSPECTIVE

Because of the unusual nature of the dollar roll transaction as a collateralized borrowing vehicle, it is only possible to estimate the financing cost (i.e., the breakeven reinvestment rate). The reason being that the speed of prepayments will affect the financing rate the investor pays by rolling the passthroughs. In our illustration, since the passthroughs are trading at a discount, faster prepayments will benefit whoever holds the securities. Thus, the investor's financing rate obtained via a dollar roll is directly related to the prepayment speed. An investor can perform a sensitivity analysis to determine the effect of varying prepayment speeds on the financing rate. Exhibit 16.5 presents a Bloomberg screen of a sensitivity analysis of the breakeven financing rate for the discount Fannie Mae passthroughs from Exhibit 16.2. Specifically, the matrix displays how the breakeven finance rate varies with prepayments speeds and the size of the drop. Each row represents a different PSA speed and each column represents a different drop. For discount passthroughs, holding the drop constant, financing rates increase as prepayments decrease. Holding the prepayment speed constant, financing rates decrease as the drop increases.

If the passthroughs are trading at a premium, the investor's financing rate will be inversely related to the prepayment speed. Exhibit 16.6 presents a Bloomberg screen of a sensitivity analysis of the breakeven financing rate for the premium Ginnie Mae passthroughs from Exhibit 16.4. As conjectured, slower prepayment speeds translate into higher breakeven rates. The maximum financing rate can be determined assuming no prepayments or an assumed PSA speed of zero. In this case, the breakeven finance rises to 2.259% or approximately 55 basis points higher than the base case.

In addition to the uncertainty about the prepayment speed, there is another risk that involves the substantially identical securities returned by

EXHIBIT 16.5   Bloomberg Screen of a Sensitivity Analysis of the Breakeven Financing Rate for a Discount Passthrough

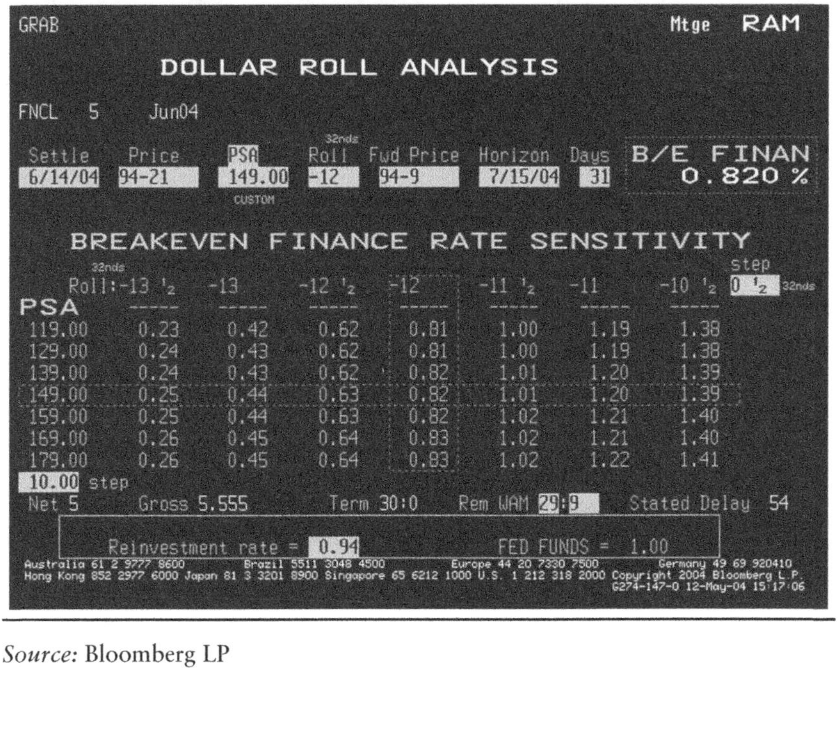

Source: Bloomberg LP

EXHIBIT 16.6   Bloomberg Screen of a Sensitivity Analysis of the Breakeven
Financing Rate for a Premium Passthrough

```
GRAB                                                          Mtge  RAM
            DOLLAR  ROLL  ANALYSIS

GNSF   6¹₂   Jun04
                            32nds
  Settle    Price    PSA    Roll  Fwd Price  Horizon  Days  B/E  FINAN
 6/22/04   103-6    341.00  -11   102-27     7/22/04   30    1.710 %
                   B.Median

     BREAKEVEN  FINANCE  RATE  SENSITIVITY
      32nds                                                step
        Roll:-12 ¹₂   -12    -11 ¹₂   -11   -10 ¹₂   -10    -9 ¹₂  0 ¹₂ 32nds
PSA     -----  -----  -----  -----  -----  -----  -----
 281.00   1.28   1.46   1.63   1.81   1.99   2.17   2.35
 301.00   1.24   1.42   1.60   1.78   1.96   2.14   2.32
 321.00   1.21   1.39   1.57   1.75   1.92   2.10   2.28
 341.00   1.18   1.35   1.53   1.71   1.89   2.07   2.24
 361.00   1.14   1.32   1.50   1.68   1.85   2.03   2.21
 381.00   1.11   1.28   1.46   1.64   1.82   2.00   2.17
 401.00   1.07   1.25   1.43   1.60   1.78   1.96   2.14
 20.00 step
 Net 6 ¹₂   Gross 7         Term 30:0   Rem WAM 28:1    Stated Delay  44

        Reinvestment rate = 0.93          FED FUNDS = 1.00
Australia 61 2 9777 8600       Brazil 5511 3048 4500      Europe 44 20 7330 7500      Germany 49 69 920410
Hong Kong 852 2977 6000 Japan 81 3 3201 8900 Singapore 65 6212 1000 U.S. 1 212 318 2000 Copyright 2004 Bloomberg L.P.
                                                                    G274-147-0 13-May-04 16:31:44
```

Source: Bloomberg LP

the dealer at the end of the dollar roll. As noted earlier, even among substantially identical securities, some pools perform worse than others. The
risk is that the dealer will deliver securities from pools that perform poorly.

MBS DOLLAR ROLL AUTOMATION[4]

While institutional investors holding sizeable agency MBS positions use dollar rolls as an alternative funding source, one key challenge of tapping into
this market is the relatively high operational barriers to entry. The complexity is due largely to the volume of mortgage pools involved. For every billion dollars out on roll, there is approximately 1,000 to 3,000 newly
created pools replacing the ones sold out on the open. TBA trading systems
can easily handle the trading, allocation, and delivery requirements. However, there are other aspects of the trade—asset/liability, accounting, and
price perpetuation—that are difficult tasks without automation.

---

[4] We thank Jim Daraio of Capital Markets Management Corp. for providing the exhibits for this section.

These automated systems must address two main objectives from a balance sheet perspective. First, the position and accounting information must be maintained for the life of the dollar roll agreement. Second, the same distribution of prices of the original pool inventory must be maintained when assigning prices to the pools purchased at the dollar roll's close.

Exhibit 16.7 presents the dollar roll life cycle and how the system of one vender, CMMC Portfolio System, can satisfy these two objectives. A

EXHIBIT 16.7   MBS Dollar Roll Automation

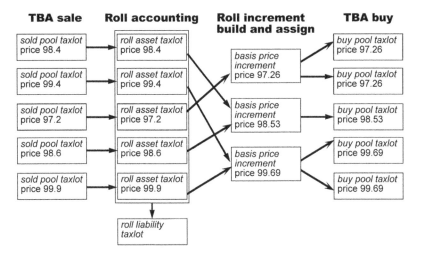

MBS Dollar Roll Automation

TBA sale	Roll accounting	Roll increment build and assign	TBA buy
sold pool taxlot price 98.4	roll asset taxlot price 98.4	basis price increment price 97.26	buy pool taxlot price 97.26
sold pool taxlot price 99.4	roll asset taxlot price 99.4	basis price increment price 98.53	buy pool taxlot price 97.26
sold pool taxlot price 97.2	roll asset taxlot price 97.2		buy pool taxlot price 98.53
sold pool taxlot price 98.6	roll asset taxlot price 98.6	basis price increment price 99.69	buy pool taxlot price 99.69
sold pool taxlot price 99.9	roll asset taxlot price 99.9		buy pool taxlot price 99.69
	roll liability taxlot		

Process

System provides complete automation required for high-volume TBA and Dollar Roll transactions.

TBA sale and TBA buy
An opening side TBA sell and future TBA buy are simultaneously done. Inventory allocation, EPN, other notifications and clearance follow standard trading practices.

Roll accounting
Each *sold pool taxlot* is assigned an accounting placeholder, the *roll asset taxlot*, with accounting done on it for the life of the roll. Accounting entries are principal, price amortization or accretion, roll prepay expense and foregone interest income.

A *roll liability taxlot* representing the sum of the *sold pool taxlots* is assigned. Accounting entries are principal, deferred income and interest expense.

Roll increment build and assign
On roll close date, *basis price increments* are created representing the distribution of basis prices from the *sold pool taxlots* with roll period price amortization/accretion.

TBA *buy pool taxlots* are assigned to *basis price increments* and inherit their basis price(s).

© 2004 Capital Markets Management Corp.

placeholder pool is created for each pool sold out and allows for detailed accounting including level-yield price amortization or accretion using the sold pool's accounting yield. The impact of prepayments on premium/discount priced pools, forgone interest and other calculations are performed. In the system, the entire dollar roll transaction is represented as a liability. Accounting for the dollar roll in this manner allows an institution to better reflect the transaction on the balance sheet and minimize operational exposure.

Maintaining the distribution of prices is accomplished by establishing price increments. Price increments are typically created using a 100 basis point range. The price distribution is maintained by assigning the sold pools to these price increment slots. When the buy pools are delivered, they are assigned to an increment(s) perpetuating the prices of the sold pools. These increment prices include price amortization/accretion of the sold pools for the span of the dollar roll agreement.

Exhibit 16.8 presents a CMMC Portfolio System summary report of a hypothetical dollar roll with an effective date of December 15, 2003. Each row of the exhibit is equal to one price increment, for example, all sold pools with a current price between 102 and 102.99999999. The "Average Book Price" column is the weighted price and the "Par Sold" is the sum of the par values of the sold pools. Correspondingly, the "Redelivered Par" is the sum of the par values from the close of the roll that are returned and assigned an increment price. The "Funding Rate" of 2.13931% located in the upper center of the screen is a simple measure that is indicative of expenses associated with a dollar roll transaction. The funding rate is calculated by dividing the principal returned at the close of the agreement by the total expenses and then annualizing. Note that this measure does not consider reinvestment from the proceeds arising from the sale of the mortgages and the value of the prepayment shield. Total expenses are simply the forgone coupon interest minus the drop adjusted for the impact of principal paydown. This impact reflects the premium amortization and discount accretion of both scheduled principal payments and prepayments not received. A CPR prepayment estimate supplied at inception of the agreement is employed in this calculation and is located at the center left-hand portion of the screen.

EXHIBIT 16.8 CMMC Portfolio System Summary Report for a Dollar Roll

CMMC Portfolio System

File   Options   Windows   Preference   Support   Help

XYZ Corporation
Dollar Roll Close Out

For Effective Date: 2003-12-15

Owner ID	10001	Business Function	27	Roll Trade	100001537		
Contra ID	14733	Contra Short Name	ZZZ CORP	Roll Sale Trade	100001536		
Product Type	RLFNF	Settlement Date	2003-11-14	Roll Buy Trade	100001538		
Coupon	6.00	Maturity Date	2003-12-15				

| Roll Principal | 20,178,487.69 | Funding Rate | 2.13931 | | | | |

Sale Price	101.25000	Lost Coupon	103,325.63	TBA Par	20,000,000.00		
Buy Price	100.90000	Prepay Impact	-3,332.45	Delivered Par	19,998,501.17	Var	-.0074942
Roll Price Drop	0.35000	Price Drop Amount	69,994.77	Received Par	19,999,994.57	Var	-.0000272
Prepay Estimate	20	Total Expense	36,663.31	Over/Under Par	-1,493.40		

Roll Increment ID Code	Par Sold	Book Value Sold	Average Book Price	Redelivered Par Allocated	Redelivered Book Value Allocated	Book Price
100000109	4,999,999.44	5,114,645.14	102.2929142	4,999,999.44	5,114,645.14	102.2929142
100000110	5,099,997.45	4,858,522.78	95.2652002	5,099,997.45	4,858,522.78	95.2652002
100000111	4,899,998.91	4,936,626.27	100.7474973	4,899,998.91	4,936,626.27	100.7474973
100000112	4,899,998.97	4,814,521.51	98.2555616	4,899,998.97	4,814,521.51	98.2555616
100000114	98,506.40	93,842.45	95.2653343	99,999.80	95,349.29	95.3494826
Totals	19,998,501.17	19,818,158.15	99.0982173	19,999,994.57	19,819,664.99	99.0983519

Calculations
Roll Principal   = Delivered Par * Buy Price / 100
Lost Coupon   = amount of pool interest payments that would have been received
Prepay Impact   = sum of the price amortization/accretion on the estimated principal payment
                amount where amortization is negative, accretion is positive
Total Expense   = Lost Coupon - Prepay Impact - Price Drop Amount
Funding Rate   = Total Expense / Roll Principal * (365 / #days of roll) * 100

Legend
• Product Type 'RLFNF' is a FNMA fixed-coupon roll liability.
• Prices are in decimal.
• Prepay Estimate is in CPR.
• Average Book Price column is basis price of sold pools plus period price amortization/accretion.
• Book Price column only differs from Average Book Price on increment blending due to overdelivery
  for one pool to avoid splitting. Other overdeliveries inherit the trade price and are treated as purchases.

© 2004 Capital Markets Management Corp.

CHAPTER 17

Evaluating the Interaction of Dollar Rolls and MBS Investments

Anand K. Bhattacharya, Ph.D.
Managing Director
Countrywide Securities Corporation

Paul Jacob
Executive Vice President
Countrywide Securities Corporation

William S. Berliner
Executive Vice President
Countrywide Securities Corporation

The dollar roll market is an important financing vehicle in the *mortgage-backed securities* (MBS) markets. The existence of a transparent and easily traded market provides a ready source of financing for many investors. At the same time, originators can sell existing loans in the pipeline forward into an active and liquid market and thereby hedge the risk of price declines. Similar to the repurchase markets, dollar rolls can also trade "special" where periodic shortages and squeezes can lead to attractive short-term financing and current yield enhancement opportunities for investors. Because dollar rolls only exist in the most liquid TBA MBS passthrough markets, the decision to buy MBS other than TBAs requires the investor to evaluate and understand the opportunity cost implicit in this decision, the impact of rolls on hedging costs and, by implication, inventory levels of dealers and financial intermediaries. This tradeoff takes place in fixed-rate passthrough products such as specified and "customized" MBS, *adjustable-rate products* (ARM), and structured MBS.

This chapter will provide a historical and analytical framework for evaluating the impact of rolls on MBS markets and strategies after providing a brief description of dollar rolls. This leads to a discussion of the impact of the dollar roll markets on MBS investment strategies and concludes by discussing the implication of dollar roll specials on valuation dynamics and technical conditions in the MBS sector.

DESCRIPTION OF THE DOLLAR ROLL MARKET

At the core level, a roll transaction is essentially a form of forward purchase. For example, the Fannie Mae 5.5 "November/December" roll represents the difference between the MBS price for November settlement and the price for delivery in December. In an efficient market, an investor should be indifferent between buying the MBS in November or, as an alternative, investing in cash for a month and taking delivery of the MBS in December. Due to the incremental carry advantage of the Fannie 5.5s as compared to cash, the price of the MBS in December (the "back month") should be lower than the price of the MBS in November (the "front month"). The roll or the "drop"—the extent to which the back month price is lower than the front month price—is meant to compensate the investor for the difference between a month of mortgage yield and a month of yield on cash, which is usually lower. If the drop is relatively large (implying that prices for December delivery are inordinately low or November settlement prices are relatively high or both) the roll is said to be "special." In this situation, the investor is better off "rolling" the MBS (i.e., selling November [front month] delivery and simultaneously buying the same position for December [back month] delivery) rather than taking delivery in November of the MBS, all other considerations being equal. The amount of the "special" represents the value of the incremental current yield on the position above and beyond the "normal" cost of funding the security. Alternatively stated, when a roll is special the effective cost of funding the MBS position in the roll market is lower than current funding cost. As a note, this effective cost of funding, often referred to as the "implied repo rate," can be calculated given the drop and a prepayment assumption effective over the holding period in question.

Rolls tend to become special as a result of four types of short-term supply/demand imbalances:

▓ Excessive demand for front-month delivery of pools. Demand pressures arise in the MBS markets due to asset allocation decisions that favor MBS exposure, particularly with respect to depositories that generally seek to put settled securities on their books. Collateral mortgage obligation (CMO) issuance also creates demand for front-month delivery, as dealers need collateral for CMO deals closing at month-end. Obviously, such conditions are exacerbated in the face of supply shortages.

▓ Forward selling by originators in order to hedge production pipelines. This type of selling pressure, which in some sense represents the genesis of the TBA market, typically takes place in the back months. During periods of heavy production or anticipated rate volatility, originators may accept a discounted value in order to effect a hedge consistent with expected loan funding schedules.

▓ The existence of a "short base" in the dealer and investor communities. These investors often use short positions in TBAs to hedge existing MBS positions, and need to roll hedges forward at settlement date. When dealers are long mortgages in the form of specified pools, CMO tranches and nonagency MBS, a key component of their hedge is a basket of short positions in TBA passthroughs. This creates a substantial short base of hedge entities in passthroughs, analogous to the short base that often exists in on-the-run Treasuries. Financial markets tend to charge a form of "rent" to a short base of hedgers in liquid instruments with large outstanding balances (or "floats"). This rent is expressed as financing specials, either in the Treasury repo markets or, in the case of MBS, in TBA rolls.

▓ The occasional short squeeze that can arise as a result of the existence of the aforementioned situations. Such squeezes can often be exacerbated by low outstanding float and limited trading activity in particular coupons. Additionally, traders who own coupons subject to squeezes may seek to profitably exploit such market conditions.

Typically, pressures on supply and demand across settlement months tend to be associated with new-production coupons around par in dollar price. Additionally, the magnitude of such imbalances, and consequently the persistence of roll specials, is also generally a function of the quantity of trade flows in the subject coupons. This implies that rolls in an environment of high origination volume and heavy CMO issuance will be more special than rolls at a time of low origination, low CMO deal flow, and reduced aggregate investor demand.

RECENT ROLL MARKET EXPERIENCE

The history of roll financing specials on 30-year Fannie 5.5s and 6.0s is depicted in Exhibit 17.1. This illustration, which shows 4-week moving averages from March 2003 through March 2005, measures the degree of roll financing "specialness," or the difference between current short-term investment rates and the effective cost of financing the TBA coupons, in 32nds per month. Additionally, the total size of primary dealer net long mortgage positions as reported by the Federal Reserve for the associated period is overlaid in the exhibit.

To some extent, the history in Exhibit 17.1 can be characterized as being comprised of three distinct periods, namely early 2003, late 2003, and the time frame ranging from 2004–2005. The 2002–2003 refinancing boom, which was characterized by historically low interest rates, peaked during early 2003. During this time frame, most TBA rolls were trading extremely special, even as mortgage rates were attaining 30-year lows and the refinancing activity was at all-time highs. This period was characterized by extremely heavy mortgage origination and high levels of issuance in CMOs and nonagency MBS. Additionally, as noted in the exhibit, MBS dealer inventories during this time attained multiyear highs. Moreover, there were significant short squeezes in the spring of 2003 in newly originated lower coupons (such as 30-year 4.5s and 5.0s) that had never been actively traded before.

It is apparent from Exhibit 17.1 that during 2003 there was a strong positive correlation between the overall size of dealer MBS positions and the degree of TBA roll specials. This is largely attributable to the effects of hedging activity, which is a driving factor in the determination of roll levels as noted previously. The bond market selloff that occurred in the summer of 2003, however, dramatically altered issuance and hedging flows in MBS. Due to the advent of higher rates, the volume of mortgage origination, new CMO production, and dealer inventories registered dramatic declines. Consequently, with reduced aggregate hedging demand, the extent of rolls on special also declined. Incidentally, this change in market sentiment and valuation is reminiscent of the transition from 1999 to 2000, when rates rose, origination and CMO activity sank, and rolls were generally not special for an extended period of time.

Since the beginning of 2004, the MBS roll markets have been influenced mainly by technical factors. The specials that have occurred from time to time have tended to reflect localized supply/demand imbalances in specific coupons. In 30-year MBS, roll specials have more frequently occurred in coupons with reduced float, i.e., 4.5s, 6.0s, and 6.5s. Specials have occurred with much less frequency in 30-year 5.0s and 5.5s, which have significantly higher outstanding supply.

EXHIBIT 17.1   Primary Dealer Net Mortgage Position versus Value of Roll Special in 30-Year Fannie 5.5s and 6.0s (4-week moving averages; weekly March 2003–March 2005)

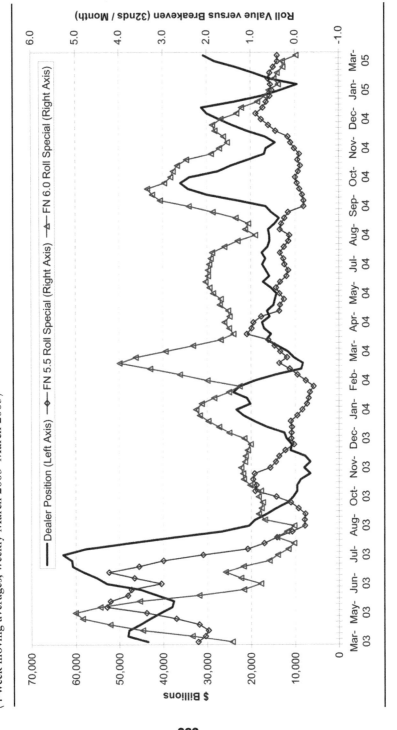

The association of TBA roll financing specials with overall hedging activity and dealer MBS inventory levels can at times result in roll valuations being correlated with MBS dollar price levels. MBS hedging needs— for origination pipelines, inventories and CMO production—are often heaviest for par and slight premium coupons. This makes specials more likely to occur for passthroughs in the 99–103 dollar price area, all other things being equal. Deep discounts and very high coupons are generally associated with reduced trading volume and tend not to experience severe hedging pressures. Therefore, rolls associated with such coupons are less likely to trade special. However, the valuation of rolls during 2004 and early 2005 has been something of an exception with respect to the observation that rolls tend to be most special for MBS just above par. To a large extent, this has been due to the extreme concentration of outstanding supply in 30-year 5.0s and 5.5s during this time. Because any short positions eventually have to be covered, securities with limited supply are much more likely to experience tight financing conditions than those cohorts with ample available supply. Therefore, coupons with larger quantities of outstanding tradeable float are unlikely to experience short squeezes, notwithstanding the earlier observation with respect to the correlation between MBS price levels and roll valuations.

TBA ROLL STRATEGIES—BENEFITS AND COSTS

For MBS investors, TBA rolls have traditionally been employed as a strategy to enhance current yield. Investors using this strategy typically own large blocks of passthroughs in TBA form, rather than as specific pools. The TBA rolls act as a financing vehicle, generating cash that is invested in short-term and floating-rate instruments, while maintaining exposure to the coupon's price performance. The overall current yield of the position is enhanced to the extent that the rate earned on the short-term investments exceeds the effective financing rate implied by TBA roll pricing. In other words, yield enhancement opportunities exist whenever the rolls are special.

While the roll strategy has been widely and successfully used for many years, it is not without risks. The main risk, highlighted in Exhibit 17.1, is that TBA roll specials are rarely stable. Specials are products of short-term supply/demand imbalances and tend to fluctuate as financing conditions tighten and ease. Therefore, investors cannot count on rolls to contribute a consistent level of incremental current yield over time. Because roll specials are, moreover, often associated with hedging flows in a coupon, the roll valuation can fluctuate considerably. Hedging activity frequently shifts as prices change. As hedging flows shift, roll specials subsequently migrate from one coupon to another. This leads to the consideration that the TBA roll strategy is associated with a hidden negative convexity cost, which is not picked up in OAS models. For those coupons, where roll levels tend to weaken in a major price move, the TBA investor effectively suffers a loss of current yield, in addition to the traditional extension or prepayment risk. A weaker roll special can also reduce demand for a coupon, causing the subject coupon to underperform other coupons. As a result, as interest rates change, the overall impact is a tendency to suffer weaker total returns due to the inherent inferior convexity.

Another related and subtle form of negative convexity is created by changes in the demand for specified or customized pools. Very large market price moves often increase the percentage of a coupon that trades in specified pool form. For example, in the case of a market sell-off, a greater proportion of a coupon's available float will trade in the market for seasoned pools. This is due to the fact that seasoned pools result in a higher return advantage when the TBA coupon is trading at a discount, as seasoned pools are shorter in duration than new production and thus trade closer to par value as rates rise. In the case of a market rally that pushes the coupon price to a significant premium, superior convexity attributes such as low loan balance will be valued higher, and a greater percentage of pools with such attributes will trade in specified form. Therefore, both the trading volume and valuations of specified pools tend to increase in a large move in rates in either direction. This represents another form of hidden negative convexity for TBA positions; this is of particular concern to index-benchmarked investors whose performance is compared to the average performance of all outstanding pools in a coupon. To the extent that a portfolio strictly holds passthroughs in TBA form and rates change, its returns may lag the average performance of a coupon or cohort with a sizable component of seasoned or convexity pools. Additionally, the likelihood of this development increases with the magnitude of the rate move.

TBA ROLL FINANCING AND SPECIFIED POOL EVALUATION

When a TBA coupon is rolling special, investors contemplating investing in specified pools face a sharper trade-off between the higher carry of the TBA position and the superior convexity of specified pools such as low-loan-balance MBS. Typically, investments in specified or custom pools involve a pay-up over TBA prices for generally slower expected prepayments and, hence, higher current yield. The TBA roll is often used as the base-case alternative in evaluating specified pool alternatives. A roll special has the effect of increasing the opportunity cost of owning specified pools. If a TBA roll is expected to deliver 2–3 ticks per month in incremental current yield for an extended period, it can be difficult to justify the purchase of a specified pool at a higher price. However, in the event the TBA roll is expected to be soft, the specified pool strategy becomes more attractive.

Exhibit 17.2 presents a scenario analysis for 30-year Fannie 5.5s that quantifies the potential trade-off between TBA rolls and convexity pools. As of February 10, 2005, TBA 5.5s in March were trading at 101-24, and the March/April roll was priced at 6.5 32nds (i.e., ticks). Assuming a prepayment speed of 20% CPR on TBA 5.5s, this roll was financing special by 0.8 ticks. In other words, the cost of financing the TBA position at this roll level, 2.40%, was below the short-term investment rate of 2.70%, generating incremental current yield equivalent to 0.8 ticks per month.

On the same date, low-balance Fannie 5.5s were trading at a pay-up of 10.5 ticks over TBA.[1] In the base case, these low-balance MBSs are projected to prepay at a rate of 15% CPR. Using this prepayment assumption, the low-balance pools generate 5.8 ticks per month in current carry above the short-term rate. When this current carry is compared to the TBA roll, the rolled TBA position generates 0.7 ticks higher in current yield. The superior base-case current yield of the TBA is wholly attributable to the roll special.

While the TBA roll in this analysis provides higher current yield in the base case, this performance may not be sustainable as interest rates change. Modeling a scenario where rates decline by 100 basis points, the price of TBA 5.5s increases to 103-29, the prepayment speed increases to 45% CPR, and the roll special disappears. In this case, the current carry on TBA 5.5s would fall to just 0.1 ticks per month. This compares unfavorably with the low-balance 5.5s that, at a slower projected speed of 28% CPR, would deliver 2.7 ticks per month in current carry. Thus, in a declining rate scenario, the combination of slower prepayments and weakness in the TBA roll leads to the low-balance pools earning the equivalent of an incremental 2.6 ticks per month in current yield. Additionally, the price pay-ups of low balance pools will likely increase as rates decline, thereby providing additional total return opportunities. In a bearish scenario where rates rise by 100 basis points, the price of TBA 5.5s drops to 97-23+, prepayments slowed to 9% CPR, and the roll special again goes to zero. In this scenario, the TBA current carry of +7.7 ticks per month was just 0.1 ticks above the current yield of the low-balance pool, which was also evaluated at 9% CPR.

---

[1] Low balance conventional MBS are composed of mortgage loans with an original balance of less than or equal to $85,000. Due to the smaller size of the loan, such obligors are less sensitive to refinancing opportunities because of the fixed costs involved in refinancing.

EXHIBIT 17.2 Low Balance ($85,000) 30-Year Fannie 5.5s versus TBA Roll: Scenario Analysis of Current Carry Base Case Market Data as of February 10, 2005. Low Balance Payup 10+/32nds over TBA.

Scenario	−100 bps		Base Case		+100 bps	
Projected Fannie 5.5 TBA Price	103-29		101-24		97-23+	
	TBA	$85,000	TBA	$85,000	TBA	$85,000
Projected Prepayment Speed	45 CPR	28 CPR	20 CPR	15 CPR	9 CPR	9 CPR
Projected TBA Roll Special (32nds/month)	0.0		0.8		0.0	
1-Month Carry (expressed as Roll Level, 32nds/month)	0.1	2.7	6.5	5.8	7.7	7.6
Difference in Current Carry: $85,000 − TBA	2.6		−0.7		−0.1	

The scenarios in Exhibit 17.2 are presented as illustrations rather than concrete projections. Certainly, the evaluation is sensitive with respect to the sustainability of TBA roll specials. However, the variability of rolls apparent in Exhibit 17.1 suggests that there are so many moving parts to the roll markets that an accurate long-term scenario projection for financing specials is probably impossible. Additionally, longer-term experience for coupons with large outstanding balances such as 30-year 5.5s suggests that roll specials are more likely to disappear if the TBA price moves to a high premium or deep discount. Nonetheless, the example illustrates the interaction of factors that drive the dollar roll versus specified pool decision; it also demonstrates that such decisions are influenced by expectations for changes in the interest rate environment.

TBA ROLL FINANCING SPECIALS AND CONVEXITY POOL PAY-UPS: HISTORICAL EVIDENCE

Financing conditions in a TBA coupon can exert a powerful influence on specified pool pricing since, as noted above, TBA roll specials can influence investment decisions in specified pools. In addition, MBS dealers tend to hedge specified pool inventories mainly with short positions in the TBA coupon, as described earlier in this chapter. As with any short sale, the more special the TBA roll financing, the more expensive the ongoing hedging costs. A very special roll will tend to make dealers reluctant to accumulate and carry large inventories of specified pools, and more eager to sell those inventories.

Although historical pricing in convexity pool markets does not have the length, depth or granularity that is associated with TBA passthroughs, recent history can be used to make some rough observations about the relationships between roll specials and specified pool pay-ups. A direct comparison of roll specials and convexity pool pay-ups is inappropriate, given that the most important determinant of convexity pool pay-ups is the TBA price level. Instead, the relevant examination is whether the historical "price/pay-up" curve for a given category of pool tends to be lower whenever the TBA roll is significantly special.

Exhibits 17.3 and 17.4 summarize the experience for low- and intermediate-balance (i.e., loans having a maximum loan amount of $110,000) 30-year Fannie 6.0s. These exhibits describe the convexity pool pay-up versus the price of the TBA on a weekly basis from August 7, 2003 through March 10, 2005. Further, the pay-up history was divided into two populations, based on the level of the roll financing special. One series represented weeks when the TBA 6.0 roll was financing special by 1.5 ticks per month or greater, while the other series represented weeks when the TBA 6.0 roll special was below 1.5 ticks per month.

EXHIBIT 17.3 $85,000 30-Year Fannie 6.0s Pool Pay-Up versus Price—in Context of Roll Special (Weekly, August 2003–March 2005)

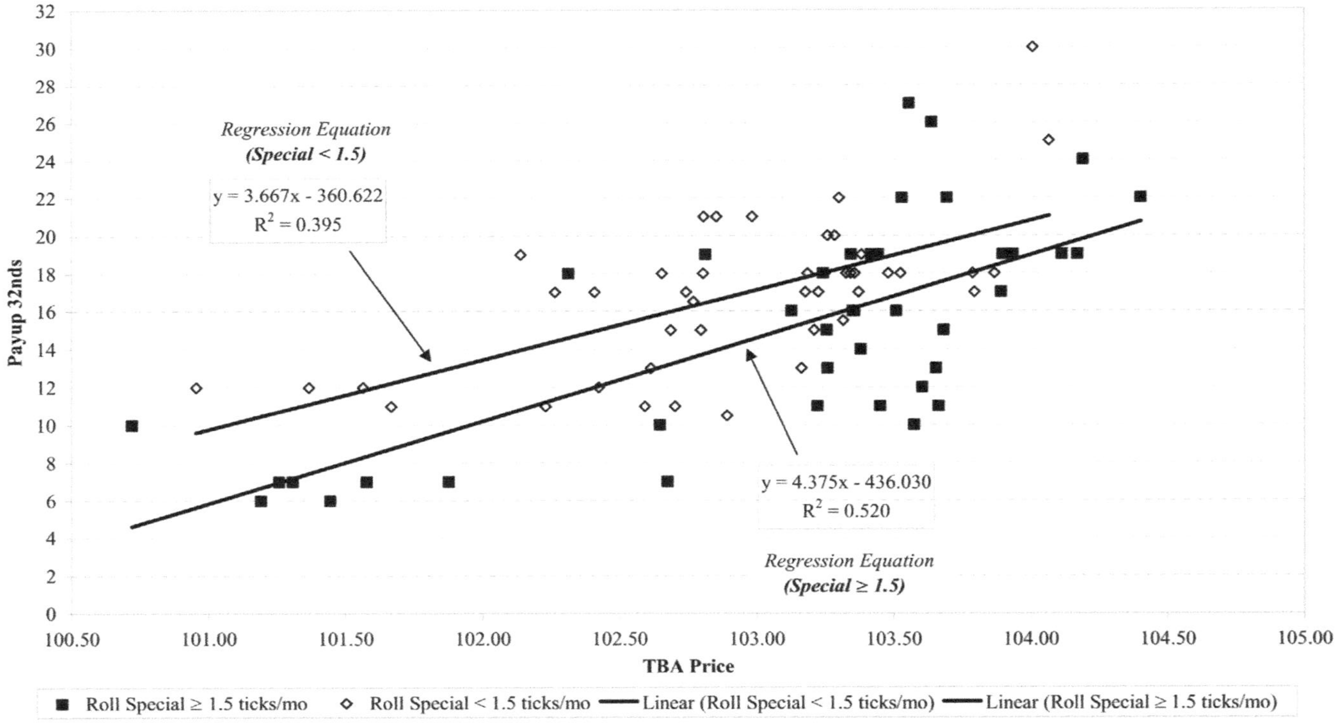

Payup 32nds
32
30
28
26
24
22
20
18
16
14
12
10
8
6
4
2
0
100.50
101.00
101.50
102.00
102.50
103.00
103.50
104.00
104.50
105.00
TBA Price
Regression Equation
(Special < 1.5)
y = 3.667x - 360.622
R² = 0.395
y = 4.375x - 436.030
R² = 0.520
Regression Equation
(Special ≥ 1.5)
Roll Special ≥ 1.5 ticks/mo
Roll Special < 1.5 ticks/mo
Linear (Roll Special < 1.5 ticks/mo)
Linear (Roll Special ≥ 1.5 ticks/mo)

EXHIBIT 17.4 $110,000 30-Year Fannie 6.0s Pool Pay-Up versus Price—in Context of Roll Special (Weekly, August 2003–March 2005)

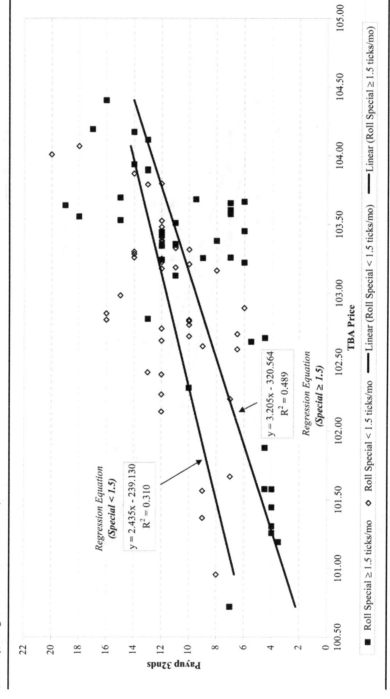

Both series show the expected positive correlation between convexity pool pay-ups and TBA price levels. (Note that seasoned pools tend to exhibit a negative correlation between pay-up and TBA price due to the fact that the value of seasoning increases as prices decline.) In all cases, while the relationship between pay-ups and TBA prices is not exact, two important observations can, nevertheless, be made from the exhibits. In both charts, a visual scan shows that the "low special" data points tend to lie above the "high special" data points. Additionally, a linear regression trend line fit to the "low special" data lies well above a trend line fit to "high special" observations for both products.

The placement of the trend lines suggests that convexity pool pay-ups tend to be higher, in the context of TBA dollar prices, when the TBA roll is less special. This is consistent with expectations since, as noted, a lucrative roll special for the TBA coupon reduces both the attractiveness of specified pools to investors and increases the cost to dealers of hedging pool inventories.

Another interesting observation comes from a comparison of the slopes of the respective trend lines in the exhibits. In both cases, the slope of the "high special" line is steeper than that of the "low special" line. The result is that the gap between the trend lines is larger at lower dollar prices and smaller at higher prices. This suggests that the impact of roll specials in suppressing pay-ups is greatest when the TBA dollar price is lower—which is also when the convexity pay-up is lower. In contrast, the trend lines suggest less of an effect at higher dollar prices, when pay-ups are higher and the effect of prepayments on yield is heightened. This indicates that when the stakes are higher for convexity pools, financing conditions have less of an impact.

In this context, it is also noteworthy that the interaction of demand considerations (i.e., the impact on demand for specified pools based on roll market conditions) and supply dynamics (specifically, the reluctance of dealers to hold inventories as hedging costs increase) is not invariable. For example, *changes* in roll market conditions often exert unique pressures on valuations. Consider a period where rolls were not particularly special, resulting in strong demand for specified pools (due to the low opportunity cost of holding such pools) along with growing dealer inventories (attributable to both the desire to meet investor demand and relatively low hedging costs). If rolls suddenly become special, demand for specified pools is likely to dry up at the same time dealers might seek to reduce inventories. The combination of these effects would likely put downward pressure on pay-ups. Alternatively, specified pool pay-ups might be expected to improve if rolls fade after a period of specialness, since demand for the product would improve at a time of relatively low dealer inventories. By contrast, the implications on specified pool valuations of a protracted period where roll valuations remain constant would arguably be mixed. A protracted period of roll specialness would likely cause tepid investor demand, offset in part by low dealer inventory levels in the product. While the historical evidence suggests that the demand effect is the primary driver of valuations, the impact of hedging costs and lower inventory levels should not be dismissed in this equation.

SUPPLY AND VALUATION IMPLICATIONS FOR OTHER MBS SECTORS

In addition to the impact on the valuation of customized MBS, roll markets often impact trading and production in other mortgage products. For some sectors, the dynamics are similar to those noted with respect to specified pools, while the effects can be more subtle for other products. For example, since prices in some sectors of the ARM market (most notably 10/1 hybrid products) track 15-year agency passthrough valuations fairly closely, ARM inventories are often hedged by shorting 15-year TBAs. When the rolls trade special and the hedge becomes more expensive, dealers may have to widen bid/ask spreads to account for the incrementally higher cost of hedging. Alternatively, dealers may choose to either reduce inventories of the product or use some other instrument as a hedging vehicle. The utilization of a different (and potentially less efficient) hedging instrument increases the likelihood for losses due to hedging errors. The incremental riskiness of the position must therefore be priced into dealer offerings through tighter spreads. However, the impact of roll specials on demand for certain MBS products may be somewhat muted; for example, since the traditional investor clienteles for ARMs (generally banks and depositories) are not active participants in the roll market, the occurrence of roll specials do not impose the same opportunity costs for such investors as experienced in the specified pool sector.

A somewhat different set of dynamics is created by roll specials in the CMO market. Agency CMO issuance is fundamentally an arbitrage where collateral (generally agency passthroughs) is purchased, and the cash flows of the collateral are tranched along various prepayment leverage and maturity spectra to meet various demand profiles in the market. For example, in a sequential CMO deal, the short cash flows might be sold to banks, the intermediate cash flows might appeal to asset managers, and the long classes would likely be targeted to insurance companies. As noted earlier in this chapter, dealers often buy pools in the front months of the TBA market to accumulate collateral for deals, which generally close at the end of the month. If the roll becomes special, it implies a higher price in the front month and thus raises the cost of the collateral. This makes such deals less profitable, which in turn leads to reduced issuance and lower dealer inventories. A countervailing factor is the relative attractiveness of the product as compared to passthroughs (which, because of roll specials, are associated with a higher current yield). This would be particularly relevant for products that serve as passthrough alternatives (i.e., intermediate PACs and sequentials). It would also be meaningful for those investors that utilize dollar rolls and evaluate the opportunity costs of holding CMOs in the same fashion as specified pools.

CONCLUSIONS

The dollar roll is an essential tool for mortgage originators and MBS portfolio managers who seek to maximize their returns. It is important for investors who utilize rolls as a financing vehicle to understand the broader relationship between dollar rolls and portfolio performance. As such, the expected direction of interest rates, loan production, and opinions on volatility should be taken into account in the development of roll strategies. Put differently, the stronger the belief that rates move substantially from current levels, the less attractive a strategy that utilizes TBA rolls will appear. This is due to the expectations that changes in the prevailing interest rate environment lead to improved relative valuation of specified pools and enhanced-convexity products. At the same time, interest rate volatility generally causes dollar roll strategies to underperform, due to the subtle negative convexity associated with these positions.

It is also important to note that while some MBS investors may systematically eschew dollar roll strategies due to investment guidelines or accounting considerations, such investors nonetheless are impacted by, and should be cognizant of, developments in the roll market. Valuations and relative performance in the markets for non-TBA products (including specified pools, ARMs, and CMOs) are affected by dollar roll specials, due to the impact on both demand and supply for these products. In the custom pool markets, for example, pay-ups for products with enhanced convexity attributes tend to cheapen as rolls become more special as the opportunity cost of holding pools in any form increases in such circumstances. The impact of roll market conditions on valuations is also affected by the willingness of dealers to hold product inventories, and the impact of inventory decisions can vary depending on both the product in question and market conditions. The roll market thus exerts a powerful effect throughout the MBS market for all investors, whether or not they actively trade dollar rolls.

Finally, both the specialness of rolls and their impact on related MBS products are the result of the interaction of various market factors and forces. This makes forecasts of roll levels under various scenarios unreliable, as there are numerous variables that can impact the extent to which rolls trade special. The impact on valuations for alternative products is also difficult to predict, as the subtle balance of supply and demand can be affected by numerous other factors. Despite these caveats, an awareness of conditions in dollar rolls is a critical aid to successfully managing and trading positions in the MBS sector.

Equity Financing Alternatives to Securities Lending

Equity Financing Alternatives to Securites Lending

Frank J. Fabozzi, Ph.D., CFA
Frederick Frank Adjunct Professor of Finance
Yale School of Management

Steven V. Mann, Ph.D.
Professor of Finance
Moore School of Management
University of South Carolina

As we have seen in previous chapters, investors who want to establish a short position in common stock can borrow the stock via a security lending transaction. Investors who want to implement a levered long position in common stock can simply buy stocks on margin. However, these positions can be replicated using derivative contracts such as contracts for differences, single-stock futures, and equity swaps as well as with equity repos. In this chapter, we describe these methods of equity financing. We discuss the advantages and disadvantages of these methods as opposed to more traditional methods employed in the cash market.

CONTRACTS FOR DIFFERENCES

Contracts for differences (CFDs) are derivative products that can be utilized to replicate both long and short positions in an underlying asset but do not carry any rights of ownership. These contracts were originally developed in the United Kingdom as a means of avoiding the stamp duty reserve tax, a tax imposed on the transfer of U.K. equities. The underlying asset for equity CFDs could be an individual common stock or an equity index.[1]

A long position in an equity CFD creates a synthetic, levered long position. Correspondingly, a short position in an equity CFD creates a synthetic short position. Investors create leverage in that when an equity CFS position is opened both the long and the short are required only to post a fraction (10%–20%) of the position's value in the form of margin. A broker loans the balance of the contract's value and the investor in a long equity CFD pays interest on the contract's full value. Conversely, the investor in a short equity CFD receives interest on the contract's full value. The margin requirement varies across stocks and is a function of such factors as the stock's market capitalization and its price volatility. At the end of each trading day, CFDs are marked to market using the closing share prices. As long as the margin requirement is maintained, the position can remain open indefinitely.

Illustration

Let us illustrate how a long position in an equity CFD works with a hypothetical example. Suppose an investor buys 1,000 shares of Citigroup as a CFD at a price of $48.65 per share. The total market value of the position is $48,650. Brokerage commission on the trade is assumed to be 0.25% or approximately $122. The margin requirement is say, 10% so the investor must deposit at least $4,865 in an account with a broker to open the position. The investor is effectively borrowing money to establish a long equity position and must pay interest on the financing (i.e., the contract's full value). Suppose the interest rate is 3-month LIBOR + 200 basis points. Accordingly, interest is charged each trading day to the investor's margin account and is determined using the following expression:

1,000 × Citigroup closing share price × (3-month LIBOR + 200bps)
× (1/360)

Now suppose that one month later the price of Citigroup stock stands at $51 a share and the investor desires to sell a CFD to close their position. The profit on this position is $2,350 (= $51,000 − $48,650) plus any cash dividends paid while the position is open less the interest paid to finance the position as well as the commissions paid to open and close the CFD. Thus, a long position in this equity CFD creates a virtual levered long position in 1,000 shares of Citigroup common stock.

---

[1] CFDs are also widely available on electricity, oil, and currencies.

A short position in an equity CFD profits when stock prices fall. The mechanics of a short equity CFD position are essentially the same as the long equity CFD with two important exceptions. First, an investor is required to post margin of, say, 10% of the total value of the position; but instead of paying interest on the contract's full value, the short CFD investor receives interest each day the position is open. This feature is tantamount to the rebate an investor who borrows a security using a security lending agreement receives for providing cash collateral.

Advantages and Disadvantages of CFDs

CFDs potentially offer several advantages to investors. First, CFDs allows the investor to avoid certain trade-related costs related to custody, clearing, and settlement. Moreover, there is no bid-ask spread because contracts are valued at the prevailing market price at the time the position is opened. Second, greater leverage is possible with CFDs as compared to taking a physical position in the underlying asset. For example, suppose a hedge fund has a negative view on a stock and desires to establish a short position. To do so, the hedge fund must borrow the stock and provide collateral based on the underlying value of the borrowed stock. Conversely, taking a short position using a CFD does entail any physical ownership of the security so an amount of collateral needed in a security lending agreement is not required. A CFD requires only a margin of 10%–20%. As a result, the CFD permits much greater leverage. In the United States, Regulation T requires that an investor shorting a stock does not receive access to the proceeds of the short sale and in addition must put up at least 50% margin to secure the position. Third, a short position in a common stock via an equity CFD avoids the uptick rule.[2] Finally, after the short position is established, a CFD offers another advantage by eliminating *recall risk*, the risk of the stock lender recalling the stock prior to the investor wanting to close out the short position.

There are some offsetting disadvantages of using CFDs as opposed to taking a long position in the underlying asset. First, equity CFDs on individual common stocks do not carry any voting rights and thus for large institutional investors taking a long position in common stock using a CFD does not present any opportunities for shareholder activism. Second, equity CFDs positions will be closed out if a takeover of the corporation underlying the CFD is consummated. The final closing

---

[2] On the New York Stock Exchange, short sales may be transacted on a zero plus tick, which occurs when a tick is equal to the preceding tick, but is greater than the most recent nonzero tick. The Nasdaq has a similar rule called the *Bid Rule,* which governs when short sales may be transacted.

price will be the prevailing market price one day prior to the final day the shares are quoted in their existing form. Third, some institutional investors, especially mutual funds, are restricted as to the type of derivative products in which they are permitted to invest and CFDs may not be available to such investors. Finally, equity CFDs on individual common stocks are nondeliverable.

Availability of CFDs

According to IFX Markets Ltd., a leading dealer in CFDs, it is estimated that CFD trading in the United Kingdom accounts for at least 30% of all equity volume traded in London. CFDs are available on equity indices (index tickers in parentheses) in the United Kingdom (FTSE 350), the United States (S&P 500, NASDAQ 100), and the following European indices: Austria (ATX), Belgium (BEL20), Denmark (KFX), Finland (HEX), France (CAC 40), Germany (DAX, MDAX), Italy (MIB30, MIBTEL), Netherlands (AEX), Sweden (OMX), and Switzerland (SMI). As for the Asian markets, CFDs are available on the major indices in the Pacific Basin. Equity CFDs on individual common stocks are available on most of the constituent stocks of the major stock indices around the world.

CFD Trading Strategies

CFDs are utilized in a number of different trading strategies. For example, if investors have a view on the prospects of a particular common stock, CFDs are a low-cost vehicle to speculate on the expected change in price. In addition, CFDs can be used to hedge short-term fluctuations in a portfolio's value. As an example, suppose an investor with a long position in a portfolio of common stocks believes that the risk of a substantial sell-off is uncomfortably high. There are several ways to hedge this risk. One obvious but relatively costly way is to liquidate the portfolio and then repurchasing the shares when the risk has subsided. Taking a short position in CFDs offers a much more cost-effective method to hedge this risk exposure and avoids the possible tax liability incurred from liquidating the portfolio.

CFDs can also be employed to lock in a profit of a physical position in common stocks. To capture a profit due to a share price increase, one need only short a CFD in an equal amount at the prevailing market price. Accordingly, CFDs can be utilized for tax management. Finally, suppose an investor needs liquidity but desires to maintain an exposure. This is easily accomplished by converting a common stock position into a CFD at the prevailing market price. In the process, the investor releases the 90% of the cash in the position (assuming a 10% margin) while remaining fully exposed to the prospects of the common stock.

SINGLE-STOCK FUTURES

Single-stock futures are equity futures in which the underlying is the common stock of an individual corporation as opposed to an equity index such as the S&P 500. These contracts received approval for trading in 2001. As of January 2005, single-stock futures are traded on two exchanges: OneChicago[3] and NASDAQ Liffe Markets.[4]

Exhibit 18.1 presents Bloomberg screens that list the single-stock futures traded on OneChicago and their open interest as of January 2005. The contracts are for 100 shares of the underlying stock. On the settlement date, physical delivery of the stock is required.

Exhibit 18.2 presents a Bloomberg Equity Futures Contract Description screen for a March 2005 futures contract on Allstate common stock. Notice the last trading of the contract is March 18 but the individual who is short this contract has until March 23 to deliver the underlying

EXHIBIT 18.1 Bloomberg Screen of Single-Stock Futures Listed on OneChicago
Panel a: Page One of OneChicago Listing

GRAB Govt SFUT

Sorting | Select Exchange | Related Functions | EQUITY STOCK FUTURES

Security	Name	Exchg	OpenInt	Security	Name	Exchg	OpenInt
1) AA US	Alcoa Inc	OC	1525	21) C US	Citigroup Inc	OC	171
2) AAPL US	Apple Computer Inc	OC	198	22) CA US	Computer Assoc Int	OC	198
3) AIG US	American Intl Grp	OC	88	23) CAT US	Caterpillar Inc	OC	52
4) ALL US	Allstate Corp	OC	2359	24) CCL US	Carnival Corp	OC	0
5) ALTR US	Altera Corp	OC	121	25) CEPH US	Cephalon Inc	OC	30
6) AMAT US	Applied Materials	OC	55	26) CHKP US	Check Point Sftwre	OC	83
7) AMD US	Advanced Micro Dev	OC	11188	27) CMCSK US	Comcast Corp	OC	13
8) AMGN US	Amgen Inc	OC	3341	28) CME US	Chicago Merc Hlds	OC	24
9) AMZN US	Amazon.com Inc	OC	195	29) CMVT US	Comverse Technlgy	OC	46
10) AXP US	American Express	OC	5844	30) CSCO US	Cisco Systems Inc	OC	661
11) BA US	Boeing Co	OC	34	31) CVX US	ChevronTexaco Corp	OC	30
12) BAC US	Bank of America	OC	5524	32) DD US	Du Pont de Nemours	OC	9
13) BBBY US	Bed Bath & Beyond	OC	42	33) DELL US	Dell Inc	OC	7723
14) BBY US	Best Buy Co Inc	OC	10	34) DIA US	DIAMONDS Trust	OC	2751
15) BGEN US	Biogen Inc	OC	0	35) DIS US	Walt Disney Co	OC	10
16) BIIB US	Biogen Idec Inc	OC	0	36) DOW US	Dow Chemical Co	OC	9
17) BMY US	Bristol-Myers Sqib	OC	33	37) DWA US	DreamWorks Animatn	OC	0
18) BRCD US	Brocade Comm Systm	OC	110	38) EBAY US	eBay Inc	OC	618
19) BRCM US	Broadcom Corp	OC	233	39) ED US	Consolidated Edisn	OC	0
20) BSX US	Boston Scientific	OC	0	40) EDS US	Electronc Data Sys	OC	45

Australia 61 2 9777 8600 Brazil 5511 3048 4500 Europe 44 20 7330 7500 Germany 49 69 920410
Hong Kong 852 2977 6000 Japan 81 3 3201 8900 Singapore 65 6212 1000 U.S. 1 212 318 2000 Copyright 2005 Bloomberg L.P.
G616-30-0 05-Feb-05 12:04:12

[3] OneChicago is a joint venture of three exchanges—Chicago Board Options Exchange, Chicago Mercantile Exchange, Inc. and the Chicago Board of Trade
[4] NASDAQ Liffe Market is a joint venture of the NASDAQ Stock Market and the London International Financial Futures and Options Exchange (Liffe).

EXHIBIT 18.1   (Continued)

Panel b: Page 2 of OneChicago Listing

	Security	Name	Exchg	OpenInt		Security	Name	Exchg	OpenInt
1)	EK US	Eastman Kodak Co	OC	6887	21)	JNJ US	Johnson & Johnson	OC	4532
2)	ELN US	Elan Corp	OC	55	22)	JNPR US	Juniper Networks	OC	117
3)	ELX US	Emulex Corp	OC	15	23)	JPM US	JP Morgan Chase	OC	3439
4)	EMC US	EMC Corp	OC	28	24)	KKD US	Krispy Kreme Dough	OC	0
5)	F US	Ford Motor Co	OC	54	25)	KLAC US	Kla-Tencor Corp	OC	62
6)	FD US	Federated Dptmt St	OC	2	26)	KO US	Coca-Cola Co	OC	8187
7)	FRE US	Freddie Mac	OC	0	27)	KSS US	Kohl's Corp	OC	0
8)	GE US	General Electric	OC	2071	28)	LEN US	Lennar Corp	OC	116
9)	GENZ US	Genzyme Corp	OC	171	29)	LLTC US	Linear Technology	OC	251
10)	GM US	General Motors	OC	1465	30)	LLY US	Eli Lilly & Co	OC	4150
11)	GOOG US	Google Inc.	OC	2329	31)	LOW US	Lowe's Cos Inc	OC	0
12)	GS US	Goldman Sachs Grp	OC	51	32)	LTD US	Limited Brands Inc	OC	40
13)	HAL US	Halliburton Co	OC	6247	33)	MCD US	McDonald's Corp	OC	10744
14)	HD US	Home Depot Inc	OC	6	34)	MER US	Merrill Lynch & Co	OC	36
15)	HON US	Honeywell Intl Inc	OC	3846	35)	MGM US	Metro-Goldwyn-Mayr	OC	0
16)	HPQ US	Hewlett-Packard Co	OC	97	36)	MMM US	3M Co	OC	10
17)	IBM US	Intl Bus Mach	OC	2331	37)	MO US	Altria Group Inc	OC	2011
18)	INTC US	Intel Corp	OC	2476	38)	MOT US	Motorola Inc	OC	73
19)	IP US	International Papr	OC	2	39)	MRK US	Merck & Co Inc	OC	2464
20)	JBLU US	JetBlue Airways	OC	40	40)	MSFT US	Microsoft Corp	OC	8945

Panel c: Page 3 of OneChicago Listing

	Security	Name	Exchg	OpenInt		Security	Name	Exchg	OpenInt
1)	MU US	Micron Technology	OC	185	21)	RIMM US	Research In Motion	OC	222
2)	MWD US	Morgan Stanley	OC	11	22)	RJR US	RJ Reynolds Tobaco	OC	0
3)	MXIM US	Maxim Intgrtd Prod	OC	266	23)	SBC US	SBC Communications	OC	5044
4)	NEM US	Newmont Mining	OC	62	24)	SBUX US	Starbucks Corp	OC	187
5)	NOC US	Northrop Grumman	OC	49	25)	SEBL US	Siebel Systems Inc	OC	127
6)	NOK US	Nokia Oyj	OC	142	26)	SGP US	Schering-Plough	OC	10059
7)	NVDA US	Nvidia Corp	OC	251	27)	SIRI US	Sirius Sat Radio	OC	125
8)	NVLS US	Novellus Systems	OC	194	28)	SLB US	Schlumberger Ltd	OC	3695
9)	NWS US	News Corporation	OC	0	29)	SNDK US	Sandisk Corp	OC	139
10)	NXTL US	Nextel Comm Inc	OC	6190	30)	SUNW US	Sun Microsystems	OC	354
11)	JPM US	Bank One Corp	OC	3439	31)	SYMC US	Symantec Corp	OC	214
12)	ORCL US	Oracle Corp	OC	381	32)	T US	AT&T Corp	OC	25
13)	PD US	Phelps Dodge Corp	OC	128	33)	TGT US	Target Corp.	OC	65
14)	PEP US	PepsiCo Inc	OC	15	34)	THC US	Tenet Healthcare	OC	10
15)	PFE US	Pfizer Inc	OC	4134	35)	TIBX US	TIBCO Software Inc	OC	107
16)	PG US	Procter & Gamble	OC	54	36)	TWX US	Time Warner Inc	OC	39
17)	PMCS US	PMC Sierra Inc.	OC	347	37)	TXN US	Texas Instruments	OC	137
18)	PSFT US	Peoplesoft Inc	OC	0	38)	TYC US	Tyco International	OC	36
19)	QCOM US	Qualcomm Inc	OC	304	39)	UPS US	United Parcel Srvs	OC	4
20)	QLGC US	QLogic Corp	OC	115	40)	USB US	U.S. Bancorp	OC	4

EXHIBIT 18.1 (Continued)
Panel d: Page 4 Page of OneChicago Listing

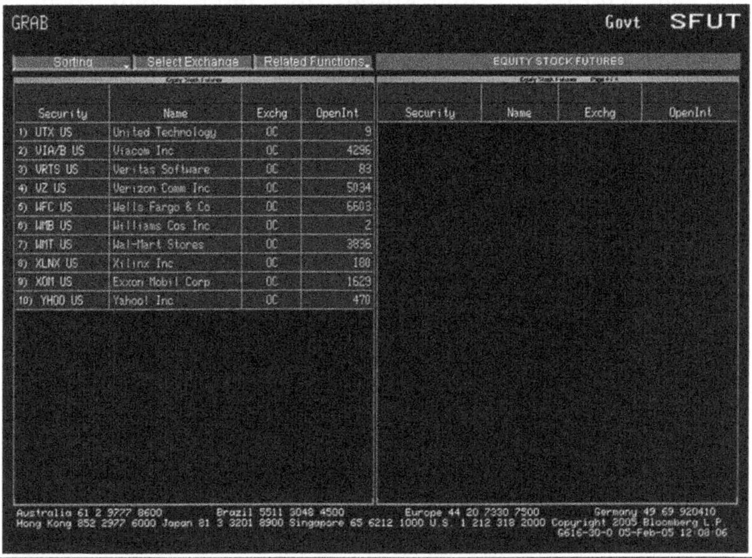

Source: Bloomberg LP

EXHIBIT 18.2 Bloomberg Description Screen of an Allstate Single-Stock Futures Contract

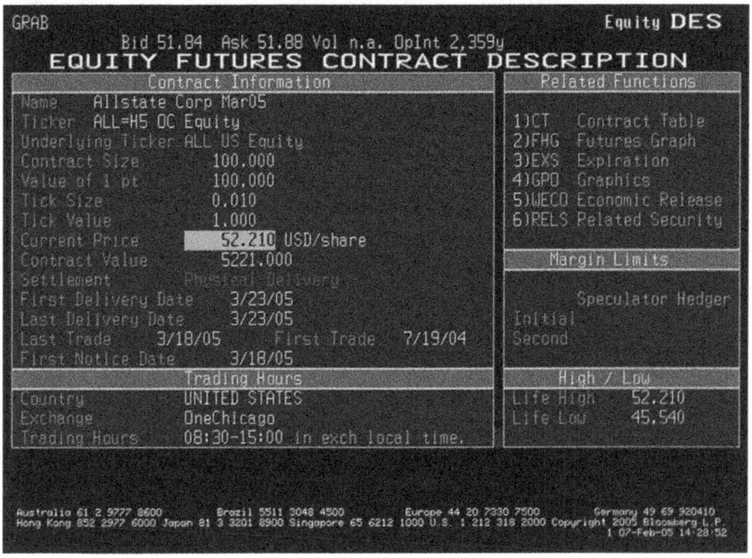

Source: Bloomberg LP

shares. The open interest of the contract[5] in early January 2005 was 2,359 contracts. Exhibit 18.3 presents a Bloomberg screen for the expiration schedule for the first four Allstate stock futures contracts in 2005.

Single-stock futures of only actively traded New York Stock Exchange and NASDAQ stocks are traded. Consequently, an investor interested in taking a short position using single-stock futures is limited to those stocks traded on either of these exchanges. There are three advantages of using single-stock futures rather than borrowing the shares in the cash market (via a stock lending transaction) if the investor seeking to short a stock has a choice.

The first advantage is the transactional efficiency that the futures contract permits. In a stock lending program, the short seller may find it difficult if not impossible to borrow the stock in question for a variety of reasons. Moreover, an opportunity can be missed as the stock loan department seeks to locate the stock to borrow. A second advantage is that like CFDs recall risk is eliminated. A third potential advantage is

EXHIBIT 18.3 Bloomberg Screen of the Expiration Schedule of an Allstate Single-Stock Futures Contract

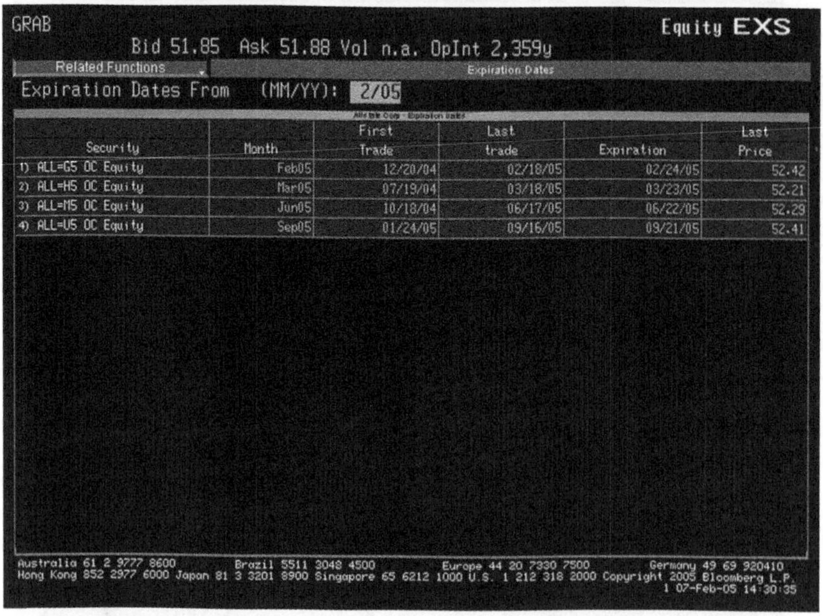
GRAB Equity EXS
Bid 51.85 Ask 51.88 Vol n.a. OpInt 2,359y
Related Functions Expiration Dates
Expiration Dates From (MM/YY): 2/05

Security	Month	First Trade	Last trade	Expiration	Last Price
1) ALL=G5 OC Equity	Feb05	12/20/04	02/18/05	02/24/05	52.42
2) ALL=H5 OC Equity	Mar05	07/19/04	03/18/05	03/23/05	52.21
3) ALL=M5 OC Equity	Jun05	10/18/04	06/17/05	06/22/05	52.29
4) ALL=U5 OC Equity	Sep05	01/24/05	09/16/05	09/21/05	52.41

Australia 61 2 9777 8600 Brazil 5511 3048 4500 Europe 44 20 7330 7500 Germany 49 69 920410
Hong Kong 852 2977 6000 Japan 81 3 3201 8900 Singapore 65 6212 1000 U.S. 1 212 318 2000 Copyright 2005 Bloomberg L.P.
1 07-Feb-05 14:30:35

Source: Bloomberg LP

[5] Open interest is the number of futures contracts outstanding at a point in time.

the cost savings by implementing a short sale via single stock futures rather than a stock lending transaction. The financing of the short sale position in a stock lending transaction is arranged by the broker through a bank. The interest rate that the bank will charge is called the *broker call loan rate* or the *call money rate*. The broker call loan rate with a markup is charged to the investor. However, if the short seller receives the proceeds to invest, this reduces the cost of borrowing the stock.

There are several factors that determine whether or not there is a cost savings by taking a short position in a single-stock futures contract. To understand these factors, we begin with the relationship between the price of the single-stock futures contract and the price of the underlying stock. The following relationship must exist for there to be no arbitrage opportunity:[6]

$$\text{Futures price} = \text{Stock price}[1 + r(d_1/360)] + \text{Expected dividend}[1 + r(d_2/360)]$$

where

r = short-term interest rate
d_1 = number of days until the settlement of the futures contract
d_2 = number of days between receipt of the expected dividend payment and the settlement date

The short-term rate in the pricing relationship above typically reflects the London Interbank Offered Rate (LIBOR). This is the interest rate which major international banks offer each other on a Eurodollar certificates of deposit (CD) with given maturities. The maturities range from overnight to five years. So, references to "3-month LIBOR" indicate the interest rate that major international banks are offering to pay to other such banks on a CD that matures in three months.

The difference between the futures price and the stock price is called the *basis*. The basis is effectively the repo rate (for the period until the settlement date) adjusted by the expected dividend. The basis is also referred to as the *net interest cost* or *carry*. The buyer of the futures contract pays the net interest cost to maintain the long position; the seller of the futures contract earns the net interest cost for financing the buyer's long position. Note the similarity between single-stock futures and equity contracts for differences. Recall, the long position in an equity contract for differences paid interest on the value of the contract while the short position received interest.

---

[6] The derivation of this relationship is found in most books that cover futures contracts.

Thus, a comparison of the cost advantage to shorting single-stock futures rather than using a stock lending transaction comes down to empirically determining which has the lower net interest cost. NASDAQ Liffe examined this issue for the period May 1991 to November 2001.[7] The results suggest that the only time when it was advantageous to use single stock futures was around August 2001 when the Federal Reserve aggressively cut interest rates. In general, the study indicates that the advantage of using single stock futures is adversely affected by low interest rates and steep yield curve environments.

EQUITY SWAPS

Yet another way to replicate either a levered, long equity position or a short sale is with an equity swap. Equity swaps are contractual agreements between two counterparties that provide for the periodic exchange of a schedule of cash flows over a specified time period where at least one of the two payments is linked to the performance of an equity index, a basket of stocks, or a single stock. Thus, investors can gain exposure to equities without entering the cash market directly.

In its most basic form, in an equity swap one counterparty agrees to pay the other the total return to an equity index in exchange for receiving either the total return of another asset or a fixed or floating interest rate. All payments are based on a fixed notional amount and payments are made over a fixed time period. Equity swaps have a wide variety of applications including asset allocation, accessing international markets, return enhancement, hedging equity exposure, and synthetically shorting stocks.

A basic swap structure is illustrated in Exhibit 18.4. In this instance, the investor owns a short-term debt instrument that delivers floating rate payments based on LIBOR plus a spread.[8] The investor then enters into a swap to exchange LIBOR plus the spread for the total return to an equity index. The counterparty pays the index's total return in exchange for LIBOR plus a spread. Assuming that the equity index is the Nikkei 225, a U.S. investor could swap dollar-denominated LIBOR plus a spread for cash flows from the total return to the Nikkei denominated in yen or U.S. dollars.

Exhibit 18.5 presents a Bloomberg SWPM (swap manager) screen of an equity swap where the total return of the Nikkei 225 Index denomi-

---

[7] "Single Stock Futures for the Professional Trader," *Nasdaq Liffe*, undated.

[8] Note the difference in the quotation convention for equity swaps compared to interest rate swaps. For the latter, the floating rate is quoted flat while the fixed-rate side is quoted as the rate on a comparable maturity Treasury plus a swap spread.

EXHIBIT 18.4   Equity Swap Structure

Basic Domestic Swap Structure

Enhanced Return Swap Structure

EXHIBIT 18.5   Bloomberg Screen of a Nikkei 225 Equity Swap

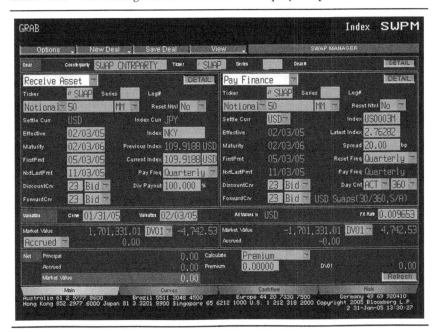

Source: Bloomberg LP

nated in dollars is exchanged for quarterly payments based on three-month LIBOR plus 20 basis points. Note that this one year equity swap has a notional principal of $50 million. The index could be any equity index in the world. A swap could also be structured to generate superior returns if the financing instrument in the swap yields a higher return than LIBOR.

An example of an equity swap is illustrated in a Bloomberg screen presented in Exhibit 18.6. This swap is a one-year agreement that starts January 31, 2005 where the counterparty agrees to pay the total return on the S&P 500 Index (SPX) in exchange for dollar-denominated LIBOR plus a spread of 50 basis points on a quarterly basis. The notional amount is $10 million. This type of equity swap is the economic equivalent of financing a long position in the S&P 500 Index at LIBOR. The advantages of using equity swaps are no transaction costs, no sales or dividend with-holding tax, and no tracking error/basis risk versus the index.

Equity swap structures are very flexible with maturities ranging from a few months to 10 years. The returns of virtually any asset can be swapped for another without incurring the costs associated with a transaction in the cash market. Payment schedules can be denominated

EXHIBIT 18.6   Bloomberg Screen of a S&P 500 Equity Swap

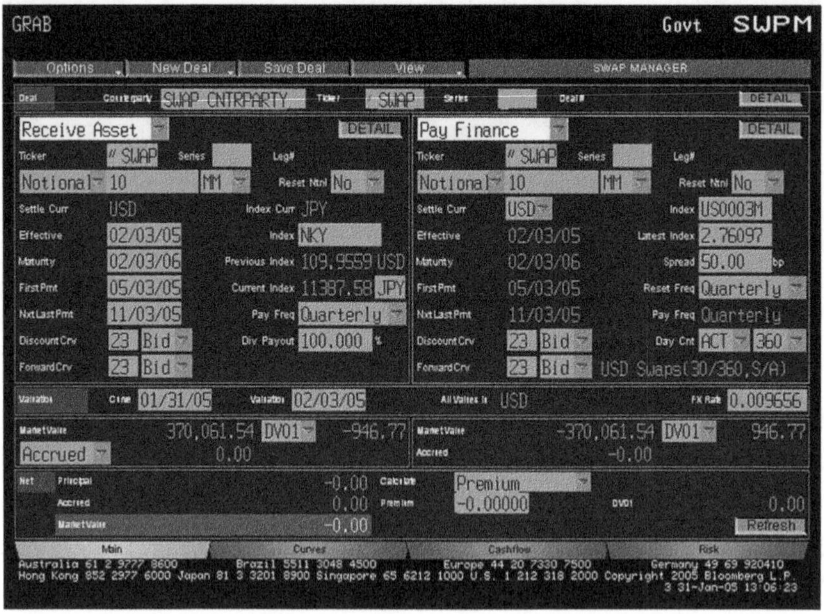

Source: Bloomberg LP

in any currency regardless of the choice of the equity asset and payments can be exchanged monthly, quarterly, annually, or at maturity. The equity asset can be any equity index or portfolio of stocks denominated in any currency—hedged or unhedged.

Variations of the basic structure include: international equity swaps where the equity return is linked to an international equity index; currency-hedged swaps where the swap is structured to eliminate currency risk; and call swaps where the equity payment is paid only if the equity index appreciates (depreciation will not result in a payment from the counterparty receiving the equity return to the other counterparty because of call protection).

The basic mechanics of equity swaps are the same regardless of the structure. However, the rules governing the exchange of payments may differ. If the investment objective is to reduce U.S. equity exposure and increase Japanese equity exposure, for example, a swap could be structured to exchange the total returns to the S&P 500 for the total returns to the Nikkei 225 Index. If, however, the investment objective is to gain access to the Japanese equity market, a swap can be structured to exchange LIBOR plus a spread for the total returns to the Nikkei Index. This is an example of diversifying internationally and the cash flows can be denominated in either yen or dollars. The advantages of entering into an equity swap to obtain international diversification are that the investor exposure is devoid of tracking error and the investor incurs no sales tax, custodial fees, withholding fees, or market impact costs associated with entering and exiting a market. This swap is the economic equivalent of being long the Nikkei 225 Index financed at a spread to LIBOR at a fixed exchange rate.

There are numerous applications of equity swaps but nearly every one assume the aforementioned basic structure. Investors can virtually swap any financial asset for the total returns to an equity index, a portfolio of stocks, or a single stock. Market makers are prepared to create structures that allow an investor to exchange the returns of any two assets. The schedule of cash flows exchanged is a function of the assets. For example, an investor who desires to outperform an equity benchmark may be able to accomplish this by purchasing a particular bond and swapping the cash flows for the S&P total returns minus a spread.

EQUITY REPO

An *equity repo agreement* is the sale of a security with a commitment by the seller to buy the same equity security (or equivalent securities) back from the purchaser at a specified price at a designated future date or at call. As with repos in the bond market (as discussed in Chapter 13), an equity repo agreement is a collateralized loan where the collateral is the equity security sold and subsequently repurchased. Equity repo is employed to finance long equity positions as well as to borrow securities to cover short positions. Although relatively small in comparison to the volume of repurchase agreements with say government securities, the equity repo market is reasonably well-developed in the United States, the United Kingdom, continental Europe, and to a lesser extent, Japan.

Let us illustrate an equity repo transaction where a hypothetical common stock, XYZ, serves as collateral for the loan. Suppose a dealer firm desires to use an equity repo agreement to finance one million shares of XYZ common stock which is currently trading at $22 per share. The term of the agreement is assumed to be one month. Assume the relevant repo rate is 5% which is the interest rate (i.e., borrowing rate) specified in the agreement. Then, as will be explained below, the dealer firm would agree to deliver 1,000,000 shares of XYZ common stock for $20,000,000. The $83,333.33 difference between the "sale" price of $20,000,000 and the repurchase price of $20,083,333.33 is the dollar interest on the financing.

In order to provide the lender of cash some cushion should the market value of XYZ common stock decline during the one-month agreement, the amount lent should be less than the current market value of XX common stock.[9] The amount by which the market value of the equity used as collateral exceeds the loan's value is called the initial margin or "haircut." While the initial margin is transaction specific, we will assume an initial margin of 10%. Accordingly, since the total market value of the common stock used as collateral is $22,000,000, this is why the purchase price (i.e., amount borrowed) in our illustration is $20,000,000 ($22,000,000/1.10). The total repurchase price is the sale price plus repo interest. Using a repo rate of 5% and a repo term of 30 days, the dollar interest is $83,333.33 as shown below:

$$\$20,000,000 \times 0.05 \times (30/360) = \$83,333.33$$

The total repurchase price is $20,083,333.33

One of the terms negotiated in an equity repo agreement is the procedures used for marking the equity collateral to market. Moreover, the conditions under which the initial margin needs to be reinstated via a margin call also needs to be determined. Usually in equity repo agreements, the party being called for additional margin has the right to deliver

---

[9] This is a term repo. An open repo has no fixed maturity date with the possibility it may be terminated daily.

the required amount in either additional securities or in cash. In addition, if the term of an equity repo includes an ex-dividend date, the lender of cash (borrower of securities) is generally contractually required to make the payment equal to the amount of the dividend to the borrower of cash (lender of securities) on that date. Finally, the agreement may also include a right of substitution which means the borrower of cash has the right to substitute equivalent collateral during the life of the equity repo agreement. This payment is termed the *manufactured payment.*

The illustration presented above is an example of a *cash-driven repo* transaction. The motivation for entering into a cash-driven repo is as a source of financing. By contrast, the motivation of a *stock-driven repo* transaction is to borrow common stock to cover a short position. There are also opportunities for arbitrage between equity repo and other forms of equity financing. For example, a dealer firm could borrow common stock using a securities lending agreement and then lend the shares via equity repo.

Common stock that is in demand in the securities lending market (commonly called *specials* just as in the fixed-income repo market) can be lent out and serve as a low-cost source of financing. Common stock that is not considered special will result in a higher repo rate. One of the differences between equity repo and the traditional repo market is that the term *general collateral* has little relevance in the equity repo market. Because common equity is more idiosyncratic than, say, U.S. Treasuries, the repo rate negotiated between counterparties will be specific to a particular transaction. Thus, while there are certainly common stocks that are specials, the balance of common stock should not be viewed as close substitutes as collateral in equity repo transactions. As a result, these equity repo transactions result in a wide range of repo rates.

One final element that requires mention is custody of the collateral. The three methods used in traditional repo agreements are also employed in equity repo agreements. The most straightforward approach is to physically *deliver-out* the securities to the cash lender, their clearing agent, or a designated third party. While this approach is logical and results in the least credit risk to the cash provider, this method is the most expensive in terms of time and administrative costs. The next method is termed *hold-in-custody*. With this method, the collateral remains in the possession of the borrower of cash. While this method is the least costly, it should be considered after a careful examination of the cash borrower's credit risk. The third method involves the use of a *collateral management facility* operated by a bank which performs the duties of holding the equity collateral, marking-to-market, margin calls, and the like, for a fee. This arrangement is akin to a tri-party repo in the bond market.

SUMMARY

This chapter discusses some recent innovations in equity financing. We discussed four methods. Contracts for differences are derivative instruments that allow investors to create a synthetic levered long or short position in a common stock. Single-stock futures are futures contracts on a single common stock which allow the user to create leverage at low cost. Equity swaps are swap contracts where the cash flows exchanged between the counterparties are based on equity price movements. Finally, equity repo is tantamount to a traditional repurchase agreement where underlying collateral is common stock.

Index

Printed and bound by CPI Group (UK) Ltd, Croydon, CR0 4YY

23/04/2025

14660925-0002